FIRST AND SECOND LANGUAGE ACQUISITION PROCESSES

Carol Wollman Pfaff, Editor
Free University of Berlin

NEWBURY HOUSE PUBLISHERS, Cambridge
A division of Harper & Row, Publishers, Inc.
New York, Philadelphia, San Francisco, Washington, D.C.
London, Mexico City, São Paolo, Singapore, Sydney

Library of Congress Cataloging in Publication Data
Main entry under title:

First and second language acquisition processes.

Proceedings of the Second European-North American
Workshop on Cross Linguistic Second Language Research
(EUNAM II), held at Jagdschloss Göhrde, West Germany,
August 22–28, 1982.
   Includes index.
   1. Language acquisition–Congresses.   I. Pfaff,
Carol Wollman.   II. European-North American Workshop on
Cross Linguistic Second Language Research (2nd : 1982 :
Jagdschloss Göhrde, West Germany)
P118.F54   1986   401'.9   85–7242
ISBN 0-88377-298-1

NEWBURY HOUSE PUBLISHERS, Cambridge
A division of Harper & Row, Publishers, Inc.

Language Science
Language Teaching
Language Learning

First Printing: September 1986
Printed in the U.S.A.   2 4 6 8 10 9 7 5 3 1
63 24693

CROSS-LINGUISTIC SERIES
ON SECOND LANGUAGE RESEARCH

Roger W. Andersen, Editor

Second language research within the United States has tended historically to focus on the acquisition of English as a second language. The purpose of this series is to expand the focus of second language research to include a wider variety of languages, and to approach such research from a more inter-disciplinary perspective. In addition to language acquisition, the series will deal with second language use and its related psychological, social and anthropological concerns. Other volumes in the series include *Second Language Acquisition by Adult Immigrants: A Field Manual*, Clive Perdue, Editor, and *Second Languages: A Cross-Linguistic Perspective*, Roger W. Andersen, Editor.

ACKNOWLEDGMENTS

Eu / USA we a step further

This is the second volume of papers from the European–North American Project on Cross Linguistic Second Language Research (EuNam), which provided an opportunity for scholars to compare and discuss their empirical studies of various first and second languages.

The first workshop was funded by The National Science Foundation (Grant No. BNS 81–05747) and the National Endowment for the Humanities (Grant No. RD–20127–81–1201) and the Second by the Volkswagenstiftung.

I am grateful to Carol Kind for her valuable assistance with editorial tasks and decisions and to Andrea Siebert for careful typing and retyping of difficult nonstandard material in various languages.

CONTENTS

FIRST AND SECOND LANGUAGE ACQUISITION PROCESSES

Introduction

In recent years the field of second language acquisition research has expanded and diversified as the number of native and target languages, the social contexts in which they are acquired, and the theoretical frameworks in which they are investigated have increased. A wealth of particular information on both products and processes of acquisition has been amassed for specific L1/L2 pairs and there have been several studies comparing acquisition of a given L2 by native speakers of several different L1 s. On the basis of such studies, a number of principles and general hypotheses for second language acquisition concerning the role of linguistic universals, cognitive development and social factors have been proposed. The purpose of the European-North American Workshops on Cross-Linguistic Second Language Research (EuNam) funded jointly by the National Science Foundation and the Deutsche Forschungsgemeinschaft is twofold: to facilitate the comparative analysis of existing and ongoing empirical studies in various settings in Europe and North America, and to foster the development of explicitly cross-linguistic designs for future comparative research.

This volume presents some of the results of EuNam II held at Jagdschloß Göhrde, West Germany, August 22–28, 1982. The workshop brought together for a second time a group of researchers, all of whom do empirical studies of language acquisition in a variety of L1/L2 contexts. As a result of our first workshop, held in 1981 at Lake Arrowhead, California (Andersen, 1984) we had achieved a broad acquaintance with each other's work – the background social contexts, research methodologies, some of the linguistic characteristics of the various interlanguages under investigation and, perhaps most significantly, the leading theoretical questions and analytic approaches to be taken to this important complex of problems. With respect to these basic theoretical issues, there turned out to be far more homogeneity of interest than the diversity of L2 acquisition contexts might indicate, so that at the end of EuNam I meeting, we were able to formulate four general research topics which were to structure the second workshop: (1) the role of input, interaction and discourse; (2) cross-linguistic perspectives on cognitive principles; (3) markedness hierarchies and typological constraints; and (4) functional approaches to the expression of categories such as temporality, conditionality, denial, case and reference.

Because we felt that the findings of cross-linguistic research on L1 acquisition were especially relevant to our work, we invited two researchers in that field, Berman and Kail, to participate not only to summarize those findings, but to discuss the implications of the similarities and crucial differences between L1 and L2 acquisition for future research. These papers, along with Hyltenstam's discussion of hypotheses relating to markedness, universals and typology, are included in Part One. The papers in Part Two represent a variety of topics focusing on theoretical interpretations of empirical studies of various linguistic features in the interlanguages of adults and children in a range of social settings (see the table, pages xvii-xviii). The papers in Part Three all deal with a single topic, reference to past events in the speech of adult immigrants. Our goal on the EuNam II Workshop was to assemble a broad cross-linguistic comparison on a relatively restricted range of linguistic features centered on the four general research topics identified above. These theoretical issues are discussed in the brief descriptions of the individual contributions given below.

I. CROSS-LINGUISTIC LANGUAGE ACQUISITION RESEARCH: REVIEW AND HYPOTHESIS FORMATION

Berman's and Kail's papers on L1 acquisition provide summaries of much of the literature, focusing particularly on the theoretical issue of the relationship between linguistic and cognitive development: the respective roles of target language structure, perceptual and pragmatic factors. Both papers discuss primarily internal linguistic-cognitive factors, rather than external factors such as social setting, motivation, etc. which play a significant role in L2 acquisition. (For some discussion of such factors in L1 acquisition, see Berman, 1984.) Both focus primarily on experimental studies, mostly of comprehension, for example, the interpretation of simple sentences. Berman also discusses the development of inflectional and derivational morphology and Kail also treats comprehension of complex sentences and presuppositions associated with adverbs and conjunctions.

There is much in these two articles to stimulate L2 researchers. Both authors identify implications for L2 acquisition research. Berman points to the importance of comparative research with young (5–8-year-old) L2 learners in "natural" conditions vs. L1 to isolate effects of various linguistic, social and motivational factors and to address the question of linguistic determinism or linguistic pace setting of cognitive development, specifically comparing L1 vs. L1/L2 in children's conceptual grasp of distinctions made in only one of the languages. This type of research is also suggested by Kail's findings that comprehension develops more rapidly in a language which marks a conceptual distinction overtly by two lexical items than in one with a single plurifunctional item.

In addition to their explicit suggestions for L2 research, many of the results and procedures presented by Berman and Kail could be generalized to L2 studies, without, however, necessarily expecting simple parallels in L1 and L2. Berman notes, for example, that in studies of the development of word formation devices in Hebrew and English, young children favor transparency and simplicity principles while older children pay more attention to principles of conventionality and productivity. This is clearly not simply a matter of age (cognitive development) but of familiarity with the target language. In L2 acquisition studies, it is frequently the case that younger learners are more familiar with more of the L2 than older learners. Kail stresses the need to focus on acquisition strategies rather than accuracy of response, as exemplified by the paradigms of L1 comprehension research which pose metalinguistic questions after the child's production or comprehension responses. This and other metalinguistic procedures could be applied more extensively in L2 acquisition research.

Researchers in second language acquisition have not simply been waiting for direction to theoretical questions from L1 acquisition and general linguistics. Although second language research has sometimes been regarded with skepticism because of its "applied" goals, the messiness of the data, and the often stigmatized nature of "incorrect" language use, it has independently incorporated many of the important approaches in linguistic theory. One of the most important of these is the attempt to account for the occurrence and nonoccurrence of linguistic transfer in terms of the notions of markedness, universals and typology.

Hyltenstam's article is devoted to exploration of this confluence of second language research and linguistic theory. He reviews the theoretical basis of the notions markedness, universals and typology, then summarizes studies of L2 acquisition which make use of these notions. Finally, he suggests four paradigms of L2 research based on the use of these notions: (1) interlanguages are natural languages in that they are subject to constraints related to language universals which are generally applicable to all languages; (2) L2 data are valid data in the search for language universals; (3) the order of acquisition for structures follows markedness conditions; and (4) the structural character of interlanguages is determined by the typological nature of the learners' L1 and L2. He then expands on the third paradigm, using the notion of markedness to generate specific hypotheses for L2 acquisition using sentence negation, yes/no questions and verbs of perception as examples.

II. THEORETICAL INTERPRETATIONS OF EMPIRICAL SECOND LANGUAGE STUDIES

Pfaff's paper on functional approaches to interlanguage, though addressed to a difference linguistic feature—determiners and reference—is closely related to the papers in Part Three in outlook and theoretical orientation. She discusses in general several uses of "functionalism" in linguistics—in synchronic analysis of adult native speakers' systems, in language change, in pidginization and creolization, and in L1 acquisition and the related notion of "plurifunctionality" of linguistic forms.

The analysis of the use of articles and pronouns by Turkish immigrant school children learning German illustrates the interplay of various functional parameters which account for the observed developmental sequences in the acquisition of determination and reference to NPs. Pfaff finds a hierarchy of acquisition of discourse functions to mark old and new information and to distinguish protagonist from other participants, case marking and, finally, gender marking. Her analysis suggests, further, that learners attempt to make systematic use of the various plurifunctional definite article forms of the target language.

Clahsen is concerned with bringing evidence from L2 acquisition to bear on alternative models of language processing proposed by Chomsky and by Bates. Taking data from the ZISA project (Clahsen, Meisel and Pienemann, 1983), on adult Italian, Spanish and Portuguese immigrants learning German, Clahsen examines their strategies in the process of acquiring the German word order rules for verb placement. He concludes that neither a "grammaticist" position (as proposed in Chomsky's work) nor a purely "cognitivist" or "strong functionalist" position (as proposd by Bates) can account for the observed developmental strategies, but that an "integrativist" model containing both an (autonomous) linguistic component and a set of nonlinguistic cognitive principles (a "general problem solver") must be adopted.

Nicholas bases his discussion of a young English-speaking child's acquisition of German in a natural setting on a "variationist" model of L2 acquisition which assumes that the acquisition process can be divided into a *developmental dimension*, with a strict sequential acquisition of target language rules common to all learners, and a *learner-type-specific dimension*, defined by social and psychological variables, which determines acquisition not tied to specific developmental stages. His focus in this paper is on one learner-type-specific interactional style in which the learner's behavior plays a crucial role in determining the input received for L2 acquisition processing. He considers, in particular, the use of "contextually defined queries" such as "hm?", "ha?", "ok", and "wa", which focus on the form of the utterance previously produced and elicit a verbal response from the interlocutor—in particular, reformulations of the content of the nonstandard utterance.

Nicholas proposes the use of such queries as one mechanism employed by what Seliger (1977) calls *high input generators*, and suggests, further, that learners who are structurally oriented make more frequent use of this feature than less structurally oriented learners. Nicholas here presents evidence that the learner, Cindy, is structurally oriented on a number of independent measures (use of redundant features, use of a variety of forms, initial functional restrictions, early development of morphological marking) and demonstrates the effectiveness of her use of contextually defined queries.

Pienemann investigates the influence of instruction on natural language acquisition processes—in particular, whether instruction can induce learning a rule out of the natural sequence. Pienemann investigates syntactic word order rules for German verbs for which there exists a well-established developmental sequence based on longitudinal studies of adult L2 and child L1 and L2 acquisition. The experimental design consisted of interviewing 7–9-year-old Italian immigrant schoolchildren learning German before and after their exposure to instruction in the word order rule of inversion.

The detailed results for two children reported here support Pienemann's claim that a certain linguistic structure (inversion) could be added to the interlanguage by formal instruction only if the learner was close to the point when this structure was acquired in a natural setting. Pienemann then explores the theoretical bases of this observation in terms of processing strategies and, finally, considers implications for further research directed to the development of instructional materials and methods.

Lightbown, like Pienemann, focuses on the effect of input in formal classroom teaching on learner performance. Using evidence from a large sample of 11–17-year-old French schoolchildren whose exposure to English is exclusively in a classroom learning context, she analyzes three aspects of their spoken and written interlanguage: (1) order of morpheme accuracy for six morphemes (copula, auxiliary, plural, -ing, 3rd pers. sing., possessive) frequently treated in L2 acquisition research on English; (2) the use of *have* as an existential introducer *(you have a clock on the wall)*, and (3) choice of preposition.

For each of these areas she finds evidence to support her claim that "acquisition" processes are not restricted to natural settings but occur also in the classroom "learning" context. In the use of -ing, she finds evidence that, as a result of intensive drill, the form but not the function is learned. Usage drops off sometimes after the input is reduced. Use of *have* as an existential introducer, based on a false hypothesis involving extension of *have* to a function of *avoir* common in French but not English, is acquired although not taught and is maintained as a stable element of the interlanguage. Prepositions used correctly in classroom activities are not carried over to use in experimental contexts outside class.

These findings support and supplement Pienemann's: teaching will not induce "acquisition" until the appropriate preceding interlanguage stage is reached, and lack of teaching will not block "acquisition-like" processing of the input, even in a formal learning context.

III. CASE STUDIES OF REFERENCE TO PAST IN A SEMANTIC/FUNCTIONAL FRAMEWORK

Von Stutterheim and Klein's paper introduces Part Three, containing case studies of reference to past, with a discussion of various functional approaches (see also Pfaff's paper in this volume). They delimit a "concept-oriented" approach to L2, i.e., one which starts from the meaning of an utterance in order to determine the role of the respective expressive devices (forms), an approach which they contrast with a purely structural analysis. Their central concern here is to present a conceptual framework for the analysis of temporality on two dimensions: (1) references to points or frames in time (deictic, durative, iterative) and (2) reference to temporal relations (event 1 after event 2, event 2 before event 1). These categories are encoded in speech either through the use of explicit linguistic devices (morphosyntax, lexicon) or by pragmatic devices or discourse organization principles (order of mention, implicit reference).

L2 learners have restricted ability to employ explicit devices, so pragmatic devices predominate. Explicit and pragmatic devices thus have different roles in interlanguage systems than they do for native speakers (and different roles in interlanguages of varying proficiency). Using examples of Turkish adult workers learning German, von Stutterheim and Klein illustrate the pragmatic devices used: implicit reference (inherent temporal reference, associative temporal reference and order of mention). Finally, they relate this work to research on L1 acquisition and creolization and argue for the necessity of extending the available data base with related studies.

Meisel pursues a similar functional approach. Before turning to his analysis of reference to past events and actions, he first provides a brief functional interpretation of the previous work of the ZISA group on the acquisition of German word order rules by Italian, Spanish and Portuguese adults (Meisel, Clahsen, Pienemann, 1981; Clahsen, Meisel, Pienemann, 1983) and the papers by Clahsen and Pienemann in this and the preceding EuNam volume, Andersen (ed), 1984). In the present paper, Meisel focuses on reference to past in the speech of one Spanish learner whose linguistic development was examined over an 80-week period—with reference also to other speakers in the longitudinal study.

After summarizing the explicit and implicit devices available in standard German and the colloquial forms which constitute the actual input to foreign workers, Meisel discusses the observed developmental sequences. In the earliest stages explicit devices are not available since verbal elements are either omitted altogether or unsystematically marked. Pragmatic devices used include: (1) *scaffolded discourse*, in which the interlocutor provides alternative reference points; (2) *implicit reference* to events in the speaker's past presupposed to be known to the hearer; (3) contrast of two or more events and (4) order of mention following natural order.

In early stages, explicit reference is provided by adverbials; the choice of type (locative vs. temporal, adverbial vs. prepositional phrase) and overall frequency varies with learner type, while the position of the adverbial appears to be related to the degree of explicit marking with verb morphology. A second explicit linguistic device employed is connectives used in connection with contrasted or sequential events. Verbal inflection (which may be highly nonstandard) arises only in connection with relating two or more events in the past. Finally, Meisel finds no evidence that early interlanguage stages are characterized by aspectual systems as is claimed for L1 and creole systems.

Trévise begins by pointing out that in the study of temporal reference—in the speech of native speakers as well as of that of interlanguage speakers— the relationship between linguistic markers and notional values is highly complex. She provides an explicit and more complete framework for the analysis of linguistic and pragmatic devices considering major types of *reference point operations* and *narrative structure* and goes on to illustrate their use in detailed analysis of narrative sequences in the speech of two adult Spanish-speaking learners of French (political refugees from Argentina and Chile).

The narrative of the first of those speakers, in contrast to those analyzed in the preceding papers, contains a highly complex intermingling of story line, commentary and narrative within the narrative. Trévise's analysis is concerned with the linguistic devices used to distinguish among them. The "structural skeleton" of the narrative reveals the "story line" (foreground) segments to be more homogeneous (primarily using active verbs in various aspectual forms) than the commentary (background) (with stative as well as active verbs marked for tense/aspect and a-temporal forms).

The second speaker has a much more rudimentary command of French verb morphology, but with the use of connectives and adverbials, and relying on the knowledge of the interlocutor, he is able to build up a rather complex narrative, as Trévise demonstrates. Here, as in the preceding papers, one of the morals for interlanguage research is that much vital information is lost in an analysis that only counts instances of this or that standard morphological marker.

Veronique analyzes conversation and narrative excerpts from North African Arabic- and Berber-speaking workers living in France who have varying degrees of proficiency in French. He focuses on their use of verb morpho-syntax and other devices to express reference to past events and actions in backgrounded and foregrounded passages. His findings support those of the other papers in Part Three—all speakers employ pragmatic means: spatial deixis, shared knowledge of the world, overt calendrical expression, adverbials. All also contrast (auxiliary) *Verb + e* forms with simple verb stems. Speakers differ in the distribution of marked and unmarked verb forms in connection with background and foreground events and in their ability to express duration, to switch temporal reference points and to violate chronological sequence in more intricate narratives.

As are the authors of the other papers in this volume, Veronique is convinced that the understanding of interlanguage is enriched by the functional approach which considers devices beyond morphological markers. However, he also expresses some problems and questions entailed by such a functional approach: (1) What are the relevant basic concepts?: How, for instance, shall we deal with reference to past vs. the notion "prior to"? (2) Speaker and hearer perspectives differ—in which crucial ways? (3) To avoid the danger of functional analysis becoming simply a taxonomy of another kind, we need to seek higher level explanations for cognitive structure that permits use of the various morpho-syntactic, semantic and discourse devices to function as reference to past.

The research findings collected in this EuNam II volume represent an important step toward the development of an empirically based theory of L2 acquisition. The papers address the most important theoretical issues of L2 research of the last decade and begin to provide crucial comparable cross-linguistic evidence.

The topic of transfer from L1, perhaps the first and most intuitively accessible hypothesis about the process of L2 acquisition, has in the last 20 years been definitively shown to be unable to account for much of the phenomena of interlanguage. However, its role cannot be denied, not only in the acknowledged areas of phonology and lexicon, but in some areas of syntax as well. The question which remains now is thus not whether L1 transfer occurs, but in what areas of grammar, and according to what underlying principles. Hyltenstam's contribution to this volume consolidates the views that linguistic universals, typology and markedness are crucial to the various phenomena of L1 transfer and clarifies the lines of future research in this field.

The sense that L2 acquisition processes are fundamentally similar to those of first language acquisition clearly underlies many of the EuNam II contributions, some of which stress the more particularly linguistic aspects, while others try to sort out general cognitive and pragmatic abilities of learners. The papers by Berman, Kail and Clahsen, which specifically address the issue of comprehensive models for language acquisition, all suggest that an integrativist approach which combines elements of all three is necessary to account for the findings of acquisition studies. Nicholas' paper, which is concerned with the role the learner plays in eliciting crucial input, adds a fourth set of factors which must be integrated—that of individual personality.

A third theme that runs through the case studies presented in this volume is that of functionalism. In each of these studies, the investigators ask the questions: How do learners accomplish their communicative ends using only the limited means available in their current interlanguages? What are the functions served by the various interlanguage forms? These questions are clearly addressed in the set of papers by von Stutterheim and Klein, Meisel, Trévise and Veronique on adult immigrants' reference to past events, in Pfaff's paper on child immigrants' expression of reference and determination, as well as in Lightbown's paper on children learning a foreign language exclusively in a classroom setting.

A final topic addressed here, by Lightbown and more explicitly by Pienemann, is the comparison of acquisition processes and patterns of usage in natural and in classroom settings. Lightbown's and Pienemann's findings—that natural acquisition sequences cannot be overridden by classroom instruction—are not only of great interest theoretically, but also have direct relevance for the teaching and assessment of second and foreign languages. These papers clearly support the position that theoretically well-founded cross-sectional and longitudinal studies of natural as well as guided acquisition, such as those in this volume, are essential to achieve applied goals effectively. Such goals have additional social importance today, as economic and political conditions have required large numbers of immigrants throughout the world to learn additional languages. The apparently objective criterion of language proficiency is easily taken as the basis for crucial educational, employment and naturalization decisions. It is hoped that the L2 research in volumes such as this will contribute to a realistic understanding of L2 production and its underlying processes that will benefit policy makers, theoreticians, and ultimately L2 speakers themselves.

Overview of Empirical Studies Discussed in This Volume

Author	Language (L1)/L2	Setting	Age (years)	Type of Data	Linguistic Feature(s)	Theoretical Focus
Berman	English, Hebrew	L1	preschool & school age	production & comprehension, experiments	morphosyntax	cognitive & linguistic factors
Kail	English, French, other	L1	preschool & school age	comprehension experiments	syntax, semantics	cognitive & linguistic factors
Hyltenstam	(various)/Swedish, English	various L2	children adults	experiments & conversation	syntax, semantics negation, question, verbs of perception	markedness, universals, typology
Pfaff	(Turkish)/German	imm...ant	school age (14-15)	structured conversation	article and pronoun, reference	discourse & grammatical function
Clahsen	(Italian)/German		adult	free conversation	word order	models of cognitive & linguistic processing
Nicholas	(English)/German		child (3)	free conversation	use of queries, morphosyntax	learner-type interactional style
Pienemann	(Italian)/German		school age (7-9)	free & structured conversation	word order (inversion)	processing account of instructional influence on developmental sequence
Lightbown	(French)/English	guide	age (11-17)	oral & written structured elicitation	grammatical morphemes, introducers, prepositions	"acquisition" & "learning" in instructional context
v. Stutterheim & Klein	(Turkish)/German	immigrant natural L2		free conversation	temporal reference	linguistic & pragmatic devices
Meisel	(Spanish)/German	immigrant natural L2		free conversation	temporal reference	linguistic & pragmatic devices
Trévise	(Spanish)/French	immigrant natural L2	adult	free conversation	temporal reference	linguistic & pragmatic devices
Veronique	(Arabic, Berber)/French	immigrant natural L2	adult	free conversation	temporal reference	linguistic & pragmatic devices

PART ONE

Cross-Linguistic
Language Acquisition Research:
Review and
Hypothesis Formation

CHAPTER 1

Cognitive Components of Language Development[1]

Ruth A. Berman
Tel Aviv University, Israel

This paper discusses certain facets of the role of cognitive factors in children's acquisition of their mother tongue, with the aim of providing a frame of reference for considering such issues in studying second language acquisition from a cross-linguistic perspective. We start by briefly reviewing positions taken by linguists and psychologists on the relation between cognitive and linguistic development (Section 1), and how such scholars have specified the content of cognitive strategies or principles in relation to language acquisition (Section 2). Subsequently, we consider how such factors interact with different facets of the acquisition process, in terms of developmental sequencing (Section 3.1), in particular domains of linguistic structure (3.2), and with respect to typological properties of the target language (3.3) as well as language universals (3.4). And we conclude by considering certain impliciations of these issues for the study of second language acquisition in early childhood and by adults (Section 4).

1. THE RELATION BETWEEN COGNITIVE AND LINGUISTIC DEVELOPMENT

Different positions can be identified in relating general cognitive development and acquisition of competence in the native language. Each stand will, in turn, reflect the protagonists' conception of the more general issue of the interrelation between language and thought. These positions can be viewed along a continuum of logically possible relations, from total identity through to a null connection, with differing degrees of interaction located between these extremes.[2] Below we note four key positions which seem to have had a major impact on language acquisition research, ignoring more specific claims which distinguish between different proponents of these broad sets of overall views.

The "language acquisition" position is associated with Chomsky's conception of linguistic competence as a highly specific knowledge domain. It is concerned with evolving a formal model of learnability, to account for the logical problem of the human ability to acquire any natural language. The child is perceived as "a little linguist" who has recourse to partial, imperfect input data in testing hypotheses about language structure, made available to the learner by linguistic universals. Research conducted within this paradigm emphasizes the independence of linguistic knowledge from other cognitive systems, and focuses on acquisition of formal rules of grammar, mainly syntax. Such studies tend to dismiss "nonstructural strategies" which may impinge on language acquisition as outside of, or at most ancillary to, the central task of the LAD: internalization of the rules of grammar. Different models within such a framework are discussed by Pinker (1979), and studies from different perspectives are reported in collections by Baker and McCarthy (1981), Tavakolian (1981), and Wexler and Culicover (1980).

A "determinist" position is associated with the so-called Sapir-Whorf hypothesis on the relation between language and thought, and also with certain behaviorist orientations in American psychology. In language acquisition research, such views have had an impact mainly within the Soviet tradition (Luria and Yudovich, 1959; Vygotsky, 1962). The strong version of this claim is that cognition depends on language, so that cognitive development is possible only on the basis of prior linguistic knowledge. Thus, knowing a word or having a linguistic form available might not only facilitate but may even be necessary for conceptualizing the notions or objects which are so expressed. This view, as well as a less extreme recognition of possible "linguistic pacesetting of cognitive development" (Slobin, in press) is, as noted, at most peripheral in current child language studies.

The "cognitivist" position is identified mainly with developmental psycholinguistics in the Piagetian tradition, as in Sinclair [de Zwart] (1973, 1975). The claim here is the logical converse of the deterministic view: Language acquisition is considered crucially dependent in both content and developmental sequencing on prior cognitive abilities. And language development is then essentially a mapping of cognitive structures onto linguistic representations. Thus, language learning is a function of more general nonlinguistic abilities, just as language is an expression of such knowledge. Clear, critical reviews of the implications of this position for child language research and theory are provided in Bowerman (1978), Corrigan (1979), and Karmiloff-Smith (1979).

An "integrative" position has emerged, too, under the combined impact of the impetus given to child language research by theoretical linguistics in the 1960s and the evolution of developmental psycholinguistics as a field of inquiry. The view here is that language acquisition cannot be accounted for as any straightforward or one-to-one mapping between cognitive representations and linguistic expressions. Yet acquisition is not, on the other hand, only internalizing formal rules of grammar analogously to a scientist constructing a theory. Rather, development of language has underpinnings in general cognitive development—and the precise role these perform needs to be identified. But the child also acquires peculiarly linguistic knowledge, since languages display formal properties and constraints which have no necessary analogue in other domains or systems of representation. This view is espoused from different perspectives in the current research of, for instance, Bowerman(1978, 1981), E. V. Clark(1977, 1981), Karmiloff-Smith (1979, 1981), Maratsos (1982, 1984), and Slobin (1981, in press).

In this paper, I try to motivate my own outlook as closely aligned with this last position. It seems to have promoted most in-depth examinations of specific linguistic subsystems as constructed by children in, and increasingly across, different languages. Its proponents consider acquisition in the domains of word formation and semantics as well as morphophonology and syntax. And, as in the seminal work of Brown (1973) and his associates, they remain concerned with language development over time. An open mind also seems warranted for a modified kind of "determinism." Thus, a conceptual distinction might intially be identified by virtue of its having overt formal marking in the learner's language. And beyond the very early stages of acquisition, language may be a determining factor in the reorganization, if not in the initial learning, of certain concepts (see Blank, 1974; Weissenborn, 1980). Besides, recognition of a partial dependence on linguistic representation as affecting conceptualization seems particularly worthwhile in the study of *second* language acquisition.

This representation of different perspectives on language development as mutually exclusive is adopted here as a heuristic device. Yet it also reflects a genuine gap, even a disaffinity, between the kinds of research questions, and hence findings, which are emerging in the field today. Those motivated by a concern for linguistic theory will focus on the formal properties of the end-state system to be learned. Those occupied with general psychological development will focus on changes in structures and processes at different stages in the history of the language-learning child. And many scholars will seek more generally "functionalist" explanations for the development of grammar, along lines not even noted above (see Bates and MacWhinney, 1982). Ideally, current attempts to provide a detailed characterization of the child's "language-making capacity" (Slobin, in press) will yield a more integrated picture than is now available of both end state and development in language acquisition of form and function; of more generally cognitive and specifically linguistic components of the language learning process.

2. TYPES OF COGNITIVE COMPONENTS

So far, notions such as *cognition, cognitive development*, and *cognitive abilities* have been treated as givens, with the term "conceptual" replacing "cognitive" in places. In the most simplistic terms, since cognition has to do with knowledge and the mind in general, *all* language learning is cognitive in essence—apart from physiological, affective, and social factors which lie outside our domain of concern. To provide a more specific frame of reference, a distinction can be drawn between different kinds of cognitive factors which might impinge on language development (Section 2.1), and different processes and strategies can be associated in current language acquisition research with various kinds of cognitive, acquisitional, or operating principles (Section 2.2).

2.1 RELEVANT COGNITIVE FACTORS

Cromer (1978) makes a useful distinction between i) cognitive *structures and processes*, ii) cognitive *operations*, and iii) cognitions or *thoughts* (see Johnston, in press). The first component encompasses underlying mechanisms such as short-term memory, production and attention span, auditory processing and other features of the sensory apparatus. These biologically conditioned mechanisms or "organizing capacities" can be shown to impinge on language acquisition by evidence from learners whose abilities are nonintact, such as aphasic children. Besides, such capacities generally manifest maturational progress during early development.

The second component entails sensorimotor operations as well as later-developing operations such as identity and reversibility. This kind of "structural prerequisite" underlies such claims as the following: The ability to put objects in spatial and temporal sequences is a precursor to the ability to order linguistic elements in strings; performance on nesting and seriation tasks is relevant to the linguistic ability to handle embedded clauses and to use comparative terms, respectively; and the ability to talk about hypothetical or timeless events, or to describe event sequences by means of grammatical clause structure that does not match the real-time temporal sequences, depends on the child's developing ability to decenter his own viewpoint from that of the speaker.

The third component—cognitions or thoughts—refers, for instance, to children's ability to make reference to immediate past time or to actions currently in progress even before they have learned the appropriate linguistic markers for these notions. This factor corresponds to what Slobin (1973) terms "conceptual and factual knowledge," and such abilities are reviewed by Johnston (in press) to show that relevant nonverbal spatial and quantitative knowledge may be prerequisite to children's learning of locative terms such as *in, next to* or comparative terms such as *more/less, big/small.*[3]

In this last domain, of conceptual content, the boundaries between cognitive and linguistic development are particularly fuzzy. And there is an unfortunate tendency of some work in child language to identify cognitive with *semantic* knowledge, and hence acquisition.[4] Yet any claim for one-to-one mappings between conceptual and linguistic content evades the critical issue of just what it is that the learner will need to map into linguistic expression (Bowerman, 1981; Slobin, 1982). For in addition to concepts, children need to acquire the semantics of their native tongue, learning which aspects and properties of entire conceptual domains are reflected in linguistically relevant categories. And they also need to learn which formal structures are deployed in expressing these categories in their native tongue: grammatical inflections, affixation or compounding in word formation, and syntactic rules of conjoining and embedding, for instance. Studies in language development thus seem to provide a unique arena for clarifying the complex layers of distinctions between i) conceptual content—cognitions; ii) linguistic content—semantics; and iii) linguistic form—structural devices.

Studies now available of the development of specific subsystems, particularly among children of different language backgrounds, help clarify interrelations between concepts, meanings, and forms. Consider, for instance, acquisition of Locatives, Determiners, Causatives, Tense-Aspect, and Gender. In each of these five domains respectively, the learner needs first of all to understand the conceptual, nonverbal nature of spatial relationships; of known versus nonspecific objects and entities; of causal relations between people, objects, and events; of categorizing events in terms of when and how they take place or are experienced; and of categorizing objects and entities into different classes. The learner also needs to master the semantics of these domains. This includes, for instance, the difference in meaning between such closely related locative terms as *below* and *under*, or *among* and *between*, and the fact that the first two but not the latter two have converse terms in *above* and *(up)on*; knowledge that determiners like *a, the, this* may function semantically to distinguish deictic and anaphoric reference as well as generic and specific object reference;[5] knowledge that the semantics of causativity distinguishes directly manipulative from indirect causation—as in *drop the doll* versus *make the doll fall* respectively; the semantics of tense may involve reference to the time of utterance as point present, but it will not serve to encode such conceptually time-related notions as distance or speed; and systems of gender or other means of noun classification may refer to a being's sex, or the animacy or even shape of an object, but never, say, its color or absolute size.

In addition, learners need to know how to match forms to meanings in their language. Thus, locative relations may be expressed by grammatical inflections, by adpositions or particles, and/or by distinct lexical items; various determiners may be used to specify such functions as the proximal/ distal distinction or generic/specific reference; various devices may be used for marking causative relations—word order as in *he broke the lamp/the lamp broke*; syntactic clause union as in *he'll cry/make the boy cry*; or morphology as in *he's lying down/laying the baby down*. Additionally, learners need to know what forms, if any, are used for classifying nouns into grammatical gender groups—by articles as in German, by the surface endings of nouns as in Hebrew, by a mixture of the two as in French, and to distinguish such lexical class markings from the marginal lexical suffixes such as *-ess* in English.

In second language learning, cognitive structures and operations may function differentially according to the general maturational level and mental capacities as well as conceptual knowledge brought to bear on the task by learners of different age levels and backgrounds (Berman, 1984). The interrelation between concept/meaning/form is clearly illustrated in cases where a learner needs to acquire two distinct forms for meanings which are subsumed under a single form in the source language. Thus, the grammar of Hebrew does not distinguish formally between present and past irrealis conditionals (e.g., *I'd buy a house if I won the lottery* versus *I'd have bought a house if I'd won the lottery*). Conceptually, it is plausible that the (adult) Hebrew speaker can recognize a difference between hypothetical situations which may still be realized should circumstances change and those that are irrevocable. And he or she may even have learned that either past tense or perfect verb forms can be used in such clauses. Yet he may not have a clear idea at all of the semantics of such constructions, hence of the form/meaning relations they entail. A lexical example is provided by a verb such as Hebrew *kibel* which can serve for both 'receive' and 'accept' in English, as in the contrastive context of *get an invitation* versus *accept an invitation*. Clearly, Hebrew speakers understand the conceptual distinction between receiving something passively and agreeing to take an offer. What they need to learn is the semantics of these two verbs in English—including the fact that *get* can mean the same as *receive* but also can be used in an accomplishment sense of 'obtain,' while *accept* is antonymous to *reject* but not to *refuse*, again by contrast with comparable Hebrew verbs. Additionally, the learner will need to realize that *get* is used as an auxiliary type verb in English causatives (*get someone to leave*), middle-voice type passives (*get taken away*), and in inchoatives (*get sick*)—all semantic categories which are typically encoded in the form of verb morphology in a Semitic language such as Hebrew.

2.2   PRINCIPLES AND STRATEGIES IN ACQUISITION

Various claims have been made for general operating principles and acquisitional strategies which are critical to an evaluation of the role of cognitive components in language development. A problem in trying to specify the content of such factors is to define the domain to which they apply. One way is by means of a "default" approach, where such factors are identified with all of language learning *minus grammar*. And in fact many variables have been noted in current attempts to integrate the study of language acquisition with general developmental processes, including such diverse parameters as cognition, communicative intent, discourse, input, nonverbal strategies, and pragmatic function. What such attempts all share is a tendency to downgrade the acquisition of language *qua* language, as a "peculiarly structured system in its own right" (Slobin, 1981).

At the other extreme, an "everything else" approach is taken by proponents of a strong version of the language acquisition position outlined at the beginning of Section 1. From this point of view, much of developmental psycholinguistics is misguided in focusing on general cognitive and other principles or learning strategies rather than on the role of grammatical theory in acquisition. Various "auxiliary hypotheses" are construed as lying outside of, even if ancillary to, the central task of language learning: acquiring the rules of grammar (Roeper, 1981). These include such factors as: *item-by-item* or rote learning of individual, unanalyzed forms (see further Section 3.1 below); *thematic analysis* in interpreting predicate-argument relations—for instance whether a noun phrase is animate or not; and *contextual interpretation*, or relying on real-world knowledge and pragmatic familiarity in processing input strings. Such an "everything else" approach is problematic, *inter alia* because it ignores the potentially critical distinction between strategies which are employed for *acquiring* language in contrast with those used for *processing* language (see Nelson, 1973). Thus rote learning is a way in which children acquire linguistic knowledge, whereas analysis of input strings in terms of the semantic content or pragmatic function associated with their constituents is a strategy which children use when processing such strings in order to interpret them appropriately.

One important orientation to the role of nonlinguistic factors in the acquisition of grammar focuses on perceptual strategies (Bever, 1970). Such principles are generally experimentally established by having children interpret specific sets of stimulus sentences. They include: the Minimum Distance Principle (C. Chomsky, 1969) to explain, for instance, the fact that young children take as subject the noun phrase which is closest to the verb, irrespective of its grammatical relation to different predicates in the main and embedded clause; the NVN Strategy (Bever, 1970), by which children initially interpret such strings as though they mirror the order Actor-Action-Object, again irrespective of the actual grammatical relations manifested; and The Parallel Function Strategy (Sheldon, 1974) to explain why children find it easier to understand relative clause sentences if the noun modified by the relative shares the same grammatical function as the head noun in the relative—in turn deriving from the complexity of processing "double function constituents" in general (Bever, 1970).

A rather different orientation is more clearly developmental. For instance, in reviewing various processing strategies deployed by children in sentence comprehension tasks, Cromer (1976) distinguishes between immature and later types of strategies. Thus, younger children around age two to three tend to interpret strings in terms of their expectations from what is familiar or likely in the real world of events—for instance, that cats *drink* milk and cows *give* milk, while mothers *put* milk *in* bottles *for* their babies, and so on. By contrast, word order strategies of the kinds noted above are more likely to be used by older children, aged around four. This suggests a possible maturationally determined hierarchy of strategies (and see, further, Section 3.1 below).

The major thrust in delineating general principles underlying how learners acquire as well as process language is associated with the seminal work of Slobin (1973). These take the form of sets of hypotheses, drawn in the main from a wide range of performance data, which are construed as underpinning language development both across and within languages (Slobin, 1982, in press). Such principles have further been delineated with attendant learning strategies in the acquisition of morphophonology and syntax (MacWhinney, 1978, 1981) as well as in word formation and lexical development (Clark, 1981, 1982). Thus, in his most recent work on operating principles which inform what he terms the child's *language making capacity*, Slobin (in press) delineates "a network of operating principles that filter and analyze speech input into the units and frames that provide the substance for grammatical structures." MacWhinney (in press) specifies a set of fifteen basic operating principles within his dialectic model, including, for instance, *rote, analogy, inference*, and *rule formation*. He distinguishes different kinds of strategies as operating with respect to each principle, differentiating between learning and processing in terms of the three processes of *application, monitoring*, and *acquisition*. Clark's recent work focuses on the role of acquisitional principles in the learning of word formation (Clark, 1981; Clark and Hecht, 1982), specifically semantic *transparency, formal simplicity, productivity*, and *convention* or how semantic categories in fact are lexicalized in a given language.

Such attempts to specify general operating principles which shape the path of language learning seem to provide the most promising research orientation to date. They make it possible to characterize overall cognitive principles and organizational strategies brought to bear on the specific task of acquiring a language, where this is viewed essentially as an expanding network of form-meaning relations. Despite differences in focus between individual scholars mentioned above, all base their claims on detailed data from spontaneous output as well as experimental designs. It is then possible to address questions concerning both language production and language comprehension, as well as the interrelation between the two. Their data refer to different domains of linguistic structure, morphophonology, the lexicon, as well as syntax, and such work is typically cross-linguistic and comparative rather than anglocentric. And such research accommodates in-depth study of the reorganization of linguistic knowledge over time (see, for instance, Karmiloff-Smith, 1979; Bowerman, 1982). In general, such studies seem to capture more of the spirit of children as learners in interaction with language as the object of their learning than other views touched on above. Their work thus seems more relevant to the cross-linguistic study of *second language* acquisition than an "everything else" approach which dismisses so-called auxiliary hypotheses as distinct from the crucial question of rule acquisition, on the one hand, or which focuses exclusively on nonlinguistic strategies of speech development on the other.

3. INTERACTION OF OPERATING PRINCIPLES WITH FACETS OF LANGUAGE LEARNING

This section considers the nature and role of various such operating principles in relation to different facets of the language-learning situation. Specifically, we discuss how various operating principles interact in terms of developmental sequencing and reorganization of strategies over time (Section 3.1), how they interact with specific domains of linguistic structure and with one another (3.2), with typological and language-specific properties of the target language (3.3), and with linguistic universals (3.4).

3.1 DEVELOPMENTAL SEQUENCES AND PATTERNS OF REORGANIZATION

An important motivation of work on operating principles, acquisitional processes, perceptual strategies, etc., has been to predict what is relatively easy or more difficult for the learner. This, in turn, should make it possible to establish developmental sequences for different kinds of acquisition. In general, it might be the case that context-anchored auxiliary hypotheses of the kind noted in the preceding section will *precede* structure-dependent rules of grammar. This is the view espoused, for instance, by Roeper (1982), by which various cognitive abilities are construed as functioning to *trigger* linguistic abilities.

Indeed there is a growing body of evidence that children proceed from an initial heavy reliance on extralinguistic cues and criteria via attention to surface features of configurational arrangements such as linear ordering of elements, and on to more independently grammatical principles in terms of word class membership, morphological markings, and syntactic relations. Thus, for the two- to three-year-old, when moving into basic command of the morpho-syntactic structures of his mother tongue, what Cromer (1976) terms "action-based" strategies might be critical for an initial construal of form-meaning relations. These include such *a priori* organizing principles as studied, for instance, by Clark in relation to the emergence of locatives (1973, 1977), and they take the form of so-called "probable event strategies" (e.g., in a sentence like *Dad hit Johnny because he was angry/crying* the pronoun will be taken to refer to the father for anger, to the child for crying), in the sense of interpreting utterances in terms of real-world likelihood or what is familiar from extra-linguistic experience. Subsequently, children will pay attention to surface forms, relying on intermediate type "word order" strategies such as NVN being identified with actor-action-patient even in a string such as *the cow is pushed by the horse*. Only later, with the emergence of a more autonomously structural command of the rules of grammar, will such strategies give way to greater reliance on formal features of morphosyntactic structure.

It is by no means clear, however, whether or how developmental patterns may function differentially in relation to specific linguistic systems, to comprehension and production processing respectively, and in different settings of experimental paradigms compared with contextualized usage. For instance, in a study of Hebrew speakers' acquisition of word formation devices for naming innovative agents and instruments (Clark and Berman, 1984), we found that preschool children rely heavily on the principles of semantic *transparency* (favoring one-to-one mapping between formal markers and semantic contents) and formal *simplicity* (favoring devices that are stem-external and/or which require minimal modifications of a basic stem form). Older children and adults, however, having a larger repertoire of both specific lexical items and the devices by which they are derived, pay relatively more attention to the principle of *conventionality* (how specific meanings happen to be encoded in the current lexicon) as well as to the relative *productivity* of a device in general colloquial usage.

One way to specify how operating principles interact with language development over time, then, is in terms of successive reorganizations of specific linguistic subsystems. I am currently working on a developmental model to account for reconstruals which children entertain en route from initial, immature acquisitions through to a normative command of their grammar and lexicon (Berman, 1985). Evidence for a very general pattern of sequencing is yielded by Hebrew-speaking children's learning of a number of different subsystems. These include: *Plural*—marked in Hebrew by the inflectional ending-*im* for masculine and-*ot* for feminine nouns, with numerous stem changes depending on the lexical subclass of different nouns (e.g., *séfer/sfar-im* "book/s," *sifra/sfar-ot* "number/s"), and applying across the syntax in Subject-Verb and Noun-Adjective agreement; *Tense/Mood*—where, for any verb, there is a five-way choice between infinitive, imperative, present, past, or future forms; *Predicate Type*—where verb morphology marks intransitive versus transitive active versus passive or middle voice, as well as causatives, reflexives, reciprocals, and inchoatives; as well as *Noun Classes*—where, again, morphology may distinguish such classes as agents, instruments, place names, and collectives (for details of such research, see the review in Berman, in press).

These distinct subsystems, in which semantics interacts with morpholexical and syntactic patterning, manifest a common developmental pattern, proceeding from *nonanalysis to productivity*, as follows:

(1) a. Rote-learned, unanalyzed amalgams or chunks
    b. Initial alternations of several highly familiar exemplars
    c. An interim schema in the form of a nonnormative rule
    d. Application of the normative rule with some deviations
    e. Appropriate rule application constrained by lexical exceptions, and other non–rule-governed limitations

This sequence pays account to *rote* as an important early acquisitional strategy, where some quite straightforward imitation is still operative, prior to any ability to analyze surface linguistic forms (as discussed, for instance, in Bowerman, 1982; R. Clark, 1974; MacWhinney, 1978, 1981). Thus, a child may use the plural forms *ca'acu-im* "toy-s" or *kubiy-ot* "block-s," the causative verb form *le-havi* "to bring" (cf. *la-vo* "to come" from the same consonantal root), or dative marking in an unsegmented string such as *tavíli* = /taviʔi li/ "bring + Fem (it) to-me" well before he or she has done any analyzing at all.

Analysis is first triggered by and for a few highly familiar lexical items or constructions (e.g., *yeled* "child" and *ylad-im* "children" both occur, as do intransitive *nixnas* "go in" and causative *hixnis* "put in," and so do different forms of a very common verb such as *la-lexet* "to go"—e.g., *lexi!* "go away!", *holxim* "are-going," and *halax-ti* "I went"). These usages are no longer fully routinized, since they are evidence of a certain amount of *alternation*—the same noun being used in both singular and plural, say, or the same verb in different tenses. But the child's construals are still heavily input-bound, and he/she is not yet capable of extracting a rule to apply beyond these few familiar exemplars.

Only in the intermediate stage will the learner show linguistic creativity in applying a rule-bound set of form-meaning alternations (1c above). This is not necessarily by means of a normative construction. For instance, in agent noun innovation, children create words in Hebrew along a pattern of present tense verb stem plus agentive ending, which does not occur in the conventional lexicon (e.g., *mistakel* "look-looker" yields **mistakl-an* "looker," *mafxid* "frighten" yields **mafxid-an* "frightener"). And in certain verb classes, children overmark present tense in talking about ongoing events by means of prefixal *m-* so that alongside of well-formed present tense verbs such as *mistakel* "is-looking," *mafxid* "frightens," or *mevi'im* "are-bringing," children will come out with forms such as **mizaher* "takes care" (cf. normative *nizhar*), or **mesim* "is-putting" (cf. normative *sam*). At this point, the child is applying a linguistic rule and making use of a *structural* strategy to do so. And it is only at this third step that there is clear evidence for the child having knowledge of the *semantics* of a given formal distinction—such as agents versus instruments, self-initiated versus causative events, or ongoing versus perfective events.

Subsequently, this interim schema or transitional bridge strategy will be replaced by the normative rule (1d above). However, constraints on its application may not yet be fully recognized. For instance, in English, nouns such as *sheep* or *deer* do not take a plural ending, and the noun *cooker* refers to an object-instrument and not a person-agent, since the latter is pre-empted by the form *cook*. Similarly, in Hebrew there is one basic intransitive verb pattern which is most generally used for reflexives, inchoatives, and also reciprocals—but verbs with a reciprocal meaning such as *lifgosh* "to meet" or *lariv* "to quarrel" do not occur in this particular pattern in the current lexicon. Only in the final stage of acquisition (1 e above) will the learner have command both of the general, normative rule of grammar and of the constraints which restrict its domain to certain constructions or sets of lexical items.

This kind of analysis devolves on highly specific subsystems of form/content mappings. It takes into account sources of "auxiliary hypotheses" such as context, input, and familiarity (e.g., in determining which items serve as triggers in Stages 1 a and 1 b above) as well as different kinds of processing operations (e.g., the role of such principles as formal simplicity and overt marking of distinct categories). And it aims to show how certain strategies interact as the child acquires the rules of grammar. Each of the five steps might have a different status depending on the specific type of knowledge involved. Clearly, they will not operate in the same way or degree across all subsystems and levels of knowledge. For instance, English-speaking children will apply interim rules of past tense formation differentially for distinct subclasses of verbs (Bybee and Slobin, 1982); and a Hebrew-learning child aged three might be at Step (d) with regard to all the major inflectional forms of the language, yet only entering Step (b) in making use of derivational patterns of word formation (Berman, 1982a; Clark and Berman, 1984).

In the present context, what seems important is not the precise nature of these claims, but the importance of detailed developmental studies— particularly ones which consider the same systems in both early and later childhood—as in Bowerman's work on causatives, Cromer's on temporal reference, and Karmiloff-Smith's on determiners and anaphoric reference. Studies which probe complex patterning of analysis and reanalysis yielding different construals along the path to end-state, adultlike knowledge seem most likely to suggest predictive models for the character of *interlanguages* in second as in first language acquisition.

3.2   DOMAINS OF LINGUISTIC STRUCTURE

As noted, account needs to be taken of how operating principles interact, or fail to interact, with different kinds of knowledge—in understanding and producing utterances, in syntax, morphology, the lexicon, and semantics respectively. Some principles might apply across the board. Thus, there seems to be a clear perceptual basis to the claim that it is difficult for learners (and users) to process *interrupted sequences*, as noted from different perspectives by Bever (1970), MacWhinney (1978), and Slobin (1973). This would explain, for instance, why vowel infix alternation typical of Semitic languages might make it difficult for Hebrew-speaking children to learn the difference in meaning between, say, *kacar* "short," *kicer* "shortened," *kucar* "made short," *kicur* "shortening"; or between *katav* "wrote," *kotev* "is-writing," *ktav* "handwriting," *ktiv* "spelling," *katuv* "written." And it might also explain difficulties English-speaking children have with discontinuous verb-particle combinations (evidenced when a child says, for instance, "turn *off* the light *off*"). Yet superficially identical "interrupted sequences" may function differently in the acquisition of different kinds of linguistic categories. Thus, in producing innovative diminutives, Hebrew-speaking children will use suffixes rather than stem-internal interrupted sequences. For instance, from *xatul* "cat" they will derive **xatul-on* "kitty" long before they use the conventional reduplicative form *xataltul*. And they also prefer suffixes to stem-internal changes in coining agent nouns: for instance, from *le-xabek* "to hug" they will give **xabkan* "hugger" or **mexabk-an* "hugs-er," but never **xabak*, even though this is a common agent-noun pattern in Hebrew, as in *cayar* "painter," *tabax* "cook" (Berman and Sagi, 1981; Clark and Berman, 1984). This confirms that Hebrew learners have difficulty with using interrupted sequences in acquiring devices for forming new words. Yet even younger children, aged two to three, do rely on alternations of infix vowels to distinguish between present versus past tense inflection for many common verbs (compare present tense *o-e* combinations in *holex* "goes, is walking," *oxel* "is eating," *shote* "is drinking," and *ose* "is doing" with past tense *a-a* in *halax, axal, shata* and *asa* respectively). Thus a straightforward operating principle—based on the perceptual salience of stem-external markers compared with linear reorganization of single constituents whose elements do not appear in sequence—may provide a stumbling block for learners in one part of the grammar but not another.

Another difficulty in attempting to validate operating principles across the board is that, as noted earlier, certain semantic categories may impinge on several different subsystems of the morphosyntax. For instance, gender marking interacts with the article systems in French and German, say, but not in Hebrew. Similarly, Bowerman (1974, 1981) has shown that for the acquisition of English causatives, children need to acquire certain kinds of lexical information (compare *I'm moving it/it's moving* but *I'm pushing it/*it's pushing*), but that this interacts with the syntax of auxiliary-type verbs (*make her sing, get it to go, have them help*) as well as with the verb-particle system (*come in* versus *bring in, go out* versus *take out*). Hebrew-learning children also have to contend with a complex interplay of morphological, syntactic, and lexical knowledge in acquiring the semantics of causatives (Berman, 1980, 1982a). But in their language, this critically interrelates with the use of verb patterns in the expression of such categories as transitivity, reflexives, and inchoatives. Thus, examination of operating principles within one linguistic category—e.g., causatives—involves consideration of other categories which impinge on that same subsystem, and it does so differentially for different languages (and see, further, Section 3.4 below).

Thus, for instance, proposals about how children learn the propositional case-role distinctions of agent versus instrument (e.g., *the boy hits the nail with a hammer* versus *the hammer hits the nail*) do not seem relevant to how they acquire the lexical classes of agent and instrument nouns, say *hitter* versus *hammer*. Yet it might be worth examining what kinds of operating principles and acquisitional strategies are at play in the development of propositional, case-role form/content mappings and encoding of related notions in lexical noun classes respectively. Or, there is evidence that certain features of Tense-Aspect marking apply across the board in children's early verb usage: present tense forms are preferred for durative verbs like *sleep, cry* or statives like *know, want,* whereas preterites are used for end-state or punctual verbs like *broke, fell* (Bickerton, 1981). Yet little is available on how this particular acquisitional strategy interacts with the development of other subsystems deployed in the expression of temporal and aspectual distinctions—for instance, time adverbs such as those meaning *now, already, soon, all the time* and conjunctions such as *when, until, as soon as.*

Such in-depth investigation of specific semantic domains as permeating different subsystems of the grammar could be based on hypotheses deriving from the kind of operating principles suggested to date. As findings emerge for different languages, order of development could be predicted for these domains in languages not yet studied. And as findings emerge for different subsystems across languages, operating principles can be reevaluated and refined (as is done in Slobin, in press). Ideally, it might be possible to establish an interactive hierarchy of the different principles which are specified. This is complicated, because of potential conflicts between one principle and another—even at a single developmental stage or in a single linguistic subsystem. Thus, the pull towards a one-to-one mapping between semantic content and surface form may compete with the demand that language be "quick and easy" (Slobin, 1977). Work on children's grasp of innovative agent and instrument nouns reveals that the principle of semantic transparency might, moreover, conflict both with the criterion of formal simplicity and with the principle of linguistic productivity (Clark and Berman, 1984). Also, reliance on the perceptually salient cue of word-level stress in a language which has regular word-initial stress may be at odds with the injunction to pay attention to what comes at the end of words (Peters, 1981). Below we consider yet one more factor which needs to be taken into account in attempting any such integrated model of operating principles in relation to development, to semantic and grammatical domains, and to one another: the nature of the language being acquired.

3.3   THE ROLE OF LANGUAGE TYPOLOGY

In acquiring a language, the learner must come to appreciate what kind of object he is engaged with, in order to set up expectations and make predictions deriving from quite general properties of the target language which are yet not common across all natural languages. Below we review studies which illuminate the role of typological predispositions in children's acquisition of their native tongue.

i) Lust (1981) reports on a series of studies of how children process anaphoric relations—for instance, in conjunction reduction working both forward (as in *kittens hop and Ø run*) and backward (*kittens Ø and dogs hide*) as well as in pronominal anaphora across complex clauses, again both forward (*Tommy ran fast because he heard a lion*) and backward (*while he was outside, Tommy saw a fire truck*). Lust concludes that her subjects' preference for forward anaphora or rightward reduction, and their reluctance to interpret coreference relations in terms of backward anaphora (leftward reduction) is a function of the basic right-branching direction of their language, English. The prediction then would be that, say, Japanese learners would be conversely affected by this factor, and that they will tend to prefer backward to forward anaphora in line with the mainly left-branching direction of their language.

ii) Hakuta (1981) reports on a series of studies of Japanese children's performance on tasks with relative clauses and other types of complex sentences selected, *inter alia*, for properties of linear ordering and direction of embedding. He finds that in English, linear order is confounded with the grammatical status of constituents owing to the strict word order requirements of English syntax. By contrast, in a language like Japanese, where word order is far more flexible, young children's construals of complex clause relations are determined crucially by considerations of linear order (what Hakuta terms "configurational arrangements"). This indicates that while similar strategies may be applied by all learners, the content of the task may be rather different for learners of different types of languages. One crucial difference in the acquisition task would then be between different types of word order languages, as shown by the findings of Bates *et al.* (1984). It is feasible, in terms of our earlier discussion (Section 3.1) that initial reliance on surface configurations will give way to considerations of structure-dependent constraints irrespective of the nature of the target language. But structural factors may have relatively different roles depending on the specific nature of word order constraints in the language in question.

iii) Stress patterns may also play a different role as perceptual cues depending on the nature of the target language. As noted earlier, for instance, languages with regular, predictable stress patterns provide learners with important cues in segmenting the overall stream of speech (Peters, 1981), in turn downgrading the importance of the recency effect of word endings. For Hebrew learners, however, the two parameters largely coincide, since word stress is usually on the last syllable, whether a stem *tarmíl* "bag" or a suffix *tarmil-ím* "bags," *tarmil-ó* "bag-his = his bag." so that they should have an important aid in segmenting the stream of speech into words. As another example, consider the fact that in English even quite young children recognize noun compounds in terms of their unique stress pattern. Yet adult Hebrew speakers who are highly proficient in English as a second language do not seem able to distinguish between, say a *dárkroom* and a *dark róom*—possibly because in Hebrew stress is simply nonfunctional in distinguishing noun-noun compounds from noun-adjective combinations (cf. the compound *xadár xoshex* "darkroom," *xadréy xoshex* "darkrooms" versus *xeder xashúx* "(a) dark room," *xadarím xashuxím* "dark rooms"). Again, at issue is not merely knowledge of isolated facts about a given target language, but more general structural cues which learners come to perceive as relevant to their processing of linguistic material. And it indeed seems to be the case, as Bates *et al.* (1984) conclude from their comparative study of sentence comprehension tasks given to English-speaking and Italian preschoolers from age 2½, that from a very early age (the authors claim "from the beginning"), children are "sensitive . . . to the information value of cues in their particular language."

iv) Knowing a language clearly entails recognizing what the available structural options are, and also how they interact with other options in the language. This is shown by cross-linguistic comparison of children's use of noun compounding in coining new words in English and in Hebrew. For English-speaking three-year-olds, a preferred device when asked to give a name to "a girl who pulls wagons" would be something like *wagon-girl*, while older children gave derived compounds such as *wagon-puller* (Clark and Hecht, 1982). Hebrew-speaking children responded to a similar task with relatively few compounds, and they did so from a later age, not before age five (Clark and Berman, 1984). Yet in terms of the task, compounding is structurally less complex for Hebrew-speaking children, since Hebrew retains the same verb-object order in the nominal form, too (compare English *the boy pulls wagons/wagon-boy* or *wagon-puller* with Hebrew *yeled moshex agalot/yeled agalot* "boy-of wagons = wagon-boy" or *mashxan agalot* "puller-wagons = wagon-puller"). The results are, rather, due to differences between the two languages: English, as a largely analytic language, makes wide use of compounding or juxtaposition of existing words to form new words (and this is even more striking in other Germanic languages such as German or Norwegian). Hebrew, as a Semitic language with a rich bound morphology and set noun patterns for different morphosemantic classes, favors use of affixation for new words. Thus, English-speaking children know from an early age how to form compounds, and they use this as a quite favored device for coining new nouns. Hebrew-speaking children come to learn that they *can* make use of compounds, but they recognize other devices as more typical or less marked for the coining of new lexical items.

v) A final example is provided by the learning of passives. There is ample evidence that children avoid passive structures in their early output (apart from rote-learned adjectivelike forms such as *broken, torn, hurt*), and that they also find them harder to understand than active sentences. This is partly due to the fact that passives are more marked constructions: they depart from canonic word order/semantic role correspondences, they have more complex verb morphology, and they focus on a nonactor noun. But there are also typological differences as to whether a passive must or should be used in a given language. Thus, in Hebrew even ten-year-olds will avoid using passive constructions, even though these are not structurally more complex than their counterparts in, say, English, German, or French. The reason Hebrew speakers do not avail themselves so widely of this formal option is that they have other highly productive constructions which fulfill the main functions of passive sentences—to downgrade agency and/or to focus on the patient-experiencer. These options include impersonal subjectless sentences with plural verbs, use of middle-voice predicates, and fronting of nonsubject nominals—all constructions well in evidence by around age four.

In other words, given the same operating principles, the same non-linguistic strategies, and similar structural options, learners also come to know which forms are favored for which functions in their language. This knowledge derives from familiarity with common input forms. But it also depends on recognition of (a) the availability of other devices for expressing the same content and (b) the congruence of these devices with the main typological predispositions of their language—for instance, morphological affixation rather than syntactic conversion or juxtaposition in forming new words; required subject-verb syntax of English or French compared with languages like Hebrew which allow experiencers to be specially marked as dative in verb-initial syntax (e.g., *hu ibed et hatik* "he lost the bag" versus *ne'ebad la hatik* "got-lost *to-him* the bag," where *he* is construed as experiencing the loss); and the relative constraints on linear ordering of major sentence constituents—as grammatically determined in strict word order languages or as pragmatically flexible in, say, Hebrew, Hungarian, or Italian.

It is likely that the kind of modified "determinism" espoused in Section 1 above may apply particularly in this connection of the formal options available to speakers for expressing certain semantic contents and/or pragmatic functions. That is, linguistic pacesetting of cognitive development may be sought in just those domains which display a particularly elaborate set of form/function correspondences—e.g., expression of different kinds of irrealis conditionals in English, various ways of highlighting nonagent nominals in Hebrew, or the ease with which compound adjectives are available in Norwegian. A very different but no less important typological parameter of language learning is discussed in some detail in Berman (in press). Learners must gain mastery of linguistic structures which have no obvious communicative function, yet are critical to the grammar of their language. Examples include the special syntactic patterning of English auxiliaries like *be, do, have,* and modals in different constructions (interrogatives, negatives, affirmations) or the pervasiveness of number and gender concord in Hebrew syntax, in Subject-Verb and Noun-Adjective-Determiner agreement. These are instances of relatively early morphosyntactic acquisitions where various nonlinguistic, context-based strategies seem minimally relevant, whereas structure-dependent rules of the grammar will soon force themselves upon the learner as he moves on to become a native speaker of a language with that particular type of patterning.

This returns us to the theme of a possible difference in interplay of operating principles in relation to different kinds of linguistic knowledge.

Evidence to this effect is provided by study of patterns of *loss* of English as a second language among Israeli gradeschoolers following their return to a Hebrew-speaking environment after a prolonged stay in the United States and attainment of nativelike proficiency in English (Berman and Olshtain, 1983). The English these children used after six months to a year back in Israel showed hardly any elementary errors of the kind common among school learners of English as a second language: omission of the indefinite article, of the copula *be* in present tense, and of -*s* marking on third person verbs in the present. However, that their English had deteriorated was evident in certain other kinds of errors which they did make: in word order both within and across major constituents, in avoidance of dangling prepositions, in omission of object pronouns where the referent is clear from context (e.g., Q: What happened to your watch? A: I lent Ø to a friend of mine), and use of lexical repetition for intensifying. We interpreted this as indicating that rather different kinds of language knowledge were involved here. Superficial markers of isolated grammatical categories, often having no overt marker at all in other languages, are learned early on, and they become so automatic that they are not so susceptible to forgetting—e.g., indefinite articles, present-tense *be*, and 3rd singular verbs marked by -*s*. By contrast, aspects of language which may be more subject to (nonpathological) attrition will reflect quite general typological properties of the language in question; they express important semantic distinctions—e.g., in Hebrew word order is used to distinguish head from modifier in noun compounds—and they perform clear pragmatic functions, such as the use of fronting to focus on a nonsubject constituent (cf. English *the decorations can go up tomorrow* with the Hebrew form *the decorátions we can put up tomorrow*).

Operating principles for language acquisition thus can be related to the language-specific predispositions that will be set up in the learner in terms of which he or she can make typologically viable predictions about how things work in that language. Such principles can, further, be examined in relation to different kinds of knowledge within a given language, comparing peripheral or incidental with more central properties of its structure, on the one hand, and purely formal systems such as gender marking with ones having clear functional correlates such as word order, on the other.

3.4 LINGUISTIC UNIVERSALS

The notion of linguistic universals, like others discussed above, will differ in terms of the theoretical and research orientation which is espoused. The term figures centrally in the first view outlined in Section 1 above. Here, the Language Acquisition Device is construed as incorporating linguistic universals which serve to constrain the learner's hypotheses about the form and content of the grammar of the language he happens to be acquiring. A major motivation of the typologically oriented study of universal grammar is to establish cross-linguistic predictions about overall trends (e.g., inflecting or isolating, verb-initial or verb-final, grammatical or pragmatic word order) as correlating with other properties and clusters of properties in a given language-type. For the cross-linguistic study of language acquisition, a key issue is the kinds of knowledge which *all* learners will acquire (or, from a more nativist perspective, bring to bear on the task) irrespective of the particular language which is being learned.

Two directions seem to afford fruitful ways of examining how nonlinguistic principles might interact with linguistic universals in acquisition. First, there is by now a large body of cross-linguistic research into semantic categories which may be differently realized on the surface—through morphology, syntax, and/or the lexicon. These include manipulative and indirect causatives (Shibatani, 1976), lexicalized versus syntactically productive reflexivization (Faltz, 1977), and different notions of path, figure, manner, and cause as mapped onto motion verbs (Talmy, 1984). General cognitive development, both structural operations and conceptual content in the sense delineated in Section 2.1 above, may account for overall similarity in the general sequence in which the relevant semantic distinctions are acquired in different languages—with English, Hebrew, and Japanese affording clear typological contrasts in these respects. Yet details of the acquisitional patterning of how semantic distinctions are mapped onto surface forms may also depend critically on language-specific properties of the target language in such cases.

A second thrust in recent work on language universals incorporates both first and second language acquisition in a single frame of reference. Such research attempts to specify universal trends of *change* in linguistic systems in some kind of transitional state: over the course of history, in early childhood, in second language learning, and in situations of language contact leading to the emergence of pidgins and creoles (Bickerton, 1981; Givón, 1979; Meisel, 1977). Again, a fruitful line of investigation is to start out with well-defined linguistic categories which manifest clear cross-linguistic patternings of form/content relations—such as those noted above, as well as tense-aspect systems, noun classification by gender and determiner systems, or devices for compounding. Certain common features can be detected in reanalyses, simplifications, regularizations, and other types of modifications of such linguistic subsystems across different transitional genres (sub-languages and/or interlanguages). This could provide a way of teasing out just those operating principles which play a role universally across situations of language learning and of language change.

Such research seems important in order to separate out linguistic universals as distinct from other kinds of general conceptual or factual knowledge. And this in turn seems necessary to establish what mental operations and processing strategies are brought to bear on the task of learning a language, as distinct from any other kind of learning. The position I have tried to elaborate in this paper, then, is that both linguistic factors and general cognitive principles must be brought to bear on learning, first, a particular language (English, Japanese, Hebrew, or Turkish) and, second, a particular linguistic subsystem (causatives, dimensional adjectives, gender marking, inflectional morphology). Cross-linguistic second language research as exemplified in this volume can best proceed from the bottom up: starting with semantic categories expressive of different concepts and functions, via typological questions of markedness and overall predispositions, on to the role of general cognitive principles and processing strategies, as all these interact with pragmatic parameters of input and discourse. Applying such an overall strategy we can best achieve the goal of specification of linguistic universals as a predictive basis for a theory of language acquisition both in the native tongue and in second languages.

4. SOME IMPLICATIONS FOR SECOND LANGUAGE ACQUISITION

The focus in this paper has been on language-internal factors concerning the patterning of form/meaning relations in the target language, on the one hand, and on learner-internal factors relating to general operating principles and processing strategies, on the other. In my paper for the EuNam I workshop (Berman, 1984), by contrast, emphasis was laid on the extent to which second language acquisition is affected by "environmental" factors such as language background, source of input, and context of the learning situation. It follows that rather different questions arise for the current study, when such external factors are taken into account, as must be done it seems to me in order to consider the nature and role of cognitive components in second language acquisition (SLA).

Thus, for instance, naturalistic SLA in childhood could provide a unique area for investigating cognitive parameters which are "transferred" from first to second language learning. This is not the issue generally considered in the study of childhood bilingualism, of cognitive effects of acquiring more than one language at an early age (e.g., Ben-Zeev, 1977). Rather, the question here is what general strategies are shared or distinct in the two learning situations. To ascertain an answer, one would need to undertake careful comparative study of how a certain language is acquired as a native tongue (in terms of specific subsystems of form/meaning relations as noted earlier) and by, say, five- to eight-year-olds acquiring that same language as a second language. Yet owing to the importance of external factors noted for SLA in general, this would also need to be compared with the learning of that same second language by children of other backgrounds—linguistic, socioeconomic, and motivational.

A second question for childhood SLA concerns linguistic determinism, or linguistic pacesetting of cognitive development (Slobin, in press). The question here would be what cognitive effect there might be to learning a language which makes distinctions not overtly marked by the grammar of the mother tongue. For instance, Hebrew lacks formal marking of naming versus nonspecific reference through use of the indefinite article (e.g., *What did you say?—doll?* versus *What did you want?—a doll?*) or between perfect and perfective past (e.g., *I've eaten an egg today* versus *I ate an egg today*). Monolingual speakers of a language like Hebrew could be compared, say, with their contemporaries who have acquired English as a second language in childhood, to test the hypothesis that the latter may have a clearer *conceptual* grasp of such distinctions than children who know only a language where this is not overtly manifested in the grammar.

A different set of questions arises in relation to postpuberty SLA. The claim could be made that adults learning another language "have presumably passed through all the developmental stages and possess all the necessary cognitive equipment" (Cromer, 1978: 120). This implies that any difficulties arising in adult second language learning are due to lack of lin- guistic rather than lack of cognitive knowledge or abilities. Findings which cast doubt on this hypothesis are provided by a pilot study conducted with native Hebrew speakers of different ages and sociocultural backgrounds. Ravid (1985) found that on a wide range of elicitation tasks there was a greater-than- chance similarity between the performance of the youngest subjects, aged three to four, and a control group of adults of low educational background. The strategies used by these adults (on such tasks as backformation of singular from plural forms or innovative coining of nouns), as well as their deviations from more normative usage, had much in common with those of young children by contrast with well-educated adults. And there is much other evidence, too, of the impact of formal schooling on linguistic construals and usages in the native tongue, particularly in situations of considerable diglossia (see Berman, in press). Moreover, apart from the impact of educational level and other such variables, it is obvious that given the importance of prior linguistic experience in general, "cognitive equipment" may work negatively in the case of language transfer from the mother tongue to the target language in SLA.

On the other hand, there may indeed be cases where adult second language learners need only to acquire *linguistic* information to encode conceptual distinctions already available to them. In such cases, language learning can indeed be isolated from merely immature or developmental strategies and "auxiliary hypotheses." Such evidence is provided, for instance, by a replication of our Hebrew agent-instrument noun study with children (Berman, Hecht, and Clark, 1982) with adults learning Hebrew as a second language conducted by Miriam Saar (reported in Clark and Berman, 1984). These learners had all the conceptual tools necessary for distinguishing agents from instruments, and as such they handled the task like our control group of native-speaking adults. But the nonnatives lacked the structural devices and conventional knowledge of the lexicon to perform even as well as native-speaking five- to seven-year-olds. Their nonlinguistic strategies were similar to those of the native-speaking adults (all alike in this case were college students), but their language was inadequate. It was not simply "immature," since they knew different kinds of things about these classes of nouns than did young preschool native speakers, nor were their infelicities due to negative transfer, since they were from a variety of first-language backgrounds.

Thus adult second language acquisition can provide insight into a special interplay between available cognitive resources and processing strategies—possibly affected by extraneous factors of level of general education and formal language study—and deficient or as yet nonaccessible linguistic rules and structures. Such research could help pinpoint a basic core of what constitutes linguistic knowledge, and it might show whether, in nonpathological cases, lack of linguistic resources can also be evidence for some cognitive deficit.

NOTES

1. This article is a revision of the position paper entitled "Cognitive Principles and Language Acquisition" presented at the Second European–North American Workshop on Cross-linguistic Second Language Acquisition Research, held at Göhrde, West Germany, in August 1982. I am grateful to participants in the workshop, as well as to Evelyn Hatch, for their helpful comments on an earlier version.

2. For such an analysis see Bates *et al.* (1977). They propose six different models for characterizing the interdependence between linguistic and cognitive, as well as social development. See, too, Roeper (1982) for a review of four views of possible interactions between language ability, cognitive ability, and pragmatic factors.

3. Both Johnston and Cromer, though from rather different perspectives, espouse a weak version of the "cognitive hypothesis" that construes language acquisition as dependent on prior cognitive development. From this point of view, factors other than conceptual development, such as frequency of input or the structural complexity of linguistic forms, will also play a role in language learning.

4. Partly this was due to the increasing impact of a pragmatic or functionalist orientation to child language studies in the 1970s. These in some cases neutralized the distinction between *meaning* in a behavioral sense, of communicative intent, social function, affective connotation and so on, and the referential sense of meaning as semantic content. The first is concerned crucially with what *people* mean, the second with what *utterances* mean.

5. Different formal devices and linguistic subsystems interact in the expression of semantic categories. For example, anaphoric reference is expressed by determiners, by pronouns, and by lexical repetition; aspectual distinctions are marked lexically by choice of verbs, inflectionally in verb forms, as well as through adverbials; and generic versus specific descriptions are distinguished by both determiners and aspect marking—as in *elephants walk slowly* versus *these elephants are walking slowly*. (For detailed examples and discussion, see Talmy, 1984).

REFERENCES

Baker, C. L., and J. M. McCarthy (eds.). 1981. *The Logical Problem of Language Acquisition.* Cambridge, Mass.: MIT Press.

Bates, E., L. Benigni, I. Bretherton, L. Camaioni, and V. Volterra. 1977. From gesture to the first word: On cognitive and social prerequisites. In M. Lewis and L. Rosenblum (eds.), *Interaction, Conversation, and the Development of Language,* New York: Wiley.

Bates, E., and B. MacWhinney. 1982. Functionalist approaches to grammar. In E. Wanner and L. Gleitman (eds.), *Language Acquisition: The State of the Art.* London: Cambridge University Press.

Bates, E., B. MacWhinney, C. Caselli, A. Devescovi, F. Natale, and V. Venza. 1984. A cross-linguistic study of the development of sentence-interpretation strategies. *Child Development* 55: 341–354.

Ben-Zeev, S. 1977. Mechanisms by which childhood bilingualism affects understanding of language and cognitive structures. In. P. A. Hornby. NY: Academic Press.

Berman, R. A. 1980. Child language as evidence for grammatical description: Preschoolers' construal of transitivity in Hebrew. *Linguistics* 18: 677–701.

Berman, R. A. 1982a. Verb-pattern alternation: The interface of morphology, syntax, and semantics in Hebrew child language. *Journal of Child Language* 9: 169–191.

Berman, R. A. 1982b. Dative marking of the affectee role in Modern Hebrew. *Hebrew Annual Review* 6: 35–59.

Berman, R. A. 1983. Establishing a schema: Children's construals of verb-tense marking. *Language Sciences* 13.

Berman, R. A. 1984. Crosslinguistic first language perspectives on second language acquisition research. In R. Andersen (ed.), *Second Languages.* Rowley, Mass.: Newbury House.

Berman, R. A. 1985. A step-by-step model of language learning. In I. Levin (ed.), *Stage and Structure: Human Development,* vol. 1. Norwood, N.J.: Ablex, 191–219.

Berman, R. A. In press. Acquisition of Hebrew. In D. I. Slobin (ed.).

Berman, R. A., B. F. Hecht, and E. V. Clark, 1982. Acquisition of Hebrew agent and instrument nouns. *Papers and Reports on Child Language Development* 21: 16–24, Stanford.

Berman, R. A., and E. Olshtain. 1983. Features of first language transfer in second language attrition. *Applied Linguistics* 4: 223–234.

Berman, R. A., and I. Sagi. 1981. Word-formation processes and lexical innovations of young children. *Hebrew Computational Linguistics* 18: 32–62 (in Hebrew).

Bever, T. E. 1970. The cognitive bases for linguistic structures. In J. R. Hayes (ed.), *Cognition and the Development of Language.* New York: Wiley.

Bickerton, D. 1981. *Roots of Language.* Ann Arbor, Michigan: Karoma.

Blank, M. 1974. The cognitive functions of language in the preschool years. *Developmental Psychology* 10: 225–245.

Bowerman, M. 1974. Learning the structure of causative verbs. *Papers and Reports on Child Language Development* 8: 142–178, Stanford.

Bowerman, M. 1978. Semantic and syntactic development. In R. Schiefelbusch (ed.), *Bases of Language Intervention.* Baltimore, Md.: University Park Press.

Bowerman, M. 1981. Beyond communicative adequacy: From piecemeal knowledge to an integrated system in the child's acquisition of language. *Papers and Reports on Child Language Development* 20: 1–24, Stanford.

Bowerman, M. 1982. Starting to talk worse: Clues to language acquisition from late speech errors. In S. Strauss (ed.), *U-Shaped Behavioral Growth.* New York: Academic Press.

Brown, R. 1973. *A First Language: The Early Stages.* Cambridge, Mass.: Harvard University Press.

Bybee, J., and D. I. Slobin. 1982. Rules and schemas in the development and use of the English past tense. *Language* 58: 265–289.

Chomsky, C. 1969. *The Acquisition of Syntax in Children from 5 to 10.* Cambridge, Mass.: MIT Press.

Clark, E. V. 1973. Nonlinguistic strategies and the acquisition of word meaning. *Cognition* 2: 161–182.

Clark, E. V. 1977. Strategies and the mapping problem in first language acquisition. In J. Macnamara (ed.), *Language Learning and Thought.* New York: Academic Press.

Clark, E. V. 1981. Lexical innovations: How children learn to create new words. In W. Deutsch (ed.), *The Child's Construction of Language.* New York: Academic Press.

Clark, E. V. 1982. The young word-maker: A case-study of innovation in the child's lexicon. In E. Wanner and L. Gleitman (eds.), *Language Acquisition: The State of the Art.* London: Cambridge University Press.

Clark, E. V. and R. A. Berman. 1984. Structure and use in the acquisition of word formation. *Language* 60: 542–590.

Clark, E. V. and B. F. Hecht. 1982. Children's coining of agent and instrument nouns. *Cognition* 11: 1–24.

Clark, R. 1974. Performing without competence. *Journal of Child Language* 1: 1–10.

Cromer, R. 1976. Developmental strategies for language. In V. Hamilton and M. Vernon (eds.), *The Development of Cognitive Processing.* New York: Academic Press.

Cromer, R. 1978. The strengths of the weak version of the cognitive hypothesis for language acquisition. In V. Lee (ed.), *Language Development.* London: Croom Helm.

Corrigan, R. 1979. Cognitive correlates of language: Differential criteria yield differential results. *Child Development* 50: 617–631.

Faltz, L. 1977. Reflexivization: A study in universal syntax. Berkeley, Ca.: University of California doctoral dissertation.

Givón, T. 1979. *Understanding Grammar.* New York: Academic Press.

Hakuta, K. 1981. Grammatical description versus configurational arrangement in language acquisition: Relative clauses in Japanese. *Cognition* 9: 197–236.

Johnston, J. In press. Cognitive prerequisites: The evidence from children learning English. In D. I. Slobin (ed.).

Karmiloff-Smith, A. 1979. *A Functional Approach to Child Language: A Study of Determiners and Reference.* London: Cambridge University Press.

Karmiloff-Smith, A. 1981. The grammatical marking of thematic structure in the development of language production. In W. Deutsch (ed.), *The Child's Construction of Grammar.* London: Academic Press.

Luria, A. R. and F. I. Yudovich. 1959. *Speech and the Development of Mental Processes in the Child.* London: Staples Press (re-issued Penguin Books, 1971).

Lust, B. 1981. Constraints on anaphora in child language: A prediction for a universal. In S. Tavakolian (ed.).

Maratsos, M. P. 1982. The child's construction of grammatical categories. In E. Wanner and L. Gleitman (eds.), *Language Acquisition: The State of the Art.* London: Cambridge University Press.

Maratsos, M. P. 1984. Some current issues in the study of the acquisition of grammar. In P. Mussen (ed.), *Carmichael's Manual of Child Psychology,* 4th ed.

MacWhinney, B. 1978. *The Acquisition of Morphophonology.* Monographs of the Society for Research in Child Development 43, Nos. 1–2.

MacWhinney, B. 1981. Basic processes in syntactic acquisition. In S. Kuczaj (ed.), *Language Development: Syntax and Semantics.* Hillsdale, N.J.: Erlbaum.

MacWhinney, B. In press. Hungarian language acquisition as an exemplification of a general model of grammatical development. In D. I. Slobin (ed.).

Meisel, J. 1977. Simplification, interlanguages, and pidgins in relation to second language pedagogy. In S. P. Corder and E. Roulet (eds.), *Actes du 5ème Colloque de Linguistique Appliquée de Neuchâtel.* Geneva: Droz.

Nelson, K. 1973. *Structure and Strategy in Learning to Talk.* Monographs of the Society for Research in Child Development 38, Nos. 1–2.

Peters, A. 1981. Language typology and the segmentation problem in early child language. *Berkeley Linguistic Society* 7: 236–248.

Pinker, S. 1979. Formal models of language learning. *Cognition* 7: 217–283.

Ravid, D. 1985. Morphophonemic change in modern Hebrew: Four cases of "therapeutic reanalysis." Paper given at First Annual Conference of Israel Society for Theoretical Linguistics, Tel Aviv University, June 9–10, 1985 (in Hebrew).

Roeper, T. 1981. Introduction to Tavakolian 1981.

Roeper, T. 1982. The role of universals in the acquisition of gerunds. In E. Wanner and L. Gleitman (eds.), *Language Acquisition: The State of the Art*. London: Cambridge University Press.

Sheldon, A. 1974. The role of parallel function in the acquisition of relative clauses in English. *Journal of Verbal Learning and Verbal Behavior* 13: 272–281.

Shibatani, M. (ed.). 1976. *The Grammar of Causative Constructions: A Conspectus. Syntax and Semantics* 6. New York: Academic Press.

Sinclair de Zwart, H. 1973. Language acquisition and cognitive development. In T. E. Moore (ed.), *Cognitive Development and the Acquisition of Language*. New York: Academic Press.

Sinclair de Zwart, H. 1975. The role of cognitive structures in language acquisition. In E. Lenneberg and E. Lenneberg (eds.), *Foundations of Language Development Vol. 1*. New York: Academic Press.

Slobin, D. I. 1973. Cognitive prerequisites for the development of grammar. In C. A. Ferguson and D. I. Slobin (eds.), *Studies of Child Language Development*. New York: Holt, Rinehart, Winston.

Slobin, D. I. 1977. Language change in childhood and history. In J. Macnamara (ed.), *Language Learning and Thought*. New York: Academic Press.

Slobin, D. I. 1981. Psychology without linguistics = linguistics without grammar. *Cognition* 10: 27–35.

Slobin, D. I. 1982. Universal and particular in the acquisition of language. In E. Wanner and L. Gleitman (eds.), *Language Acquisition: The State of the Art*. London: Cambridge University Press.

Slobin, D. I. (ed.). In press. *Crosslinguistic Study of Child Language*. Hillsdale, N.J.: Erlbaum.

Talmy, L. 1984. Lexicalization patterns: Semantic structure in lexical forms. In T. Shopen (ed.), *Language Typology and Syntactic Descriptions*, Vol. 3. London: Cambridge University Press, pp. 57–149.

Tavakolian, S. (ed.). 1981. *Language Acquisition and Linguistic Theory*. Cambridge, Mass.: MIT Press.

Vygotsky, L. S. 1962. *Language and Thought*. Cambridge, Mass.: MIT Press (1st publ. 1934).

Weissenborn, J. 1980. L'acquisition de prépositions spatiales: Problems cognitifs et linguistiques. Nijmegen: Max Planck Institute for Psycholinguistics, ms.

Wexler, K., and P. Culicover. 1980. *Formal Principles of Language Acquisition*. Cambridge, Mass.: MIT Press.

CHAPTER 2

The Development of Sentence Interpretation Strategies from a Cross-Linguistic Perspective

Michèle Kail[1]

University of Paris, France

INTRODUCTION

Developmental psycholinguistics is a part of cognitive psychology. Its purpose is to define how linguistic knowledge is elaborated and actualized in language performance. Its goal is to characterize which psychological procedures are utilized by children at different moments of their linguistic development and how these procedures reveal the level of integration of the various phonological, syntactic, semantic and pragmatic processing systems. Language may be characterized by its double function of representation and communication. My studies are primarily devoted to the former, attempting to understand how children analyze the linguistic signal and extract the covariation relations between form and meaning. I have attempted to determine the processes by which children acquire language and the mechanisms underlying these processes, by integrating them into the more general framework of cognitive development. This objective implies the preferential recourse to those linguistic models which stress the underlying structures and rules. However, one should keep in mind that the child simultaneously develops linguistic and nonlinguistic abilities and that it is extremely difficult to dissociate "general knowledge" from linguistic knowledge. My studies dealing with the psycholinguistic processing of coreference assignment and especially my work on the presuppositions of certain connectives emphasize the necessity of taking into account pragmatic dimensions in the analysis of performance, both in children and adults. Since it represents a stable stage of the linguistic subsystems considered, I also studied adults' performance.

The representative perspective has been largely influenced by Chomsky and is mainly centered on the analytical unit constituted by the sentence. The communicative perspective, deriving from the work of Halliday (1967) among others, is focused on discourse in context. My general approach claims the existence of a relation among surface grammatical devices, communicative functions and processing constraints. This functionalist view contests the competence/performance distinction. "In a functionalist theory, there is no competence other than competence-to-perform" (Bates, McNew, MacWhinney, Devescovi and Smith, 1982). The strict distinction between semantics and grammar has been questioned by certain authors, such as Lakoff and Thompson (1975), who defended the view that

> there is a direct and intimate relation between grammars and mechanisms for production and recognition. In fact we suggest that grammars are just collections of strategies for understanding and producing sentences. From this point of view, abstract grammars do not have any separate mental reality: they are just convenient fictions for representing certain processing strategies (p. 295).

The functionalist perspective assumes that the child acquires grammatical forms, for instance that of subject, via the topicalization function. It also stresses the fact that discursive relations participate in the construction of sentences. For example, word order or pronominalization constitute linguistic procedures which express certain relations between "new information" and "old information" (MacWhinney and Bates, 1978).

In syntactic theories, however, especially transformational generative grammars, "subject" or "word order" are primitive concepts, a priori categories; they are derived neither from the agent role nor from the topic/comment distinction.

Certain points mentioned by Bates and MacWhinney support the functionalist approach concerning acquisition:

— longitudinal data concerning word order indicate that in their two-word utterances children already use the topic/comment distinction and the concept of agent;
— data from different languages reflect two functional tendencies concerning word order: (1) a tendency to order information in terms of agent–action; (2) a very early tendency to place new information (comment) before old information (topic) regardless of semantic roles or formal class.

Their hypothesis is that topic initialization is based mainly on the recognition of the listener's needs, whereas comment initialization is based on how salient or new the information is from the child's point of view (see Greenfield and Zukow, 1978). The transition from comment/topic order to topic/comment order corresponds to the ability of the child to take into account the listener's perspective. This has been tested in different paradigms (Krauss and Glucksberg, 1969). Many results support the hypothesis that in very young children the pragmatic comment/topic order (especially used in production) reflects more general attentional processes (Bates, 1976).

It should also be mentioned that many data, as indicated by Bowerman (1973) and Brown (1973), may be interpreted equally well in terms of word order rules of abstract "subject-verb" categories or in terms of word order rules of semantic "agent-action" categories. In order to determine if the child utilizes the syntactic "subject" category, the only pertinent cases are those in which the agent or topic and the grammatical subject are not confounded, as is the case in passive sentences. According to Bates and MacWhinney (1979), the "subject" category apparently has no psychological reality for English-speaking children before the age of 4–5 years.

In the first part of the present paper, the main characteristics of processing strategies in children are summarized (typology of strategies; methodological problems raised in their study). The second part presents a synthesis of studies devoted to strategies—with particular emphasis on French—for interpreting simple and complex sentences (relative and pronominal clauses) and a summary of my own work on the development of strategies of comprehension of utterances involving presuppositions. The third part mentions several cross-linguistic experimental studies of processing strategies. These studies attempt to determine to what extent processing strategies depend on the specific structural characteristics of a language, in other words to determine the manner in which the structure of a given language influences the very process of learning.

1. SOME CONSIDERATIONS OF SENTENCE INTERPRETATION STRATEGIES IN CHILDREN

Fodor and Garrett (1966) and Bever (1970) first stressed that the essential operation in sentence processing consists of discovering the deep semantic relations. To do this, the subject has at his disposal discovery procedures enabling him to use the information contained in the surface structure to recover the configurations of the deep structure. During the past ten years, developmental psycholinguistic studies dealing with processing strategies had various objectives. I will mention only the most important.

1. One objective was to attest to the reality of strategies of comprehension (or production), in other words, to understand the development of the general procedures used by the child in order to attribute agent-patient functions, by selecting certain cues in the surface structure of the utterance: semantic information, information given by the order of lexical elements, and information on potential deep structure conveyed by a given lexical element. In agreement with many authors, especially Bronckart (1983), I distinguish sets of strategies according to the subject's "centration" on one or another type of cue. These strategies presuppose the knowledge of the lexical elements of the utterance.

a. Pragmatic strategies These strategies depend on the establishment of a relation between linguistic and extralinguistic entities and concern general knowledge and acquisition of facts elaborated by the child. The attribution of functions in this case is based on certain characteristics of the situation, for example the plausibility of events or their reversible or nonreversible character. For instance, to understand the sentence "it's the baby that the mother is washing" the very young child refers to his own experience of the regularity of events (Bronckart et al., 1976; Noizet, 1977; Vion, 1980). These pragmatic strategies are observed very early, before 3 years of age.

b. *Word order strategies*   These are processing strategies in which the essential cues concern the position of the two nouns, without taking into account the other available morphosyntactic cues. Various studies (Fraser et al., 1963; Slobin, 1966; Turner and Rommetveit, 1967; Sinclair and Ferreiro, 1970; Bever, 1970) have led to the formulation of a general interpretation rule emerging at around 4 years of age. It consists of attributing the interpretation "agent-action-patient" to all noun-verb-noun sequences. In fact, Segui and I have shown however (Kail and Segui, 1978) that certain results are not interpretable in terms of absolute order strategy but rather in terms of partial order strategy. Lempert and Kinsbourne (1978, 1980) report similar results. Sinclair and Bronckart (1972) mentioned a procedure which occurs at an earlier age and is based on the proximity in relation to the verb: the noun which is the closest to the verb is the agent.

c. *Morphosyntactic or syntactic strategies*   These strategies consist of attributing agent and patient functions on the basis of strictly morphological and syntactic cues (verb, noun, grammatical morpheme forms) other than word order. This type of processing coincides with the complete comprehension of a simple sentence (Noizet, 1977; Bronckart, 1977). Most results agree in pointing out the early character of pragmatic strategies and the progressive occurrence of others, order strategies being reported as occurring earlier than morphosyntactic strategies.

2. A second objective of developmental psycholinguistics was to specify the domains in which such strategies appear. These strategies are most often investigated in the context of a particular linguistic structure (simple sentences, relative sentences, causal, temporal, conditional subordinates) and depend on the level of analysis (isolated sentences or sentences in extended discourse), the methods of investigation (acting out, sentence-picture matching) and the psychological activities involved (comprehension vs. production). From this point of view, it should be mentioned that most conclusions were based on experimental research devoted to the comprehension of utterances.

3. A third objective of research concerning strategies was the analysis of their modes of functioning during development. This involves detecting their emergence and their organizational relations: exclusivity, relative dominance, complementarity, interaction. Many studies point out children's dependence on some strategies, as opposed to the liberty of choice of adult speakers. However, it should be noted that in the procedures used by the adult speakers, there are many indications of their "submission" to the

constraints of the linearity of the discourse. Furthermore, it has been shown (Kail, 1976; Farioli, 1979) that children are capable of adapting the processing strategies at their disposal at a given moment according to the nature of the operations required by the task for example. In addition, it seems that one of the dominant modes of functioning of these strategies is overgeneralization, in other words the application of a previously efficient strategy to cases where it is not required. The acquisition of a given linguistic structure implies the acquisition of restrictive rules concerning the use of these strategies, as emphasized by Sheldon (1974): ". . . learning a language also involves learning not to rely on certain strategies, but learning to restrict the use of certain strategies in those sentences where they do not apply" (p. 280).

4. A fourth objective of developmental psycholinguistics was to characterize the psychological status of strategies in their relation to the general cognitive procedures of information processing: perceptual laws, order rules and operations. Such a characterization, which attempts to define cognitive invariants (operating principles, for example), implies cross-linguistic comparisons. Languages indeed vary considerably in the constraints on word order in the surface structure. This question of the interrelations between cognitive and linguistic dimensions will be dealt with in the third part.

SOME METHODOLOGICAL REMARKS CONCERNING THE IDENTIFICATION OF PROCESSING STRATEGIES

First, it is necessary to underscore the fact that most comprehension studies ask the child to act out the event referred to by the utterance, using toys. The actions produced by children are grouped in categories, the cues chosen by them being inferred from their responses. In this type of investigation, psycholinguists are more interested in the procedures used by the children when acting out an event than by the accuracy of their responses. Although such a method permits the emergence of actions which could not be predicted a priori, it concerns only a restricted set of utterances.

Second, the identification of processing strategies raises some questions as shown by Bronckart, Gennari and De Weck (in press), who recently formulated an interesting distinction between cue intake and effective use of cues in the interpretation of simple sentences. One of the major results of their research was to show that children as young as 4 years old take into account different types of cues: the agentivity of nouns, their position, and the morphosyntactic marks of the sentence. Although the use of pragmatic cues occurs very early, the use of morphosyntactic cues is rather late, between 6 and 10 years of age. The use of word order cues, less frequent than predicted, is observed when the two latter are no longer efficient. These authors proposed, as does Vion (1980), to reserve the term "processing strategy" for those cases in which the same subject uses the same category of cues for attributing agent and patient functions in a stable and systematic way. A subject-by-subject analysis of responses is required to give evidence of the existence of strategies. With a few exceptions (Sinclair and Bronckart, 1972; Lempert and Kinsbourne, 1980; Bridges, 1980; Vion, 1980), however, most authors analyze the responses of groups of subjects of the same age. In this case, it would be preferable to speak of a processing mode.

Whether strategy or mode of processing, the basic question is to determine if the processing procedures result from rules internalized by the child or rather reflect a dominant choice at a given age. As far as I know, the analysis of individual differences concerning the strategies of production and comprehension has not been developed to an appreciable extent, except for the work of Bloom (1975), Nelson (1980) and Lieven (1980). Studies conducted with a differential perspective (concerned for example with the preferential use of a given mark—intonation or word order—in languages presenting redundancies, e.g., Finnish, Polish) should shed some light on our comprehension of the acquisition of language structure. Instead of analyzing the consequences of preferential uses on the subject's subsequent linguistic development, however, studies too often lead to typologies with no special interest (for example, word babies vs. intonation babies, fast learners vs. slow learners, expressive vs. referential, pronominal vs. nominal). It is nonetheless clear that individual differences within a native language, as well as cross-linguistic differences, constitute essential information for the knowledge of universals in language acquisition.

2. CHILDREN'S INTERPRETATION OF SENTENCES

A. THE INTERPRETATION OF SIMPLE SENTENCES

Suppose the following sentences are presented to children:

1. *la fille mange la pomme*   "the girl is eating the apple"
2. *l'indien renverse le soldat*   "the Indian knocks over the soldier"
3. *la pomme est mangée par la fille*   "the apple is eaten by the girl"
4. *le soldat est renversé par l'indien*   "the soldier is knocked over by the Indian"
5. *c'est une pomme que la fille mange*   "it's an apple that the girl is eating"

In children younger than 2½ years, most authors have observed incomplete processing; either the child interprets the action as intransitive, or he himself acts as the agent, the proposed utterance thus being interpreted as noun phrase (NP)–verb (V) or V-NP. Various interpretations have been advanced, some stressing perceptual and cognitive limitations, others referring to linguistic determinations (Sinclair and Bronckart, 1972; De Villiers and De Villiers, 1973; Bridges, 1980).

From the age of 2½ or 3 years, the choice of agent and patient is based on the event plausibility (probable event strategy). Empirical knowledge in (1), (3) and (5) is sufficient to attribute the agent function to *fille* "girl." This is not the case in (2) and (4), however, since both lexemes can fulfill the function of agent (reversible sentences). Event plausibility is itself actualized in certain lexical features (animate vs. inanimate) or in certain characteristics of the action expressed by the verb (Sinclair and Ferreiro, 1970; Cambon and Sinclair, 1974; Lempert, 1978). Evidence of pragmatic strategies is also given for English. Strohner and Nelson (1974), for example, have shown that improbable active sentences of the type *the fence jumps over the horse* are interpreted by 2–3-year-old children as "the horse is jumping over the fence." Five-year-old children, on the other hand, who use word order to a much greater extent when decoding the sentence, act out the "silly" action of the fence jumping over the horse.

Word order strategies   Word order strategies were demonstrated as early as 1963 by Fraser, Bellugi and Brown in the comprehension of passive sentences that 4-year-old children interpret as the corresponding active sentences. This observation was subsequently confirmed by a number of authors.

According to Bever (1970), this behavior would result from the interpretation of all NVN sequences in terms of agent-action-patient. For utterances which do not have the canonical form, the interpretation becomes: the first noun of the sequence corresponds to the agent, the second to the patient.

As summarized by Vion (1980), psycholinguistic studies have shown three types of word order processing:

— strict order: N1 = agent; N2 = patient (Sinclair and Bronckart, 1972; Abrams *et al.*, 1978; Bronckart, 1979);
— partial order: the position of the nouns relative to the verb is taken into consideration: the noun immediately preceding the verb is the agent, that which follows it is the patient (Lempert and Kinsbourne, 1978; Kail and Segui, 1978);
— proximity: the closest noun to the verb is the agent (Sinclair and Bronckart, 1972).

In a study of passive reversible sentences, Sinclair, Sinclair and Marcellus (1971) suggested that children's comprehension depends on their capacity to consider the same event from two distinct points of view. Beilin (1975) assumes that children's capacity to comprehend and to produce such sentences is related to the development of operational reversibility and "decentration." However, the relations between cognitive and linguistic development are too vague and do not enable one to respond to a very important question: are these order rules (very evident in English and French where canonical order is SVO) "linguistic," inferred from regularities of the language, or are they independent of them, and do they consequently depend on perceptual and cognitive constraints? Partial responses to this question will be given in the third part.

Very little developmental research, with the exception of Hornby (1971), Bates (1976) and Parot and Kail (1980), has related the question of word order to that of the topic/comment distinction in the processing of passive sentences. Hornby studied the evolution of cues used by 6- to 10-year-old children for topic and comment identification (in active, passive, cleft and pseudocleft sentences). At 6 years of age, the main factor is the contrastive stress. From 8 years of age on, the child develops a procedure for topic identification based on word order within the sentence. With increasing age, a variety of procedures for distinguishing old information (topic) from new information (comment) are observed.

In a series of experiments, Tannenbaum and Williams (1968) and Turner and Rommetveit (1968) asked children to describe a picture after having heard an introductory text focusing on a given "topic." It was shown that 3- to 7-year-old children answered more rapidly in the passive voice when the introductory topic corresponded to the subject of the passive. This result was partially contradicted in my own work (Parot and Kail, 1980) where it was shown that there was no effect of topicalization on the recall of passive sentences in 8;6-year-old children and that in 9;7-year-old children the effect was the reverse of the one described by Tannenbaum and Williams (1968).

Morphosyntactic strategies   As mentioned above, these interpretation strategies are based on taking surface structure cues into consideration. Contrary to pragmatic strategies, these strategies are specific to a given structure of a language and have been studied to a lesser extent than the former. Bever (1970) gave an example of morphosyntactic strategies when describing a strategy based on the presence of the relative pronoun *that* which enables a role to be attributed to each noun phrase of an utterance. In a surface sequence such as the following:

C'est le garçon que la fille pousse
NP1   NP2   V

NP1 is the object of a basic sentence in which NP2 is the subject. As can be seen, the use of this strategy is in contradiction with the use of word order strategy according to which NP1 is the agent.

Studying the understanding of reflexive and passive sentences with *se faire* (e.g., *la fille se fait battre par le garçon* as opposed to *la fille est battue par le garçon*), Jakubowicz and Segui (1980) showed that young children (4;4) are capable of utilizing the information conveyed by the grammatical morpheme *se*. The use of the reflexive pronoun *se* as a cue of the logical functions of noun phrases would explain that passive sentences with *se faire* are mastered earlier than simple passive sentences.

Other authors (Maratsos and Abramovitch, 1975) also demonstrated the importance of certain grammatical surface structure morphemes: by 3–4 years of age, the absence of a verbal auxiliary in a passive sentence does not modify the interpretation of the sentence. The ellipsis of the preposition *by*, however, leads children to interpret the passive sentence as an active one.

B. THE INTERPRETATION OF COMPLEX SENTENCES

Relative sentences   In studies of the comprehension of relative sentences, the parallel function strategy (sometimes referred to as the no-shift-role strategy), which consists of attributing the same grammatical function to a relative pronoun as to its antecedent, is dominant in children between 3;6 and 6 years of age.

Sheldon (1974), Chipman (1974), and Amy and Vion (1976) indeed showed that relative sentences in which the coreferential NPs have identical functions—SS and OO types as in (6) and (9)—are easier to understand than those in which the coreferential NPs have different functions— SO and OS types as in (7) and (8). (In the examples, PF = parallel function; NPF = nonparallel function.)

Subject relatives:
   6. *The dog that jumps over the pig bumps into the lion* (SS) (PF)
   7. *The lion that the horse bumps into jumps over the giraffe* (SO) (NPF)

Object relatives:
   8. *The pig bumps into the horse that jumps over the giraffe* (OS) (NPF)
   9. *The dog stands on the horse that the giraffe jumps over* (OO) (PF)

It is interesting to note that the same results are obtained in French and English. This strategy accounts for early correct comprehension of some sentences (those which contain parallel functions), as well as for the nature of errors produced by overgeneralizing it to structures which do not contain parallel functions. Improper use of the parallel function strategy is responsible for 66 percent of errors. These results contradict the supposedly universal principle according to which the interruption or rearrangement of linguistic units should be avoided (Slobin, 1966).

To say it is dominant does not mean that other strategies do not come into play during the same period of development, as Amy and Vion (1976) pointed out. Sheldon's study (1974) showed that in right-branching sentences 64 percent of errors were due to the strategy of extraposition (children interpret the relative clause that follows the matrix clause as modifying the subject NP rather than the object NP). Use of this strategy explains the lack of improvement with age on object relatives (OO type) as opposed to performance with subject relatives (SS type).

What becomes of the remarkable coherence provided by the parallel function strategy when one turns to the studies of the production and repetition of relative clauses? It is difficult to answer this question given the small number of studies, the heterogeneity of age groups and the very limited number of studies which required children to describe the action acted out by the experimenter.

A review of the relevant literature (Deyts and Noizet, 1973; Morsly and Mahmoudian, 1973; Amy, 1975; Kail, 1975a, 1975b; Ferreiro, Othenin-Girard, Chipman, and Sinclair, 1976) shows the following results: using different techniques (spontaneous production vs. induced production), Ferreiro *et al.* (1976) found that very young children (4 to 5 years of age) produce mostly coordinate sentences. Relative sentences are not produced at a significant level before 7 years of age. These comparative studies clearly indicate that subject relatives are easier to produce than object relatives. In the case of the former, the easiest are those in which the action to be described refers to an event in which the same agent carries out two distinct actions on two different patients. On the other hand, children have difficulties in using relative sentences when asked to describe events in which two agents carry out two actions on the same patient, or in which the agent of an action plays the role of the patient in another part of the event. These studies reveal a very interesting result: when the relative clause has a determinative function in the sentence it cannot be used at the same time for the narration of an event; this fact explains the "redundant" nature of some productions (e.g., *the elephant washed pushed the monkey*).

These are examples of productions that highlight certain difficulties encountered in the comprehension of relative clauses and which have to do with their functional value. It should also be noted that many 8-year-old children prefer to use a passive rather than an object relative (for studies with adults see Noizet, Deyts and Deyts, 1972). I wish to emphasize that even though the parallel function strategy plays a role, the consistency of data obtained in comprehension and production tasks concerns only the function of agent, as will be shown below, when dealing with the processing of pronominal sentences. For English-speaking children as for French-speaking children, the relative clauses that interrupt the main clause seem to be harder to produce and to imitate than those that do not interrupt it (Kail, 1975a, 1975b; Deyts and Noizet, 1973). I also found that relative clauses introduced by *que* (object relatives) are harder than those introduced by *qui* (subject relatives) and that object relatives where word order is not canonical (e.g., *la fille que la maîtresse appelle gifle le garçon*) are harder than those where the order is canonical (e.g., *la fille qu'appelle la maîtresse gifle le garçon*). This last result is accounted for by the fact that the verb-subject inversion maintains at the surface level an NVN sequence which could induce the use of the NVN adjacency strategy. I also found that with delayed imitation younger children (6 years old) omit relative pronouns; older ones (7;6 years old) substitute *qui* for *que* (*que* is very often changed into *qui*) and simplify the sentence (main clause and relative clause) by producing two separate sentences (Kail, 1975b).

Pronominal sentences   The mastery of the pronominal system implies the integration of information coming from different levels of analysis: that concerning the speaker/listener distinction, that concerning the lexical characteristics of the referent (gender and number) or that concerning syntactic rules. The child must also master the distinction between identity and equivalence, especially since the pronoun can have a function different from that of its antecedent. In a study devoted to comprehension, I showed that a dominant fact is the rather late use of the lexical marks (gender and number) of pronouns and noun phrases in the assignment of coreference (Kail, 1976; Kail and Léveillé, 1977).

Using a variety of techniques, I found that in very young children (between 2;8 and 3;6 years old) the minimal distance strategy is dominant; the coreferent is the closest noun phrase. From 3;6 years of age on, the parallel function strategy predominates. The use of this strategy accounts for the early mastery of utterances involving parallel functions (e.g., *le lapin pousse la souris et il renverse le chat*) and for the errors observed in other cases (e.g., *la vache pousse le chat et il renverse le lapin*); it also accounts for the preferential coreference assignment in the case of anaphoric ambiguities (e.g., *le lapin pousse le chien et il renverse la tortue*).

In a study devoted to the role of stress on pronouns in the comprehension of the corresponding referent, Maratsos (1973) showed that the presence of a contrastive stress changes the pronoun coreference. In young children from 3 to 5 years of age, the comprehension of unstressed pronouns was tested by asking children to act out sentences of the following type: *Susie jumped over the old woman and then she jumped over Harry* and *Susie bumped into the old woman and then Henry bumped into her*. These sentences are interpreted by the use of a no-shift-role strategy. On the other hand, since the comprehension of stressed pronouns implies an inhibition of this strategy, it is difficult for very young children to interpret them as unstressed pronouns. Chipman (1974) also reports that in 3- to 7-year-old children, comprehension of sentences in which the personal pronoun has the same function as its antecedent is better than that of sentences in which the functions of the personal pronoun and its coreferent differ (e.g., *the boy washes the girl and then he knocks over the other boy* vs. *the boy washes the girl and then she knocks over the other boy*). It is as though younger children would prefer to violate lexical rules rather than shift roles. However, I have shown (Kail, 1976) that the generality of the parallel function strategy has two limitations.

a. Using an acting out technique, I found that comprehension of sentences in which the referent of the pronoun is the patient of both clauses (e.g., *la vache pousse le lapin et le chien le renverse*) is more difficult for children under 6 years of age than comprehension of sentences in which the referent of the pronoun is the patient in one clause and the agent in the other (e.g., *la vache pousse le lapin et le chien la renverse*). I suggest that variables influencing topicalization (i.e., a shift in the topic of sentences in which the pronoun is the object) might explain results that are at variance with the general hypothesis according to which children use a cognitive strategy whose purpose is to introduce as little change as possible between the two actions.

b. Using a questioning technique (who knocks over Y? who pushes X?) for both subject (*il, elle*) and object pronouns (*le, la*) with ambiguous coreference, I did not find that children selected the coreferent which the parallel function strategy would predict. The so-called minimal distance strategy, which consists of taking the nearest NP as the coreferent of the pronoun, accounts for the results as well as the parallel function strategy. This dependency on situational variables was confirmed by Farioli's (1979) findings, using a task which required children to judge the accuracy of paraphrases. This study carried out on children from 5 to 11 years old casts doubt upon the privileged status of the parallel function strategy. Farioli suggests that children use a "subject strategy" which consists of selecting as a coreferent the subject of the clause which accompanies the clause containing the pronoun, regardless of the function of the pronoun. The "subject strategy" can be explained by the notion of coreference to the topic. Children probably use this strategy when they become capable of detecting the topic of a sentence, at about 7 years of age according to Hornby, Hass and Feldman (1970). The importance of the topic for determining coreference in sentences with ambiguous pronouns has also been shown in adults both in paraphrase judgment tasks and in sentence completion (Kail, 1979a). A recent study by Grober, Beardsley and Caramazza (1978), however, considers the parallel function strategy as fundamental in coreference assignment. I have shown that this strategy is sometimes employed by adults when the coreferent is ambiguous and when the verb of the main clause does not bring about a privileged interpretation.

In a recent paper (Kail, 1983), I criticize the studies which consider the parallel function strategy as a "natural" general cognitive strategy, independent of situational parameters. One can refer to the parallel function strategy only in the processing of isolated sentences. The importance of topic factors appears when the linguistic units considered are not restricted to such sentences (Kail and Karmiloff-Smith, 1980). In children's narrations, it is observed that only the topic subject is the privileged candidate for pronominalization and the additional referents are not pronominalized (or when they are, a defined noun is added (e.g., *il lui donne un ballon, le marchand* (Karmiloff-Smith, 1981)).

Within the framework of this limited review of sentence comprehension (or production) strategies in children, the following observations can be made: the study of strategies is centered on performance and not on the preliminary conditions which make them possible. One should not underestimate the interest of processing strategies since they intervene in the complex processes governing the passage from sound to meaning and since they may work as a local model of behavior, but one is obliged to point out that no general developmental model has yet been proposed. Studies have indeed determined the age at which a given strategy is first used and the processes of its maturation, but even the most systematic studies fail to make explicit the development of strategies and the cognitive processes which govern the passage from one strategy to another. The manner in which cognitive development plays a role in the maturation and elaboration of a particular strategy remains unclear. It should be noted that most studies, by centering on syntactic variables, accentuate the metalinguistic character of the tasks put to the child.

As Cromer (1981: 62) stated,

> Strategies then are merely ways of answering the psycholinguist's questions or interpreting sentences in the real world when the structure of these sentences is not yet understood and the child does not know what else to do. They do not explain how the child acquires those structures.

Nelson (1973) proposed the distinction between strategies for acquiring language and strategies for processing language. The former are strategies consisting of adding new elements to the original repertoire, whereas the latter match elements to the existing repertoire.

I consider that the study of strategies should go beyond the structural level and should incorporate the functional level, if the many relationships between the child and his language as well as the operations which determine the acquisition of language are to be understood. Concerning coreference, for example, this will involve analyzing aspects of the input which have often been neglected, such as presuppositions which lie at the intersection of problems of interpretation and of language use. Those types of presuppositions are one example of contextual and functional aspects of language to which developmental psycholinguistics should now turn.

THE INTERPRETATION OF SENTENCES CONTAINING CONNECTIVES WITH A PRESUPPOSITIONAL VALUE

Recent work has shown that the meaning of an utterance is not limited to the explicit information conveyed, but is also influenced by implicit information, the processing of which is indispensable for complete comprehension. A speaker expresses in part what he considers to be already known, what he believes is knowledge shared with the listener—in other words, what he presupposes.

Following Ducrot's (1972, 1977) definition, I shall say that the presupposed information in the utterance *John continues to smoke* is: "John used to smoke" and the asserted information: "John smokes presently." Let us recall that whereas sentence negation modifies the asserted information, it does not alter the presupposed information.

As is known, adults are able to make inferences about the speaker's intentions by taking into account the grammatical structure or the choice of particular words. How do young children become capable of making these subtle inferences? Developmental studies devoted to presuppositional processing are limited in number. Of particular interest for us are those which consider presuppositions within the general framework of the communicative act, more specifically the work of Bates (1976), Greenfield and Smith (1976) and Greenfield and Zukow (1978), analyzed in detail by Kail and

Plas (1979). For the present purposes, it suffices to say that the above authors emphasize the early use of presuppositions, at about 18 months, as evidenced by children's one-word utterances. Bates maintains that presuppositions rely on very general cognitive mechanisms which govern strategies used in effecting distinctions between figure and ground, the latter underlying topic/comment distinctions which serve as the basis for the differentiation of presupposed and asserted information. In the same perspective, Greenfield and Zukow (1978), borrowing concepts from information theory, suggest that presupposition as such is rooted in a state of certainty in which something is taken for granted, while the cognitive basis of assertion is uncertainty or change.

In several studies (Kail, 1978, 1979b; Kail and Léveillé, in press) I tried to specify the strategies of comprehension and of recall of sentences with adverbial presuppositions at different developmental stages. An additional goal was to determine how children become aware of the existence of presupposed information. The adverbs used were: *encore* "more, again," *aussi* "also," *même* "even," and *seulement* "only," in sentences like: *je veux aussi des X*. These studies used an experimental setting which simulated a situational context. Children from 5;6 to 8;1 years old were examined.

As predicted, the comprehension of sentences with lexical presupposition depends on the complexity of the inferential operations which link asserted and presupposed information. More specifically, sentences with *encore* are mastered at an earlier age than sentences with *aussi* or *seulement*, since in the first type there is a direct relationship between the meaning of the asserted component ("I want Xs") and the meaning of the presupposed information ("I already have Xs").

The analysis of responses and their justifications lead to the distinction of three stages. In a first stage (before 5;10) the presupposed information is ignored. It is as though children process only the asserted component of the sentence. At this stage, children justify their response on the basis of emotional reasons. In the second stage (from 6 to 8 years of age) there is a partial intuition of the presupposed information. Correct responses are justified by arguments which have no generality and are based on the specific characteristics of the situation or on the anticipated results of the action implied by the sentence. One of the most frequent strategies consists of reducing the complex presupposed information to something simpler, which leads children to interpret *aussi* as *encore*. In the third stage (from 8 years on) the presupposed information is understood, as evidenced by the justifications given by the children and their ability to discuss the conditions of use of a particular sentence. Justifications are no longer based on the characteristics of the situation, but rather on the characteristics of several possible situations defined by the asserted and presupposed information. Furthermore, at this stage children define the conditions of use of the different utterances.

The aim of another study (Kail, 1980) was to see whether sentences which run counter to presupposed information are considered unacceptable to children and if so, at which age children first begin to reject them. In order to answer this question, sentences of the type P *mais* Q were submitted to children's judgment. French linguists (Ducrot, 1977, 1980; Anscombre and Ducrot, 1977) claim that "P but Q" sentences presuppose that the P clause can be an argument leading to an R conclusion and that the Q clause is an argument which cancels this conclusion. Such sentences correspond to only one of the two meanings of *mais* in French, as shown by Anscombre and Ducrot (1977). This particular meaning corresponds to *pero* in Spanish and *aber* in German. (The second meaning of *mais* corresponds to *sino* and *sondern*.) It was particularly interesting to see how children react when confronted with "unacceptable" sentences containing a Q argument which, instead of canceling the conclusion, reinforces it (e.g., *le crayon est neuf mais il écrit bien* "the pencil is new but it writes well"). Children from 6;8 to 9;5 years of age participated in a completion task and a judgment task. The results supported the hypothesis that the comprehension of the argumentative value of *mais* develops gradually, and that the youngest children interpret *mais* as *et* "and." In a second stage *mais* is interpreted as having a weak implication. Children from 6;8 to 8;6 years of age consider the sentence "the pencil is new but it writes well" as acceptable. In order to reject this sentence, the child has to know that the appropriate use of "but" requires the second clause to be a contradiction of a proposition that can be inferred in a specific context from the connective and from P. The context may consist of general world knowledge and/or particular situational information (linguistic and nonlinguistic). The justifications these children give are based on pragmatic regularity: "if a pen is new, it writes well. That's normal." This pragmatic regularity constitutes an obstacle to the decision that the only acceptable sentences are those that express an exception. From 8:6 years on children make comments on the sentence itself. For instance, they say: "one should delete 'but' or replace it with 'and' for the sentence to be correct."

These results underscore the importance of cognitive factors in these experiments even though the experimental conditions used necessitated metalinguistic decisions which are rather different from those usually made by young children in their verbal exchanges. These particular experimental conditions explain the discrepancy between my results and those obtained by Bates (1976), who showed that children make early use of presuppositions in "natural" conditions of communication. Bates emphasized that children make use of their knowledge concerning the particular characteristics of the listener and the situation at an early age. It should be pointed out, however, that the acquisition of language also consists of acquiring competence for evaluating the appropriateness of an utterance.

One of the issues raised by the studies reported here is to determine how and to what extent the cognitive strategies underlying the discovery of presuppositions may be influenced by the structural characteristics of a particular language. The syntactic and lexical organization of a language might facilitate the appraisal of the presupposed information. It should be interesting to determine for example if in German, which has two distinct lexemes for *mais* (*sondern* and *aber*) and in English, which has two distinct lexemes for *seul* (*alone* and *only*) and *même* (*even* and *same*), the lexical differentiations modify the developmental stages in the comprehension of presupposition.

Evaluation of the generalizability of my findings with French-speaking children requires the establishment of similarities based on conceptual or communicational universals as well as possible differences linked to specific linguistic characteristics. Such an approach should contribute to our understanding of how children gain access to the conventions which govern the form and content of language utterances.

3. CROSS-LINGUISTIC STUDIES OF SENTENCE COMPREHENSION IN CHILDREN

The purpose of my work is to explain the development and mastery of linguistic knowledge. Two classes of variables are considered: those depending on the conceptual and factual knowledge of the child and those concerning the cognitive processing mechanisms participating in the formation of linguistic rules. The first group of variables enables us to predict a universal sequence for semantic development which would reflect universals of cognitive development interacting with prototypical communication settings. The second group of variables enables us to predict differences in the developmental rhythm and stages of certain linguistic forms related to the specific organizational system of a given language.

This perspective was widely developed in Slobin's Berkeley Cross-linguistic Acquisition Project. Analyzing data collected since 1960 in about 40 different languages, Slobin (1973) inductively formulated seven very general operating principles which guide the child in the development of two types of strategies: for the production and interpretation of language and for the construction of the system of linguistic rules. For example, he advanced the principle that underlying semantic relations should be marked overtly and clearly and the principle that postposed markers (suffixes and postpositions) are more salient than preposed markers (prefixes and prepositions).

Slobin (1977) also suggested that, although these principles reflect highly general cognitive laws which limit the forms that natural languages may take, they also orient modifications of languages with time. Finally, they govern the manner in which languages interact and become modified through bilingual practice. Thus, for example, those structural aspects of a particular language which are easy for the child to learn tend to persist in the historical evolution of that language and to resist the erosion of bilingual contact. Conversely, those aspects which are difficult for the child to acquire are less stable with time and will have a greater tendency for rapid modification in conditions of prolonged bilingual contact.

A new version of these operating principles is based on data gathered from different languages (Romance languages, English, Turkish, Hebrew, Japanese, Hungarian, Finnish, German, Samoan, Kaluli, Slavic languages), using a questionnaire (Slobin, 1981); the following questions were investigated:

1. What sorts of errors typically occur? How can they be accounted for? (Include discussion of repairs and self-corrections if relevant.)
2. What systems are learned relatively error-free? How can this be accounted for? (Include discussion of "non-occurring errors" if relevant.)
3. What systems are acquired strikingly early or strikingly late in comparison with general cross-linguistic or English-based expectations?
4. What evidence is there for cognitive pacesetting of linguistic development?
5. Is there any evidence for linguistic pacesetting of cognitive development?
6. What general operating principles for language development are suggested by study of a language of this type? (This is an invitation to confirm or modify proposed operating principles and suggest new ones.)
   (a) perceptual (receptive) principles governing attention and comprehension of speech
   (b) speech production principles
   (c) rule-formational principles governing both grammatical achievements and consistent error types
7. Are there significant reorganizations in the course of development?
8. What are the features of input and adult-child interaction influencing development?
9. Are there data on individual differences that cast light on developmental processes?
10. What issues could be illuminated by further study of languages of this type, or by explicit comparison with other types of languages?

In a recent paper (Kail, 1983), I analyzed the scope of the theoretical proposals advanced in the field of cross-linguistic studies, especially Slobin's operating principles (see also Berman's contribution to the present book). In the following part, I shall deal with the comprehension of simple sentences (to which many studies are devoted) and with the comprehension of presuppositions from a cross-linguistic point of view.

WORD ORDER, CASE MARKING
AND SEMANTIC STRATEGIES IN SENTENCE INTERPRETATION

Most cross-linguistic studies of the comprehension of simple sentences, of which several examples will be given, do not support the hypothesis according to which there exists a priority of strategies based on word order as formulated by Pinker (1982, 78): For case-inflected languages, children will utter sentences in the dominant word order and will use the dominant word order as a cue in comprehending sentences before they have mastered their language's morphology.

Slobin and Bever (1982) have shown that the priority of word order is not a language universal. They have conducted a cross-linguistic study in the development of sentence comprehension from 2;0 to 4;4 years of age in Serbo-Croatian, Turkish, English and Italian, four languages which vary in regard to the use of word order and inflections to signal agent-patient relations. Two of the languages, Serbo-Croatian and Turkish, are inflectional and therefore allow 6 word orders of subject-verb-object (in reversible triplets). These languages differ in that the inflections in Turkish are always explicit and regular, while in Serbo-Croatian there are several declensions, as well as forms that do not differentiate agent and patient phonetically. The other two languages, English and Italian, are noninflectional but Italian shows considerably more flexible word order than English, relying on pragmatic and contextual cues. Analysis of collected data showed that in the two inflectional languages, the sentences included combinations of word order and case inflections. In the word order languages, sentences included combinations of word order and contrastive stress, word order developing faster and being used more consistently than contrastive stress. However, Italian children made greater use of contrastive information than English children. In the inflectional languages, case inflections were learned earlier and used more consistently than word order. Serbo-Croatian children, however, showed a strong dependence on word order comprehension strategies, even in inflected sentence forms where such strategies would be unnecessary.

The most rapid acquisition of all took place in Turkish. Turkish children had acquired almost all their case system by age 2½, well before case acquisition in Serbo-Croatian, and before word order systems in English or Italian.

Slobin and Bever concluded that the main result of this investigation is that children seem prepared to learn both inflectional and word order languages. Contrary to expectations based on the alleged naturalness of fixed SVO order, the acquisition of Turkish is not impaired by the fact that word order is not a cue for semantic relations.

Another interesting result in Slobin and Bever is that in all four languages, the word order strategy is predominant at around 3½ years of age, which is the usual age at which overgeneralization of word order strategies has been reported for English. The authors propose two explanations: a linguistic one, based on the fact that it is only at this stage that the child can process utterances with three major constituents (5 words in Italian or English; 3 words in Turkish and Serbo-Croatian), and a more general one, according to which the development of immediate memory would account both for the development mean length of utterances and the emergence of the order strategy.

Finally, Slobin and Bever assume that the sequence of acquisition in a given language will depend upon the clarity, regularity and information value of grammatical cues in that language.

In their study of word order as an important means for Hebrew children to assign sentence relations, Frankel, Amir, Frenkel and Arbel (1980) asked children from 3 to 11 years old and adults to interpret utterances consisting of two nouns and a verb. Some utterances included only word order cues while others included direct object marker and subject-verb gender agreement cues. Even though Hebrew word order is relatively free, when it is used as an interpretative cue, subjects generally assigned sentence relations according to the dominant SVO order of modern Hebrew. There was no evidence of a developmental sequence for word order strategies (contrary to results obtained in French). In addition, there was no evidence that word order, for any age group, was necessarily a dominant cue when other linguistic information was available.

Another proposed universal in the development of sentence comprehension is that semantic strategies are relatively "primitive" (semantic information and knowledge of world events) while reliance on word order reveals a more sophisticated and metalinguistic way of processing language.

In an attempt to shed some light on this question of a "universal" priority of one type of information over another, Bates, McNew, MacWhinney, Devescovi and Smith (1982) have compared adult interpretation of sentences, varying word order (NVN, VNN, NNV), lexical animacy (animate, inanimate and reversible sentences with two animates), contrastive stress (first noun stress, second noun stress, no stress on either noun), and topicalization (first noun topicalized, second noun topicalized, sentences in which neither noun is introduced in advance) in Italian and English. Although both are SVO word order languages without case inflections, Italian permits far more variations in word order for pragmatic purposes.

The results showed that Italians rely overwhelmingly on lexical animacy (with a main effect accounting for 42% of the variance compared to 4% for the main effect of word order). English subjects, by contrast, relied overwhelmingly on word order (with a main effect accounting for 51% of the variance compared to only 3% for animacy). In addition, Italians made greater use of topicalization and stress information. Finally, Italians were slower and less consistent in applying their standard SVO order, even on reversible items when no lexical contrasts were available.

Bates *et al.* (p. 246) concluded: "Italian is 'less' an SVO language than English. Semantic strategies apparently stand at the 'core' of Italian to the same extent that word-order stands at the 'core' of English."

These results are discussed in the light of the competition model, a functionalist model (Bates and MacWhinney, 1982) in which decisions in sentence interpretation are made by evaluating the relative weight of the cues present in the stimulus. In this model, no role is assigned to universal predispositions or to underlying separations of autonomous processing components: for example, "semantic contrasts are integrated into the parsing system on an equal footing with grammatical cues" (word order for example).

In a further study by Bates, MacWhinney, Caselli, Devescovi, Natale and Venza (in press), English and Italian children from 2 to 5 years of age were asked to enact sentences with combinations of word order, animate/ inanimate nouns, and contrastive stress. From 2;6 years of age the two linguistic groups begin to have entirely different strategies, as reflected in their respective adult models, and this permits them to assume that the data are globally compatible with an acquisition model based on the impact of *cue validity* (MacWhinney, 1978). Cue validity is characterized by the degree of cue "applicability" on the one hand and cue "reliability" on the other hand. In sentence comprehension, cues are highly "applicable" if they are available and highly "reliable" if they are not ambiguous. The most valid cues are those which are both applicable and reliable.

As far as developmental studies are concerned, the main hypothesis is that the order in which cues for sentence comprehension emerge in children speaking different languages is largely a function of the relative validity of cues in that language. Comparing French data (Kail and Charvillat, 1984) to English and Italian, we found that word order and semantic information were the most important cues for children in their interpretation of simple sentences.

Even though French children make a greater use of semantic information than English children and a smaller use than Italian ones, their choices are closer to those of English children. In the same way they make a smaller use of syntactic information than the English but a greater use than the Italians while remaining closer to the English.

From all these developmental studies taken as a whole we can draw the following conclusion: in the course of development, children constantly adapt their initial strategies according to the differential weight of cues in adult speech. But the results obtained with French speaking adults run partially against some predictions of the Competition Model: we found that French adults' strategies relied more on semantic (animacy) than on syntactic (word order) cues, especially when these cues are presented in competition.

In our cross-linguistic comparisons we came to the conclusion that French was less canonical (if by canonical we mean a tendency to equate NVN with SVO) than English but more than Italian; besides, while English subjects manage to have consistent choices in NNV and VNN structures where syntax is the only available cue with a second noun strategy, the French, like the Italian are far less systematic and slower in processing them. And while the English continue to decide in favor of syntax when it competes with semantic information, the prevalence of the latter is practically as dramatic in French as in Italian and this constitutes a rather unexpected finding in a language which, all things considered, has a comparatively strict SVO order. Therefore, the linguistic proximity between French and English, as far as SVO order prevalence is concerned, is not reflected in our data, which appears to potentially constitute a case in which sentence interpretation cannot be directly connected to cue validity (here word order) even though this is one assumption of the competition model.

These data suggest the integration of *"cue cost"* within the competition model. This notion, which must be distinguished from that of "cue validity," is centered on the distinction between *local processing* and *topological processing* in sentence comprehension. In French, order and animacy are both valid cues but the results indicate that local processing using semantic information from nouns is less costly (as revealed in situations of word order and animacy competition) than topological processing.

This distinction transgresses the classical boundaries among syntactic, semantic and pragmatic cues and raises in different terms the question of the autonomy of language processors. Local processing may indeed use grammatical (morphological) and semantic cues, and topological processing may use syntactic information and also suprasegmental information usually associated with topicalization and focusing of information. Let us note that this typological distinction that allows us to characterize different languages was initially put forward by MacWhinney, Bates and Kleigl (1984):

> languages seem to divide themselves into those that favor local cues and those that favor topological cues. If a language searches for grammatical cues locally, topological structure is then free to express meanings other than basic case relations. If a language searches for grammatical cues topologically, local features will not figure as prominently in grammatical processing, but may be available for use in entirely different ways.

What appears to be decisive is that whatever language a subject speaks, he does not seem capable of searching for grammatical cues *simultaneously* at these two levels.

CROSS-LINGUISTIC STUDIES OF THE ROLE OF LEXICAL DIFFERENTIATION IN SENTENCE PROCESSING BY CHILDREN

The origin of a series of my comparative studies is the question of determining to what extent and by what modalities the cognitive strategies underlying the activities of discovery and comprehension of the presuppositional components of utterances can be modified by the structural characteristics of a particular language. As a result of its specificities, the syntactico-lexical organization of a particular language may or may not favor access to the relevant cues from which the child identifies the presupposed component of an utterance.

In a recent work (Kail and Léveillé, in preparation), I compared the comprehension of utterances in French and English which included lexical presuppositions introduced by *seul* and *même*. As mentioned above, the English language has two distinct morphemes for *seul*: *only* and *alone*, and two for *même*: *even* and *same*, so that the morphemes with adverbial function (*only* and *even*) imply presuppositions which differentiate them from the morphemes with adjectival function (*alone* and *same*). The results of a preliminary study with 4- to 10-year-old English-speaking children indicate that utterances in which the modifier has an adjectival function (*alone, same*) are understood earlier and more easily than those in which the modifier introduces a presupposition (*only* and *even*). This is consistent with the errors observed in young French children who utilize a strategy of substitution of the adverbial lexeme by the adjectival lexeme, thus transforming the proposed utterance. As hypothesized, the existence of two distinct morphemes in a language seems to facilitate the detection of the presuppositional component associated with one of them. This type of result corroborates Slobin's proposal (1980) that direct matching between a notion and its linguistic form would favor acquisition. I also showed that this facilitation interacts with the nature of the required cognitive operations. *Only*, which implies the comprehension of complementarity relations, is mastered later than *even*, which requires the comprehension of inclusion relations. The same results were obtained in French.

In a second series of experiments (Kail and Weissenborn, 1984) the processing of the connective "but" was studied in French and German, since the latter has two distinct lexemes: *sondern* and *aber* with different conditions of use. "P *sondern* Q" implies that the proposition P contains an explicit negation (syntactically marked) and its use indicates that the speaker denies a certain meaning. "P *aber* Q," on the other hand, does not imply a syntactic negation. In the experimental material, the presupposition was inferred from the linguistic context (a short text) preceding the utterance children were asked to complete and to judge. The main results of this work underline the identity of the cognitive processes utilized by children of the two linguistic groups but also indicate differentiations which need further investigation. This study showed that utterances which are less complex from a presuppositional viewpoint and whose topic is that of the prior linguistic context are easier to process for both the judgment task and the completion task. This result underlines the functional relationship between the presupposition and the topic (old information). When processing utterances of the type "P *mais* Q," the youngest children processed only the contents of P and Q. In this case, the connective played a very limited role. This result is consistent with other findings from studies of the acquisition of connectives. In addition, we confirmed the hypothesis according to which utterances with *mais-aber* are mastered later than those with *mais-sondern*. The greatest difficulties with utterances containing *mais-aber* are explained by the greater cognitive complexity of the contrast *aber*. In the case of utterances with *mais-sondern* the explicit negation of P indeed provides the necessary information enabling the child to determine the class of predicates within which he must construct the opposition between P and Q. In the case of *mais-aber* utterances, the child must use the context to construct a proposition P', presupposed by P. The results apparently indicate that the mastery of the semantics of *aber* implies that of *sondern*. In other terms, the comprehension of the presupposition attached to utterances with *aber* requires the prior mastery of adversative type oppositions, such as those existing in *sondern*. Finally, the prediction according to which the lexical differentiation existing in German would lead to an earlier distinction between *et* "and" and *mais* "but" was partially confirmed. In the judgment tasks of "P *mais-sondern* Q" type utterances, however, German children showed better performance than French children in the corresponding utterances.

Several international programs devoted to the study of processing strategies are in progress. Whether these programs aim at the validation of a general model of processing (Bates and MacWhinney's competition model), or whether they aim at the determination of psycholinguistic universals (Slobin's operating principles), they all sustain the view that children use those cues which are more stable, more informative in their own language. Such a view runs counter to schematic claims concerning the primacy of syntax or of semantics in linguistic development.

NOTE

1. I am very grateful to Madeleine Léveillé for her invaluable help in preparing this manuscript.

REFERENCES

Abrams, K. H. *et al*. 1978. The relation between mother to child speech and word-order comprehension strategies in children. In R. N. Campbell and P. T. Smith (eds.), *Recent Advances in the Psychology of Language: Language Development and Mother-Child Interaction*. New York: Plenum Press, 337–347.

Amy, G. 1975. Expérience de production d'une phrase relative a partir de trois phrases simples. Document renéoté, Département de Psychologie, Aix-en-Provence.

Amy, G. and M. Vion. 1976. Stratégies de traitement des phrases relatives: quelques considérations d'ordre génétique. *Bulletin de Psychologie*, numéro spécial "La mémoire sémantique," 295–303.

Anscombre, J.-C. and O. Ducrot. 1977. Deux "mais" en français? *Lingua* 43: 24–40.

Bates, E. 1976. *Language and Context: Studies in the Acquisition of Pragmatics*. New York: Academic Press.

Bates, E., S. McNew, B. MacWhinney, A. Devescovi, and S. Smith. 1982. Functional constraints on sentence processing: A cross-linguistic study. *Cognition* 11: 245–299.

Bates, E. and B. MacWhinney. 1979. A functionalist approach to the acquisition of grammar. In E. Ochs and B. Schieffelin (eds.), *Developmental Pragmatics*. New York: Academic Press.

Bates, E. and B. MacWhinney. 1982. Functionalist approaches to grammar. In L. Gleitman and E. Wanner (eds.), *Language Acquisition: The State of the Art*. New York: Cambridge University Press.

Bates, E., B. MacWhinney, C. Caselli, A. Devescovi, F. Natale, and V. Venza. In press. A cross-linguistic study of the development of sentence interpretation strategies.

Beilin, H. 1975. *Studies in the Cognitive Basis of Language Development*. New York: Academic Press.

Berman, R. 1984. Cross-linguistic first language perspectives on second language acquisition research. In R. Andersen (ed.), *Second Languages: A Cross-Linguistic Perspective*. Rowley, Mass.: Newbury House.

Bever, T. G. 1970. The cognitive basis for linguistic structures. In J. R. Hayes (ed.), *Cognition and the Development of Language*. New York: John Wiley and Sons, 279–362.

Bloom, L. 1975. *One Word at a Time: The Use of Single Word Utterances Before Syntax*. The Hague: Mouton.

Bowerman, M. 1973. *Early Syntactic Development*. Cambridge: Cambridge University Press.

Bridges, A. 1980. SVO comprehension strategies reconsidered: The evidence of individual patterns of response. *Journal of Child Language* 7: 89–104.

Bronckart, J.-P. 1977. *Théories du langage: une introduction critique*. Bruxelles: Mardaga.

Bronckart, J.-P. 1979. L'élaboration des opérations langagières: un exemple à propos des structures casuelles. *Cahiers de l'Institut Linguistique de Louvain* 5: 139–157.

Bronckart, J.-P. 1983. La compréhension des structures à fonction casuelle. In J.-P. Bronckart, M. Kail, and G. Noizet (eds.), *Psycholinguistique de l'enfant*.

Bronckart, J.-P., M. Gennari, and G. De Weck. In press. The comprehension of simple sentences. *International Journal of Psycholinguistics*.

Bronckart, J.-P. and I. Idiazabal. Les stratégies de compréhension des énoncés transitifs en basque (in preparation).

Bronckart, J.-P., H. Sinclair, and I. Papandropoulou. 1976. Sémantique et réalité psycholinguistique. *Bulletin de Psychologie*, numéro spécial, "La mémoire sémantique," 295–303.

Brown, R. 1973. *A First Language*. Cambridge: Harvard University Press.

Cambon, J. and H. Sinclair. 1974. Relations between syntax and semantics: Are they "easy to see," *British Journal of Psychology* 65: 133–140.

Chipman, H. 1974. The construction of the pronominal system in English. Thèse de Doctorat de Psychologie, Genève.

Cromer, R. F. 1976. Developmental strategies for language. In V. Hamilton, and M. D. Vernon (eds), *The Development of Cognitive Processes*. New York: Academic Press, 305–358.

Cromer, R. F. 1981. Reconceptualizing language acquisition and cognitive development. In D. Schiefelbusch, and B. Brinker (eds.), *Early Language Acquisition and Interventions*. Baltimore: University Park Press.

De Villiers, J. G. and P. A. De Villiers. 1973. Development of the use of word-order in comprehension. *Journal of Psycholinguistic Research* 2: 331–341.

Deyts, J.-P. and G. Noizet. 1973. Etude génétique de la production des subordonnées relatives. *Cahiers de Psychologie* 16: 199–212.

Ducrot, O. 1972. *Dire et ne pas dire*. Paris: Herman.

Ducrot, O. 1977. Note sur la présupposition et le sens littéral. Postface à P. Henri, *Le mauvais outil: langue, sujet et discours*. Paris: Klincksieck.

Ducrot, O. 1980. *Les mots du discours*. Paris: Ed. Minuit.

Farioli, F. 1979. L'identification de la coréférence pronominale chez les enfants de 5 à 11 ans. *L'Année Psychologique* 79: 87–104.

Ferreiro, E., C. Othenin-Girard, H. Chipman, and H. Sinclair. 1976. How do children handle relative clauses? *Archives de Psychologie* 172: 229–267.

Fodor, J. and M. Garrett. 1966. Some syntactic determinants of sentential complexity. *Perception and Psychophysics* 2: 289–296.

Frankel, D., M. Amir, E. Frenkel, and T. Arbel. 1980. A developmental study of the role of word-order in comprehending Hebrew. *Journal of Experimental Child Psychology* 29: 23–35.

Fraser, C., U. Bellugi, and R. Brown. 1963. Control of grammar in imitation, comprehension and production. *Journal of Verbal Learning and Verbal Behavior* 2: 121–135.

Greenfield, P. and J. Smith. 1976. *The Structure of Communication in Early Language Development.* New York: Academic Press.

Greenfield, P. and P. Zukow. 1978. Why do children say what they say when they say it? An experimental approach to the psychogenesis of presupposition. In K. Nelson (ed.), *Children's Language,* vol. I. New York: Gardner Press, 287–336.

Grober, E. H., W. Beardsley, and A. Caramazza. 1978. Parallel function strategy in pronoun assignment. *Cognition* 6: 117–133.

Halliday, M. A. K. 1967. Notes on transitivity and theme in English, part II. *Journal of Linguistics* 3: 199–244.

Hornby, P. 1971. Surface structure and topic-comment distinction: A developmental study. *Child Development* 42: 1975–1978.

Hornby, P., W. Hass, and C. Feldman. 1970. A developmental analysis of the psychological subject and predicate of a sentence. *Language and Speech* 13: 182–193.

Huttenlocher, J. and S. Strauss. 1968. Comprehension and a statement's relation to the situation it describes. *Journal of Verbal Learning and Verbal Behavior* 7: 300–304.

Huttenlocher, J. K. Eisenberg and S. Strauss. 1968. Comprehension: Relation between perceived actor and logical subject. *Journal of Verbal Learning and Verbal Behavior* 7: 527–530.

Jakubowicz, C. and J. Segui. 1980. L'utilisation des indices de surface dans la compréhension d'énoncés chez l'enfant: les phrases passives. In *Approches du Langage.* Paris: Ed. de la Sorbonne, 63–75.

Kail, M. 1975a. Etude génétique de la reproduction des phrases relatives. Reproduction immédiate. *L'Année Psychologique* 75: 109–126.

Kail, M. 1975b. Etude génétique de la reproduction des phrases relatives. Reproduction différée. *L'Année Psychologique* 75: 427–443.

Kail, M. 1976. Stratégies de compréhension des pronoms personnels chez le jeune enfant. *Enfance,* numéro 3–4, 447–466.

Kail, M. 1978. La compréhension des présuppositions chez l'enfant. *L'Année Psychologique* 78: 425–444.

Kail, M. 1979a. Coréférence et thématisation. *L'Année Psychologique* 79: 411–427.

Kail, M. 1979b. Compréhension de seul, même et aussi chez l'enfant. *Bulletin de Psychologie,* numéro spécial "La compréhension du langage," 763–771.

Kail, M. 1980. Etude génétique des présupposés de certains morphèmes grammaticaux. Un exemple: mais. In *Approches du Langage.* Paris: Ed. de la Sorbonne, 55–64.

Kail, M. 1983. L'acquisition du langage repensée: les recherches interlangues. Partie I. Principales propositions théoriques. *L'Année Psychologique* 83. Partie II. Spécificités méthodologiques et recherches empiriques. *L'Année Psychologique* 83.

Kail, M. (in press). Stratégie des fonctions parallèles et coréférence des pronoms. In J.-P. Bronckart, M. Kail, and G. Noizet. *Psycholinguistique de l'enfant.* Paris: Delachaux et Niestlé.

Kail M., Charvillat A. 1984. Linguistic cues in sentence processing in French from a cross-linguistic perspective: A study of children and adults. International conference on Knowledge and Language, Warsaw. To appear in J.H. Danks, I. Kurcz and G.W. Shugrar. *Knowledge and Language,* Amsterdam, North Holland.

Kail, M. and A. Karmiloff-Smith. 1980. Recherches de psycholinguistique génétique sur l'anaphore: conduites métalinguistiques ou conduites langagières? Document ronéôté. Paris: Université de Paris V.

Kail, M. and M. Léveillé. 1977. Compréhension de la référence des pronoms personnels chez l'enfant et l'adulte. *L'Année Psychologique* 77: 79–94.

Kail, M. and M. Léveillé. In press. A developmental study of recall and comprehension of presupposition. In Studies on Background Knowledge. Göteborg.

Kail, M. and M. Léveillé. In preparation. A developmental cross linguistic study on comprehension of lexical presuppositions.

Kail, M. and R. Plas. 1979. Psycholinguistique des présuppositions: Eléments pour une critique. *Semantikos* 3: 1–26.

Kail, M. and J. Segui. 1978. Developmental production of utterances from a series of lexemes. *Journal of Child Language* 5: 251–260.

Kail, M. and J. Weissenborn. 1984. A developmental cross-linguistic study of adversative connectives: French "mais" and German "aber-sondern." *Journal of Child Language* 11: 143–158.

Karmiloff-Smith, A. 1981. The grammatical marking of thematic structure in the development of language production. In W. Deutsch (ed.), *The Child's Construction of Language*. London: Academic Press.

Krauss, R. and S. Glucksberg. 1969. The development of communication competence as a function of age. *Child Development* 40: 225–266.

Lakoff, G. and H. Thompson. 1975. Introducing cognitive grammar. *Proceedings of the Berkeley Linguistic Society* 1.

Lempert, H. 1978. Extrasyntactic factors affecting passive sentence comprehension by young children. *Child Development* 49: 694–699.

Lempert, H. and M. Kinsbourne. 1978. Children's comprehension of word-order: A developmental investigation. *Child Development* 49: 1235–1248.

Lempert, H. and M. Kinsbourne. 1980. Preschool children's sentence comprehension: Strategies with respect to word-order. *Journal of Child Language* 7: 371–379.

Lieven, E. V. M. 1980. Different roots to multiple-word combinations. *Proceedings of the 1980 Child Language Research Forum*. Stanford, Ca.

Maratsos, M. P. 1973. The effect of stress on the understanding of pronominal coreference in children. *Journal of Psycholinguistics* 1: 1–8.

Maratsos, M. P. and R. Abramovitch. 1975. How children understand full, truncated, and anomalous passives. *Journal of Verbal Learning and Verbal Behavior* 14: 145–157.

MacWhinney, B., Bates, E. and R.P. Kleig. 1984. Cue validity and sentence interpretation in English, German and Italian. *Journal of Verbal Learning and Verbal Behavior* 23, 127–150.

MacWhinney, B. 1978. Processing a first language: The acquisition of morphophonology. *Monographs of the Society for Research in Child Development* 43 (1–2). Serial no. 174.

MacWhinney, B. and E. Bates. 1978. Sentential devices for conveying givenness and newness: A cross-cultural developmental study. *Journal of Verbal Learning and Verbal Behavior* 17: 539–558.

Morsly, D. and M. Mahmoudian. 1973. L'emploi des relatifs "qui" et "que." *Recherches Pédagogiques* 49: 131–143.

Nelson, K. 1973. Structure and strategy in learning to talk. *Monographs of the Society for Research in Child Development* 38 (n. 1–2, serial 149).

Nelson, K. 1980. Individual differences in language development: Implications for development and language. Paper presented at the Fifth Annual Boston University Conference on Language Development, October 1980.

Noizet, G. 1977. Les stratégies dans le traitement des phrases. *Cahiers de Psychologie* 20: 3–14.

Noizet, G., F. Deyts, and J.-P. Deyts. 1972. Producing complex sentences by applying relative transformations: A comparative study. *Linguistics* 89: 49–67.

Parot, F. and M. Kail. 1980. Topicalisation et thématisation dans le rappel de phrases. Etude chez l'adulte et chez l'enfant. *L'Année Psychologique* 80: 99–120.

Pinker, S. 1982. A theory of the acquisition of lexical interpretive grammars. In J. Bresnan (ed.), *The Mental Representation of Grammatical Relations*. Cambridge, Mass.: MIT Press.

Sheldon, A. 1974. The role of parallel function in the acquisition of relative clauses in English. *Journal of Verbal Learning and Verbal Behavior* 13: 272–281.

Sinclair, H. and J.-P. Bronckart. 1972. SVO—a linguistic universal? A study in developmental psycholinguistics. *Journal of Experimental Child Psychology* 14: 329–348.

Sinclair, H. and E. Ferreiro. 1970. Etude génétique de la compréhension, production et répétition des phrases au mode passif. *Archives de Psychologie* 160: 1–42.

Sinclair, A., H. Sinclair, and O. de Marcellus. 1971. Young children's comprehension and production of passive sentences. *Archives de Psychologie* 161: 1–22.

Slobin, D. I. 1966. Grammatical transformations and sentence comprehension in childhood and adulthood. *Journal of Verbal Learning and Verbal Behavior* 5: 219–227.

Slobin, D. I. 1973. Cognitive prerequisites for the development of grammar. In C. A. Ferguson and D. I. Slobin (eds.), *Studies of Child Language Development*. New York: Holt, Rinehart and Winston.

Slobin, D. I. 1977. Language change in childhood and history. In J. Macnamara (ed.), *Language Learning and Thought*. New York: Academic Press, 185–214.

Slobin, D. I. 1980. Universal and particular in the acquisition of language. In E. Wanner and L. R. Gleitman (eds.), *Language Acquisition: The State of the Art*. New York: Academic Press.

Slobin, D. I. 1981. The origins of grammatical encoding of events. In W. Deutsch (ed.), *The Child's Construction of Language*. New York: Academic Press.

Slobin, D. I., and T. G. Bever. 1982. Children use canonical sentence schemas: A crosslinguistic study of word-order and inflections. *Cognition* 12: 229–265.

Strohner, H. and K. E. Nelson. 1974. The young child's development of sentence comprehension: Influence of event probability, nonverbal context, syntactic form and their strategies. *Child Development* 45: 565–576.

Tannenbaum, P. and F. Williams. 1968. Generation of active and passive sentences as a function of subject or object focus. *Journal of Verbal Learning and Verbal Behavior* 7: 246–250.

Turner, E. A. and R. Rommetveit. 1967. The acquisition of sentence voice and reversibility. *Child Development* 38: 649–660.

Turner, E. A. and R. Rommetveit. 1968. Focus of attention in recall of active and passive sentences. *Journal of Verbal Learning and Verbal Behavior* 7: 543–548.

Vion, M. 1980. La compréhension des phrases simples chez le jeune enfant. Thèse de 3ème cycle, Université de Provence, Aix-en-Provence.

CHAPTER 3

Markedness, Language Universals, Language Typology, and Second Language Acquisition

Kenneth Hyltenstam
University of Stockholm, Sweden

INTRODUCTION

During the last few years, the notions of *language universals* and *markedness* have been frequently referred to in second language acquisition studies, and the area of *language typology* in general has attracted considerable attention within the field. Among other things, typological facts and purported markedness conditions have been used in attempts to augment the predictive validity of the concept of language transfer (e.g., Eckman, 1977, 1981; Kellerman, 1978, 1979).

The notions of language universals and markedness are not at all simple and clear-cut, since these terms have been applied to various phenomena in different branches of linguistic research. They have also been used within different theoretical frameworks, and accordingly, bear different assumptions in these various uses. As regards language typology, its place in a theoretical discussion of second language acquisition can be characterized as somewhat unclear. Therefore, an analysis of the use and utilization of these concepts in L2 research is in order.

The present article is an attempt at such an analysis. It starts by giving a broad sketch of how the above-mentioned terms have been used in linguistics generally. A number of studies within second language acquisition will then be reviewed in order to illustrate the use of the terms in this field. Finally, one specific approach to the use of markedness in second language acquisition research will be suggested. Here, the notion of markedness is primarily seen as helpful in the hypothesis-generating phase of L2 research. At the same time, however, the present approach underscores the reciprocal nature of second language acquisition and language typology and universals research. As illustrative examples, three linguistic phenomena are used, two syntactic and one lexical-semantic:

1. sentence negation
2. yes/no questions
3. verbs of perception

THE NOTIONS

LANGUAGE UNIVERSALS

The notion of *language universals* has been a central theme in theoretical reasoning about language and languages as far back as we can trace. A characteristic feature of the discussion over centuries is the question whether language universals exist, or whether, on the contrary, each language has its own unique structure. During the last decades, the discussion has not so much centered around the question whether universals exist or not—enough similarities in structural patterning between different languages have been demonstrated to convince linguists of the existence of language universals—but rather to what extent different languages are structured according to universal principles. Also, what is salient in the theoretical discussion is how we can gain information about the universal properties of language. This latter question is an important one, and it has great consequences for how work is carried out in the area.

As regards the ways we gain information on language universals, there are presently two major methodological approaches (cf. Comrie, 1981). One of these approaches is a straightforward one in terms of methodology; data from a representative sample of the world's languages are analyzed in order to extract universal patternings. This approach is closely associated with the work of Joseph H. Greenberg and has been strongly influenced by his article on language universals (1963). The second approach goes back to Chomsky's (1965) version of transformational grammar and can be considered less straightforward in that its methodology relies on the validity of the theoretical construct of linguistic innateness. Here, the argumentation is briefly as follows: Children can be observed to learn their mother tongue in a "remarkably" short period of time. It is difficult to understand how this would be possible, if language were not innate. It is an empirical fact, however, that not all aspects of a particular language can be innate, since children learn the language they are exposed to rather than that of their biological parents. Therefore, what is innate must be a number of abstract principles that constrain language. These principles can be equated with language universals, and are specified in universal grammar (UG). The question then arises of how these principles can be studied. Since they are abstract principles, they must be arrived at through a detailed analysis of a specific language, focusing on the relationships between abstract and more concrete levels of representation. Ideally, in order to see whether purported universal principles are in operation in all languages, we need detailed analyses of a number of languages, but resources seldom allow this. In most cases, universals have been suggested on the basis of an analysis of a few languages—sometimes of a single language.

Both approaches, i.e., the Greenbergian and the transformational, have a number of drawbacks, which we cannot, however, go into here (cf. Comrie, 1981). Different studies within second language acquisition research are related to one, or in some cases, both of these approaches (see below).

MARKEDNESS

The notion of *markedness* also has different meanings in the two approaches mentioned above. Before we go into these differing views, we will very briefly look at the history of the concept.

The notion has been used in discussions about various phenomena of language structure in many different ways. Expressed at a very general level, one can say that linguistic phenomena that are common in the world's languages, that seem easier for linguistic processing, and that are more "natural" than others, are unmarked as opposed to their marked variants.

Within a stricter theoretical framework, the notion was first used by the Prague school of linguistics, primarily in phonology (Trubetzkoy 1939) but also in morphology. The notion of markedness was adopted early in generative phonology (Chomsky and Halle, 1968), and has been built into various approaches to theoretical phonology, e.g., Bailey (1973). Greenberg (1966) discusses the mainly European structuralist reasoning about markedness with regard to criteria for what should be identified as unmarked and marked categories in phonology, grammar, and lexicon. His summary of criteria should not be seen as anything other than a useful taxonomy: The discussion does not, for example, address questions such as possible conflicts between criteria. Greenberg points to the fact that different criteria have been used in phonology on the one hand and in grammar and lexicon on the other, but sees a possibility of equating the two sets. The following five criteria, which have been used for identifying the markedness values in phonology, are mentioned:

1. Neutralization: in positions where an otherwise upheld contrast is neutralized (e.g., the voice distinction in obstruents in word final position in German), it is the unmarked value that appears (i.e., [−VOICE] is unmarked, whereas [+VOICE] is marked in this case).

2. Frequency: the unmarked category appears with greater frequency.
3. Allophonic variation: the unmarked member has greater allophonic variability.
4. Phonological features: the number of phonemes with the unmarked feature is always greater than that with the marked feature, e.g., the number of nasal vowels is smaller than that of oral vowels.
5. Allophones: the basic allophone, defined in terms of phonological independence of its environment, is the one with the unmarked feature.

According to Greenberg, those criteria that have been suggested for markedness conditions in grammar and lexicon can be identified and equated with those used in phonology (note that his discussion mainly concerns morphological features, rather than syntactic):

1. Neutralization—contextual neutralization (an example is the use of the unmarked singular form of nouns when they appear in the context of cardinal numbers in Turkish and Hungarian).
2. Frequency—frequency.
3. Allophonic variation—allomorphic variation (the unmarked category shows greater allomorphic variation than the marked one, except when it is expressed by zero (see below)).
4. Phonological features—syncretization (some oppositions that are upheld in the unmarked category, e.g., oral vowels, are neutralized in the marked category, viz. nasal vowels); a corresponding example from grammar is the opposition between masculine and feminine in the singular (the unmarked category) which is syncretized in the plural (the marked category).
5. Basic allophones—basic allomorphs (agreement is the example mentioned by Greenberg. Here the unmarked masculine appears in contexts like Spanish *cuello y camisa blancos* "white (masc.) collar (masc.) and shirt (fem.)").

Besides these five criteria, a sixth is the zero expression of the unmarked category.

All these criteria can be applied to the categories of a single language, and markedness conditions for various structures of that particular language can be arrived at. The same categories will in many cases, however, turn out to be characterized as marked or unmarked in a number of languages, which is, of course, also what this theory hopes for. Had this not been the case, the notion of markedness could not be given a general definition in universal grammar other than at an uninterestingly general level.

On the basis of the observation that the same categories turn out to be marked and unmarked in various languages, a further step can be taken in the formulation of markedness conditions where cross-linguistic facts are taken into account more systematically. Greenberg (1966:60) makes this point in passing:

> Whenever a statement of one of the above five types can be put in terms of a universal implication, it is the unmarked member which is the implied or basic term and the marked which is the implying or secondary.

In other words, whenever the existence of a category A in a language implies the existence of a category B (A → B), A is considered more marked than B. For example, if a language has the category of voiced stops (A), it also has the category of voiceless stops (B).[1]

Since the implicational definition takes more facts into account than any of the other criteria, it can be considered to give a more narrow, and therefore stronger, definition of the notion of markedness. For many structural phenomena, however, it is not possible to define cross-linguistic markedness conditions on the basis of implicational relationships, since there are no two categories, A and B, which both occur in the same language and where one is implied by the other. This is the case with, for example, sentence negation and interrogation, where a given language exhibits one or more of the structural possibilities that exist. Even in these areas, however, cross-linguistic markedness conditions can be formulated, albeit in a weaker form. As regards categories where an implicational relationship holds, it is a natural consequence that the implied category (B) is more *frequent* among languages than the implying category (A). In the same way, frequency can be used as a criterion for cross-linguistic markedness also for categories where no implicational relationship holds. In this formulation, categories that occur more frequently among languages are identified as unmarked, whereas those that occur less frequently are marked. However, it is only when the frequency of a given category is not dependent on, or related to, a certain basic word order type that the markedness conditions can be said to have a universal validity.

When the notion of markedness is used within the Greenbergian approach to language universals, it bears assumptions of the kind just discussed. I will reserve the notion of *cross-linguistic markedness* for this use.

To sum up this section so far, cross-linguistic markedness conditions can be given two formulations, one that is stronger and another that is weaker. In the stronger formulation, markedness conditions are arrived at through observation of the implicational relationship between categories. As a resulting effect of this relationship, one category is more frequent among languages than the other. In the weaker formulation, the basis for the formulation is only the frequency criterion. The markedness values arrived at in both formulations are of course strongly sensitive to what language sample is used, and the criteria which have been used to arrive at this sample.

Now, within the framework of transformational grammar, the notion of markedness is given a fundamentally different definition—just as is the related notion of language universal. Historically, within this approach, there has always been some distinction made between more central and more peripheral aspects of language structuring. Recall the notion of *kernel sentences* (Chomsky, 1957), generated by the central devices of phrase structure rules and obligatory transformations only, or the distinction between the *base component* and the *transformational component* of most versions, notably in Chomsky (1965). These distinctions bear some resemblance to markedness distinctions, although the notion of markedness itself was not used as a defined theoretical concept until in more recent developments of the extended standard theory (EST). Here, the notion of *core grammar* has developed during the last few years (Koster, 1978; Chomsky, e.g., 1980). The basic principle of this approach is the division in the grammar of any language between a *core*, which is unmarked, and a more marked *periphery*. The grammar of a particular language is related to UG (see p. 56 above) in that the core grammar is one of the possible manifestations of UG. The principles of UG are seen as parameters with a finite number of values which have to be "fixed" in the core grammar of any particular language. The values of the parameters are formulated at a very general level. For example, one parameter concerns word order phenomena, and the values in this case are approximately either a head-modifier order or a modifier-head order, which makes possible the incorporation of word order generalizations of the kind formulated in Greenberg (1963).

The periphery contains "borrowings, historical residues, inventions, and so on" (Chomsky, 1980:126), i.e., elements and structures that are not derivable from UG.

Even if the part of a language which is generated by the core grammar is considered unmarked in relation to the marked structures and items of the periphery, degrees of markedness are considered to exist both within the core grammar on the one hand and within the periphery on the other. However, the theory has not yet developed clear criteria for ascribing markedness values to specific structures of the core or the periphery, which is of course not so strange if one considers the recency of this development. "Ultimately, the answers to the question of the theory of markedness will have to come from the deep study of particular languages within a principled theory of UG" (Chomsky, 1980:127).

LANGUAGE TYPOLOGY

With regard to the notion of *language typology,* there is less to say in our context. Language typology can be seen as a field of study where patterns that exist among the languages of the world are researched, and where the possible variation that can be found in human languages is described. Of course, the specification of language universals is based on discerned patterns in this variation; the limits of the variation are specified in the universals (cf. Comrie, 1981).

SECOND LANGUAGE ACQUISITION STUDIES

Although the establishment of *second language acquisition universals*, i.e., universally valid acquisitional sequences and general principles. has been the aim of a large number of studies (an early discussion of these principles is found in Hatch (1974)), and although these universals have a certain connection with language universals in general, they will not be dealt with here. Rather, in this section, I will deal with a number of studies where insights from the field of language typology, language universals, and markedness conditions have been drawn on in discussions of second language acquisition.

The relationship between the typological patterning of languages and first language acquisitional patterns was extensively discussed in Jakobson's influential work (1941), where phenomena of segmental phonology were dealt with. Jakobson's thinking has been influential also in second language acquisition research. An early example of this is Johansson (1973), where phonological data from nine groups of learners of Swedish were analyzed with the aim of testing whether those phonological distinctions in the target language which were marked in Jakobson's system also constituted the largest acquisitional difficulties in general.

Although Jakobson's work has also influenced later studies, the new interest in universals and language typology in general has of course been incorporated into the field.

The relationship between typological facts and second language acquisition patterns has been noted in a large number of studies within the field of interlanguage research, sometimes more or less in passing. The studies that will be reviewed here are characterized by the fact that this relationship is a central theme of the discussion. Table 1 displays the studies that will be considered. Information is also given about the linguistic phenomenon, the type of approach to language universals, and the kind of empirical data involved in each study.

It can be noted that the relative clause construction has been a favored phenomenon to look at. This does not come as a surprise, since it is essential to be able to work with areas where the typological facts are fairly well described. Keenan and Comrie's (1977) article on the NP Accessibility Hierarchy has been used in exactly this way. The article was circulated as early as 1972 and was first considered in second language acquisition contexts by Schachter (1974).

Classifying the various studies according to one of the two major methodological approaches mentioned earlier in this article has involved a certain amount of idealization. The classification is based on whether the universal type which the second language pattern is related to is arrived at through a survey of various languages or through a deep analysis of one language.

TABLE 1   Second Language Acquisition Studies with Focus on Language Typology, Language Universals, and Markedness Conditions

	Linguistic phenomenon	*Approach*	*Empirical data*
Eckman (1977)	pronominal copies in relative clauses, voicing in obstruents	Greenbergian	Schachter's 1974 data free written production
Eckman (1981)	pronominal copies in relative clauses, voicing in obstruents	Greenbergian	Schachter's 1974 data
Gass (1979)	relative clauses, in particular the use of pronominal copies	Greenbergian	17 learners of English: 9 L1's grammatical judgments, sentence combining
Gass (1980)	relative clauses, in particular the use of pronominal copies	Greenbergian	17 learners of English: 9 L1's grammatical judgments, sentence combining + free written production
Gass and Ard (1980)	relative clauses, in particular the use of pronominal copies	Greenbergian	English 1st language perceptual data from Sheldon (1974) compared to the sentence combining task in Gass 1979 and 1980
Hyltenstam (1981a)	pronominal copies in relative clauses	Greenbergian	45 learners of Swedish L1's: Persian, Greek, Spanish, Finnish elicited production
Hyltenstam and Magnusson (1983)	voicing in stops	Greenbergian	10 normally developing L1 learners of Swedish, 10 retarded L1 learners of Swedish, 9 adult L2 learners of Swedish, 6 child L2 learners of Swedish, L1 of L2 learners: Finnish elicited production
Ioup and Kruse (1977)	relative clauses, in particular the use of pronominal copies	Greenbergian	learners of English grammatical judgments
Johansson (1973)	vowel and consonant systems	Greenbergian	160 learners of Swedish, 9 L1's imitation

TABLE 1 (continued)

	Linguistic phenomenon	Approach	Empirical data
Mazurkewich (1981)	to- and for- dative structures	transformational	45 French L2 learners of English, 38 Inuktitut L2 learners of English, 12 L1 English as a control group grammatcial judgments
Ritchie (1978)	the right roof constraint	transformational	12 Japanese learners of English, 6 L1 English as a control group grammatical judgment
Rutherford (1981)	arrangements of (S, O, V) in different languages, topic-prominence vs. subject prominence, grammatical vs. pragmatic word order	Greenbergian	L1's: Mandarin, Japanese, Korean (Arabic and Spanish)
Rutherford (1982)	morpheme acquisition order, wh-questions, negation, "complex constructions"	various approaches to markedness	various data from the literature
Schachter (1974)	relative clauses	Greenbergian	Persian, Arab, Chinese, and Japanese learners of English free written production
Schmidt (1980)	deletions in coordinated structures	transformational (Greenbergian)	9 learners of English L1's: Japanese (5), Chinese, Finnish, German and Arabic (1 each) picture description, imitation, sentence combining, grammatical judgment
Wode (1981a)	negation	Greenbergian	various data from L1 and L2 acquisition and pidgins and creoles, language change

TABLE 1 (continued)

	Linguistic phenomenon	Approach	Empirical data
Wode (1981b)	negation	Greenbergian	various data from L1 and L2 acquisition and pidgins and creoles, language change
Zobl (1982a)	definiteness, negation, subject deletion, FOR as an infinitive marker (modifier-head structure)	typologically con-strained historical change	data from various sources, mostly free oral production
Zobl (1982b)	relative clauses, subject and object deletion	Greenbergian and transformational, acquisitional data as criteria for marked-ness	data from Gass (1979) and Zobl (1982a)

We will now proceed to look at how universals or markedness conditions have been used in the different studies to throw light on phenomena in second language acquisition. In many studies, typological facts have been used to arrive at a more restricted view of what language phenomena are subject to transfer from the native language. According to this view, in order to decide whether a certain L1 structure can possibly be transferred to the learner's interlanguage, it is necessary to establish what role this structure plays typologically, whether it is marked or unmarked.

This is the main theme of Eckman's studies, where it is claimed that L1 structures that are different from L2 structures *and* typologically less marked will be transferred to the target language. This explains, for example, why German-speaking learners of English will have difficulties with the distinction between voiced and voiceless obstruents in word-final position, while it is not difficult for English-speaking learners of German to acquire the pattern of final devoicing in German. There is independent implicational evidence that it is the typologically more marked case to maintain the voice distinction in obstruents in word final position: Any language that maintains this distinction in word final position also maintains it in medial and initial position (Dinnsen and Eckman, 1975). The same kind of reasoning is applied to the phenomenon of pronominal copies in relative clauses. Eckman concludes that "different and more marked will constitute difficulty"; as can be seen, he discusses the phenomenon of transfer in terms of "degree of difficulty."

Eckman does not mention the possibility that typologically unmarked structures turn up in situations where both L1 and L2 have marked structures.

Interestingly enough, this phenomenon has been observed independently by Ioup and Kruse (1977), Gass (1979, 1980), and Hyltenstam (1981 a) in the grammatical area discussed by Eckman – pronominal copies in relative clauses. What is observed is that learners of English (Ioup and Kruse, Gass) and Swedish (Hyltenstam) accept or produce pronominal copies in the target language – where they should not occur – irrespective of whether their native language contains such elements. Gass notes a statistically significant difference in positions high on the accessibility hierarchy (the relativized element is (subject), direct object, indirect object or object of preposition) between learners whose L1 has and those whose L1 does not have pronominal copies in relative clauses. Gass formulates an initial hypothesis on the outcome of her study in the following terms: "if Chinese, Arabic and Persian subjects retained pronouns in English in that position to a significantly greater degree than the other subjects, language transfer was hypothesized to be present." The interpretation of the subsequent results in relation to the initial hypothesis leads her to infer that transfer occurs in the higher positions of the accessibility hierarchy but not in the lower. Universal principles and transfer are seen as two nonoverlapping processes in this interpretation. In the study by Ioup and Kruse, similar results were reached.

Very similar patterns were obtained in Hyltenstam (1981 a). In this study, the results were interpreted in terms of cooperation between transfer and markedness conditions, i.e., no attempt was made to distinguish structures due to transfer from structures due to universal patterns, as they were not seen to be mutually exclusive. Rather, it is possible to view the factors underlying the appearance of pronominal copies in the L2 data as conspiring to the effect that a higher frequency of a structure was found in the learners' output if both factors, i.e., low degree of markedness and existence in L1, were present, than if only one of these was present.

In Rutherford's study (1981), it was observed that learners with different *types* of native languages (in terms of topic vs. subject prominence) differ in their use of certain structures at different stages of learning. In data from Chinese learners of English, the phenomenon of nonextraposed sentential subjects is present quite early, while this phenomenon appears late in other groups of learners. Chinese is described as a topic-prominent language, and one characteristic of such languages is the use of sentential subjects. Topic-prominency is thought to account for the differential learning structures found in the field of sentence syntax for Chinese and other learners—what Rutherford calls *typological transfer*. Another example of this type of transfer is Japanese learners' use of extraposed sentential subjects with *it* as a subject placeholder. Such dummies do not exist in Japanese, but since this language utilizes grammatical word order principles (rather than pragmatic), Japanese learners are taken to be more sensitive to syntactic constraints on word order in general.

Another line of approach utilizing the concept of markedness to account for transfer effects in second language learning is that represented by Kellerman in various articles (e.g., 1978, 1979). Although Kellerman uses markedness in order to delimit what structures are transferred, and although he discusses typological distance between languages as providing the framework for transfer, his characterization of markedness is formulated in psycholinguistic terms, and language-typological facts are given secondary importance. Structures that the learner perceives as marked in the native language in relation to a given target language will not be transferred.

Rutherford (1982) uses the notion of markedness in an extremely unrestricted way, which allows any definitional basis of the notion such as psycholinguistic complexity, structural patterning ("contextual neutralization"), linguistic redundancy, typological markedness, and observations of acquisitional orders ("learner assumptions"). This is of course not satisfactory, since it is impossible to know what these various uses of the term have in common; the concept itself remains too vague and undefined to be of any practical use. Rutherford also suggests that markedness theory should be applied to discourse aspects of language.

Zobl (1982b) argues that the notion of markedness should be incorporated directly in second language acquisition research by arriving at markedness conditions from observed acquisitional data themselves. This approach relies heavily on the concept of *projectability,* i.e., the process by which a learner arrives at a solution for a specific target language structure without any direct experience with the actual structure in the input. For example, from the sentences *I can, You eat this,* and *You can eat,* the learner can project to NP–Aux–Vb–NP, *I can eat this,* which is more complex than any of the sentences in the input. Now, projectability is used as a central notion in the definition of markedness in the sense that the easier it is for a learner to project to the structure in question, the less marked the structure. Markedness conditions for a given structure are calculated on the basis of three criteria: (1) the accessibility/inaccessibility of the structure to a projected analysis; (2) the amount of data required by a learner to fix the structure in his grammar; and (3) the number of revisions a learner is required to introduce into his original assumption about the structure. Disregarding the problem of circularity and the difficulty in operationalization of the suggested criteria, *the projection model of markedness*—which Zobl chooses to call it—is interesting in that it operates with a well-defined notion of markedness.

As noted above, all of the studies referred to in Table 1 take some stance on the relation between typological facts and second language acquisition. However, different studies emphasize, or focus on, different aspects of this relation. Four such different aspects can be discerned in the studies mentioned here:

1. *Interlanguages are natural languages in that they are subject to constraints related to language universals which are generally applicable to natural languages.* Most studies conducted within the transformational approach fall naturally into this category (this is the case for

Ritchie (1978) and Schmidt (1980), but also studies such as Wode (1981a, b), which do not discuss general principles but specific structures found to characterize interlanguages, belong here. In both these groups of studies, interlanguage data are examined specifically to find structures that either violate universal principles or that are nonexistent in the languages of the world, respectively. In these studies the conclusions have been that interlanguages *are* natural languages.

2. *L2 data are valid data in the search for language universals.* Different kinds of data have been used as a basis for formulating language universals and markedness conditions. Traditionally, data on language typology, first language acquisition, aphasia and other language pathologies, as well as psycholinguistic data on language production and perception, have provided the impetus for generalizations. More recently, data on pidgins and creoles, and particularly on second language acquisition, have also been applied to this question. Among the studies considered here, Gass and Ard (1980) and Wode (1981a, b) argue that L2 data have a certain advantage to this end in that the learning of a second language constitutes a purer case of language development where some confounding variables such as simultaneous cognitive development—as in first language acquisition—are absent.

3. *The order of acquisition for structures follows markedness conditions as defined either in the transformational approach or in the Greenbergian approach.* Studies that take this stance are represented in Table 1 by Mazurkewich (1981), Hyltenstam (1981), and Hyltenstam and Magnusson (1983) in that they claim to show that less marked structures are acquired earlier than more marked structures.

4. *The structural character of interlanguages is determined by the typological nature of the learners' L1 and L2.* Rutherford (1981) discusses some basic typological differences between languages at a general level such as subject or topic prominence, adherence to pragmatic vs. grammatical word order, and the order of basic clausal constituents. From these parameters, the study can predict a number of structural characteristics of interlanguages. Eckman (1977, 1981) distinguishes languages according to whether they have marked or unmarked structures in certain structural areas; and proceeding from this characterization, he attempts to predict what structures will characterize interlanguages in each direction for a certain L1/L2 pair.

It would be interesting to work out in greater detail the empirical claims about second language acquisition implicated in each of the four approaches discussed here. However, for the purposes of this paper, I intend to develop only one of them, i.e., number 3. This approach implies the use of knowledge from one area of research in predicting the form data should take in another. In this way we obtain an independent basis upon which to build hypotheses and predict second language acquisition patterns. A further consequence is that we can then test the explanations used for language-typological facts on language acquisition data (explanations such as ease in producing and perceiving unmarked structures due to a transparent correspondence between surface and underlying structure). Should the outcome of this research satisfactorily indicate a parallelism between typological facts and language acquisition facts, it would seem feasible to use language typology directly in the prediction of acquisitional patterns.

The more precise main prediction, then, is that unmarked categories will be preferred to marked ones in early stages of second language acquisition, irrespective of the learner's L1 and L2. This accounts for the uniformity across various L1/L2 constellations in second language acquisition patterns. However, the learner's L1 and L2 also result in differences, for example in the frequency with which unmarked structures occur and in the rate at which unmarked structures are replaced by marked ones, if the target language contains the marked structure. These similarities and differences are stated in the following consequent predictions:

1. Where both L1 and L2 have typologically unmarked categories in a certain area, no acquisitional difficulties will be experienced.
2. Where L1 has an unmarked and L2 a corresponding marked category, the unmarked category will often be transferred from L1 to L2, and this unmarked category will in many cases remain as a feature of the learner's interlanguage for a long period of time.
3. Where L1 has a marked and L2 a corresponding unmarked category, transfer from L1 will be much rarer. If the marked category *is* transferred, it will not remain as a feature of the learner's interlanguage, since the corresponding unmarked category in the target language will be easy to acquire.
4. Where both L1 and L2 have a marked category, the unmarked category can still turn up in the learner's interlanguage. It will, however, fairly quickly be abandoned in favor of the marked category.

The following chart from Hyltenstam (1981a) summarizes the main prediction given above. The consequent predictions 1–4 should be seen as comments to the main prediction.

Native language	Target language	Initial stages of interlanguage
1. unmarked	unmarked	unmarked
2. unmarked	marked	unmarked
3. marked	unmarked	unmarked
4. marked	marked	unmarked

To conclude this article, three examples will be given of how this reasoning can be applied to particular language structures. These examples are *sentence negation, yes/no questions* and, in the lexical area, *verbs of perception.*

SENTENCE NEGATION

In Dahl (1979), typologies for placement of sentence negation have been discussed in the light of data covering 240 languages from 40 language families. Dahl's study is summarized and its implications within the field of second language acquisition are discussed in Hyltenstam (1981a). Here, both the summary and the discussion are repeated in an abridged form for the purposes of this article.

It is possible to distinguish at least three language types that must be considered separately with regard to sentence negation. One of these types uses morphological negation. Different subtypes can be distinguished here, but languages with affixation are the most frequent. Suffixation seems to be somewhat more frequent than prefixation, but neither of these can be said to be more marked than the other, since the affixation pattern is correlated with the basic word order type of the language: morphological negation is more frequent in verb-final languages on the whole, and the preference for suffixation is stronger there.

The other two types of language use syntactic negation, i.e., the negation is expressed by a particular free form in the sentence. In one of the types, this free form is a negative auxiliary, i.e., the negator is inflected for some or all categories of the finite verb, and it is thus a member of the class of auxiliaries in those languages. The typological patterns for negative auxiliaries conform to those of auxiliaries in general with regard to placement, which means postverbal placement in most verb-final languages and preverbal placement in verb-initial and verb-second languages (Greenberg, 1963).

For the language types mentioned so far, then, we have not been able to formulate any markedness conditions for sentence negation. For the remaining group, however, those with uninflected negative particles, it is possible to formulate such conditions based on frequency. According to Dahl's study, there is a clear tendency for preverbal placement of the particle. In the actual sample, the proportions were 84 languages with preverbal placement of the particle as against 20 with postverbal placement. Since this tendency is valid for all basic word order type languages, the value of unmarked can be given to preverbal placement and marked to postverbal placement of the negation.

According to our prediction, preverbal placement should be preferred in initial phases of acquisition for learners with an L1/L2 pair where both languages use negative particles. Depending on the particular L1/L2 constellation, frequency differences should be discernible.

Studies of sentence negation are not conclusive on this point, primarily due to the lack of data from the earliest stages of acquisition (Hyltenstam, 1977; Noyau, 1981), but preverbal placement of the negative element seems to be an extremely common learner solution (Schumann, 1979; Wode, 1981c; Hyltenstam, 1981b; Zobl, 1982a). These observations seem fruitful for further investigation.

YES/NO QUESTIONS

In Ultan (1978), characteristics of interrogative systems are researched in a sample of 79 languages, selected randomly in terms of geographical, genetic, and typological distribution. Yes/no questions, information questions (i.e., wh-questions), and alternative questions are treated in Ultan's article, but only yes/no questions are considered here.

There are three main devices to express yes/no questions in Ultan's sample—and probably universally (Greenberg, 1963): intonation, a question particle or affix, and inversion. These three can occur in isolation or combined with each other; it is particularly common to use intonation and one of the other two together.

With regard to frequency, intonation "holds the first rank." Even if intonation is not the prime or the only device with which to express yes/no questions in many languages, the possibility of distinguishing interrogatives from their corresponding declaratives solely by means of intonation seems to exist "in most (perhaps all?) languages."

"After intonation, interrogative particles are the most widespread device for marking YN clauses or sentences." As noted above, interrogative particles include both free forms, i.e., particles proper, and interrogative affixes. (As already noted by Greenberg (1963), the position of the particles is dependent on what basic word order type the particular language belongs to, but this question does not concern us here.)

Least frequent is the device of inversion. Most of the languages in Ultan's sample that have inversion are modern European languages; one exception is Malay. Inversion does not occur in VSO languages, which means that the resultant order is always VSO. Only one verb-final language in the sample exhibits inversion, and this language is Hungarian, where it is questionable whether SVO or the SOV order is favored. There are certain implicational restrictions on the occurrence of inversion in yes/no question, i.e., inversion in yes/no questions occurs only if inversion also occurs in information questions, and inversion in information questions occurs only if the interrogative word is placed initially (Greenberg, 1963:83). Since the interrogative word is placed in initial position less frequently in SOV languages than in SVO languages, the frequency of the device of inversion must also be lower in the former type. Therefore, markedness conditions are difficult to establish for inversion at a general level. However, since this device seems to be uncommon also in SVO languages, it must be considered marked. In fact, if we use the weaker basis of frequency for the formulation of what is typologically marked, it seems possible to have the devices of interrogation ordered from least to most marked in the following way: intonation, interrogative particle, inversion.

Our predictions would be that intonation is the preferred means of expressing yes/no questions with particle and inversion coming later.

Observations to this effect can be found for example in Wode (1981c) and Hyltenstam (1981b).

VERBS OF PERCEPTION

Typological patterning in the area of lexical arrangement has been investigated for a small number of semantic areas. The most well-known and influential work is that by Berlin and Kay (1969) on the topic of basic color terms. In this semantic field, a hierarchy of lexicalization was found to accord to the following pattern.

$$\begin{Bmatrix} black \\ white \end{Bmatrix} > red > \begin{Bmatrix} yellow \\ green \\ blue \end{Bmatrix} > brown > \begin{Bmatrix} purple \\ pink \\ orange \\ grey \end{Bmatrix}$$

According to this hierarchy, the authors suggest, predictions can be made about what color terms a particular language makes use of: if the language uses only two basic color terms, these are always *black* and *white*, if three, *red* is added, and so forth. Primary data for Berlin and Kay's investigation was collected from 20 languages. Additionally, secondary data from other investigations were used. Altogether, the sample consisted of 98 languages.

The typological investigation that will be considered here is one by Viberg (1981, 1982). In this investigation typological patterning in verbs within the semantic field of perception was researched in a sample of approximately 40 languages, selected as representatively as possible in terms of areal and genetic distribution. The data from the sample languages were analyzed according to how the notions in a so-called basic paradigm of perception are expressed lexically. The basic paradigm takes the following form (examples from English are given):

VERBS OF PERCEPTION
Basic paradigm:

	Activity	*Experience*	*Copulative*
SIGHT	John was looking/ looked at the birds	John saw the birds	John looked happy
HEARING	John was listening/ listened to the birds	John heard the birds	John sounded happy
TOUCH	John was feeling/felt the tyre (of his bike)	John felt a stone under his foot	The stone felt sharp
TASTE	John was tasting/ tasted the soup	John tasted garlic in the soup	The soup tasted < of garlic / good/bad
SMELL	John was smelling/ smelt the cigar	John smelt cigars in the room	John smelt < of cigars / good/bad

The degree of lexical differentiation within this basic paradigm varies in languages. Compare for example English and Swedish.

English

	Activity	Experience	Copulative
SIGHT	look at	see	look
HEARING	listen to	hear	sound
TOUCH		feel	
TASTE		taste	< good/bad *of* onions
SMELL		smell	< good/bad *of* onions

Swedish

	Activity	Experience	Copulative
SIGHT	titta på	se	se . . . ut
HEARING	lyssna på höra på	höra	láta
TOUCH	känna på	känna	kännas
TASTE	smaka på	känna (smaken av)	smaka< gott/illa lök
SMELL	lukta på	känna (lukten av)	lukta< gott/illa lök

This lexical differentiation is, however, not random. At least two implicational hierarchies are supported by the data.

The first hierarchy concerns the lexical differentiation between the notions of "activity" and "experience":

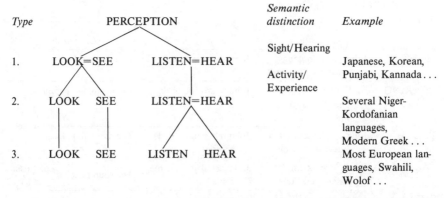

Type	PERCEPTION		Semantic distinction	Example
			Sight/Hearing	
1.	LOOK=SEE	LISTEN=HEAR		Japanese, Korean,
			Activity/ Experience	Punjabi, Kannada . . .
2.	LOOK SEE	LISTEN=HEAR		Several Niger-Kordofanian languages, Modern Greek . . .
3.	LOOK SEE	LISTEN HEAR		Most European languages, Swahili, Wolof . . .

As this diagram states, perceptual verbs are always differentiated lexically in the modalities of sight and hearing. (Viberg cites assumed exceptions to this,

where the same verb together with certain nouns is used for both modalities.)
It is not, however, always the case that different lexical elements are used for
"activity" and "experience," i.e., between lexical elements such as *look/see*
and *listen/hear*. Japanese, Korean, Punjabi, and Kannada are examples of
languages that do not make this distinction. Languages that have a lexical
differentiation of "activity" and "experience" in only one of the modalities of
sight and hearing make this differentiation in the modality of sight rather
than hearing. Examples of such languages are given in the graph. Most
European languages differentiate lexically between "activity" and "experience" in both modalities.

It is much more common not to differentiate between "activity" and
"experience" in the modalities of touch, taste, and smell. As can be seen from
the chart above, English is an example of such a language. In terms of
markedness, then, it is the least marked case not to distinguish lexically
between "activity" and "experience" and most marked to make this
differentiation in the modalities of taste and smell.

Where no lexical differentiation is made between the notions of "activity,"
"experience," and "copulative," Viberg interprets the facts as a case of
neutralization rather than a case of polysemy, since none of the meanings can
be considered the basic meaning.

The second hierarchy, on the contrary, concerns patterns of polysemy
within perceptual verbs of experience. A lexical differentiation according to
different modalities is more frequently made in verbs of experience than in
verbs of activity. In English, for example, there is one verb of experience for
each modality: *see, hear, feel, taste, smell*. The following chart (p. 74) from
Viberg (1982) (modified) shows the patterns of polysemy in a number of languages, and the basic meaning of each lexical element is circled.

The general pattern that can be seen from this chart is summarized in the
following hierarchy of polysemy:

$$\text{SIGHT} > \text{HEARING} > \text{TOUCH} > \begin{Bmatrix} \text{TASTE} \\ \text{SMELL} \end{Bmatrix}$$

The markedness conditions in this case follow the hierarchy of polysemy,
which means that it is the least marked case to have only one verb of
perception with the basic meaning of "see" (this type is actually not attested
in Viberg's sample, as noted above). The second degree of markedness is to
have two verbs of perception with the basic meaning of "see" and "hear."
Next in degree of markedness come systems which also have a verb with the
meaning of "feel" and most marked are those systems which include words
for "taste" and "smell" as well.

Note that in the area of verbs of perception, the typological markedness
conditions can be formulated in their stronger version, since an implicational
relationship holds between the different systems in this case.

For second language acquisition, then, these typological facts would
predict that learners would prefer few verbs to express meanings in the

PATTERNS OF POLYSEMY

Sense modality	Kurdish	Swahili	Hausa	Swedish	Malay	Seneca	English
SIGHT	ditin	ona	gan(i)	se	lihat	-kE-	see
HEARING	bistin	sikia	ji	höra	dengar	-athO:te-	hear
TOUCH	ditin	sikia	ji	känna	rasa	(-ka?EyO-)	feel
TASTE	ditin	ona	ji	känna	rasa	-hsO:wi-	taste
SMELL	ditin	sikia	ji	känna	hidu	-hsO:wi-	smell

Hausa	Swedish	Malay	Seneca	English
Hausa	Swedish	Malay	Seneca	English
Birom	(Icelandic)	Indonesian	W Greenlandic	German
Chibemba	Polish	Bengali		Danish
Mambwe	Serbo-Cr.	Modern Greek		Arabic
Setswana	Bulgarian			Chinese
Luo	Finnish			Vietnamese
Turkish	Estonian			
(duymak)	Hungarian			Tigrinya
??Italian	Turkish			Oromo
	(hissetmek)			Wolof
	?Suryoyo			
				Hindi
				Punjabi

semantic field of perception in early phases of acquisition. The phenomenon of semantic extension of lexical elements in the learner's interlanguage is well attested. Furthermore, the way semantic extension operates is not random. A plausible hypothesis is that semantic extension in the learner's interlanguage follows the patterns of lexicalization found in typological studies. For example, the pattern of nondifferentiation of perceptual verbs of activity and experience can be discerned in a lexical study of a number of second language learners of Swedish (Kotsinas, 1982:79). The form that was most often chosen by these learners for the modality of sight was *titta*, i.e., the equivalent of English *look*, rather than *se* (= *see*). Kotsinas' study also reveals a number of systematic semantic extensions in other fields (see Kotsinas, 1983, 1984, forthcoming).

SUMMARY

In this article, it has been pointed out that the field of language typology and the notions of language universals and markedness have attracted considerable attention in second language acquisition research. A central concern here has been to elucidate the notion of markedness in more detail. One main problem in the application of markedness concepts to L2 studies is the extreme diversity of uses the term has generally had in linguistics. An overview of how the notion of markedness has been utilized in L2 research revealed that there has been a great deal of vagueness in the definition of the term, and that there is often no explicit discussion about what theoretical assumptions the notion bears in each application.

The article suggests one way of restricting the use of markedness— recognizing other alternatives. Here, cross-linguistic—or typological— markedness is used in the phase of formulating hypotheses about second language acquisition patterns: cross-linguistically unmarked structures and elements are hypothesized to turn up in early phases of acquisition, irrespective of the markedness conditions of the L1 and L2 involved. The markedness conditions for L1/L2, however, are hypothesized to play an important role in the learner's further development: the transfer patterns are likely to be dependent on L1/L2 markedness constellations. It is further suggested that the explanations that have been proposed to account for typological patternings might be considered also for acquisitional patterning, where parallels between the two fields have been observed.

NOTE

1. This formulation in actual fact is too broad and needs to be qualified for gaps in phonological systems (Gamkrelidze, 1973) and for phonotactic constraints (Dinnsen and Eckman, 1975); for purposes of exemplification, this formulation might be justified here.

It is important to note that most of the implicational universals formulated in Greenberg (1963) are of a totally different kind from those we consider here. They concern the cooccurence of various structural phenomena, typically word order phenomena such as if a language is verb-initial, then it uses prepositions (rather than postpositions). Cross-linguistic markedness conditions cannot be formulated for the categories that occur in these universals.

REFERENCES

Bailey, C.-J. N. 1973. *Variation and Linguistic Theory*. Arlington, Va.: Center for Applied Linguistics.
Berlin, B. and P. Kay. 1969. *Basic Color Terms: Their Universality and Evolution*. Berkeley: University of California Press.
Chomsky, N. 1957. *Syntactic Structures*. The Hague: Mouton.
Chomsky, N. 1965. *Aspects of the Theory of Syntax*. Cambridge, Mass.: MIT Press.
Chomsky, N. 1980. Markedness and core grammar. In Proceedings from the GLOW Meeting, Pisa, April 1979: *Markedness and Linguistic Theory*, pp. 123–146.
Chomsky, N. and M. Halle. 1968. *The Sound Pattern of English*. New York: Harper & Row.
Comrie, B. 1981. *Language Universals and Linguistic Typology*. Oxford: Basil Blackwell.
Dahl, Ö. 1979. Typology of sentence negation. *Linguistics* 17: 79–106.
Dinnsen, D. A. and F. R. Eckman. 1975. A functional explanation of some phonological typologies. In R. Grossman et al. (eds.), *Functionalism*. Chicago: Chicago Linguistic Society.
Eckman, F. R. 1977. Markedness and the contrastive analysis hypothesis. *Language Learning* 27: 315–330.
Eckman, F. R. 1981. Markedness and degree of difficulty in second language learning. In J.-G. Savard and L. Laforge (eds.), *Actes du 5ᵉ congrès de l'Association Internationale de Linguistique Appliquée*. Québec: Les Presses de l'Université Laval.
Gamkrelidze, T. V. 1973. Uber die Wechselbeziehung zwischen Verschluss- und Reibelauten im Phonemsystem. Zum Problem der Markiertheit in der Phonologie. *Phonetica* 27: 213–218.
Gass, S. 1979. Language transfer and universal grammatical relations. *Language Learning* 29: 327–344.
Gass, S. 1980. An investigation of syntactic transfer in adult second language learners. In R. C. Scarcella and S. D. Krashen (eds.), *Research in Second Language Acquisition*. Rowley, Mass.: Newbury House.
Gass, S. and J. Ard. 1980. L2 data: Their relevance for language universals. *TESOL Quarterly*, vol. 14., no. 4.
Greenberg, J. H. 1963. Some universals of grammar with particular reference to the order of meaningful elements. In J. H. Greenberg (ed.), *Universals of Language*. Cambridge, Mass.: MIT Press.
Greenberg, J. H. 1966. *Language Universals, with Special Reference to Feature Hierarchies*. Janua Linguarum, Series Minor 59. The Hague: Mouton.
Hatch, E. 1974. Second Language Learning-Universals? *Working Papers on Bilingualism* 3: 1–17.
Hyltenstam, K. 1977. Implicational patterns in interlanguage syntax variation. *Language Learning* 27: 383–411.
Hyltenstam, K. 1981a. The use of typological markedness conditions as predictors in second language acquisition: the case of pronominal copies in relative clauses. Paper presented at the European-North American Workshop on Cross-Linguistic Second Language Acquisition Research. Los Angeles, September 7–14, 1981.

Hyltenstam, K. 1981 b. Dynamic change in the acquisition of a second language as exemplified by negation and interrogation. In J.-G. Savard and L. Laforge (eds.), *Actes du 5ᵉ congrès de l'Association Internationale de Linguistique Appliqée*. Quebéc: Les Presses de l'Université Laval.

Hyltenstam, K. and E. Magnusson. 1983. Typological markedness, contextual variation, and the acquisition of the voice contrast in stops by first and second language learners of Swedish. *The Indian Journal of Applied Linguistics* 9: 1–18.

Ioup, G. and A. Kruse. 1977. Interference versus structural complexity in second language acquisition: Language universals as a basis for natural sequencing. In H. D. Brown, C. A. Yorio and R. H. Crymes (eds.), *On TESOL '77: Teaching and Learning English as a Second Language*. Washington D.C.: TESOL.

Jakobson, R. 1941. *Kindersprache, Aphasie und allgemeine Lautgesetze*. Uppsala: Almqvist & Wiksell.

Johansson, F. A. 1973. *Immigrant Swedish Phonology. A Study in Multiple Contact Analysis*. Travaux de l'institut de linguistique de Lund, IX. Lund: CWK Gleerup.

Keenan, E. and B. Comrie. 1977. Noun phrase accessibility and universal grammar. *Linguistic Inquiry* 8: 63–99.

Kellerman, E. 1978. Giving learners a break: Native language intuitions as a source of predictions about transferability. *Working Papers on Bilingualism* 15: 59–89.

Kellerman, E. 1979. Transfer and non-transfer. Where are we now? *Studies in Second Language Acquisition*, 2/1.

Koster, J. 1978. Conditions, empty nodes, and markedness. *Linguistic Inquiry* 9: 551–593.

Kotsinas, U.-B. 1982. *Svenska svårt. Några invandrares svenska talspråk. Ordförrådet*. Meddelanden fran Institutionen för nordiska sprak vid Stockholms universitet, 10.

Kotsinas, U.-B. 1983. On the acquisition of vocabulary in immigrant Swedish. In H. Ringbom (ed.), *Psycholinguistics and Foreign/Second Language Learning*, Turku: Åbo Akademi.

Kotsinas, U.-B. 1984. Semantic over-extension and lexical over-use in immigrant Swedish. *Scandinavian Working Papers on Bilingualism*, 2: 23–42.

Mazurkewich, I. 1981. Second language acquisition of dative structures and linguistic theory. Paper presented at the Sixth Annual Boston University Conference on Language Development, October 11, 1981.

Noyau, C. 1981. French negation in the language of Spanish-speaking immigrant workers: Social acquisition/variability/transfer/individual systems. Paper prepared for the 1st European-North American Workshop on Cross-Linguistic Second Language Acquisition Research (Lake Arrowhead), September 1981.

Ritchie, W. C. 1978. The right front constraint in an adult-acquired language. In W. C. Ritchie (ed.), *Second Language Acquisition Research. Issues and Implications*. Perspectives in Neurolinguistics and Psycholinguistics: A Series of Monographs and Treatises. New York: Academic Press.

Rutherford, W. E. 1981. Language typology and language transfer. University of Southern California, Los Angeles (mimeo).

Rutherford, W. E. 1982. Markedness in second language acquisition. *Language Learning* 32: 85–108.

Schachter, J. 1974. An error in error analysis. *Language Learning* 24: 205–214.

Schmidt, M. 1980. Coordinate structures and language universals in interlanguage. *Language Learning* 30: 397–416.

Schumann, J. H. 1979. The acquisition of English negation by speakers of Spanish: A review of the literature. In R. W. Andersen, *The Acquisition and Use of Spanish and English as First and Second Languages*. Washington D.C.: TESOL.

Sheldon, A. 1974. *The acquisition of relative clauses in English*. Bloomington, Ind.: Indiana University Linguistics Club.

Trubetzkoy, N. S. 1939. *Grundzüge der Phonologie*. (3rd ed. 1958) Göttingen: Vanderhoek & Ruprecht.

Ultan, R. 1978. Some general characteristics of interrogative systems. In J. H. Greenberg (ed.), *Universals of Human Language, Vol. 4. Syntax.* Stanford: Stanford University Press, pp. 211–248.

Viberg, Å. 1981. En typologisk undersökning av perceptionsverben som ett semantiskt fält. SSM Report 8. Stockholms universitet: Institutionen för lingvistik.

Viberg, Å. 1982. The verbs of perception. A typological study. Paper presented at the Linguistics Universals Workshop, Cascais, Portugal, January 3–10, 1982.

Wode, H. 1981a. Language acquisitional universals: A unified view of language acquisition. Paper presented at the conference on Native Language and Foreign Language Acquisition, New York, January 15–16, 1981.

Wode, H. 1981b. Psycholinguistische Grundlagen sprachlicher Universalien: Möglichkeiten eines empirischen Paradigmas. *Arbeitspapiere zum Spracherwerb*, 28.

Wode, H. 1981c. *Learning a Second Language. 1. An Integrated View of Language Acquisition.* Tübingen: Gunter Narr.

Zobl, H. 1982a. Variations across developmental continua and language contrast. Paper presented at the conference on Language Universals and Second Language Acquisition. University of Southern California, February 6–7, 1982.

Zobl, H. 1982b. Markedness and the projection problem. Université de Moncton (manuscript).

PART TWO

Theoretical Interpretation of Empirical Second Language Acquisition Studies

CHAPTER 4

Functional Approaches to Interlanguage

Carol Wollman Pfaff

Free University of Berlin (West), Federal Republic of Germany

INTRODUCTION

The central idea behind the concept of interlanguage is that underlying the observable surface utterances produced by L2 learners are cognitive and linguistic processes or strategies for communication and for the construction of internalized linguistic systems. To begin to ask and answer questions about such interlanguage processes and strategies, we have had, in recent years, to redirect our attention from the surface products to the underlying pragmatic and linguistic functions and semantic intentions speakers are attempting to communicate.

In this paper I examine some of the theoretical issues implicitly or explicitly treated under the rubric of "functionalism" and explore the possibilities of functional analysis of interlanguage systems of determiners and reference in immigrant children's acquisition of German interlanguages. In the first section, I briefly consider the various uses of "functionalism" in linguistics: in synchronic analysis of adult systems, in language change, pidginization and creolization, and in L1 acquisition. In the second part I focus on the linguistic expression of functions pertaining to the identification of NP's in discourse, including reference, topic/focus marking and semantico-grammatical case in standard and native colloquial German. The third section presents some of the results for six Turkish adolescents' use of articles and pronouns in narratives to mark discourse functions, case and gender. The final section draws conclusions and examines the consequences for design of experiments and further studies of functional principles in L2 research.

1. FUNCTIONALISM IN LINGUISTICS

"Functionalism" is hardly a unitary, well-defined concept in linguistics. In recent years, this term has been used in several distinct (though not totally unrelated) ways. The following is not intended to be an exhaustive catalogue or to present a thorough discussion of all the theoretical issues, but merely to identify some of the major issues and approaches to functionalism, particularly those that seem especially applicable to the study of second language acquisition.

SOCIAL FUNCTION

A great deal of sociolinguistic work has focused on alternation among varieties in the verbal repertoire of a community, e.g., Ferguson's (1959) study of diglossia, Fishman's (1972) identification of typical social domains of L1 and L2 use by bilinguals, and Gumperz's (1982), Elías-Olivares' (1976), Pfaff's (1979) and Poplack's (1980) studies of the use of code switching and language mixing. There are two functional aspects to such alternation. On the one hand, the social function of each variety is to be appropriate in the given social domain, to identify the speaker's social status, role or attitudes vis-à-vis the hearer and topic. It is in this connection that Weinreich, Labov and Herzog (1968:101) point out that "in a language serving a complex (i.e., real) community, it is absence of structured heterogeneity that would be dysfunctional." Further, each variety has a range of linguistic devices commensurate with its social function and characteristic communicative intentions of its speakers. Thus, as Ochs' (1979) work on planned and unplanned discourse shows, varieties used in formal and written styles display greater syntactic complexity, while varieties used in informal styles are characterized by greater reliance on context, intonation and other prosodic devices.

The work on pidgins by Bickerton (1981), Sankoff (1980), etc. and on early or fossilized L2 interlanguages by Hatch, Schumann, Dittmar, Meisel, etc. has related their syntactically simple structure to their socially restricted function, primarily to refer to events and states in the "here and now." The analyses of foreign workers' attempts to communicate about the "not here, not now" in narrative and conversation relating to past events in the papers by von Stutterheim and Klein, Meisel, Trévise, and Veronique in the present volume dramatically illustrate the difficulties of effectively communicating with limited linguistic resources.

PRAGMATIC FUNCTION

"Pragmatic" is a term that has several different meanings in linguistics. On the one hand, it refers to functions such as assertion, denial, question, command, etc. identified by speech act theory as developed by Austin, Searle, Grice and others and can be applied to the type of conversational analysis developed by Sachs, Schegloff, etc. which is concerned with how speakers "do" these and other routines such as openings, closings, turn-taking and repair in face-to-face interaction. Givón's (1979a) use of the term "pragmatic mode" to refer to the opposite end of the continuum from syntactically complex speech can be related to speakers' extensive reliance on the Gricean (1975:45) cooperative principle assuming that hearers will be able to interpret their utterance in terms of the conversational maxims of quantity, quality, relation and manner. Givón, while suggesting that *pidgins employ the pragmatic mode exclusively*, nonetheless paradoxically gives as one reason for this a *lack of common pragmatic background*, yet another use of the term:

> Members of the Pidgin community come from different cultural and racial communities, they share relatively little of the general, pragmatic presuppositional background which forms the general context for human communication" (Givón 1979a:225–6).

The present papers on temporality in the German and French interlanguages of foreign workers, however, indicate that North African, Italian, Spanish and Turkish workers and their linguist interlocutors often share a great deal of the presuppositional background about the structuring of sequences of events; it is this which makes possible communication in the absence not only of morphological marking of temporality on verbs, but often of adverbial temporal marking as well.

An additional use of "pragmatic function" (e.g., Givón 1979a:144) is synonymous with "discourse function," discussed below.

DISCOURSE FUNCTION

Although the pragmatic functions identified in conversational analysis certainly pertain to discourse, the term "discourse function" usually refers to notions like topicality, focus and cohesion in text. Unfortunately, here too there is terminological confusion in the literature. While many authors use "topic" vs. "comment" as equivalents of the functional sentence perspective terms "theme" vs. "rheme" (Firbas, 1966) in the sense of given, old, or background information vs. new information or information deemed by speaker to be difficult for the hearer to identify at the time of utterance, the terms have almost diametrically opposite meanings in other work. Thus "topicalization transformations" may be used to focus or emphasize constituents, and "focus" is used in the sense of "topic" by Zubin (1979) and others. To further complicate matters, the everyday sense of "subject" (what the discourse is about) as opposed to "grammatical" or "logical" subject is often used to explain the terms "topic" and "focus."

Chafe (1976) provides a good introduction to the substantive issue of the linguistic expression of discourse functions, and Givón (1979a) treats in detail how the distinction between background and new information is realized through several interrelated linguistic devices such as subordination, word order, explicit morphological marking, verbal aspect, definite vs. indefinite NP, pronominalization, etc.

CASE FUNCTION

The surface grammatical functions "subject" and "object" and their underlying semantic deep case functions "agent," "recipient," "goal," "instrument," etc., more commonly called grammatical relations or roles, have been treated extensively in "case grammar" by Fillmore (1968, 1977) and in "relational grammar" by Johnson (1979) and Cole and Saddock (1977). Case functions are clearly not independent of discourse and semantic function. The quantitative analysis of English presented in Givón (1979a) demonstrates that the surface case roles subject and object are related to discourse functions. Subjects in sentence-initial position are typically part of the background, and thus definite. New information is introduced as direct object, or, if as subject, then noninitially in existential-presentative constructions. Thus, the indefinite NP's *a woman* in the existential-presentative and *a dog* as direct object are new, while *the woman*, the definite NP subject is old information in the following: (There was a *woman ... the woman* heard a *dog* barking). Quantitative work on Russian by Greenberg (1974) and on German by Zubin (1979) has shown that case function is closely linked to inherent semantic properties of nouns, e.g., that animates occur more frequently as subjects or indirect objects, while inanimates occur more often as direct objects or objects of prepositions. Zubin, further, demonstrates that entities which occur frequently within a discourse tend to occur in the nominative, and suggests that such correlations are reflections of the egocentricity of natural language, of human concerns in general. It is noteworthy that a wide range of other linguistic phenomena, from relativization (Keenan and Comrie, 1977) to word order in idiomatic compounds (man and beast/*beast and man) (Cooper and Ross, 1975) appear to follow closely related hierarchies of case, animacy, and distance from self.

PLURIFUNCTIONALITY

Adult linguistic systems typically depart from a one-to-one relationship between function and form in both directions. On the one hand, one function may correspond to many forms, as for example with redundant marking of subject with case-marked NP's and with agreement markers on verbs; functionally equivalent paraphrases, synonyms or alternative pronunciations may coexist. On the other hand, one form often corresponds to more than one function. Plurifunctional forms may be ambiguous, as with homophonous or syncretic items, or may express several functions simultaneously, as in the synthetic Indo-European languages (including German) where case, number and gender expression are inflectionally fused.

Bates and MacWhinney (1979:168–9, 174) sketch out a functionalist approach to child first language acquisition of such systems as follows:

> Although the relation between form and function may be complex, it is not so complex that it cannot be learned by a child. Thus, according to the functionalist proposal, the child's acquisi-

tion of grammar is guided, not by abstract categories, but by the pragmatic and semantic structure of communications interacting with the performance constraints of the speech channel. No one aspect of the communication situation is sufficient to motivate surface forms.

At this point, we can put forward two versions of the functionalist hypothesis. The weak version suggests only that surface grammatical devices are "correlated" with various communicative functions and processing constraints. . .

The strong version goes a step further, to suggest that grammatical forms are "determined" and "maintained" by these same communicative functions and processing constraints. The strong version leads to a developmental model in which children discover the structure of grammar through their experience with competing communicative factors.

Slobin (1973) has presented evidence from studies of first language that in acquiring the forms and functions of their language, children follow the basic principle: new forms first express old functions and new functions are first expressed by old forms (Slobin, 1973:184). He later suggested (1977) that this response to the charge of clarity is one of four major constraints on language change in general.

PLURIFUNCTIONALITY OF DETERMINER AND REFERENCE SYSTEMS

One area in which plurifunctionality is particularly evident is the article and pronoun subsystems, which as noted above express a number of discourse, semantic and grammatical functions. Children's acquisition of the functions of determiners and reference in French L1 has been investigated by Karmiloff-Smith (1979) in a series of experiments designed to isolate the various functions (descriptor, determinor, naming ...) of articles and adjectives. Karmiloff-Smith (1980, 1981) further investigates the functions of NP vs. pronoun in narratives.

Karmiloff-Smith (1979) established the following sequence of acquisitional stages of the various determiner functions in French L1. At stage 1, the child acquires a generalized article, undifferentiated for definite/indefinite, which has two main functions: (i) it permits the distinction of proper vs. common nouns, a semantic function; and (ii) it permits the distinction of "thinglike" from "actionlike" words, a syntagmatic function. At stage 2, indefinite and definite articles are acquired, with distinct functions: indefinite for naming, definite for deictic focus on the object of attention. At about the same time, or slightly earlier, the child acquires demonstrative adjective and simple modifiers, another source of referential function. At stage 3, the singular vs. plural function of determiners is acquired, whereas their gender-marking function is acquired later, the first cues to gender coming from noun endings. At stage 4, the exophoric function of definite articles to indicate a single entity in the extralinguistic context is acquired. At stage 5, the function of class inclusion is acquired. At stage 6, the child distinguishes nonspecific reference with indefinite from anaphoric reference with definite. The generic function of articles is acquired later, at stage 7.

Summarizing the principles which appear to underlie this development, Karmiloff-Smith (1979:224-6) suggests that "children first approach language as if morphemes were unifunctional and that development consists in conferring on a series of unifunctional homophones the status of plurifunctional morphemes." Between 5 to 8 years, "there is a tendency to use a separate morpheme for each function," giving rise to redundant marking and the creation of slightly ungrammatical forms before pluri-functional status is established between 8 to 12 years.

Throughout her discussion, Karmiloff-Smith, while relating her work to the cognitivist theory of Piaget and his followers (see Berman and Kail, this volume), emphasizes the role of the surface form of the target language—the specific facts of its plurifunctional system as well as the development of the child's general cognitive abilities.

It is of interest to pursue cross-linguistic investigation of the development in various L1's and in L2 interlanguages, both in cases where acquisition is begun late and cognitive abilities can be assumed to be present from the outset, and in cases of earlier L2 acquisition where cognitive and linguistic development in the L1 are still incomplete. In the rest of this paper, I begin to explore this area for German interlanguage of Turkish immigrant children.

2. FUNCTIONAL ANALYSIS OF DETERMINERS AND PRONOUNS IN GERMAN

Determiners and pronouns in German have much the same discourse function as previously described by Givón (1979a), Karmiloff-Smith (1979, 1980, 1981), and Hawkins (1978). Following Givón (1979a:57), two separate communicative functions are involved in the identification of referents:

(i)   the general difference between a "known" argument and an argument introduced for the first time (definite vs. indefinite)

(ii) for arguments that have already appeared in the relevant linguistic or extralinguistic context, the degree of difficulty of assigning their correct reference upon reintroduction into discourse (definite NP vs. pronoun).

Additionally, definite and indefinite article and pronoun forms mark the semantico-grammatical categories of case, number and gender as shown in Table 1. The indefinite article forms also function as the numeral "one."

One of the major obstacles to the learner of the German determiner and reference system is the fact that the relation between form and function is highly opaque, as indicated in Table 1. In addition to the semantically motivated role-related cases, nominative for subject, accusative for direct

TABLE 1 Article and Pronoun Forms of Standard German

| | Indefinite Articles | | | | Definite Articles | | | | Personal Pronouns | | | |
	Masculine	Neuter	Feminine		Masculine	Neuter	Feminine	Plural		Masculine	Neuter	Feminine	Plural
Nominative	ein	ein	eine		der	das	die	die		er	es	sie	sie
Accusative	einen	ein	eine		den	das	die	die		ihn	es	sie	sie
Dative	einem	einem	einer		dem	dem	der	den		ihm	ihm	ihr	ihnen
Genitive	eines	eines	einer		des	des	der	der		sein-	sein-	ihr-	ihr-

object and dative for indirect object, there are also cases governed by verbs and by prepositions, some of which take dative, some accusative, some either dative or accusative, depending on whether location or motion is expressed. *Die Katze sitzt auf dem Tisch* (location); *Die Katze springt auf den Tisch* (motion).

When dealing with L2 acquisition in a community where the language is in general use, spoken as well as standard written forms must also be considered as relevant input. German colloquial speech is characterized by the following additional plurifunctionality:

1. definite article forms are also used as personal pronouns—e.g., *die geht nach Hause* "she goes home" alongside *sie geht nach Hause* (see Pfaff (1984) for discussion of this usage in Turkish and Greek children's interlanguage.)
2. In Berlin dialect, as in other northern and eastern dialects, accusative and dative are not consistently distinguished (König 1978:154–5).
3. genitive forms are rarely used, frequently being replaced by datives— e.g., *der Hut von seinem Vater* alongside *der Hut seines Vaters*.

3. PLURIFUNCTIONALITY OF DETERMINERS AND REFERENCE IN TURKISH ADOLESCENTS' GERMAN INTERLANGUAGE

METHODOLOGY

This paper focuses on the functional development of the determiner and reference systems of the German interlanguages of seventh-grade Turkish pupils in Berlin. The social background of the pupils, who were enrolled in an integrated class with one-third Turkish, two-thirds German pupils, and the elicitation instrument, the Soziolinguistisches Erhebungsinstrument zur Sprachentwicklung (SES), are described in detail elsewhere (Pfaff, 1984; Portz and Pfaff, 1981). For the present analysis, a subsample of six children is considered.

The children are typical of their classmates with respect to length of time in Berlin and number of years of school in Turkey prior to (or in one case interspersed with) years of school in Berlin, as shown below:

Girls	Age	Years in Berlin	School years in Turkey	Boys	Age	Years in Berlin	School years in Turkey
AA	13	6–7	1,2,4	BB	14	4	1–5
AB	13	2	1–5	BL	13	7	none
AF	13	6	none	BO	15	7	1

These speakers' linguistic performance and interlanguage characteristics are also typical of the larger group analyzed in Pfaff and Portz (1979) and Pfaff (1984).

For three of the pupils (AA, AB, BO) longitudinal material is also analyzed, based on follow-up interviews in the second and third years of the experimental integrated program. The first follow-up interview repeated the SES, the second used a similar directed conversational technique.

For the investigation of the marking of discourse function, thematicization, figure (background) vs. ground, etc., two short connected narratives were elicited from each speaker, using pictorial stimuli. The narratives differ in (a) thematic subject, (b) number of characters, (c) animacy, (d) extent of characters' active participation, and (e) whether or not the participants are represented in the picture, as indicated in the following summaries:

> *The cat and the milk:* The cat sees a glass of milk on the table, thinks about what to do, jumps up, knocks over the glass, drinks the milk, some of which runs onto the floor, and jumps down.
>
> The setting is familiar from a preceding set of pictures, representing the cat and glass of milk in various locations relative to the table. All noun participants are present throughout; only the cat is active.
>
> *The snowman:* (A) Some children make a snowman, giving it eyes and buttons of coal, a carrot nose, a hat, and a broom. They admire their work and leave. (B) The hat, broom and carrot are taken by a man, woman and rabbit, respectively. (C) The children return and are distressed.
>
> The pictures are presented out of sequence: A, C, B. The snowman, in various states, is present throughout but never acts. The other participants are all transitory. For most speakers, empathy is with the children, although the actions of the others are frequently rationalized.

For the investigation of case and gender marking functions, the following singular nouns were selected, representing standard German masculine, feminine and neuter grammatical gender assignment for humans, animals and inanimates (small objects and objects large enough to function as locations):

masculine: *Junge* "boy", *Mann* "man", *Hase* "rabbit", *Ball* "ball", *Besen* "broom", *Hut* "hat", *Tisch* "table", *Zug* "train"

feminine: *Frau* "woman", *Mutter* "mother", *Katze* "cat", *Milch* "milk", *Mohrrübe* "carrot", *Nase* "nose"

neuter: *Kind* "child", *Kücken* "chicken", *Glas* "glass"

These nouns were all relatively frequently mentioned in various grammatical roles: as subject, direct object, indirect object and object of preposition. Except for *Kücken*, *Besen*, and *Mohrrübe*, which were sometimes supplied by the interviewer, all were known to the speakers.

DISCOURSE FUNCTION

The cat and the milk   For the relatively simple narrative of the story of the cat and the milk, the interlanguage systems appear to be functionally similar for all speakers, though the article and pronoun forms used differ from speaker to speaker. All speakers use only definite descriptions (definite article + noun or pronoun), as is entirely appropriate both linguistically and extralinguistically: the story elements are all pictured, thus permitting deictic definite reference, the pictured setting is familiar, and, further, the interviewer uses definite reference in introducing the picture sequence as "the story of the cat and the milk."

All speakers clearly distinguish the protagonist, the cat, from the other subjects linguistically: reference to subject with a pronoun is limited to the cat, and, if both "cat" and "milk" (as object) are pronominalized, the pronoun forms are always distinct, though in standard German both are feminine so reference to either subject or object would be with *sie* or *die*. Except for speaker AB, who introduces the cat as pronoun, subjects are introduced as definite article + noun. Repeated reference to the same subject continues with pronoun until a new subject or a frame exchange with the interviewer intervenes. Objects are introduced with definite article + noun and repeated reference either continues with definite article + noun or with pronoun. Two sample narratives are given below:

BO2

1.	*Der Glas* steht da	"*The glass* stands there
2.	*der Milch* steht da auf dem Tisch	*the milk* stands there on the table
3.	*der Katze* steht neben der Tisch	*the cat* stands beside the table
4.	und denkt, *er* will *die Milch* trinken	and thinks *he* wants to drink *the milk*
5.	dann springt *er* auf den Tisch	then *he* jumps onto the table
6.	dann kippt *er die Milch* . . . Tasse,	then *he* tips *the milk* . . . cup
7.	und trinkt *die*.	and drinks *it*.
8.	Dann lauft *er* wieder zurück.	Then *he* runs away again."

This narrative by BO2 shows one typical pattern. Subject article is *der,* object article is *die.* Pronominalized reference to the subject is limited to the cat *(er),* the object pronoun is *die.*

AF

1.	Ja, *der Milch* ist auf der . . . Tisch	"Yeah, *the milk* is on the table
2.	und *der Katze* ist neben *ihn*	and *the cat* is beside *it*
3.	und *der* denkt	and *he's* thinking
4.	wie *sie das Milch* trinken soll	how *she* should drink *the milk*
5.	und springt auf dem Tisch	and jumps on the table
6.	und *der Glas* fällt um	and *the glass* falls over
7.	und *der Milch* ist . . . um—runter—unten	and *the milk* is . . . over—down—under
8.	und *der Katze* hat . . . ist/ißt trinkt *ihn* wieder	and *the cat* has . . . is/eats drinks *it* again
9.	und geht *sie* wieder unten.	and *she* goes down again."

Again, though AF makes more extensive use of pronominalization, subject and object are kept distinct: *der* + noun as subject, *das* + noun as object, both *der* and *sie* as subject pronouns, *ihn* as object pronoun.

The Snowman   The snowman story is much more complex, involving not only a thematic subject or protagonists, the children, but agents in the complicating action as well—the man, the woman, the rabbit. With the exception of speaker AB, the speakers' treatment of the complex structure reveals rather well-developed means of narrative expression, involving appropriate alternation between NP and pronoun and between definite + noun and indefinite + noun.

Although it is difficult to speak of stages on the basis of so few examples, evidence from repair and longitudinal comparison indicate certain developmental pattern for first mention and reintroduction of arguments. These patterns suggest an interlanguage system which is sensitive to animacy and givenness.

Two illustrative narrative texts are given below and all narratives are summarized in Tables 2, 3, and 4.

AA2

1. *die Kinder* erstmal bauen *den Schneemann*	*"The children* first build *the snowman*
2. haben *sie* jetzt gebaut äh	now *they've* built—uh
3. haben *sie* jetzt gebaut	now *they've* built
4. und haben dann *Ø Nase* gemacht und auch *Ø Mund Ø Knöpfe* und so wie was und so weiter	and (they) made *Ø nose* also *Ø mouth Ø buttons* and such like
5. dann haben *sie einen Hut* gebracht und *ein*	then *they* brought *a hat* and *a—*
6. ähm wie sagt man das auf Deutsch	um—what do you call it in German?
7. ich wei*ß* nicht	I don't know
INT Besen	
8. Besen ja	broom, yeah
9. ach (unverständlich) haben *sie* gut gebaut	oh (unintelligible) *they've* built (it) well
10. und jetzt Hause gegangen	and now gone home
11. weil drau*ß*en kalt ist	because it's cold outside
12. und ist fertig	and (it's) finished
13. und ist *es* fertig?	and it's finished?
INT nee es geht noch weiter, was ist jetzt wohl mit dem Schneemann passiert?	no it goes on—what's happened to the snowman here?
14. *sie* haben	*they* have
15. ach *sie* haben *die Nase* geklaut	oh, *they've* stolen *the nose*
16. und *sie* haben *die Mohrrübe* abgerißt	and *they've* ripped off *the carrot*
INT wer hat das gemacht?	who did that?
17. *einer, irgendeiner*	*one, someone*
INT mh	
18. oder *die Schneemann*	or *the snowman*
19. *sie* haben *den Hut* genommen äh geklaut	*they've* taken *the hat*—uh stolen
20. und *den Besen* auch geklaut	and also stolen *the broom*
21. jetzt weinen *sie* hier	now *they're* crying here
INT mh, so jetzt jetzt erkennen wir was hier passiert ist was	uhah, so we see what happened here, what
22. ach so	ach so
INT passiert denn?	happened then?
23. *die Junge* äh äh *die Mann den Mann* nimmt *den Hut* in sein Kopf	*the boy*—uh uh—*the man, the man* takes *the hat* in his head
24. weil drau*ß*en kalt ist	because it's cold outside

INT	mh	
25.	*die Frau* nimmt *den Besen*	*the woman* takes *the broom*
26.	weil *Ø* hat *kein Besen* oder so was	because *Ø* has *no broom* or something like that
27.	*den Morrübe* nimmt *die Hase*	*the rabbit* takes *the carrot*
28.	weil *dies* hungrig ist	because *it's* hungry
29.	und *die Kinder* kommt jetzt	and *the children* comes now
30.	*sie* gucken *den* äh	*they* look *the*—uh—
31.	*die Hut* und *die Besen* und so weiter sind nicht hier	*the hat* and *the broom* and so on aren't here
32.	und jetzt weinen *sie* hier	and now here *they're* crying
INT	mh	
33.	richtig?	right?
INT	ja richtig so	yeah, that's right

snowman BO1

1.	*Die Kinder* machen *Ø Schneemann*	*The children* make *Ø snowman*
2.	*Sie* rollen ein . . . zwei Schneebälle	They roll one . . . two snowballs
3.	und stellen *Ø* aneinander	and put *Ø* on top of each other
4.	und *sie* machen *die Nase, die Augen, die Knopf* auf'm Hemd oder wie	and *they* make *the nose, the eyes, the button* on *the shirt* or whatever
5.	und *sie* stellen *eine . . . ein Sauger zur Hand*	and *they* put *a—a cleaner* on *the hand*
6.	und stellen *ein Hut* (unverständlich)	and put *a hat* (unintelligible)
7.	dann gehen *sie* wieder zu Haus.	then *they* go home again.
INT	Q	
8.	*Die* kommen und sehen	*they* come and see
9.	da gibts *keine Hund*	there is *no dog*
10.	da gibts *keine Hut* mehr auf'm Kopf	there is *no hat* on his head any more
11.	da gibts *keine Sauger* auf sein Hand	there is *no cleaner* in his hand
INT	und was ist passiert?	and what's happened?
12.	*der Mann* hat *sie,*	*the man* has *them*
13.	*eine Mann* hat *die Hut* abgenommen und *die Sauger* auch	*a man* has taken *the hat* and *the cleaner* too
INT		
14.	weil *der Mann das* gefreßt hat—genommen oder wie	because *the man* ate *it*—took or whatever
15.	*der Hase das* gefreßt haben	*the rabbit* ate *it*.

First mention of animates The animate agents (Table 2) are introduced as subjects in all cases, while, with one exception (AB2) inanimates are introduced as objects (Table 3), though they may subsequently assume the role of subject. Subjects are never introduced with *Ø* article + noun, objects sometimes are. There is a clear distinction in the treatment of the protagonists, the children, and other agents, the man, woman and rabbit. The children are always introduced in sentence-initial position as definites, either with definite article + noun, *die Kinder,* or with pronoun *sie* or *die,* which is appropriate in the context of the interviewers question *Was machen die Kinder?* "What are the children doing?"

Agents other than the children are introduced in two contexts. In the first, no picture stimulus is available—the speakers must speculate as to why the

TABLE 2   First Mention of Animates in Snowman Story

Speaker	Children (pictured)	Unspecified Agent (speculation beyond pictures)	Specified Agent (man, woman, rabbit)
AB1	PRO	DEF not completed	DEF + N, PRO
AB2	PRO	INDEF PRO	DEF + N
AA1	DEF + N		INDEF + N-Presentative
AA2	DEF + N	INDEF PRO	DEF + N
BO1	DEF + N		DEF + N, INDEF + N
BO2	PRO		INDEF + N-Presentative
BL	DEF + N	DEF + N	DEF + N-Presentative
AF	PRO	INDEF PRO, PRO	INDEF + N-Presentative

TABLE 3   First Mention of Inanimates in Snowman Story

Speaker	Schneemann	Hut, Besen	Nase	Augen Knöpfe
AB1	Ø + N	Ø + N	Ø + N	—
AB2	INDEF + N	DEF + N OBJ, DEF + N SUBJ	—	—
AA1	INDEF + N	DEF + N, INDEF + N	Ø + N	Ø + N
AA2	DEF + N	INDEF + N	Ø + N	Ø + N
BO1	Ø + N	INDEF + N	DEF + N	DEF + N
BO2	INDEF + N	INDEF + N	DEF + N	DEF + N
BL	INDEF + N	INDEF + N	INDEF + N	DEF/Ø + N
AF	INDEF + N	INDEF + N	INDEF + N	Ø + N

TABLE 4   Subsequent Mention of Animate and Inanimates in Snowman Story (in continuous *chains* and *reintroduction* after other nominal)

Speaker		Kinder	Mann, Frau, Hase	Schneemann	Other (inanimates)
AB1	chain	PRO	—	PRO	PRO
	reintro	—	—	DEF + N	DEF + N
AB2	chain	PRO, Ø	PRO	—	—
	reintro	DEF + N	—	—	DEF + N, PRO
AA1	chain	PRO, Ø	PRO	—	—
	reintro	DEF + N, PRO	—	DEF + N	DEF + N
AA2	chain	PRO, Ø	PRO	—	—
	reintro	DEF + N, PRO	—	—	DEF + N
BO1	chain	PRO	DEF + N	—	—
	reintro	—	—	—	—
BO2	chain	PRO, Ø	DEF + N	PRO	—
	reintro	—	—	PRO	—
BL	chain	PRO, Ø	PRO	PRO	PRO
	reintro	DEF + N	—	DEF + N	DEF + N, Ø + N
AF	chain	PRO, Ø	PRO	—	PRO
	reintro	DEF + N	INDEF + N*	DEF + N, Ø + N	—

*AF is recycling a part of the story, not reintroducing in continuation of narrative.

snowman is denuded on the final frame. Subsequently, the sequence showing the action is revealed and the speakers describe what happened. Only the unspecified agents are introduced as pronouns, definite or indefinite; the specified agents are always full definite or indefinite article + noun. There are no Ø article + noun introductions of animates.

Unspecified agents   There are several strategies for dealing with unspecified agents. Several speakers simply avoid mentioning them as in the narrative by speaker BO, given above. Other speakers promote the inanimate snowman or hat and broom to subjects at this point (AB2, BO1, BO2, AF).

Two speakers attempt to handle the unspecified agents without prompting. One speaker, AB, seems to be introducing a definite expression with *die*, either interpretable as definite article (+ noun) or colloquial pronoun form, but breaks off her sentence and does not pursue it, in (1):

(1)   vielleicht haben die—nee—(AB1 (8))   "maybe the—/they have—no"

The other speaker AA2, whose narrative is given above, introduces the unspecified agent first as *sie* "they" in line 14. When asked "who?" she supplies an indefinite pronoun *einer, irgendeiner* in line 17, then continues with unspecified *sie* in line 19.

Two further speakers produce indefinite pronoun *jemand* in response to interviewer queries, AB2 successfully in (2) and AF in an ungrammatical structure with no object—she continues with pronoun *sie*—in (3):

(2)   also—p—und—pp also
       jemand hat den Hut weggenommen (AB2 (8))   "somebody took the hat away"
(3)   Na, *jemand* hat abgenommen das haben *sie* auch weggenommen (AF (15–16))   "Well, *somebody* took (it) off; *they* took that away too"

One speaker solves the problem with a definite article + noun by postulating that the previous agents, *die Kinder*, have done it themselves (4). When confronted with the counterevidence in the pictures, he maintains the rationale for definite article + noun by postulating a relationship between the new and old agents in a presentative sentence with the man introduced as predicate nominal (5):

(4)   *die Kinder* habe sie . . . geklaut (BL (14))   "*the children* have stolen it . . . "
(5)   das ist *der Vater von den Kindern* (BL (15))   "that is *the father of the children*"

Specified agents   The introduction of specified nonprotagonist agents varies between definite article + noun and indefinite article + noun, depending on whether or not an unspecified agent has previously been introduced. If the speaker has introduced an unspecified agent as in (AB2, AA2), the specified agent is typically definite, usually definite article + noun: *der Mann, die Frau, der Hase.* The only exception is speaker AF, who uses an indefinite pronoun which, however, appears to be part of a framed exchange with the interviewer rather than integrated into her narrative.

If unspecified agents have not been introduced, there appears to be development toward introduction of nonprotagonist agents as indefinite article + noun, with the subject in noninitial position as a presentative—as in (6):

(6)   da kommt *ein Mann* (AA (15))
      "there comes *a man*"

Development toward this pattern can be seen in comparison of earlier and later narratives of speaker BO. In the first interview, BO1 introduces the man with definite article + noun in initial position, repairing to indefinite article + noun in initial position in (7). Ten months later, he uses indefinite article + noun presentational in (8):

(7)   *der* hat sie
      "*he* has it"
      eine Mann hat die Hut abgenommen und die Sauger auch (BO1 (12–13))
      "*a man* has taken the hat and the cleaner, too"
(8)   da hat *einer Mann* die Besen und die Hut weggenommen (BO2 (10))
      "there *a man* has taken away the broom and the hat"

Only one speaker(AB) introduces a nonprotagonist with a pronoun—in her first interview(9). In her later version she has adopted a system which distinguishes unspecified vs. specified agents (10–11):

(9)   *der* klaut den (AB1 (13))
      "*he* steals it"
(10) *Jemand* . . . hat den Hut weggenommen und den Besen (AB2 (8))
      "*someone* . . . took away the hat and the broom"
(11) *die Hase* hat ihm weggenommen (AB2 (13))
      "*the rabbit* took it away"

First mention of inanimates   The predominant strategy for introducing inanimates is as objects, with one exceptional example from speaker AB2. From their development as evidenced by longitudinal comparison, ((12) vs. (13) and (14) vs. (15)), it appears that $\emptyset$ article + noun is an earlier stage, followed by definite article + noun:

(12) die Kinder machen *Ø Schneemann* (BO1 (1))
      "the children make *Ø snowman*"
(13) die bauen *(ei)ne Schneemann* (BO2 (1))
      "they build *a snowman*"
(14) und der Schneemann hat *Ø Nase* und *Ø Hut* auf dem Kopf (AB1 (5))
      "and the snowman has *Ø nose* and *Ø hat* on his head"
(15) die wollen also den . . . und dann *den Besen* (AB2 (2))
      "they want the . . . and then *the broom*"

The variation between definite article + noun and indefinite article + noun is not random, but appears to be related to whether the content is new or unpredictable information as opposed to background or predictable information (see Table 3).

The snowman, although pictured and thus eligible for deictic definite reference, is totally unpredictable in the narrative; most speakers introduce it with indefinite article + noun. The choice of indefinite article + noun vs. definite article + noun for the objects given to and taken from the snowman can be related to their degree of prototypicality, as described in Chafe (1976: 40), who notes that definiteness can be established in discourse where some previously mentioned particular entails another later mentioned as definite. *Augen* "eyes" and *Knöpfe* "buttons" of coal are usual for snowmen; they are introduced with Ø article + noun (grammatical for plural NP's) or definite article + noun, while the carrot-nose and even more clearly the hat and broom are "extras"—and more likely to be introduced by indefinite article + noun: *eine Mohrrübe, eine Nase, einen Hut, einen Besen.* The fact that the carrot functions as a nose, an inalienable possession of an anthropomorphic snowman, is reflected in its more frequent introduction as definite article + noun by B01, B02, AA1, AA2, AB1.

Subsequent mention   The treatment of reference to nominals already introduced is much less complex than first mention (Table 4). Again, there is a difference in how the protagonists are treated. Reference to the children in contiguous chained sentences is realized either with pronoun or with null anaphora. After an intervening subject, the children are introduced with definite article + noun or pronoun. All other nominal references chain with definite article + noun (or infrequently with pronoun) after introduction as an indefinite article + noun. After definite article + noun, they chain with pronoun, as do protagonists. Reintroduction of nonprotagonists, however, is always realized with definite article + noun, while protagonists are sometimes reintroduced with pronoun.

CASE/GENDER REALIZATION

In light of the fact that grammatical gender is arbitrary (except for the human adults *Junge, Mann, Frau, Mutter*), and that the case marking system for articles is highly opaque, it is not surprising that the results are far from standard. For definites (Tables 5 and 6) a maximum of 54 percent overall have standard form[1]; for indefinites (Tables 7 and 8) the figure is lower, 40 percent. These percentages are notably lower than the results for standard realizations of other linguistic features investigated for these speakers (copula, auxiliary, verb inflection, word order, etc.—see Pfaff and Portz, 1979; Pfaff, 1984) where standardness was at a level of at least 90 percent for most speakers.

TABLE 5   Case/Function Distribution (Percent) for Definite Article Forms

		Subject	Direct object	Indirect object	Locative
der	(n = 59)	92%	—	2%	7%
die	(n = 67)	85%	13%	—	1%
das	(n = 10)	60%	40%	—	—
den	(n = 46)	—	61%	9%	30%
dem	(n = 51)	—	—	2%	98%
Ø	(n = 31)	32%	52%	—	16%
other	(n = 7)	43%	14%	—	43%

TABLE 6 Case/Function Distribution (Percent) for Indefinite Article Forms

		Subject	Direct object	Indirect object	Locative
ein	(n = 26)	58%	38%	4%	—
eine	(n = 7)	57%	28%	—	14%
einen	(n = 1)	—	(100%)	—	—
'n	(n = 1)	(100%)	—	—	—

TABLE 7 Case/Gender Distribution (Percent) for Definite Article Forms
(Standard forms are boxed.)

		der	die	das	den	dem	Ø	Other
SUBJECTS								
std. masc. subjects:	(n=67)	57%	28%	7%	0%	0%	4%	3%
(std. form *der*)								
std. fem. subjects:	(n=42)	14%	71%	2%	—	—	12%	—
(std. form *die*)								
std. neut. subjects:	(n=21)	48%	38%	—	—	—	10%	5%
(std. form *das*)								
OBJECTS								
std. masc. objects:	(n=38)	—	13%	5%	50%	—	29%	3%
(std. form *den*)								
std. fem. objects:	(n=42)	—	20%	7%	47%	—	27%	—
(std. form *die*)								
std. neut. objects:	(n= 5)	—	20%	20%	40%	—	20%	—
(std. form *das*)								

TABLE 8 Case/Gender Distribution (Percent) for Indefinite Article Forms
(Standard forms are boxed.)

		ein	eine	einen	'n
SUBJECTS					
std. masc. subjects:	(n = 12)	67%	25%	—	8%
(std. form *ein, 'n*)					
std. fem. subjects:	(n = 4)	75%	25%	—	—
(std. form *eine*)					
std. neut. subjects:	(n = 4)	(100%)	—	—	—
(std. form *ein, 'n*)					
OBJECTS					
std. masc. objects:	(n = 12)	75%	17%	8%	—
(std. form *einen*)					
std. fem. objects:	(n = 1)	(100%)	—	—	—
(std. form *eine*)					
std. neut. objects:	(n = 0)	—	—	—	—
(std. form *ein*)					

The distribution of forms is far from random, however. For the definite articles, the following generalizations can be made:

Subject: Der and *die* occur, for all genders: *die Junge, der Frau, die Glas* as well as *der Junge, die Frau, der Glas. Das* never occurred appropriately with neuters and is, in fact, rare as an article in general, occurring most frequently as a pronoun. *Den* and *dem* never occur as subject article forms, though they do occur with rather high frequency in other roles.

Direct Object: Den is the most frequent form for all genders, standard only for masculine. The most frequent form is $\emptyset$; *die* and *das* occur rarely. *Der* never occurred as direct object.

Indirect Object: Indirect objects occurred only rarely. *Dem/den* (see note 1) are used for masculine, *der* for feminine. No other forms occur.

Object of Preposition: Dem/den are used for masculines, *die* and *der* for feminines. Null is also found, even more frequently in the whole corpus than in this sample. Evaluation of standardness for prepositions which take dative or accusative, lexically or depending on static location vs. motion, has not been carried out.

From these results, it appears that, even for male and female humans where gender is not arbitrary, acquisition of case marking precedes gender marking in German L2 interlanguages, i.e. the function of marking grammatical role takes precedence over exploiting the lexical gender marking which would facilitate marking reference. The snowman narrative provides examples of nonstandard but systematic use of article and pronoun forms for case and reference marking.

Form/function distribution in snowman narrative: case and reference

As in the story of the cat and the milk discussed above, speakers distribute the article and pronoun forms so as to mark case function. Subjects and objects are marked with distinct forms, and often as in (16–17) departing from standard— where gender and syncretism are complicating factors:

(16) sie haben *den Hut* genommen und *den Besen* auch geklaut (AA2 (19–20))
   "they have taken *the hat* and also stolen *the broom*"
(17) *die Hut* und *die Besen* und so weiter sind nicht hier (AA2 (31))
   "*the hat* and *the broom* and so on are not here"
   (*der Hut* und *der Besen* would be standard)

Similarly, different forms are used to keep different subject referents distinct from each other. For example, in the narrative given above for speaker AA2, we find *sie* for "children" in line 2ff, *es* for "story" line 13 and *dies* for "rabbit." In BO1's narrative, we find a repair of *sie* to refer to *Hut* and *Sauger* in (18) in lines 12–13 as *sie* has already been used as subject pronoun for "children" in line 2ff:

(18) der Mann hat *sie*, eine Mann hat *die Hut* abgenommen und *die Sauger* auch.
   "the man has *it*, a man has taken off *the hat* and *the cleaner* too."

Sie would have been a standard plural object pronoun form; the repair introduces a nonstandard form *die* due to lack of masculine gender concord.

Further functional factors in interlanguage case marking systems

Examination of the results for individuals in greater detail reveals distinctions by the alternation of article forms. Three of the speakers, AF, BL and BO, use alternations between *der* and *die* as subject or as object for the same form in ways which appear to be related to the degree of participation of the noun in question.

Subjects: The stimulus pictures represent static scenes and scenes in which some action is represented. In several, items which can be grammaticalized as subject occur in both roles. Some speakers mark this distinction systematically but non-standardly with alternative forms of the definite article, as shown in the pairs (19–20), (21–22), (23–24), (25–26).

Context A
Subject as Agent or Active
Participant in Motion

(19) *der Katze* geht wieder nach unten
(AF (126))
"the cat goes down again"

(21) *der Hase* hat den Mohrrübe
(BL (173))
"the rabbit has the carrot"

(23) wie *der Hase* das gefreßt haben
(BO (95))
"as the rabbit has eaten it"

(25) dann fällt *der Glas* runter (BL (201))
"then the glass falls down"

Context B
Subject as Nonactive Participant

(20) *die Katze* ist unter den Tisch
(AF (130))
"the cat is under the table"

(22) *die Hase* gehört den kleinen Hase
(BL (282))
"the rabbit belongs to the little rabbit"

(24) *die Hase* und die kleine Hase is
Unterschied nich (BO (139))
"the rabbit and the little rabbit, there's no difference"

(26) *die Glas* ist auf dem Tisch (BL (188))
"the glass is on the table"

For natural gender items, for which gender agreement of articles is more frequently standard, use of the nonstandard, alternative subject-marking form appears to mark occurrences of non-topic nominatives in special constructions such as predicate nominals, comparatives or after conjunctions, as in (28, 30, 32) while normal subject topics are marked with the standard forms (27, 29, 31):

Context A: Topic
(27) *der Mann* hat sie (BO (93))
"the man has it"

(29) *der Junge* ist auf'm Wagen gestiegen
(BO (61))
"the boy got on the wagon"

(31) *die Mutter* gibt dem Junge den Ball
(AF (79))
"the mother gives the boy the ball"

Context B: Non-topic
(28) er hat keine selbe Anzug wie *die Mann*
(BO (118))
"he doesn't have the same suit as the man"

(30) danach *die Junge* (BO (63))
"then after the boy"

(32) das ist *der Mutter* (AF (158))
"that is the mother"

Objects: A similar phenomenon is observed for BO's direct objects. In (33) and (34), the ball is more immediately affected than in (35) and (36). In the first two examples the action is accomplished, but not in the second.

(33) dieser Junge werft *den Ball* zu seinen Freund (BO1 (71))
"this boy throws the ball to his friend"
(34) der Junge werft *den Ball* zu Mädchen (BO1 (74))
"the boy throws the ball to girl"
(35) der Junge versucht *die Ball* zu halten (BO1 (73))
"the boy tries to catch the ball"
(36) die Mädchen versucht *die Ball* zu halten (BO1 (76))
"the girl tries to catch the ball"

CONCLUSIONS AND PERSPECTIVES

From the preceding, it appears that there is an orderly sequence of acquisition of determiners and pronoun functions and forms in Turkish childrens' German interlanguage:

1. Discourse functions develop before grammatical functions. Thus children mark (a) protagonist vs. other participants by means of pronominalization vs. article + noun, (b) new vs. old information by means of pronoun or definite article + noun vs. indefinite article + noun. In addition, they appear to recognize a kind of prototype or associative semantics as determining old or predictable information in addition to previous explicit mention.

2. Case marking, which is semantically motivated, develops before gender marking, which is arbitrary. Thus the formal differences between the definite article forms are nonstandardly, but in a semantically well-motivated manner, predominantly associated with subject and object: *der* and *die* with subject, *dem* and *den* with objects.

3. There are indications of developing interlanguage-specific form-function relations, again exploiting the variety of definite article forms, e.g., distinguishing the subject of a sentence with dynamic verb (using *der*) from the subject of a sentence with stative verb (using *die*). These tendencies, while not statistically significant, are important because they seem to be examples of "creative constructions" based on universal categories such as motion or animacy which are reflected elsewhere in the grammar of standard German and Turkish (and other languages). It is especially interesting that these categories may have been significant in the historical development of case and gender marking.

More generally, these results support the functional approach to the analysis of interlanguage. Such an approach has both theoretical and practical advantages. On the theoretical side, functional analysis can provide evidence of species-specific linguistic and/or cognitive universals, whether couched in Chomskian terms as "constraints on possible human language" or as "core grammar dictated by the bioprogram" (Bickerton, 1981). On the practical side, it would seem that such study could be applied to coordinating the natural processes of language learning with language instruction provided by the schools.

NOTE

1. *Den* and *dem,* the standard masculine accusative and masculine/neuter dative forms are difficult to distinguish acoustically, however they are clearly distinct from *der, die* and *das.* Provisionally, both *den* and *dem* have been regarded as "standard" for purposes of estimating degree of standardness of case realization.

REFERENCES

Austin, J. L. 1962. *How to Do Things with Words*. Cambridge, Mass.: Harvard University Press.
Bates, E. and B. MacWhinney. 1979. A functionalist approach to the acquisition of grammar. In E. Ochs and B. Schieffelin (eds.), *Developmental Pragmatics*. New York: Academic Press.
Bickerton, D. 1981. *Roots of Language*. Ann Arbor: Karoma.
Chafe, W. 1976. Givenness, contrastiveness, definiteness, subjects, topics and point of view. In Li, Charles N. (ed.), *Subject and Topic*. New York: Academic Press, pp. 25–55.
Cole, P. and J. Saddock (eds.). 1977. *Syntax and Semantics 8: Grammatical Relations*. New York: Academic Press.
Cooper, W. E. and J. R. Ross. 1975. Word order. In R. Grossman, J. San and T. Vance (eds.) *Papers from the Parasession on Functionalism*. Chicago Linguistic Society, pp. 63–111.
Dittmar, N. 1979. Semantic features of pidginized learner varieties of German. Paper presented to Romanistentag, Saarbrücken. Revised version distributed June 1982.
Elías-Olivares, L. 1976. Ways of speaking in a Chicano community: A sociolinguistic approach. Unpublished Ph.D. Dissertation, University of Texas, Austin.
Ferguson, C. A. 1959. Diglossia. *Word* 15.325–40.
Fillmore, C. 1968. The case for case. In E. Bach and R. Harms (eds.), *Universals in Linguistic Theory*. New York: Holt, Rinehart and Winston.
Fillmore, C. 1977. The case for the case reopened. In P. Cole and J. Saddock (eds.), *Syntax and Semantics 8*. New York: Academic Press.
Firbas, J. 1966. On defining the theme in functional sentence analysis. *Travaux linguistique de Prague*, 1. 267–80.
Fishman, J. A. 1972. The sociology of language: an interdisciplinary social science approach to language in society. In Fishman, J. A. (ed.), *Advances in the Sociology of Language*, Vol I. The Hague: Mouton, pp. 217–404.
Givón, T. 1979a. *On Understanding Grammar*. New York: Academic Press.
Givón, T. (ed.), 1979b. *Syntax and Semantics 12: Discourse and Syntax*. New York: Academic Press.
Greenberg, J. 1974. The relation of frequency to semantic feature in a case language (Russian). *Working Papers on Language Universals* 16.21–45. Stanford University.
Grice, H. 1975. Logic and conversation. In P. Cole and J. Morgan (eds.), *Syntax and Semantics, 3: Speech Acts*. New York: Academic Press, pp. 43–58.
Gumperz, J. J. 1982. Conversational code-switching. In J. J. Gumperz, *Discourse Strategies*. Cambridge: Cambridge University Press.
Hatch, E. 1978. Discourse analysis and second language acquisition. In E. Hatch (ed.), *Second Language Acquisition: A Book of Readings*. Rowley, Mass.: Newbury House.
Hawkins, J. 1978. *Definiteness and Indefiniteness. A Study in Reference and Grammaticality Prediction*. London: Croom Helm.
Johnson, D. E. 1979. *Toward a Theory of Relationally Based Grammar*. New York and London: Garland Publications.
Karmiloff-Smith, A. 1979. *A Functional Approach to Child Language: A Study of Determiners and Reference*. Cambridge: Cambridge University Press.
Karmiloff-Smith, A. 1980. Psychological processes underlying pronominalization and non-pronominalization in children's connected discourse. In J. Kreiman and A. Ojeda(eds.), *Papers from the Parasession on Pronouns and Anaphora*. Chicago Linguistic Society, pp. 231–250.
Karmiloff-Smith, A. 1981. The grammatical marking of thematic structure in the development of language production. In W. Deutsch (ed.), *The Child's Construction of Language*. London: Academic Press.
Keenan, E. and B. Comrie. 1977. Noun phrase accessibility and universal grammar. *Linguistic Inquiry* 8: 63–99.
König, W. 1978. *dtv-Atlas zur deutschen Sprache*. München: Deutscher Taschenbuch Verlag.
Meisel, J., H. Clahsen and M. Pienemann. 1979. On determining developmental stages in natural second language acquisition. *Wuppertaler Arbeitspapiere zur Sprachwissenschaft Nr. 2 1–53*.

Ochs, E. 1979. Planned and unplanned discourse. In T. Givón (ed.), *Syntax and Semantics 12*. New York: Academic Press, pp. 51–80.

Pfaff, C. W. 1979. Constraints on language mixing *Language* 55. 291–318.

Pfaff, C. W. 1981. Incipient creolization in "Gastarbeiterdeutsch"?: An experimental sociolinguistic study. *Studies in Second Language Acquisition*. 3. 165–78.

Pfaff, C. W. 1984. On input and residual L1 transfer effects in Turkish and Greek Children's German. In R. Andersen (ed.), *Second Languages*. Rowley, Mass.: Newbury House., pp. 271–298.

Pfaff, C. W. and R. Portz. 1979. Foreign children's acquisition of German: Universals vs. interference. Paper presented at the Linguistic Society of America Annual Meeting, Los Angeles. In N. Dittmar and P. Königer (eds.), *Proceedings of the Second Scandinavian-German Symposium on the Language of Immigrant Workers and Their Children*. Berlin: Fachbereich Germanistik der Freien Universität Berlin.

Portz, R., and C. W. Pfaff. 1981. SES—Soziolinguistisches Erhebungsinstrument zur Sprachentwicklung: Ein Instrument zur Beschreibung der Sprach- und Kommunikationsfähigkeit ausländischer Schüler in deutschen Schulen. Berlin: Pädagogisches Zentrum.

Poplack, S. 1980. Syntactic structure and social function of codeswitching. In R. Durán (ed.), *Latino Language and Communicative Behavior*. Norwood, N.J.: Ablex.

Sachs, H., E. Schegloff, and G. Jefferson. 1974. A simplest systematics for the organization of turntaking in conversation. *Language* 50. 696–735.

Sankoff, G. 1980. *The Social Life of Language*. Philadelphia: University of Pennsylvania Press.

Schumann, J. 1982. Simplification, transfer and relexification as aspects of pidginization and early second language acquisition. *Language Learning 32*. 337–366.

Searle, J. 1969. *Speech Acts*. Cambridge: Cambridge University Press.

Slobin, D. 1973. Cognitive prerequisites for the development of grammar. In C. Ferguson and D. Slobin (eds.), *Studies of Child Language Development*. New York: Holt, Rinehart and Winston, pp. 175–208.

Slobin, D. 1977. Language change in childhood and in history. In J. Macnamara (ed.), *Language Learning and Thought*. New York: Academic Press.

von Stutterheim, C., and W. Klein. This volume. A concept-oriented approach to second language studies.

Trévise, A. This volume. Toward an analysis of the (inter)language activity of referring to time in narratives.

Veronique, D. This volume. Reference to past events and actions in narratives in L2: Insights from North African workers' French.

Weinreich, U., W. Labov and M. Herzog. 1968. Empirical foundations for a theory of language change. In W. Lehmann and Y. Malkiel (eds.), *Directions for Historical Linguistics*. Austin: University of Texas Press.

Zubin, D. 1977. The semantic basis of case alternation in German. In R. Fasold and R. Shuy (eds.), *Studies in Language Variation: Papers from the Third Annual Colloquium on New Ways of Analyzing Variation*. Washington, D.C.: Georgetown University Press, pp. 88–99.

Zubin, D. 1979. Discourse function of morphology: the focus system in German. In T. Givón (ed.) *Syntax and Semantics 12*. New York: Academic Press, pp. 469–504.

CHAPTER 5

Connecting Theories of Language Processing and (Second) Language Acquisition[1]

Harald Clahsen

Düsseldorf University, Federal Republic of Germany

INTRODUCTION

A major objective of cross-linguistic second language acquisition research is to discover universal principles which can be assumed to govern the acquisition process. Among such principles, universal cognitive processing strategies and constraints appear to me to be most important to explain the linguistic outcome of second language acquisition. In a recent study (Clahsen, 1984), I suggested a set of three processing strategies which have been shown to account for the emergence of certain rules of German syntax in various acquisitional settings (adult L2, child L2 and child L1 acquisition). Given that such correspondences could not be accidental, it has been concluded that the suggested processing strategies may be regarded as constraining all kinds of language acquisition, whether L1 or L2, whether by children or adults. Such an approach also seems to be relevant for a cross-linguistic perspective on L2 acquisition, even though I studied only one language. Given that (a) the suggested explanations are based on constraints inherent in the mental systems with which linguistic structures are perceived and produced and that (b) the empirical evidence stems from various types of acquisition, we may hypothesize that the three processing constraints are universal principles of language acquisition.

In the present paper I will try to further extend this approach. Moreover, the approach will be compared with other proposals for a cognitive explanation of (second) language acquisition. A crucial requirement for an adequate cognitive explanation of acquisition processes is to account for how the suggested cognitive strategies/principles operate within the language processing system when linguistic structures are perceived and produced.

As can be seen from the review of literature presented in Berman (this volume), the assumptions about linguistic processing underlying the suggested cognitive strategies are often not dealt with explicitly; the problem is that the question of how the learner actually employs the proposed strategies when language data is processed has to be left unanswered. Therefore, I suggest that we should explicitly connect our attempts to explain acquisition processes (cognitively) with current psycholinguistic theories of linguistic processing. It will be argued that, by applying such theories to (second) language acquisition data, we may ultimately arrive at universal constraints for the kinds of learner languages observed in our data.

In what follows, I will first outline the approach developed in Clahsen (1984). This approach, which might be labeled integrativist, to use a term taken from Berman (this volume), requires a processing model which contains both an autonomous linguistic component consisting of task-specific grammatical processors, and a set of general problem-solving strategies. Then, I will contrast this approach with the so-called functionalist position to acquisition/processing. As will become evident from a discussion of the underlying processing assumptions, the crucial difference between these two approaches is the role attributed to grammar in linguistic processing. According to the functionalist position, abstract grammars do not have any separate mental reality (Bates et al., 1982:243). I will argue against such claims, and, in particular, I will try to show that the intergrativist approach provides a more adequate theoretical framework for (cognitively) explaining (second) language acquisition processes.

1. THE INTEGRATIVIST APPROACH

Let me begin by briefly summarizing the claims and suggestions which were made in my earlier paper. I tried to show that the development of certain German word order and negation rules by adult L2, child L2 and child L1 learners can be explained by assuming a set of three sentence processing strategies plus a developmental principle according to which linguistic structures and rules which require a high degree of processing capacity will be acquired late. As the predictions which could be derived from the strategies and the developmental principle turned out to be correct, it was concluded that the suggested approach offers an adequate explanation, at least for the acquisition of German word order. Clearly this approach presupposes a certain model of sentence processing, as developed mainly by Fodor, Bever and Garrett (1974), Bever (1970), Bever and Townsend (1979) and Forster (1979). As the explanation proposed in my earlier paper only makes sense within the processing model which has been developed by the authors mentioned above, I will illustrate two tenets of their model.

(a) The model assumes an autonomous linguistic level of processing. Speech comprehension and speech production are seen as mental activities which involve actively mapping internal structures onto external sequences (see Bever, 1970:286). Fodor et al., 1974:388 ff. call the level of internal structures "mentalese"; "external sequences" are the surface forms of particular languages. As an intermediate step in the mapping procedures from "mentalese" to "external sequences" the speaker/hearer constructs a representation which corresponds to (linguistic) underlying structure. In other words, underlying structure is seen as an interlevel between the surface forms and the abstract formulas of "mentalese." The third component of the model is a grammatical processor consisting of various subcomponents (syntactic and lexical processors) which are applied serially and which are capable of mapping underlying configurations onto surface forms.

(b) The model contains an additional problem-solving component with a set of strategies which allows direct mappings between underlying structure and surface forms, thus short-circuiting the grammatical processor. Fodor et al. (1974:395) claim that the application of grammatical procedures in sentence processing "is computationally expensive, and heuristic procedures which narrow the set of transformations that need to be searched would be desirable." Forster (1979) proposes a model of speech comprehension containing autonomous linguistic processors which are applied serially and a "general problem solver" (GPS) which "is capable of some kind of rudimentary processing of linguistic material" (Forster, 1979:52). Forster's GPS is similar to the heuristics and strategies which were suggested by Fodor et al. (1974) and by Bever (1970). These devices can be seen as ways of short-cutting the process of speech production and comprehension by avoiding the application of certain grammatical operations; the strategies thus provide for "efficient parsability" (Berwick and Weinberg, 1982:166). As the GPS consists of "general conceptual knowledge" (Forster, 1979:34) and is thus also responsible for solving nonlinguistic problems, the strategies used by the GPS are not task-specific, which means that certain (complex) linguistic structures cannot be processed by the strategies of the GPS. The use of these linguistic structures involves a task-specific processor, i.e., a grammar in the sense of Forster's model. The different components and the way they interact (in speech comprehension) may be illustrated by the following (highly simplified) sketch of the model:

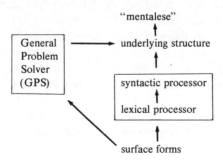

In my earlier paper, three processing strategies were described. We may now argue that linguistic structures which conform to these strategies can be processed by the GPS, whereas task-specific processing devices, for example syntactic rules, are needed for structures that violate the suggested strategies and can thus not be processed by the GPS.[2] As far as acquisition is concerned, the suggested developmental principle predicts that linguistic structures and rules which can be processed by the strategies of the GPS should be easy in language use and early in language acquisition. In turn, linguistic structures which require a task- and language-specific device, for example within the syntactic processor, should be hard to use and acquired late. This developmental principle was derived from first language acquisition research, which suggests that

> linguistic forms that constitute exceptions to relatively general procedures for sentence processing are hard for the child to learn just as they are hard for the adult to understand. (Fodor, Bever and Garrett, 1974:499)

In Clahsen (1984), I tried to demonstrate, using the acquisition of German word order as a test case, that this approach not only contributes to an adequate explanation of first language learning but is also necessary in order to adequately explain natural second language acquisition.

2. THE FUNCTIONALIST APPROACH

The approach presented in the previous section obviously differs, in certain respects, from other suggestions which might be summarized under the heading of cognitive explanations. M. Kail (this volume) argues that it is possible to explain (second) language acquisition within the so-called functionalist model suggested by Bates et al. (1982). These authors adopt a processing model which assumes "non-autonomy of components" (Bates et al., 1982:259), a conception which is obviously not compatible with the proposals mentioned above, for example with Foster's suggestion of an autonomous syntactic processor, and with Fodor et al. (1974) claim concerning the interlevel function of deep structure in sentence processing. In contrast to these approaches, Bates et al. (1982) regard the principles of grammar as "collections of strategies for understanding and producing sentences" (p. 248); cf. Lakoff and Thompson (1977:295). Following experimental results and theoretical considerations by Marslen-Wilson and Tyler (1980), the processing model adopted by Bates et al. (1982) assumes "parallel processing" (p. 257 f.), which is a second tenet obviously contradicting the serial autonomous models presented by Forster as well as Fodor et al.

Clearly the application of a parallel nonautonomous processing model to the explanation of second language learning has far-reaching consequences for acquisition research. Let me mention just one example. If, as Bates et al. (1982:249) claim, "there is no competence other than competence-to-perform," then the study of the acquisition of grammatical principles, which are meant to represent linguistic competence, is a priori not sensible. Since grammatical principles are fully explicable in terms of (nonlinguistic) cognitive constraints, the study of the acquisition of grammar should not be a research objective in its own right; rather, the acquisition of grammar can only be sufficiently described within the more general framework of cognitive development, which implies that the acquisition of grammatical principles must be regarded as corollaries of new cognitive developments. Bates and MacWhinney (1979:174) call this approach the "strong version of the functionalist hypothesis." In the following, I will argue against such claims by questioning some of the prerequisites of this approach.

A central controversy of the speech processing literature concerns the existence of serial vs. parallel and autonomous vs. nonautonomous production and comprehension procedures. It is simply not possible to present this debate within the present paper, but let me just illustrate the claim that the controversy between the different processing models is far from being solved, so that there are no grounds on which a parallel nonautonomous processing model, as proposed by Marslen-Wilson and Tyler (1980), has to be preferred to the serial autonomous models suggested by Forster (1979), Fodor et al. (1974) and others.[3] It is quite obvious that the processing model suggested in the previous section is closely related to the subcomponents of a transformational generative grammar (TGG). The aim of Marslen-Wilson and Tyler's research is to show that any processing model which tries to maintain its links to TGG has to be abandoned. This is the position also held by Bates et al. (1982). More particularly, Marslen-Wilson and Tyler try to provide experimental evidence for the following two claims:

(a) Nonautonomy of grammatical processing: Syntactic and semantic decisions continuously interact as a sentence is processed.
(b) Parallel processing: Processing subcomponents interact on-line to build a single representation.

Their experiments (see Tyler and Marslen-Wilson, 1977) consist of asking subjects to repeat the last word of an ambiguous phrase, such as *landing planes*. Context clauses were given to semantically bias the ambiguous phrases. Reaction latencies were measured in order to evaluate the biasing effect. The result was that semantic biasing was effective, thus showing that the listener combined the interpretation of the context clause with the meanings of the words *landing* and *planes* into some unified representation. This result indicates that semantic variables can interact with ongoing syntactic decisions and that these decisions depend on the on-line interaction of semantic context in the syntactic interpretation of the ambiguous fragment (see Tyler and Marslen-Wilson, 1977:45–47).

Claims (a) and (b) above have been extensively discussed in the psycholinguistic literature. Let me just briefly mention three studies in which substantial doubts have been expressed as to the processing model proposed by Marslen-Wilson and Tyler. First, Berwick and Weinberg (1983:36 ff.) argue that their experimental results provide no evidence for determining whether Marslen-Wilson and Tyler's hypothesis (a) or the "autonomy-of-grammatical-processing" thesis adopted in Forster's and Fodor et al.'s models is correct. By Tyler and Marslen-Wilson's own description, their subjects had to compute both syntactic and semantic representations:

> These semantic representations were checked for compatability with the preceding context phrase. Thus we see that Tyler and Marslen-Wilson also assume (similarly to the autonomy thesis, HC) that their subjects had knowledge of two distinct kinds, both of which were involved in parsing the experimental sentences. (Berwick and Weinberg, 1983:42)

Second, in a study reinterpreting Marslen-Wilson and Tyler's (1980) results, Norris (1982) argues against claim (b) mentioned above. He suggests that serial models which account for all of the data generally cited in support of parallel processing theories can be devised only by permitting that at each processing stage multiple outputs are produced (Norris, 1982:98); such a model is offered in Norris (1982). He therefore concludes that there is no evidence in favor of the suggested processing model and that the experimental results could be equally well explained within the alternative serial approach.

Third, a similar conclusion is reached by Cowart (1982) for Marslen-Wilson and Tyler's claim (a). In a study also reanalyzing their experimental results, Cowart demands that

> two processors within the language processing system may be said to be autonomous just to the extent that the procedures implemented by each are defined over different vocabularies and show contrasting characteristics. (p. 116)

Like Berwick and Weinberg (1983), Cowart convincingly demonstrates that the experimental results could equally well be interpreted in terms of autonomy defined above. He therefore concludes that Marslen-Wilson and Tyler's model is not necessarily superior to the "autonomy-of-grammatical-processing" thesis.

Summarizing the previous discussion, we notice that there is still ongoing debate in the psycholinguistic literature as to the processing approaches mentioned above. What appears to be particularly controversial is the role of grammars in models of language processing. Provided that the arguments against Tyler and Marslen-Wilson's theory can be maintained, a processing model like that of Bates et al. (1982) in which grammar does not have any separate mental reality (p. 248) has to be rejected. It follows that we are not forced to adopt a parallel nonautonomous processing model for our attempts to develop cognitive explanations of (second) language acquisition; rather, it appears to be *at least* equally sensible to build explanatory principles on a model which contains an autonomous grammatical processor.

3. TESTING COGNITIVE APPROACHES
TO SECOND LANGUAGE ACQUISITION

The weakest conclusion which can be drawn from the previous discussions is that, given the lack of clear evidence from psycholinguistic experimentation, both positions, the functionalist as well as the integrativist approach, can be applied when trying to establish cognitive processing strategies of second language learners. The stronger hypothesis would be that approaches which provide for an autonomous grammatical processor (cf. section 1) have to be preferred. In what follows, I will try to argue in favor of this stronger claim. More particularly, I will present some data from our longitudinal study of the acquisition of German by adult foreign workers[4] which cause some problems for the functionalist approach and suggest that the processes involved in the (second) language acquisition of German word order can more adequately be explained within a model which contains an autonomous grammatical processing component.

The data gathering procedures and the methods we used to analyze the data have been described elsewhere in detail (see Clahsen, 1984). In the cross-sectional as well as in the longitudinal study, we found that the acquisition of German word order can be represented in a strictly ordered developmental sequence consisting of several stages which are defined in linguistic terms. At the first stage of the suggested sequence, none of the Standard German rules for verb placement is applied. Rather, the learners use strict SVO order during the initial phase of the acquisition process. In Clahsen (1984), I presented data from Spanish and Portuguese learners. In the following, I will supplement these materials with data from Italian learners; I will focus on the initial stage of the suggested developmental sequence.

The quantitative results of the analysis[5] are presented in Tables 1 and 2. The vertical dimension displays the time of observation; the numbers in brackets represent duration of stay (in weeks) counted from the day of arrival. Table 1 displays the whole period of observation for Bongiovanni I, showing that he does not acquire any of the Standard syntactic rules for verb placement throughout the period of observation. In contrast, Giovanni I acquires the rule PARTICLE (see Clahsen and Meisel, 1979) during his fiftieth week of stay; Table 2 displays the period of observation up to this point of Giovanni's acquisition process.

Word order in the learners' utterances was classified according to the following three categories:

(S) V X
(1) du *kommen* in arbeit freitag   (Bongiovanni I, seventh week)
    ("you *come* in work Friday?")
    (= Are you coming to work on Friday?)
(2) meine schwester *kaufen* baum   (Giovanni I, fourteenth week)
    ("my sister *buy* tree")

S X V

  (3) Pauli immer *schlafen*   (Bongiovanni I, fortieth week)
       ("P. (=name of a dog) always *sleep*")
  (4) wann mein vater kaufen fernsehn   (Giovanni I, twenty-first week)
       ich auch *gucken*
       ("when my father buy TV I also *look*")

V S X / V X S

  (5) nix *gucken* chef.   (Bongiovanni I, sixteenth week)
       ("not *look* boss")
       (= The boss didn't see (that something
         happened).)
  (6) nix *sprechen* in deutschland meine   (Bongiovanni I, forty-second week)
       freunde
       ("not *speak* in Germany my friends")
       (= My friends cannot speak German.)

The examples of the (S) V X type are further classified according to clause type (main or embedded) and verb type (simple or complex). Note that verb-second is ungrammatical in Standard German in embedded clauses and with complex verbal elements like AUX + V and MOD + V structures (cf. my earlier paper for more details). Tables 1 and 2 present relative frequencies for the category (S) V X. As there were only very few examples of the S X V and the V S X / V X S type, a similarly detailed analysis of these categories was not possible. Note that in examples 5 and 6 *nix* is treated as an operator on the verb rather than an independent constituent. The following conventions were used for these two categories:

O: There is *no* example.
(X): There is *one* example.
X: There are *two* examples.

When there were more than two examples for one of the two categories, relative frequencies were calculated.
    The tables show:

a) (S) V X is the dominant word order. The alternative orders are practically nonexistent: either there is no example or, at most, two examples for the other two categories.
b) (S) V X is used for all clause types and for all verbal elements, even in cases where Standard German requires one of the alternative orders.

These results confirm the observations made in the earlier paper for José S., Ana S., and Zita P. From this we may conclude that the use of a dominant SVX order also characterizes the initial hypothesis of *Italian* learners acquiring German as a second language, a claim which is also confirmed by Pienemann's (1981) results from child L2 acquisition.
    Now, how can these results be explained within a cognitive approach to second language acquisition? The integrativist position outlined in section 1 of the present paper offers a straightforward explanation of these facts: Italian has SVX at the level of underlying structure. The use of the basic

TABLE 1   Word Order/Bongiovanni I

Duration of stay in weeks	(S) V X*	Main clause	Embedded clause	Simple verb	Complex verb	S X V**	V S X/ V X S**
B (7)	0.90	0.88	0.12	0.88	0.12	(X)	0.00
B (16)	0.80	1.00	0.00	0.73	0.27	(X)	X
B (19)	0.90	1.00	0.00	0.90	0.10	(X)	0.00
B (27)	1.00	0.78	0.22	1.00	0.00	0.00	0.00
B (39)	0.93	0.93	0.07	0.93	0.07	0.00	0.00
B (40)	0.91	0.90	0.10	0.97	0.03	X	0.00
B (42)	0.88	0.89	0.11	0.83	0.17	0.00	0.10
B (47)	0.79	1.00	0.00	0.84	0.16	(X)	X
B (51)	0.88	1.00	0.00	0.86	0.14	X	0.00
B (57)	0.88	1.00	0.00	0.86	0.14	X	0.00
B (63)	0.87	0.85	0.15	0.95	0.05	(X)	0.00
B (68)	0.96	0.96	0.04	0.91	0.09	X	0.00
B (72)	0.85	1.00	0.00	1.00	0.00	0.00	(X)
B (78)	0.91	0.80	0.20	0.95	0.05	0.00	(X)
B (83)	0.84	0.94	0.06	0.92	0.08	X	(X)
B (91)	0.87	0.95	0.05	1.00	0.00	X	0.00

*The following four columns represent the frequencies of (S) V X that occurred in main vs. embedded clauses, with simple vs. occurrences of complex verbs.
**0.00 = noninstance   (X) = one instance   X = two instances

TABLE 2   Word Order/Giovanni I

Duration of stay in weeks	(S) V X*	Main clause	Embedded clause	Simple verb	Complex verb	S X V**	V S X/ V X S**
G (3)	1.00	0.83	0.17	0.86	0.14	0.00	0.00
G (4)	0.97	0.91	0.09	0.97	0.03	(X)	0.00
G (8)	0.90	1.00	0.00	0.78	0.22	(X)	0.00
G (10)	0.95	1.00	0.00	0.78	0.22	(X)	0.00
G (12)	1.00	1.00	0.00	0.92	0.08	0.00	0.00
G (14)	0.93	0.69	0.31	0.96	0.04	X	0.00
G (16)	1.00	1.00	0.00	0.91	0.09	0.00	0.00
G (21)	0.89	0.83	0.17	0.93	0.07	X	0.00
G (23)	1.00	1.00	0.00	1.00	0.00	0.00	0.00
G (31)	0.92	0.83	0.17	1.00	0.00	0.00	(X)
G (36)	1.00	0.63	0.37	0.63	0.37	0.00	0.00
G (38)	0.93	0.82	0.18	0.64	0.36	0.00	0.00
G (45)	0.90	0.83	0.17	0.77	0.23	X	0.00

*The following four columns represent the frequencies of (S) V X that occurred in main vs. embedded clauses, with simple vs. occurrences of complex verbs.
**0.00 = noninstance   (X) = one instance   X = two instances

order at the level of surface structure short-circuits the grammatical processor and permits direct mappings between internal structures and surface forms; these operations can be processed by the GPS. Note that underlying structure has the function of an autonomous interlevel in language processing according to the model adopted in section 1. The fact that Italians learning German as a second language use strict SVX word order in the initial phases can thus be explained within a cognitive approach which attributes a processing function to underlying structure.

Let us now try to explain the results of L2 acquisition within the alternative (cognitive) approach (cf. Bates et al. (1982), among others). Recall that these authors do not ascribe a separate processing function to any grammatical level. As an empirical test of their claims, Bates et al. (1982) compared strategies of sentence comprehension used by Italian- and English-speaking subjects. Starting with the observation that "in Italian . . . all possible orders of subject, verb and object can and do occur in informal discourse, under certain [pragmatic-HC] conditions" (Bates et al., 1982:252), whereas word order in English is far more rigid, the authors hypothesize that the higher flexibility of word order in Italian also plays a role in sentence comprehension (p. 253). In fact, the experiments carried out by Bates et al. confirm their suspicion: Italian subjects (adults) use mainly semantic information, namely animacy, in sentence interpretation, whereas the English-speaking subjects relied overwhelmingly on word order. Bates et al. conclude that "clearly *SVO is not at the core of Italian sentence processing*" (p. 294, my emphasis -HC). Rather, noncanonical word orders have systematic effects in both comprehension and production and should thus be integrated as "systematic facts about semantic and pragmatic contributions to syntactic processing into one unified model" (p. 295).

The theoretical considerations and the experimental results gathered by Bates et al. are valuable for second language acquisition research, since they allow us to make certain predictions about the linguistic structures which are most easily accessible to the learners. As far as Italian subjects acquiring German word order are concerned, the following predictions could be made: If

1. SVO is *not* at the core of Italian sentence processing, and if
2. the learners are exposed to a large variety of word orders in the input (note that German is a language with a relatively high degree of word order flexibility), and if
3. noncanonical word order strategies are regarded as the central mechanisms of the Italian processing system,

then Italians should use variable word orders when they start to learn German. Clearly this prediction is only valid if the additional assumption can be made that the learners transfer processing strategies of their L1 to the task of second language acquisition. Meisel has shown, in various publications, that this assumption seems to be correct. In particular, Meisel (1983) argues that "a learner can only transfer what is psychologically real." Thus:

Intermediate representations and habitualized operations of L1 processing may be used in L2 performance, provided they reduce or, at least, do not increase processing complexity. (Meisel, 1983:23)

Given the evidence for a transfer of processing strategies and the fact that Italians use noncanonical word order strategies in sentence processing, the Standard German word order devices should be easily accessible to Italian subjects. The empirical results mentioned above show that these predictions are clearly false. Similar to the Portuguese and Spaniards, the Italians do *not* simply transfer surface structure orders of their L1 to the second language. Rather, the learners use word orders which can best be described by underlying (linguistic) representations.[6] Thus the empirical results mentioned above can be more adequately explained within a model which attributes a processing function to an autonomous linguistic level.

This conclusion is also confirmed by some results of Slobin and Bever's (1982) cross-linguistic study of L1 acquisition. Using spontaneous and experimental data, the authors demonstrate that children produce canonical sentence schemas which exhibit the basic word order of the target language and that such schemas "play a central role in processes of perception and interpretation of utterances" (p. 257). As far as Italian children are concerned, Slobin and Bever (1982:234f.) found that even though Italian allows for variable word orders, the children still use the SVO pattern most frequently. This result is in accordance with the above-mentioned obser-vations of L2 acquisition (by Italian learners), since the L2 learners, as well as the Italian children, clearly prefer the basic SVO patterns, even though they are exposed to a language (German) with a relatively high degree of word order flexibility. The fact that both L1 and L2 learners use canonical sentence schemas shows that they are sensitive to the underlying (linguistic) structure of the language.

4. CONCLUSION

The impetus for carrying out this study came out of the present author's conviction that it is necessary for (second) language acquisition researchers to connect their (cognitive) principles and strategies of acquisition with current psycholinguistic theories of language processing. We may now draw a preliminary conclusion as to the question of what kind of theoretical framework might reasonably be adopted. Two types of cognitive explanations of (second) language acquisition have been discussed: (a) the integrativist approach and (b) the functionalist approach. It has been shown that these two approaches are based on different kinds of processing models. One of the crucial features by which these models can be distinguished is the role attributed to grammars in language processing. Whereas the model under-lying (a) maintains the "autonomy-of-grammatical-processing" thesis, the model underlying (b) assumes nonautonomy of grammatical processors.

The approach I have been advocating is the integrativist position. Two arguments have been suggested. First, I referred to recent psycholinguistic research which casts doubts on some of the basic assumptions of the processing model underlying (b). In particular, these studies suggest that the role of grammatical processors has been considerably underestimated in the model adopted by the functionalist approach. The second argument for the integrativist position is based on empirical evidence from (natural) second language acquisition. I have tried to argue that particular phenomena related to the acquisition of German word order can be easily accounted for within a model which ascribes a processing function to grammatical representations. Morever, the empirical data do not coincide with the predictions derived from the functionalist approach since the underlying processing model does not provide for autonomous grammatical processors.

Finally, I should emphasize that the present research can only be regarded as a first step towards connecting second language acquisition research and theories of language processing. Clearly, more attempts have to be made, dealing with various sorts of linguistic phenomena, to explain second language acquisition processes within different processing theories. It appears evident to me, however, that even if we try to find processing explanations for second language acquisition processes, the study of the acquisition of grammatical knowledge remains a research objective in its own right (contrary to what is suggested by the functionalist approach).

NOTES

1. Revised version of a paper presented at the Second European-North American Workshop on Cross-Linguistic Second Language Acquisition Research, Jagdschloß Göhrde, August 1982. I want to thank all the participants especially Ruth Berman, Michèle Kail, Jürgen Meisel, Pieter Muysken and Howard Nicholas for their corrections and helpful remarks. I am also grateful to the editor of this book for helping me to improve the preliminary draft presented at the workshop.

2. The three strategies only represent a small part of the whole set of GPS strategies. The GPS contains general "pragmatic devices," for example Bates and MacWhinney's topicalization strategies (cf. Bates and MacWhinney, 1979:179 ff.), as well as cognitively based strategies which are more specific to the processing of linguistic material, for example operating principles (cf. Slobin, 1973). Thus it appears to be necessary (for an adequate description of the GPS) to divide this processor into various subcomponents.

3. Bates et al. (1982:257f.) assume, *without further justification,* that Marslen-Wilson and Tyler's model is superior to the alternative approach.

4. A detailed description of the cross-sectional study is given in Clahsen et al. (1983); the results of the longitudinal study will be published in Clahsen et al. (in prep.); a brief description of this study is given in Meisel (1981).

5. Some information about the conditions under which the two learners acquire their knowledge of German can be found in the following table:

	Bongiovanni I.	*Giovanni I.*
Date of birth	1960	1955
Origin	village close to Agrigento, Sicily	village close to Catania, Sicily
Educational background	elementary school	high school, university (medicine, 2 years)
Date of immigration	1978	1978
Job in FRG	unskilled factory worker	grinder
German language classes	no	rarely

6. This argument does not require any commitment to a specific type of underlying linguistic representation. As mentioned earlier, it is merely claimed that this component of the processing model has an interlevel function between the abstract formulas of "mentalese" and surface structure. The "task" of the underlying representations is to assign linguistic categories and serial order to the abstract (nonlinear) formulas.

REFERENCES

Bates, E. and B. MacWhinney. 1979. A functionalist approach to the acquisition of grammar. In E. Ochs and B. Schieffelin (eds.), *Developmental Pragmatics*. New York: Academic Press, pp. 167–211.

Bates, E., B. MacWhinney, S. McNew, A. Devescovi, and S. Smith. 1982. Functional constraints on sentence processing: a cross-linguistic study. *Cognition* 11. 245–299.

Berman, R. this volume. Cognitive components of language development.

Berwick, R. and A. Weinberg. 1982. Parsing efficiency, computational complexity and the evaluation of grammatical theories. *Linguistic Inquiry* 13. 165–191.

Berwick, R. and A. Weinberg. 1983. The role of grammars in models of language use. *Cognition* 13. 1–61.

Bever, T. 1970. The cognitive basis for linguistic structures. In J. R. Hayes (ed.), *Cognition and the Development of Language*. New York: John Wiley and Sons, pp. 279–362.

Bever, T. and D. Townsend. 1979. Perceptual mechanisms and formal properties of main and subordinate clauses. In W. Cooper and E. Walker (eds.), *Sentence Processing: Psycholinguistic Studies Presented to Merrill Garrett*. New York, pp. 159–226.

Clahsen, H. 1984. The acquisition of German word order. A test case for cognitive approaches to second language acquisition. In R. W. Andersen (ed.), *Second Languages: A Cross-Linguistic Perspective*. Rowley, Mass.: Newbury House.

Clahsen, H. and J. M. Meisel. 1979. Eine psycholinguistische Rechtfertigung von Wortstellungsregeln. *Papiere zur Linguistik* 21. 3–25.

Clahsen, H., J. M. Meisel and M. Pienemann. 1983. *Deutsch als Zweitsprache*. Tübingen: Gunter Narr Verlag.

Clahsen, H., K.-M. Köpcke, J. M. Meisel, H. Nicholas, and M. Vincent. In preparation. Sprachentwicklung in der zweiten Sprache.

Cowart, W. 1982. Autonomy and interaction in the language processing system: A reply to Marslen-Wilson and Tyler. *Cognition* 12. 109–117.

Fodor, J., T. Bever, and M. Garrett. 1974. *The Psychology of Language*. New York: McGraw-Hill.

Forster, K. 1979. Levels of processing and the structure of the language processor. In W. Cooper and E. Walker (eds.), *Sentence Processing: Psycholinguistic Studies Presented to Merrill Garrett*, pp. 27–85.

Kail, M. This volume. The development of sentence interpretation strategies from a cross-linguistic persective.

Lakoff, G. and H. Thompson. 1975. Introducing cognitive grammar. Papers of the Berkeley Linguistic Society 1.

Marslen-Wilson, W. and L. Tyler. 1980. The temporal structure of spoken language understanding. *Cognition* 8. 1–71.

Meisel, J. M. 1981. A description of the research program and the subjects of the ZISA longitudinal study. Ms. Hamburg.

Meisel, J. M. 1983. Transfer as a second language strategy. *Language and Communication* 3. 11–46.

Norris, D. 1982. Autonomous processes in comprehension: A reply to Marslen-Wilson and Tyler. *Cognition* 11. 97–101.

Pienemann, M. 1981. Der Zweitspracherwerb ausländischer Arbeiterkinder. Bonn.: Bouvier (Gesamthochschule Wuppertal. Schriftenreihe Linguistik, vol. 4).

Slobin, D. I. 1973. Cognitive prerequisites for the development of grammar. In C. Ferguson and D. I. Slobin (eds.), *Studies of Child Language Development.* New York: Holt, Rinehart and Winston, pp. 175–208.

Slobin, D. I. and T. Bever. 1982. Children use canonical sentence schemas: A crosslinguistic study of word order and inflections. *Cognition* 12. 229–265.

Tyler, L., and W. Marslen-Wilson. 1977. The on-line effects of semantic context on syntactic processing. *Journal of Verbal Learning and Verbal Behavior* 16. 683–692.

CHAPTER 6

Contextually Defined Queries: Evidence for Variation in Orientations to Second Language Acquisition Processes?[1]

Howard Nicholas
LaTrobe University, Bundoora, Australia

1. INTRODUCTION

Variation in the course of second language acquisition as related to personality types and interaction patterns has been a matter of speculation for at least a decade. Gardner and Lambert (1972:54) suggested that "certain personality types may be more gifted for languages than others." Five years later, Seliger (1977:274) suggested that for second language learning adults,

> active learners who utilize all language environments, both formal and natural, for practice by interacting and getting others to use language with them are termed *high input generators*. The end result of their behavior is a competence which develops at a faster and perhaps qualitatively better rate. By getting more focussed input, the *high input generator* is able to test more hypotheses about the shape and use of L2.

A similar suggestion was made for children by Wong-Fillmore (1976), but in addition she pointed out that there was some differentiation between the areas attended to by different learners, e.g., "The syntactic play that Nora and Ana engaged in was indicative of their attention to structural matters" (1976:712).

The majority of these approaches nevertheless failed to consider two aspects of the personality/L2 acquisition relationship: (1) How would personality variation manifest itself linguistically, i.e., is there a qualitative as well as a quantitative difference in the styles of language produced by or types of interaction engaged in by different learner types? (2) Does the personality variation result in more than just a variation in the speed with which or the extent to which the second language is acquired? This report will be an attempt to examine the linguistic manifestations of one particular style of interaction in the course of second language acquisition under the assumption that different learners will adopt different strategies in their attempts to come to terms with or obtain data about the language which they have to simultaneously acquire and use. The suggestion is that a particular orientation will be marked by a particular variety of language produced in the course of second language acquisition.

The discussion will be based on a "variationist" model of second language acquisition (see Nicholas and Meisel, 1983). This type of model assumes that the acquisition process can be divided along a developmental and a learner-type-specific dimension. The claim (see Meisel, Clahsen, and Pienemann, 1981; Clahsen, Meisel, and Peinemann, 1982) is that the developmental dimension is common to all acquirers of a second language and is defined by the sequential acquisition of particular rules of the second language. The learner-type-specific dimension consists of a range of varieties of the language which are not tied to specific developmental stages and cannot be sequentially ordered. Different groups of learners will use different varieties according to their needs as defined by a mixture of social and psychological variables.

In this paper I will examine one aspect of a young child's second language acquisition process which I will claim reflects a particular orientation to that process. As such, I will claim that the (relatively frequent) use of this particular feature, the "contextually defined query,"[2] is a feature of a specific variety produced by a group of acquirers with a definable orientation to the second language acquisition process. The question which I will to an extent leave unanswered is whether such a feature is also a feature of a "good" (in the sense of "rapid" or "complete") second language acquirer.

In line with the "variationist" approach and in contrast to the claims made by Seliger (1977), I will claim that learners with certain (as yet unspecified) personality and social characteristics will possess specific interactional styles which will (1) have linguistic manifestations and (2) result in their use of a particular variety of the second language in the course of their acquisition of that language. Given that there will be a range of orientations to the second language acquisition process, I will claim that it will be possible to differentiate between different groups of second language acquirers according to the way in which they obtain information about their second language and that it will thus be possible, regardless of whether it is possible to differentiate between the results of the second language acquisition process, to differentiate between the ways in which acquirers attained those results.

CINDY

The learner examined in this paper is Cindy, a native speaker of English with an English-speaking mother and a bilingual German/English-speaking father. The language of the family up to the time of arrival in West Germany,[3] two weeks before recordings began, had been English. Cindy was 3;4 years old when she reached West Germany. Cindy's three older siblings were all bilingual (English and German) with varying degrees of command of the two languages. The home (where the majority of the recordings were made) was an English language domain and remained so throughout the period of observation, although there was a gradual shift in the amount of German directed at Cindy by the bilingual members of the family as Cindy's command of her second language increased. The continuing use of English by the mother in effectively all situations, combined with the periodic absence of Cindy's father for extended periods while he fulfilled professional commitments, led to the maintenance of the role of English on a permanent basis. Although the mother later learned some German and attempted to direct some remarks at native (Bavarian) German-speaking children who came to play with one of Cindy's older sisters, she was never observed to use that language to address a remark with serious communicative intent to Cindy. It thus seems reasonable to conclude that Cindy was in a situation very favorable to second language acquisition. The first language environment remained secure while at the same time the second language could be used in situations parallel to the first language situations by people Cindy perceived as nonthreatening to her linguistic identity since they were able to demonstrate bilingual abilities. A further aspect of the favorable environment was provided by the kindergarten teacher who initially spoke English with Cindy, until she felt that Cindy could cope in German.

2.   CONTEXTUALLY DEFINED QUERIES

DEFINITIONS AND DESCRIPTIONS

Contextually defined queries consist of interrogative markers such as "hm?", "ha?", "wa?", "ok?" which are produced after a main clause uttered by (in this case) the person in the process of acquiring the second language. They are not produced after every main clause, nor (presumably) to the same extent by all acquirers. They may follow statements, questions, or imperatives and appear designed to elicit verbal responses from the interlocutor. They are most frequently used in the following manner:

(1) 6:127   C: mama *ha?*/
            H: willst du das der mama zeigen?/
                 "do you want to show that to your mother?"
            C: mm/
                 (C. prepares to run off to show the picture to her mother.)
(2) 9:329   C: das göts (=gehört) dir *hm?*/
                 "that's belongs to you"
            H: gut. dann nehme ich die weißen teilchen/
                 "good. then I'll take the white pieces"

Such contextually defined queries appear to fall between, on the one hand, what have been called "clarification requests" (see Corsaro, 1976; Langford, 1981; Hustler, 1981) or "contingent queries" (see Garvey, 1977; Gallagher, 1981) and, on the other hand, the better known category of "tag questions" (see Brown and Hanlon, 1970) or "tag constructs" (see Berninger and Garvey, 1982).

Garvey (1977:67) defines contingent queries as dependent speech acts which request a verbal response. This verbal response constitutes a recognition of the fact that the poser of the query has requested a specific type of information. Corsaro (1976:185) states:

> The clarification request is defined as an interrogative which calls for the clarification, confirmation, or repetition of the preceding utterance of a co-interactant. The CR serves no substantive topical function in interaction in that its production does not contribute information in line with the established topic; it is employed rather as a device to keep interaction running smoothly or to repair disruptions in conversation.

Berninger and Garvey (1982:151) provide the following definition of tag constructions:

> A tag construction has been defined as a MATRIX CLAUSE (any syntax) and a TAG FORM (reduced interrogative in elliptical constructions; or interrogative expression in stereotypical constructions) produced WITHIN THE SAME TURN. The discoursal functions of tag constructions include requests for information, agreement, permission, compliance, responsiveness, and attention.

Lexically, *contextually defined queries* resemble both contingent queries and a subgroup of tag constructions use for "permission requests," "compliance requests" and "verbal response requests" (see Berninger and Garvey, 1982:157). Their range of forms appears to more closely resemble that of contingent queries than that of tag constructions.

Structurally, contextually defined queries resemble tag constructions in as much as they are produced by the speaker in the same conversational turn as the matrix clause. In this they differ from contingent queries or clarification requests which are posed by the interlocutor in reaction to a remark made by the speaker. Contingent queries thus appear in a subsequent turn to that of the matrix clause whereas contextually defined queries and tag constructions appear in the same turn as the matrix clause.

Functionally, contextually defined queries display similarities to both contingent queries and a subgroup of the tag constructions. The most significant factor in establishing a closer link between contingent queries and contextually defined queries than between the latter and tag constructions is that both contingent queries and contextually defined queries have the overriding function of eliciting a verbal response from the interlocutor and focus on the form of the utterance previously produced. The majority of tag constructions require no explicit verbal response apart from affirmation or denial.

FEATURES OF USE/FUNCTION OF CONTEXTUALLY DEFINED QUERIES

The feature of eliciting a verbal response can be seen in the following two examples.

    (3) 14:28   C: warte hier. *ok?*/
                      "wait here. ok?"
                H: hier soll ich warten?/
                      "you want me to wait here?"
                C: mm/
    (4) 14:75   C: *weiß du?*/ kann nik laufen. dann . . . . .
                      "you know? (a dog) can not run. then . . . . . ."
                H: ja/ ein auto kann den hund überfahren/
                      "yes/ a car can run over the dog"

It can be seen that the above examples of queries gain meaning only from the context in which they are embedded. Additionally it seems possible to suggest that their main function in the above contexts is the elicitation of a response from the interlocutor. In example (3), one would not normally expect to have to give a verbal response to an imperative, especially when issued by a child. If any response at all were required, a simple sign of acceptance or rejection would normally suffice. Given that condition, any additional request for a response would seem to indicate that special attention is being paid to the response itself by the poser of the query. Similarly in example (4) the addition of "weiß du?" is a marker of the fact that Cindy wants to be replied to in a more explicit manner than might normally be expected. Whereas, again, given that her message is clear, a response containing no more than a signal of acceptance might be deemed adequate, by including the contextually defined query in her utterance, Cindy has ensured that her interlocutor will supply a more detailed or explicit response to her statement. In addition, she has ensured that the interlocutor will be required to supply an expansion of her initial utterance. This thus establishes another parallel to the use of contingent queries. As Gallagher (1981:51) points out: "Unlike other utterance sequences which can rely more primarily upon extralinguistic and nonverbal cues successful participation in a contingent query exchange entails the *processing of the linguistic form of messages*" (my emphasis: H.R.N.). Whereas the requirement of a contingent query is that the speaker pay attention to the form of the query posed by the interlocutor, the requirement of the contextually defined query is that the interlocutor provide an utterance related to that of the poser of the query which enables (in this case) the learner to focus on the form of the response provided by the interlocutor.

As such, I wish to suggest that contextually defined queries can fulfill a potentially very valuable role for those second langauge learners/acquirers who make use of them. The majority of such queries do not consist of such explicit forms as "weiß du?", but rather of vague interrogatives which *by their very vagueness* require the addressee to provide an explicit response in a clearly defined form. In the following example it is possible to see how the imprecise formulation of Cindy's contextually defined query forces the interlocutor to provide an explicit response which therefore requires an explicit and structured utterance on his part.

> (5) 11:18   C: das is Marc. *wa?*/
> "that is Marc (C's brother)"
> H: mhm/ das gehört Marc und der elefant gehört Marc auch glaub ich/
> "mhm/ that belongs to Marc and the elephant also belongs to Marc I think"

In order to respond to Cindy's query and to simultaneously ensure that he had understood what Cindy had been trying to communicate, the interlocutor was forced to expand and reformulate what Cindy had said. This reformulation was then available to Cindy as additional information about the language. Given that she posed the query, it is reasonable to assume that she was also attending to the response and thus was able to better focus on the new/additional information contained in the response. Since the intention of both participants was apparently to express the same content, the additional information would have been at the level of the way in which that content was expressed. Thus, this type of query sequence would appear to enable the learner to acquire *input* that is probably much closer to *intake* than is normally the case. While this does not imply that the learner will automatically be able to make use of this information in his or her own productions, it would seem to indicate that the learner had a better chance of integrating the additional information into his existing linguistic knowledge since it had been (more or less) explicitly requested and this presumably indicates that he/she is "primed" to receive it. Since language learners are normally attempting to grapple with both the form and content of an utterance (both productively and receptively), it would seem that any mechanism which allowed attention to focus primarily on one of these aspects (even if only temporarily) would be a significant strategy for obtaining usable input in the course of the language acquisition process.

An example of the way in which this process works is provided below (see also example (1)):

> (6) 9:240   C: das nit kapuperl—das nit pupperl. *eh?*/
> "that not (ka) doll—that not doll. eh?"
> H: ok. das gehört der puppe nicht/
> "ok. that doesn't belong to the doll"

In the above example (and even more clearly in example (1)), an utterance is produced which has a meaning that is clear in the context, but the form of the utterance does not accord with target norms. In response to Cindy's contextually defined queries the interlocutor provides an explicit reformulation of the content of Cindy's utterance using the target structure. The use of the target structure is not as significant as the fact that a structured utterance has been provided which expresses what Cindy was trying to express in a manner different from that which she used. The content thus remains "known" and therefore Cindy does not have to devote any additonal effort to determining what is being discussed. She can therefore devote her attention to the way in which this content is expressed. This strategy enables her to gain access to a much broader range of structural information than she might normally do; she has a mechanism which enables her to attempt to express something and then obtain information about other ways in which the same content can be expressed.

Since contextually defined queries, in contrast to contingent queries, are not essential for the clarification of the native speaker's meaning and, further, are not essential to the attainment of the acquirer's communicative goals, we can assume that they are not an essential step in the development process of (second) language acquisition. As such, they can be assigned to the range of features optionally available to acquirers of a second language. Thus, it appears likely that learners will make variable use of this feature according to their orientation towards second language acquisition processes. I will suggest that those learners who are more structurally oriented will make greater use of this feature than learners who are less structurally oriented. Whether the difference between "greater" and "lesser" is a difference between "some" and "no" use is not yet known. This is an exploratory study which examines one learner's use of this feature and attempts to develop some hypotheses related to that usage pattern. It is not yet known to what extent other second language acquirers make use of this feature or whether this feature is specific to child second language acquisition. Further, it is not known how to define (relatively) frequent use of such features since we have no idea of what range of frequencies is likely or possible. Thus, the examination of the hypothesis that the use of contextually defined queries will correlate with particular features of interactive style and thus with a structural orientation to the process of second language acquisition will involve the consideration of the following areas:

(1) the contexts in which such queries are used,
(2) the frequency of use of such queries,
(3) the forms that the queries take,
(4) other features of the learner's interlanguage which might correlate with the assumption of a particular orientation to the process of second language acquisition.

Whereas Garvey (1977:90) points out that variation in the status relations between interlocutors or in the situation can result in the use of terms such as "I beg your pardon" instead of "what?" in contingent queries, this type of variation was not observed in Cindy's contextually defined queries. Whether this is due to the fact that all the recordings were made in informal play sessions or to the fact that Cindy was too young to have acquired such fine distinctions cannot be determined. The form of her utterances appears to vary randomly across all situations and contexts. There does not appear to be any correlation between different forms and different purposes of the various queries, either. The one feature which does appear to remain constant is the focus on the attempt to elicit a verbal response from the interlocutor. In the following examples I fail to respond to contextually defined queries posed by Cindy. In each case she persists in her attempts to obtain a verbal response until one is provided.

<ul>
<li>(7) 9:137   C: wa:t mal du/. . . . . du da. ha?/. . . . .wart mal du?/
"wait 'a bit' you/. . . . .you there. ha?/. . . .wait 'a bit' you/"
H: ich warte hier aber. wo möchtest du hin?/
"I'll wait here but. where do you want to go?"</li>
<li>(8) 10:181 C: und bla:ngget/ un blanget. ha?/ un bla:nket a?/
"and blanket etc. . . . ."
H: lang gut??/
"long good??"
C: ja/
"yes"</li>
</ul>

In each case, Cindy's response is different, but both examples demonstrate the same pattern. In the first example, Cindy wants me to wait where I am while she goes away to do something else. When I do not respond to her first command (not something I would "normally" be required to do), she issues the command again and reinforces the fact that she is waiting for a verbal response by adding a contextually defined query. Again she waits for a response and when it is not forthcoming she repeats her command in its original form. This time I respond verbally so the sequence is concluded. This is probably *not* a permission request since Cindy was not used to having to wait for permission before she did something. Normally she would simply stand up and go to get a new toy or talk to someone else. Thus it seems that the crucial aspect that is missing is my verbal response to her command. Unfortunately, it is not possible to determine what would have happened if I had not responded to her second repetition of the command. There is perhaps an indication of what might have happened in example (8).

In example (8), Cindy and I are putting a doll to bed and Cindy decides that it would be a good idea if we had a blanket as well so that the doll can sleep better. Since she is "meant" to use German, she attempts to pronounce the English word in a German manner. When I neither understand nor respond to this attempt, she again makes the suggestion, but this time she adds a contextually defined query (thus making this utterance rather resemble example (1)). Once again, confused by the meaning of her word, I do not respond so she again makes the suggestion and retains the contextually defined query. Compelled to respond, I make a despairing attempt to determine what she has in fact said so that I can respond appropriately. Needless to say, my response in no way reflects what Cindy has been trying to say, but nevertheless she responds in turn by saying "ja." The exchange then continues as follows:

H: wer is lang gut?/
      "who is long good?"
C: da/
      "there"
H: wo?/
      "where?"
C: em.m.m/

Cindy then leaves the scene and returns with a blanket, at which stage I finally grasp what she has been trying to say. This shows that Cindy misunderstood me in the same way in which I misunderstood her. She accepted my approximation to my understanding of "blanket" as an attempt to determine what she had said and (parallel to many similar situations) accepted the pronunciation of the "native speaker" as an appropriate rendering of her attempts. When this leads to further complications resulting from the phonological similarity of "where" and "wer" the conversation breaks down and Cindy solves it in the only way possible—by getting the blanket. This thus explains her acceptance of my attempt at pronunciation. The normal continuation of this exchange—had my utterance made any sense to me—would have been that I attempted to formulate a question or statement about her intentions. This would have had the effect of giving Cindy the sort of response that it can be assumed she was seeking, thus she accepted my attempt at clarification.

While these can hardly be regarded as extensive examples of Cindy's intentions when uttering such queries, it is indicative of their effectiveness in eliciting verbal responses that there are so few examples of queries to which the interlocutor does not respond. One further example is provided below where the response provided is not the one that Cindy is seeking:

(9) 9:123   C: put them back/
             H: da is noch ein briefträger/schau mal/ ich hab hier ganze familien=
                   "there is another postman/ look/ I have whole families here"=
             C: =put
                   them all back. ha?/
             H: schau mal was ich hier machen kann/
                   "look at what I can do here"
             C: all put them all back. ha?/ komme gleich. ha?/
                                              "be right back. ha?"
             H: alle weg?/
                   "all away?"
             C: nit=
                   "not"
             H: =nicht?=
                   "not"
             C: =alle weg/
             H: mm?/
             C: nit alle weg/
             H: welche lassen wir dann draußen?/
                   "which ones do we leave out then?"

Cindy's first attempt to get me to put the toys away is in English, to which I do not respond; in fact I begin talking about the animals which I have been collecting and show every sign of wanting to continue the game. In an effort to focus my attention on what Cindy wants to achieve, she repeats her utterance and adds the normally effective contextually defined query. Again I do not respond and try and attract her attention to what I am doing. Cindy again repeats her suggestion complete with the query and when I again fail to respond she suggests that she will alter the situation by leaving. How serious a threat this is cannot be estimated since her utterance also contains another contextually defined query inviting a response from me. This time I respond, not to the second, but to the first query (presumably since that is more in line with what I am trying to achieve). A discussion now starts which focuses on a common topic and at the end of the sequence I come around to accepting Cindy's view of the way in which things should proceed. Again, the vital role of the verbal interaction is emphasized. Had Cindy only wanted to ensure that the toys were put away, her easiest means of doing so would have been to start packing them up herself. One gains the distinct impression that Cindy not only wanted to put the toys away, but also to *talk* about that activity.

However, Cindy was not content to merely talk about events; the talking had to be of a particular type. There had to be a close link between what she was trying to say and the response provided by the interlocutor—she maintained her right to determine the interpretation of her own and the subsequent utterances, e.g.:

(10) 12:188   C: sweepen. *he?/* sweepen/
                    (sweep + verbal inflection)
              H: ja. zuerst machen wir das hier sauber/
                   "yes. first we'll clean this here up"
              C: you must sweepen/ wa:te/
                   "wait"
              H: ich warte hier aber ich will das buch lesen/
                   "I'll wait here but I want to read this book"
              C;   look!/ da is ein sweeper/
                   "there is a broom"

Here Cindy is suggesting that I sweep up the area. When I interpret this in a manner which suggests that we both participate in the cleaning-up operation Cindy clarifies the meaning of her original utterance and then—telling me to wait—disappears to fetch a broom. Thus she is not satisfied with any response to her query, but appears to be seeking one which accurately reflects what she was trying to communicate. If my response deviates too much from what is anticipated then Cindy will return to the original utterance in order to clarify the meaning of the interaction. Note that my particular reaction in this situation does not provide Cindy with the information which she needs to formulate her original suggestion in an explicit manner—despite the fact that she has an approximate idea of how this should be done (note the appropriate infinitive marker on the English verb).

As can be seen in the utterances in Appendix 1, there is some variation in both the forms of the contextually defined queries and of the speech acts in which they are embedded. Thus, these queries can be used in a large number of different situations and are not something which have to be formulated in any complex way. Potentially, they are available from the beginning of the acquisition process. In addition to the function which they have in common with contingent queries—that of eliciting a verbal response—they have a function which is not present in contingent queries. They seem to have a limited turn-assigning function. Garvey (1977:68) claims that a contingent query "does not affect the turn-at-speaking" since the speaker continues with his turn after responding to the interlocutor's query. In the case of contextually defined queries, the same automatic resumption of the speaker's turn is not guaranteed.

(11) 8:157   C: nit kaputt. *ha*?/
                 "not 'broken'. ha?"

              H: ne das machen wir nicht kaputt/ was machen wir da?/
                 "no we won't destroy that/ what will we do there?"

              C: das/
                 "that"

(12) 11:190 C: und mir/ *wa*?/ (=was)
                 "and me/ wa? (=what)"

              H: jetzt sollst du mal versuchen den hubschrauber zu fangen/
                 "now you try and catch the (toy) helicopter"
                 auf die plätze .. fertig .. los!/
                 "on your marks .. get set .. go!"
                 ne-ne-ne-ne-ne. den hubschrauber mußt du ansehen. mm?=
                 "no-no-no-no-no. you have to look at the helicopter. mm?"

              C: =ja=
                                                  "yes"

              H: =den
                 hubschrauber

                                                              "the
                 helicopter"
                 so. hier schau mal den hubschrauber an/
                 "this way. here look at the helicopter/"

              C: ja/
                 "yes"

In both example (11) and example (12) it can be seen how the control of the conversation passes to the interlocutor, who expands Cindy's original utterance, but then continues to determine what is said. Unlike contingent queries, contextually defined queries create a situation where such behavior is possible. The interlocutor is expected to respond in accordance with the requirements of the query as imposed by the speaker (witness the continuing questioning in example (9)), but once this requirement has been fulfilled (as it has been in both of the above examples), the interlocutor is free to discuss other features of the topic or move on to different topics. There is no absolute requirement that the conversation return to the topic referred to by the poser of the query. Thus, perhaps, it is more appropriate to say that contextually defined queries have a limited turn-retention right; i.e., the right of the speaker to insist that he/she be replied to in a manner which conforms to the conditions of the query. If a satisfactory response is provided by the interlocutor then it is possible for him/her to retain the turn and develop the conversation in another direction. Thus, despite being dominated by the speaker, the contextually defined queries seem to have the function of sharing the conversational load between two speakers. In such a situation they seem to mean something roughly equivalent to "I am looking for you to say something on this topic at this point, but I retain the right to ask again if you do not provide the sort of information that I am seeking." As such, they provide the second language acquirer with a means of controlling some of the aspects of the input to which he/she is exposed and of obtaining more detailed information about certain aspects of that input. An example of this sort of usage is provided below:

(13) 13:158   C: da ist ein ball/
                    "there is a ball"
              H: dankeschön/ jetzt habe ich den ball./
                    "thank you/ now I have the ball/
              C: (tasel) dies weg/ *ha*?/
                    "(take all??) this away/ ha?"
              H: bitte?/
                    "pardon?"
              C: dein ball/
                    "your ball"
              H: was soll ich mit dem ball machen?/
                    "what should I do with the ball?"
              C: take all this weg (danksden)/
                            "away (thank you?)"
              H: soll ich den ball weg-wegschmeißen?/
                    "should I throw the ball away/out?"
              C: da/ dun (=tun) dein stuhl/
                    "there/ do your chair"
              H: ach so!/ ich soll den ball zu dem stuhl werfen. oder rollen?/
                    "aha!/ I have to throw the ball to the chair. or roll it?"
              C: stuhl. rollen/
                    "chair. roll"

In the above example, Cindy uses a contextually defined query following an utterance which I do not understand. The topic of the utterance is then redefined by Cindy and then my question provides the basis for the predication. Gradually in the process of reformulation the type of action which Cindy is suggesting is made explicit and the meaning of the original utterance becomes clearer (at least by implication). We can see, however, how (aided by my *contingent query*) the operation of the contextually defined query becomes clear. As the contingent query returns the right of speaking to Cindy she follows up her "rights" by explicating the whole process. She retains control of each individual pair of utterances and steers the conversation along a path which she considers appropriate.

The further point of this type of query, of relevance when considering the sort of orientation that their use might reflect, is the fact that such queries enable the acquirer to separate the form from the content of the utterances which follow them. In this situation, Cindy was able to concentrate on the form of my response knowing roughly what I was going to say. This can be seen in an indirect way in the above example, but more clearly in example (1). In that example, Cindy provides a single word representation of a complex topic/comment unit. Her query after having said "mama" puts the emphasis on the interlocutor to try and formulate her intention (if only to confirm his own interpretation) and thus provides Cindy with additional information about the structure of her desired utterance. In the first utterance, the meaning is contextually clear, but the form which is used to explicitly express the meaning is not available to Cindy. In his interpretation of Cindy's utterance, the interlocutor provides Cindy with this explicit formulation. The interlocutor provides no new content information; this is already available to both participants through the context. The only new information is that about the strcuture used to convey this meaning. Thus, there seems to be a link between the use of contextually defined queries and an orientation towards structural information on the part of the second language acquirer. We will return to this point later.

The frequency with which these queries are produced is variable and there are not sufficient data from other studies at the moment to make any firm predictions about the average frequency with which various acquirers make use of this feature. Thus, it is not possible to determine whether Cindy's usage of these features is in any way different from normal usage patterns. To date, the frequencies appear as follows (remembering that the interviews are of variable length).

TABLE 1   Frequency of Use of Contextually Defined Queries

Interview	Contextually defined queries	Total queries	Percentage of total queries	Total utterances
1	1	19	5.3	70
2	0	6	—	53
3	6	14	42.9	196
4	2	14	14.3	64
5	0	0	—	12
6	8	20	40.0	77
7	25	59	42.4	228
8	10	31	32.3	203
9	25	82	30.5	371
10	33	65	50.8	447
11	22	56	39.3	405
12	31	87	35.6	538
13	14	41	34.1	277
14	8	21	38.1	138
15	0	0	—	0
16	0	1	0.0	13
17	1	9	11.1	194
18	18	30	60.0	518

At least for the interim period, the contextually defined queries appear to constitute around 30 to 50 percent of the questions which Cindy poses. The results from interviews 15 to 17 are confounded by the fact that Cindy spent two weeks in the hospital with pneumonia and thus it was impossible to conduct play sessions (!). Further, this period was one of intense exposure to German so that any developmental trends which might have been present would have been intensified by Cindy's continuous exposure to the second language. It is thus not possible to determine whether the frequencies obtained here are high or low, relative to the total number of queries/questions. The data from the eighteenth interview would seem to suggest that the data from the fifteenth to seventeenth interviews are not necessarily representative of Cindy's normal language usage patterns. There does not seem to be any general trend towards either more or less frequent usage of contextually defined queries, so it could well be the case that they are part of the general language usage strategies rather than a feature of language development. We lack, however, sufficient data to prove this assumption.

3. STRUCTURAL ORIENTATION

The fairly obvious tendency of the above sections was to suggest that (frequent) use of contextually defined queries reflects a structural orientation on the part of certain second language acquirers (see Clahsen, Köpcke, Meisel, Nicholas, and Vincent, in preparation). By this I do *not* necessarily mean a learner who is concerned with "formal correctness," but rather one who is concerned to determine the structural means by which something is expressed. There is no necessary corollary that there is an interest in formal accuracy—in fact the interest could be just the opposite (see Wong-Fillmore 1976:714):

> Where Juan worked on one problem at a time and did not attempt to use what he was learning until he had most of the details worked out, Nora tended to work whatever she picked up into as many sentences as she could as a way of figuring out the potentials of the new form.

If the claim that Cindy is structurally oriented has validity, it ought to be possible to find other features of her interlanguage which reflect the same orientation. Some other features (see Clahsen et al., in preparation) might be (1) the frequent use of redundant features, (2) the use of a variety of forms to express a particular function, (3) the initial functional restriction of language until a catalogue of forms has been acquired, or (4) an "early" development of morphological features (although what constitutes "early" has still to be defined).

For all the above areas, I wish to suggest that Cindy shows indications of being structurally oriented. Any one of these features, on its own, would be insufficient to classify her as being structurally oriented, but a range of similarly interpretable indices lends some credibility to such a conclusion.

The list cannot be regarded as definitive since there are many features which would be potential candidates for such analysis and even the conclusions drawn here are dependent on the results of comparative studies. One question which cannot be addressed directly in this paper, but is critical to the whole discussion, is the question of when orientations to the (second) language acquisition process become apparent.[4]

Two claims could be made: either that children will provide less evidence of interpersonal variation in that they all have similar orientations, or that the children are not "aware" enough of language to orient themselves to particular aspects of language. Both of these claims will be confounded by the possibility of distinguishing between adults and children in a number of different ways according to different criteria. In addition, it is not clear that orientations are either "present" or "absent." Given the evidence from both first and second language acquisition studies (see Bloom, Lightbown, and Hood, 1975; Clahsen, 1982, Nelson, 1973; Pienemann, 1981; Wong-Fillmore, 1976), it is hard to argue that there is no variation in children's language acquisition processes. However, those studies which have provided evidence of interpersonal variation in the course of second language acquisition (Pienemann, 1981; Wong-Fillmore, 1976) have studied children at least five years old. A study by Lightbown (1977) showed that for at least some acquirers there was less variation in the second language acquisition of pronouns than there was in the first language acquisition of the same feature. There was, however, variation in the L2 acquisition of other features. Given, however, that other studies have not examined the question of structural orientation in contrast with functional orientation in children of Cindy's age, all that this study can claim is that there does appear to be evidence for structural orientation in children under four years of age in the course of second language acquisition. The question that remains is whether there is also evidence for functional orientation.

REDUNDANT FEATURES

The analysis of this feature will be carried over from previous work (see Nicholas, 1984) in which the rate of supply of the copula in the early phases of L2 acquisition is discussed. The copula element will be regarded as redundant since its presence in a copula structure adds no additional information which would not be present if the element were to be deleted.[5] The extension of those earlier results are shown in Table 2. As can be seen in Table 2, the rate of supply of this feature far exceeds fifty percent, indicating that this element is supplied far more frequently than it is deleted despite the fact that it is functionally irrelevant in the sorts of structures which Cindy uses. This would seem to indicate that Cindy pays more attention to formal elements than can be justified by the principle of only providing that structure which is essential to the conveying of meaning. Cindy pays attention to formal elements even where they are not essential to the communication of functional content.

TABLE 2   Rate of Supply of Copula Element in Copula Structures

Interview	Supplied	Total	Percentage supplied
1	5	8	62.5
2	0	8	—
3	26	40	65.0
4	9	14	64.3
5	0	0	—
6	8	8	100
7	43	58	74.1
8	13	21	61.9
9	62	80	77.5
10	42	49	85.7
11	26	32	81.3
12	68	81	83.9
13	29	33	87.9
14	9	11	81.8
15	0	0	—
16	3	6	50.0
17	13	21	61.9
18	48	61	78.7

VARIETY OF FORMS

Cindy begins to mark the completion of events consistently as of the sixth interview (see Nicholas, 1985). Her baseline strategy for this marking is the use of *so*. This form is roughly equivalent in its meaning to "there you are" in contexts where somebody has just been given something, but has much wider use in spoken German and in addition includes a range of other meanings. It can be used very satisfactorily to mark the completion of an event. However, from very early on Cindy makes use of an additional form to mark such "action end" situations. This additional form is later dropped. The form which Cindy uses — even when *so* would have been more appropriate — is *hast gemacht* or minor variants of this form. She even makes use of both forms in the same situation, e.g.:

(14) 9:57   C: so=
             H: =mhm=

             C: =hast du gemacht . . un das hast du gemacht/
                        "have you done . . and that have you done"

Example (14) follows the completion of a game where similar toy animals are sorted into "families."

Some further examples of variation in form are to be found in Appendix 2. As far as I can determine, there is no attempt to systematize the forms that are presented. If that is the case, the question remains as to why Cindy "bothers" to produce varied forms. Why, for example, does she "bother" to phonologically adjust lexical transfers from her first language so that they correspond to appropriate forms in her second language? (see page 136).

INITIAL FUNCTIONAL RESTRICTION

Figures 1 and 2 show the extent to which Cindy's early use of her second language is weighted in its functional distribution. Figure 1 shows that for a period extending into her second month of residence in West Germany, Cindy produces approximately 90 percent "topic focus" utterances. It is only after the seventh interview that this percentage begins to vary significantly. In fact, it could be argued that such alteration does not begin until after the ninth interview. Not until the thirteenth interview do we find dominant use of "comment" or "topic/comment" *function* utterances.[6]

Figure 2 shows an initial dominance of copula structures in topic-focusing function, but again this distribution appears to begin to alter at approximately the time of the ninth interview. (The initial variation in the second interview can be attributed to statistical distortion caused by a restricted number of examples; a total of ten multiple constituent utterances was recorded in this session.) In the seventeenth and eighteenth interviews we observe in both Figures 1 and 2 that there is a significantly different distribution of the utterance functions compared to that observed in the earlier interviews. As can be seen in Figure 1, topic/comment utterances have come to dominate in Cindy's productions, and as Figure 2 shows, copula structures have lost their initial functional restriction and in these two later interviews are also used to express topic/comment function. (The dotted lines in the period between the thirteenth and the sixteenth interviews mark the fact that interpretation of the data in this period is subject to a large number of conflicting factors such as the extended absence of the researcher and Cindy's stay in the hospital, where the recording was anything but ideal.) Thus we see that there is an initial functional restriction in two specific ways. In the first place there is a one form–one function relationship with copula structures being reserved for topic focus function and full verb structures being used to express topic/comment function. In the second place, there is an initial restriction to the almost exclusive expression of the topic focus function, i.e., pointing out a topic of conversation without providing any additional information about that topic. These two factors combined would seem to provide evidence for an orientation towards structural aspects of the language – even if only to the extent that there is almost no attempt to express a wide range of functions in the early utterances. Looked at in another way, the restriction of utterances to copula structures satisfies two further requirements: (1) it allows Cindy to engage in lots of conversation (despite the functional restriction) and (2) it allows her to produce utterances which have an overt syntactic structure. All of this would seem to permit an interpretation which claims that Cindy's language usage reflects a structural orientation.

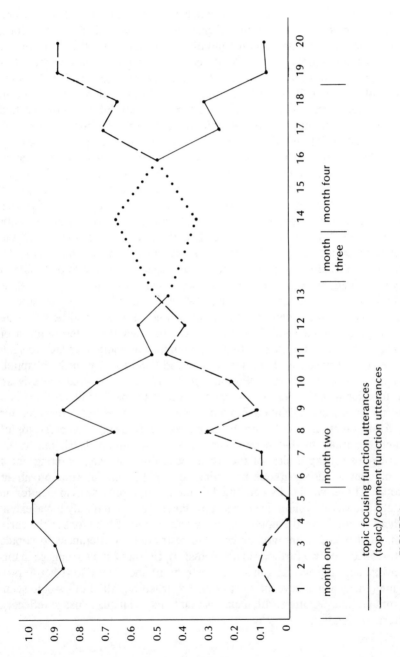

topic focusing function utterances

(topic)/comment function utterances

FIGURE 1

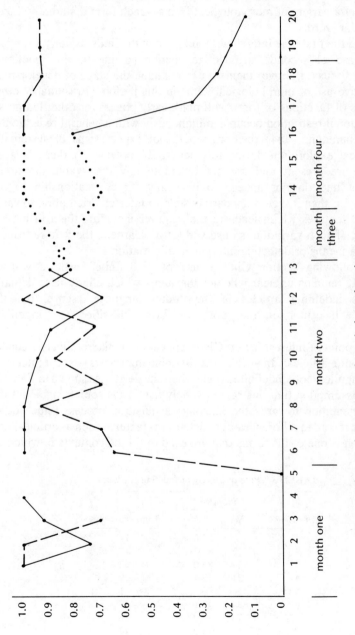

% cop. & loc. "to be" structures in topic focus function
% full verb structures in (topic)/comment function

FIGURE 2

EARLY DEVELOPMENT OF MORPHOLOGICAL MARKING

As has been pointed out elsewhere (see Meisel, this volume), the initial phases of (adult) second language acquisition are marked by noncreative production of a variety of morphological forms—each form apparently linked to a particular word.

If we take the first nine interviews conducted with Cindy as constituting an "early" phase of second language acquisition (owing to the functional restrictions discussed above) then we can examine the stage of development of the creative use of morphological items in this period. (Presumably other distributions of functions or forms will mark early phases for other learners.) If this functional restriction occurs similtaneously with a general reduction of L2 (see Schumann, 1984) then we would not expect signs of systematic morphological exploration during this period. If, however, indices of such exploration are present and are not linked to any observable functional development and do not appear to bear any direct relationship to the available input, then it would appear possible to infer an orientation towards such formal features which leads to the acquirer including them in his/her productions. If such variation is observed for all learners, the feature loses it validity as a means of detecting interpersonal variation.

In the following section Cindy's use of "indefinite" articles will be discussed. It remains unclear whether the items which Cindy uses actually function as indefinite articles in the "adult language" sense, but the discussion will center on the group of forms classified as "indefinite articles."

The first point of interest is that Cindy appears to make relatively frequent use of indefinite articles.[7] In each of the first nine interviews (except interview 5), Cindy supplies more indefinite articles than she deletes as shown in Table 3. Given the assumption that this rate of supply itself says something about the learner's orientation towards the language acquisition process (since other studies have recorded different rates of deletion of features such as articles), the next question is one of the forms that are used to fill the contexts in which an

TABLE 3   Rate of Supply of Indefinite Articles

Interview	Supplied		Total (contexts)
	No.	%	
1	7	63.6	11
2	12	85.7	14
3	49	86.0	57
4	21	72.4	29
5	0	—	1
6	34	97.1	35
7	73	84.9	86
8	17	73.9	23
9	21	60.0	35

"indefinite article" is supplied. If it can be shown that there is no functional variation which correlates with the variation in the forms used (and assuming that the variation in form is not merely random), then we would appear to have another index of exploration of the formal aspects of the language system in preference to an exploration of the functional aspects.

With the exception of four items, the forms used by Cindy in this context are either *eine* or *ein*, respectively marked for feminine or masculine/neuter gender. This is not a surprising finding since both are frequent forms in the language used around Cindy. The distribution in Cindy's language is as shown in Table 4. While it is possible that the target system is being used in the first interview (the only nouns which are used with indefinite articles are either masculine or neuter), the same claim cannot be made for later interviews. Within any given interview there does not appear to be a systematic basis for the allocation of the different forms of the indefinite articles to specific nouns. There is, however, variation across time which appears to be systematic. From interview 2 to interview 6 inclusive the *eine* form dominates in Cindy's second language usage. After this period, Cindy returns to the dominant usage of the *ein* form. Given the fact that the final *e* of the *eine* variant is salient (being at the end of the word and syllabic) adds to the likelihood that if a variety of forms is adopted this will be one of the selected forms. However, the question still remains of why such a variety would be adopted. Given that various forms will be produced, the saliency argument provides us with a basis for predicting which forms will appear, but in order to explain why this variety itself appears we have to resort to an argument which suggests that certain learners are oriented towards such structural aspects of the language. The fact that the observed variation in the use of these forms occurs at a time when there is comparative functional restriction adds additional weight to the argument that Cindy's language usage in this area reflects a structural orientation.

It thus seems possible to argue that for a limited period, before Cindy is aware of any system in the distribution of these particular features, she experiments with the use of these features. Failing to detect any system in their distribution, she resumes her dominant use of the base form in the

TABLE 4 Absolute Frequency of Use of Different Forms of the Indefinite Article

Interview	"ein"	"eine"	"ein(e)s"
1	7	0	0
2	2	10	0
3	2	46	1
4	3	18	0
5	0	0	0
6	12	22	0
7	68	3	2
8	15	2	0
9	18	2	1

seventh, eighth and ninth interviews. The fact that she moves from almost exclusive use of one form to almost exclusive use of the alternative form seems to indicate that the variation is neither random (a more equal distribution of the forms would appear if this were the case) nor a matter of trying to match the productions to the distribution in the input. It is worth emphasizing that Cindy's use of the forms does not correlate with target usage except by chance in this early phase.

4. DISCUSSION

As was stated earlier, any of the above features in isolation would not provide adequate evidence to assume any specific orientation. However, the linking of a number of diverse features which all seem to point in the same direction constitutes much more solid evidence for the presence of a particular orientation to the second language acquisition process in Cindy's second language usage. It is not claimed that such features will not appear in the interlanguages of other second language acquirers, nor is it claimed that the features discussed here are part of an invariant developmental sequence. However, it is claimed that a particular orientation to the second language acquisition process will result in variation between second language acquirers at the same stage of second language acquisition. It is thus suggested that certain of the features produced by people in the course of second language acquisition will not be common to all acquirers but will reflect systematic patterns of language usage corresponding to the orientations of the learners.

If the evidence of the other indicators can be assumed to point towards a structural orientation, then the linking of contextually defined queries and such an orientation also appears more plausible. If this conclusion is valid, then the suggestion is that certain second language acquirers can engage in manipulation of the interaction in which they participate to obtain the sort of input which best suits their requirements. To the extent that this is successful, it is likely to aid their long-term language acquisition success, but more importantly—in the short term—it is likely to influence the features which they produce in the course of the acquisition process. Further, this implies that second language acquirers can influence the sort of language to which they are exposed and can thus play a more important part in the nature of the acquisition process than has perhaps been assumed to date.

APPENDIX 1

VARIATION IN FORM AND FUNCTION OF CONTEXTUALLY DEFINED QUERIES

1:65   C: wo is the first one?/ *ja*?/
             "where"   "yes"
        H: oh. wo ist der junge?/ da ist der junge/
             "where is the boy?/ there is the boy"

3:48   C: das hier/ *ah*?/
             "this here"
        H: das da-da oben/
             "that one there-up there"

3:170 C: das (x) ein haus/ *ja*?/
             "that (x) a house/ yes?"
        H: baust du ein haus jetzt?/
             "are you building a house now?"

3:172 C: ja. das ist eine haus-das ist eine haus-*eh*?/ das ist eine haus *ja*?/
             "yes. this is a house . . . . "
        H: und das hier ist auch ein haus?/
             "and this here is also a house?"

3:179 C: das nein kaputt/ *ha*?/
             "that no 'broken'/ ha?"

6:20   C: da Heidi/ *ha*?/
             "there Heidi/ ha?"/
        H: ist das Heidi?/
             "is that Heidi?"
         C: ja/

6:75   C: wart mal/ *ah*?/
             "wait 'a bit'/ ah?"

7:93   C: komm mal gleich/ tutsi/ *ja*?/
             "be right back/ tutsi (=name of pet dog)/ yes?"

7:281 C: das mach/ *ha*?/
             "that do" ha?/
        H: wo denn?/ da?/
             "where?/ there?"

8:177 C: ein tissue/ *ha*?/
         H: ein weißes taschentuch. mhm/
             "a white handkerchief, mhm"

9:36   C: ist es not yours?/ *ha*?/
         H: diese gehören mir. alle diese (x) spielzeuge/
             "these belong to me. all these toys"

9:145 C: nich kaputt/
        H: nicht kaputt?/
        C: das is nit kaputt/ *ha*?/
        H: was ist nicht kaputt?/
             "what is not broken?"
        C: das is nit kaputt/
        H: ach so. der arme eine vogel. jetzt ist er aber-jetzt liegt er da auf dem tisch
             "ah! that one poor bird. now it is but-now it is lying there on the table"

9:334 Cindy is distributing toys
        H: gehört das mir?
             "does that belong to me?"

C: mhm/ es göt mir/ das göt dir/ *a*?/
"mhm/ it belongs to me/ that belongs to you/ a?"

H: wieviel?/ das ist glaub ich ein bi*ß*chen unfair/ da hast du vier und ich habe fünf-
neun-ich habe vierzehn und du hast nur-ich hab hier fünfzehn und du hast nur
drei/
"how much?/ I think that's a little bit unfair/ you've got four there and I have
five-nine-I have fourteen and you have only-I have fifteen and you only have
three"

9:409   C: it's raining/ *a*?/

H: es regnet.ja.es regnet schon wieder!/
"it's raining.yes.it's raining again"

APPENDIX 2

"STRUCTURAL" MARKERS

7:298   H: und kannst du vielleicht einen zweiten vogel da malen?/
"and can you perhaps draw a second bird there?"

C: zweiten vogel/
"second bird"   (inflectional ending)

8:102   C: komm*st* du mit . . zu spielplatz . . do you want to go to the spielplatz?/
"playground"   (inflectional ending)

8:126   H: hier haben wir es Cindy/
"here we have it Cindy"

C: da hast du die noch/
"there you still have it"   (SV inversion/formula)

8:190   H: ganz neues haus mu*ß*t du mir bauen/
"you have to build me a whole new house"

C: du (ch) hab*ent* haus/ da is er gebau/ schau/
"you (ch) have + house/ there is he built/ look"   (invented inflection)

9:233   C: ja. göts dir/ all gi-das iß dich-das iß dirs/ *a*?/ das git mir/
"yes.belongs to you/ all be-that is you(+ACC)-that is you" (+DAT+Poss. 's)

9:318   H: wo sitzt du mal?/
"where are you sitting?"

C: da.sitz*e* da.da/
"there.sit there.there"   (inflectional ending)

10:181 C: so/ sleep*n*/
"'there"/ sleep + infinitive marker)

H: mm?

C: slafen/
"sleep"

10:199 C: ein fisch!/ zwei fische!/
"a fish/ two fishes!"   (redundant plural marker)

10:309 C: dein fisch is beitsen=
"your fish is biting"

H: =mm?=

C: =dein fisch bites.dein fisch is beitsen/
(phonological integration of L1)

12:292 C: nie du talk/
"no/never you talk"

H: mm?/

C: nit talken du!/ nit!/
         "not talk (+infinitive marker) you/ not!"   (phonological integration)
13:192   C: ich heide/
                  "I'm hiding (+ first person singular inflection)"
13:231   C: o:o: beitze!/ ich beitze/
                  "bite!/ I bite - I am biting"   (inflection + phonological adjustment)

NOTES

1. Revised version of a discussion paper presented at the Second European–North American Workshop on Cross-Linguistic Second Language Acquisition Research; Göhrde, August 1982. Many of the ideas presented in this paper were initiated by the ZISA group in which I worked from March 1981 to March 1982. Other members of the group should not be held responsible for this interpretation.

2. In the version of this paper presented at the conference I called these queries "contingent queries" to reinforce some of the parallels between the functions of the two types of queries. Discussion resulting from that has led me to the conclusion that the two types of query are in fact distinct. I thank Sandra Kipp, Jürgen Meisel, and Margaret van Naerssen for discussion on this point.

3. The recordings were made while I was carrying out fieldwork in Passau, West Germany. I would like to thank Sascha Felix (Universität Passau) for his generous support of that work. In the examples cited in this article the number before the colon is the number of the interview. The number after the colon is the number of the utterance in that interview. A slash (/) is used to mark the end of an utterance. An equals sign (=) is used to mark the location of an interruption by the other speaker.

4. I thank Michael Clyne and Jürgen Meisel for drawing my attention to this point.

5. In the earlier analysis, the definition of copula also included locative "to be." Although the distinction between the two functions of the verb "to be" are distinguished in the analysis currently being undertaken, the earlier lack of distinction has been maintained here since similar "redundancy" arguments can be advanced in both cases (Clahsen, Meisel, and Pienemann, 1982).

6. I wish to emphasize that I am *not* describing topic/comment *structures*. Rather, I am describing those utterances which have a *function* other than just focusing on the topic, i.e., those that have a function of providing additional information about whatever topic is the focus of conversation at the time. In fact, Cindy produces comparatively few utterances which could be uniquely described as having a topic/comment structure.

7. Compare Klein and Dittmar (1979:144): "In the beginning, noun phrases do not have any modifier or determiner.... Within the class of determiners, there is a continuous shift from simple numbers ... and quantifiers ... to articles ... articles occur mainly in later stages."

REFERENCES

Berninger, G., and C. Garvey. 1982. Tag constructions: structure and function in child discourse. *Journal of Child Language* 9. 151–168.

Bloom, L., P. Lightbown and L. Hood. 1975. Structure and variation in child language. *Monographs of the Society for Research in Child Development* 40 (2).

Brown, R. and C. Hanlon. 1970. Derivational complexity and order of acquisition in child speech. In J. R. Hayes (ed.), *Cognition and the Development of Language*. New York: John Wiley & Sons.

Clahsen, H. 1982. *Spracherwerb in der Kindheit: Eine Untersuchung zur Entwicklung der Syntax bei Kleinkindern.* Tübingen: Gunter Narr Verlag.

Clahsen, H., K-M. Köpcke, J. M. Meisel, H. R. Nicholas, and M. Vincent. In preparation. *Sprachentwicklung in der zweiten Sprache.*

Clahsen, H., J. M. Meisel, and M. Peinemann. 1982. *Deutsch als Zweitsprache: Der Spracherwerb ausländischer Arbeiter.* Tübingen: Gunter Narr Verlag.

Corsaro, W. 1976. The clarification request as a feature of adult interactive styles with young children. *Language in Society* 6. 183–207.

Gallagher, T. M. 1981. Contingent query sequences within adult-child discourse. *Journal of Child Language* 8. 51–62.

Gardner, R. C. and W. E. Lambert. 1972. *Attitudes and Motivation in Second Language Learning.* Rowley, Mass.: Newbury House.

Garvey, C. 1977. The contingent query: a dependent act in conversation. In M. Lewis and L. A. Rosenblum (eds.), *Interaction, Conversation, and the Development of Language.* New York: John Wiley & Sons.

Hustler, D. 1981. Some comments on clarification requests: a response to Langford. In P. French and M. Maclure (eds.), *Adult-child Conversation.* London: Croom-Helm.

Jefferson, G. 1972. Side sequences. In D. Sudnow (ed.), *Studies in Social Interaction.* New York: The Free Press.

Klein, W. and N. Dittmar. 1979. *Developing Grammars: The Acquisition of German Syntax by Foreign Workers.* Berlin: Springer.

Langford, D. 1981. The clarification request sequence in conversation between mothers and their children. In P. French and M. Maclure (eds.), *Adult-Child Conversation.* London: Croom-Helm.

Lightbown, P. 1977. Consistency and variation in the acquisition of French: A study of first and second language development. Ph.D. thesis, Columbia University.

Meisel, J. M. This volume. Reference to past events and actions in the development of natural second language acquisition.

Meisel, J. M., H. Clahsen, and M. Pienemann. 1981. On determining developmental stages in second language acquisition. *Studies in Second Language Acquisition* 3/2. 109–135.

Nelson, K. 1973. Structure and strategy in learning to talk. *Monographs of the Society for Research in Child Development,* 38, No. 149.

Nicholas, H. R. 1984. "To be" or not "to be": Is that really the question? Developmental sequences and the role of the copula in the acquisition of German as a second language. In R. Andersen (ed.), *Second Languages.* Rowley, Mass.: Newbury House.

Nicholas, H. R. 1985. "Functional forms": A young child's acquisition of a second language. Paper presented at the Second National Child Development Conference. In T. Cross and L. Riach (eds.), *Proceedings.*

Nicholas, H. R. and J. M. Meisel. 1983. Second language acquisition: The state of the art (with particular reference to the situation in West Germany). In S. Felix and H. Wode (eds.), *Language Development at the Crossroads.* Benjamins. North American.

Pienemann, M. 1981. *Der Zweitspracherwerb ausländischer Arbeiterkinder.* Bonn: Bouvier.

Schumann, J. H. 1984. Nonsyntactic speech in the Spanish-English basilang. In R. Andersen (ed.), *Second Languages.* Rowley, Mass.: Newbury House.

Seliger, H. W. 1977. Does practice make perfect? A study of interaction patterns and L2 competence. *Language Learning* 27. 263–278.

Wong-Fillmore, L. 1976. The second time around: cognitive and social strategies in second language acquisition. Ph.D. thesis, Stanford University.

CHAPTER 7

Psychological Constraints on the Teachability of Languages

Manfred Pienemann
University of Sydney, Australia

1. RESEARCH QUESTION AND RELATED STUDIES

The question underlying this study is whether the process of natural L2 acquisition can be influenced by formal instruction.[1] Our research is intended to contribute to making explicit the view that all instances of language acquisition are constrained by the same factors. This study is not concerned with properties of *formal* language learning and their dependence on principles of natural acquisition as are the other studies in the field, which will be outlined below. Rather, it takes the reverse view and investigates the influence of instruction on *natural acquisition processes*. Consequently, the data are drawn from an experiment in which we tried to force other than "natural" learning processes in learners' natural acquisition of a second language (for further details see section 2 below). Thus the underlying question is: can processes of natural acquisition be influenced (in other than the "natural way") by formal instruction?

It seems to me that this question is of outstanding importance for two reasons. First, if we follow the above hypothesis about common principles for formal learning and natural acquisition, L2 curricula must be based on these principles. This is especially apparent if L2 development takes place in a context where natural acquisition is the predominant (or exclusive) source of linguistic development (as is the case with most immigrant workers and their children in Europe). Under this condition it is of immediate importance to discover in what way possible pedagogical options for L2 curricula are restricted by principles of language acquisition; i.e., whether the effect of formal instruction is *exclusively predetermined* by acquisition principles or whether (and if so, in what way) acquisition processes can still be manipulated by means of instruction.

The second reason is directly connected to the latter question. By investigating to what extent acquisition processes can be manipulated by instruction, we can specify some of the properties of those factors which are hypothesized to constrain language learning (and possibly also teaching).

The question underlying this research is *one* special case of the general view that *all instances of language learning, change, loss etc. might be determined by the same factors (in the individual)*. This main line of research is represented by the first left "node" in Figure 1, which gives an overview of the related research. Such a research perspective has been worked out by several scholars from different theoretical points of view (esp. Wode, 1981; Slobin, 1973, 1975; Felix and Wode, 1983). The number of studies which have been conducted in this framework (with particular reference to formal L2 learning) is relatively small. Leaving aside theoretical differences in the explanation of acquisition processes for the moment (for discussion see esp. Berman, 1982; Clahsen, 1982; Felix, 1982) we can differentiate two approaches within this "branch", which also reflect some of the differences of the underlying question (cf. Figure 1).

One of them is my approach; the other is represented by the work of Felix and Simmet (Felix, 1978, 1981; Felix and Simmet, 1981; Hahn, 1982) which has been carried out within the tradition of the "integrated perspective of language acquisition" (see Wode, 1981). These authors primarily compare the structures of utterances which appear under conditions of formal instruction with the types of structures known from natural acquisition. In this research they found a considerable number of structural parallels and similar learning strategies, although the learners had been exposed to an input sequenced in contradiction to findings from natural L2 acquisition. As these similarities of structures appear in the two different types of language acquisition (although the input was substantially different) the authors have a relatively strong empirical basis for concluding that the principles underlying natural acquisition also apply to the formal learning of a language.

The strength of this argument is reduced somewhat by the following two weaknesses: (1) The data from formal instruction are not related to individual learners of the longitudinal observation. So the comparisons of structures from different acquisitional types is (in this work)[2] not a comparison of acquisitional sequences, but, rather, of error types to natural orders of acquisition. (2) The

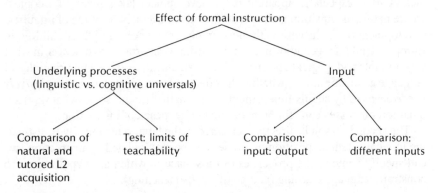

FIGURE 1 Characterization of Related Research

above conclusion (that the principles of natural acquisition also apply to formal L2 learning) only states the *general* role of those principles in formal learning, but it does not make explicit *in what way* formal L2 learning is constrained by them.

The primary difference between the above-mentioned research and the other main line of investigation I want to characterize (cf. Figure 1) is that the former concentrates on underlying acquisition principles in different types of acquisition whereas the latter is concerned with the question of the extent to which acquisition/learning processes depend on the structure of formal input. Obviously, this question is related to investigations of input in *natural* acquisition. This research again is – as I will show in some more detail in section 5 – related to a nonnativist view of first language acquisition which investigates the role of "motherese" (see Snow and Ferguson, 1977).

Many of the studies in this section were comparisons of two or more of the following variables:

(1) the language to which the learner is exposed
(2) the language he produces
(3) the language of learners with a different input
(4) the order of accuracy in natural acquisition

(See Lightbown, this volume; Long, 1982). A widespread research method among these studies (see Snow and Ferguson, 1977), which is also common in L2 research, is to compare the *frequency* of structures in the input language with their frequency/accuracy in the output. Consequently, the effect of input is measured in a quantitative manner (see also the study by Dietrich et al., 1979).

The results of these studies have not always been in agreement with each other. However, on the basis of a review of thirteen empirical studies, Long (1982) points out that in systematizing these studies according to the absolute and relative effect of input and to the amount of natural versus formal input, a general tendency can be found which indicates a positive effect of instruction for L2 acquisition.

In this context I want to point to a general weakness of this "branch" of research: On the basis of the methods which are applied (especially measuring frequency/accuracy) only a very specific type of question can be answered, namely, *how much* effect instruction has on the interlanguage. As the effect is measured on the basis of linguistic units which are not clearly related to acquisition processes, the focus of these studies is on *learning success* and not on *acquisition processes* (see also the critique of acquisitional criteria and morpheme order studies in Meisel, Clahsen, and Pienemann, 1981).

"Input" is also the heading of another line of research which is more clearly rooted in behaviorist learning psychology and which has been conducted in Germany for a number of years (see Jungblut, 1974; Heuer, 1976; Vogel and Vogel, 1975; Hüllen and Jung, 1979; for discussion see Hahn, 1982). The overall question of this research is "What is the optimal input for learning purpose x?" To some extent this question is also addressed in the line of research outlined above (see Long, 1982).

However, here the question is not *what type of structures* in the input has the optimal effect on the learner's L2 development, but what is the *optimal way of presenting* any set of structures which has been selected as a learning objective, independently of the actual state of the learner's interlanguage. Concentrating exclusively on the formal learning situation (i.e., normal foreign language classes), these studies investigated correlations between external variables such as teaching method, teaching material, teacher's behavior, etc., and learning success in terms of error-free L2 learning.

The general tendency of this line of research is to hypothesize that the formal setting of tutored L2 learning allows for language learning processes which are structurally different from natural L2 acquisition and which can be controlled by the appropriate structure of the input. As the learning process is "a priori" regarded to be fully dependent on input variables, the question "whether teaching makes a difference" does not arise. Instead, research in this framework is devoted to the search for the optimal teaching method.

2.   RESEARCH DESIGN

The informants are 10 Italian children of migrant workers, aged 7–9 years, attending elementary school in Munich in an Italian language class with supplementary instruction in German as a second language. All children had relatively intensive contact with German-speaking peers (compared to most of the informants that the Canadian studies reported, see for instance Swain and Lapkin, 1982; Lightbown, this volume).

The research method was a relatively controlled experiment. The main idea of this experiment, which had also been the structuring principle for the method applied in the study by Dietrich, Kaufmann, and Storch (1979), is that the children's interlanguage is recorded before and after a period of formal instruction so that the changes in the interlanguage can be investigated.

The learning objectives for the experiment were taken from (1) a well-investigated area of German L2 development and (2) a domain in which substantial structural differences between learner types are known to be frequent. As we will concentrate on the developmental rather than the variational dimension in this paper, I want to outline briefly some of the structural characteristics of the special developmental stages on which this study is based.

The structural domain I refer to is German word order. The development of these structures has been investigated in a number of longitudinal and cross-sectional studies (see Clahsen, Meisel, and Pienemann, 1983; Clahsen, 1980, 1981, 1982; Meisel, 1980; Meisel, Clahsen, and Pienemann, 1981; Pienemann, 1980, 1981). In this context I simply want to illustrate some structural features of the first four stages by giving a literal translation of example sentences:

1st stage: canonical word order
(1) *die kinder spielen mim ball* (Concetta)[3]
    "the children play with the ball"
2nd stage: adverb fronting (ADVERB)
(2) *da kinder spielen* (Concetta)
    "there children play"
3rd stage: particle shift (PARTICLE)
(3) *alle kinder muß die pause machen* (Concetta)
    "all children must the break have"
4th stage: subject-verb inversion (INVERSION)
(4) *dann hat sie wieder die knoche gebringt* (Eva)
    "then has she again the bone bringed"

For the arguments which follow it should be kept in mind that each rule does not replace the one preceding it. Rather, all rules are required subsequently so that, (on the basis of the *complete* acquisitional sequence), they can together account for the majority of positions of verbal elements in German main clauses.

For better understanding of the following section, I also want to mention the basic idea of the acquisitional criterion which underlies the above studies and which will be applied again to the analysis below. The main purpose is not to describe the point in time during the process of language development when a structure is *mastered* (in terms of correct use of target norms), because this is only to pinpoint the *end* of the acquisition of a certain structure. Rather, the above criterion is intended to define the *first systematic use* of a structure, so that the point in time when the learner has – *in principle* – grasped the learning task can be located (for further discussion see Meisel, Clahsen, and Pienemann, 1981).

The learning objective for the experiment was INVERSION which, like PARTICLE, is an *obligatory* permutation in German. As we wanted to test whether INVERSION can be taught before it is acquired naturally, we could include in our study only informants who had not acquired this rule. For this purpose all 100 children of the above-mentioned school were investigated in order to determine the actual acquisitional stage of their interlanguage. From these children we selected 10 informants whose interlanguages were at a stage below INVERSION.[4]

As a supplementary issue, we investigated the behaviorist hypothesis which predicts that in a formal setting structures can be learned in other than the natural order. Within this perspective the only question is whether this learning will be transferred to natural communication. In order to test this hypothesis we gathered data in normal outdoor conversation (with radio microphones) in addition to the usually more formal linguistic interviews. All steps of the data-gathering procedure are summarized in Table 1. All steps were tape recorded. In line with the hypothesis to be tested, the experiment contains two different types of data-gathering techniques (plus the recordings of the instruction period): (I) The *linguistic interviews* were dialogues between pairs of (a) informants and (b) student interviewers. The interviewers selected topics (in any suitable order) from a list of topics and had some toys and picture stories at hand in order to get the "con-

TABLE 1   Data Gathering Procedure

Step	No. of interviews	Time (days)
selection of informants	100	7
first interview	10	1
first hidden recording	10	2
first instructional period		5
second interview	10	1
second instructional period		5
third interview	10	1
second hidden recording	10	2

versation" going. These interviews were conducted in separate sessions in the school environment. (II) The *hidden recordings* were gathered in the children's play environment (playground, backyard, etc.). These recordings contained no preplanned interactional, thematical or other structure.

Besides the question of whether L2 learning can be manipulated in the developmental dimension our instructional experiment also included a learning objective, which is typical for the dimension of systematic variation, in order to test the extent to which this dimension of L2 acquisition is resistant to formal instruction. For reasons of space we shall not report on this aspect here.

The Bavarian Department of Education was kind enough to support this experiment, and made it possible for our informants to be taught as a special class using the teaching material that we had developed.

The recordings are transcribed in full. Some aspects of the linguistic analysis will become clear in the following section, which summarizes the effects of the experiment on two of our informants.

3.   RESULTS

The main findings about the effect of the instruction in the experiment on Teresa's and Giovanni's interlanguages are summarized in Tables 2 and 3. In these tables the first column on the left-hand side represents the features of the acquisitional stages as presented in section 2. Tables 2 and 3 show all experimental steps in their chronological order from left to right. The resulting squares contain either an "X" for applied optional rules, or the probability of rule application for obligatory rules. If the structural description of an obligatory rule is never met in one interview (or informal conversation, etc.) or if an optional rule is never applied, the appropriate square is left blank.

As we have concentrated on INVERSION in our experiment with the developmental dimension, we have separately analyzed some pseudoapplications[5] of this rule which are reported to appear at earlier stages (see Clahsen,

TABLE 2   Teresa

	Hidden recording I	Interview I	Instruction (copula)	Interview II	Instruction (INVERSION)	Interview III
ADVERB	X	X		X		X
PARTICLE	(0.0)	0.0		0.0		0.00
INVERSION	0.0	0.0		0.0		0.83
"INVERSION"						
da is	(X)	X		X		X
was/wo is?	(X)	X		X		X
da V	(X)	(X)				

1981; Pienemann, 1981; Clahsen et al., 1983). These structures are summarized at the bottom of both tables. Table 3 also contains one additional line at the very bottom which I will refer to later on.

Table 2 shows clearly that Teresa's interlanguage is in stage 2 (adverb fronting), since adverb fronting is applied consistently in all phases of the experiment, while the obligatory rules PARTICLE and INVERSION (stages 3 and 4) are consistently applied with a zero-probability except for the last interview. As the list at the bottom of Table 2 shows, pseudoapplications of INVERSION appear throughout the whole experiment.

The crucial point in this table is the interview after the second instructional experiment, which was devoted to the instruction of INVERSION. It might really come as a surprise that the probability of application has jumped from zero to 0.83, which is an enormously high figure. At first glance this seems to confirm the above-mentioned behaviorist hypothesis that the learning of a structure is only dependent on the right input. It seems to contradict the view that structures can only be learned if the whole system is sufficiently developed, since INVERSION seems to have been learned without the prior acquisition of PARTICLE.

However, this critical figure refers to very special data: (I) One-third of the corresponding sentences consist of speech formulae which have been presented in the instructional experiment:

> (5) *was soll ich tun?* (Teresa, interview III)
> "what shall I do?"
> (6) *wie geht's?* (Teresa, interview III)
> "how goes it?" = "how are you?"

(II) All other sentences in which INVERSION is applied are *copies* of sentences which had been learned in the instructional experiment. To illustrate this point I quote two dialogue fragments from the postinstructional interview with Teresa. (Teresa and an interviewer are playing with hand puppets. Teresa is "Anna," the interviewer is "Klaus.")

> (7) Teresa: *grüß dich Klaus* "hello Klaus"
> Interv: *grüß dich anna* "hello Anna"
> Teresa: *komm du morgen zu meine geburtstag?* "come you tomorrow to my birthday?"[6]
> Interv: *du hast geburtstag* ↗ "you have birthday")

(8) Interv: *du bist anna, kommst du zu meinem geburtstag?*
"you are Anna. Come you to my birthday?"
Teresa: *ja, wann?* "yes, when?"
Interv: *ah, morgen* "ah, tomorrow"
Teresa: *komm giovanni auch?* "come Giovanni too?")

Quite obviously, Teresa's utterances in (7) and (8) are transferred from one of the dialogues which have been drilled in the instructional period. For comparison, the relevant part of this "model dialogue" from the instruction is quoted below:

(9) Anna: Grüß dich, Klaus.
Klaus: Grüß dich, Anna.
Anna: Kommst du morgen zu meinem Geburtstag?
Klaus: Oh ja! Kommt Giovanni auch?

As we can see, the first three turns in (7) are identical with the ones in (9), except for some morphological deviations in Teresa's question. As the interviewer did not know the "model dialogue," she could not follow the drilled conversation pattern in her second turn. But after some minutes of unsuccessful conversation she introduced the birthday topic again (cf. dialogue (8)), and Teresa managed to get a turn in (8) where another of the drilled patterns fits (i.e., *komm Giovanni auch?*).

As in (8), Teresa finds meaningful ways to apply the drilled patterns to other contexts (but all in situations with the same hand puppet characters centering around the topic of the "model dialogue"). But the structures of these sentences are neither lexically nor morphosyntactically varied. This is especially apparent with the morphological deviations in these sentences, which are typical for this acquisitional stage (see Pienemann, 1982b).

Thus the critical figure in the last interview does not really reflect a high probability of rule-governed application of INVERSION; it is caused by some sort of transfer of drilled structures. This assumption also seems reasonable with respect to the memory load involved in such a transfer, since the interview was conducted one day after the instruction ended.

This interpretation is strongly supported by the fact that in all other sentences of the crucial interview which are not described under (I) or (II) and which meet the structural description of INVERSION this permutation rule is *not applied*, as the following sentence demonstrates:

(10) *ja mensch, warum ø du nix gesagt von die deine mutti?*
"yes man, why you no told about your mommy?"
(Teresa, interview III)

Therefore the result of the experiment is just the contrary of what it appears to be at first glance: the instruction has *not* added a syntactic rule to Teresa's interlanguage. From this alone, of course, we cannot conclude that Teresa *could not* learn INVERSION at this point in time, because the instruction might simply have been bad. I will come back to this point later on.

TABLE 3 Giovanni

	Hidden recording I	Interview I	Instruction (copula)	Interview II	Instruction (INVERSION)	Interview III	Hidden recording II	Hidden recording III
ADVERB	X	X		X		X	X	X
PARTICLE	0.47	0.31		0.14		0.50	0.61	0.56
INVERSION	0.17	0.11		0.20		(0.67)	1.00	0.67
"INVERSION"								
da is	X	X		X		X	X	X
jez is	X						X	X
wo is?							X	X
VERB AND COMPLEMENT SEPARATED	0.00	0.00		0.00		(0.50)	0.29	0.36

The picture that emerges from Table 3 for Giovanni's interlanguage is quite different. Not only does he consistently apply ADVERB, but also PARTICLE and to some extent INVERSION. It thus seems that — according to our acquisitional criterion — he *has* already acquired INVERSION. But as the line at the very bottom of Table 3 shows, the application of this rule is restricted to structures in which the verb and its complement are not separated by the rule. These are mainly structures like (11):

(11) *morgen komm ich*
"tomorrow come I"

which can be produced by a strategy which simply brings the subject NP into final position, as suggested by Clahsen (1984). As such a strategy is already implied in PARTICLE, these structures do not involve cognitive principles which are more complex than the ones that were applied until stage 3 (PARTICLE) (see Clahsen, 1984).

The linguistic teaching objectives of the experiment, however, *do* consist of structures in which the verb and its complement are separated by the rule INVERSION. This can be seen from the following example sentences which are taken from the teaching material:

PP + V + NP$_1$ + NP$_2$

(12) *Jetzt bauen die Kinder eine Bude.*
"Now build the children a hut."
(13) *Aus Brettern machen sie Wände.*
"From boards make they walls."

WH + V + NP$_1$ + NP$_2$

(14) *Wo ißt Klaus Spaghetti?*
"Where eats Klaus spaghetti?"

The crucial question is whether Giovanni applies the INVERSION rule in such structures after they are taught. The answer to this question can be found in the line at the very bottom of Table 3, which clearly shows that the above-mentioned exclusive use of a "subject-final strategy" is in fact abandoned after the instruction. This means that after the instruction, Giovanni's interlanguage for the first time contains an operation which separates the verb from its complement, as illustrated by the following examples:

(15) *wo bring sie der säcke?*
"where bring they the sacks?"
(16) *has du noch eine bonbon?*
"have you another sweet?"
(17) *jez schreib ich hausaufgabe*
"now write I homework"
(18) *das geschenk kauf die mama*
"the present buy the mommy"

Of course, it can be argued that Giovanni's learning simply reflects his normal progress in his L2 development because he was close to the crucial stage anyway.

This interpretation, however, can be ruled out on the basis of available observational data.

First, we know from several longitudinal studies (see Clahsen, 1984; Pienemann, 1981) that the acquisition of INVERSION is a protracted process which takes months before the relative frequency of rule application develops from around 0.2 to 0.7. With Giovanni this process has taken only a few days. Certainly, this does not prove that Giovanni's learning process is not the result of natural acquisition, but it makes clear that — assuming this process to be exclusively the result of natural acquisition — it would be a rare exception to the findings about the speed of this acquisition process which we obtained from longitudinal studies.

Second, in natural acquisition INVERSION is usually not simultaneously acquired for all possible structural contexts which are preposed adverb/adverbial, preposed object NP, *wh*-questions, yes/no questions, preposed subordinate clause. Giovanni, however, immediately applies the rule to four out of five possible structural contexts (cf. sentences (15)–(18)), once the object-final strategy is abandoned. This shows that Giovanni's learning process would be an exceptional instance of natural acquisition from a structural point of view as well.

And finally, there is a third learner in our study who learned INVERSION in a manner similar to Giovanni. It would be a fairly improbable coincidence if this exceptional natural learning process should have taken place in two individuals and just at the very point in time immediately after the crucial experiment was conducted.

So we have to face the situation that in one learner the result of the experiment was positive and in the other it was negative. As we know from our observations during the instructional period, this is not due to Teresa's poor learning; she actively participated in the lessons and passed all learning checks. This is supported by the stereotype application of learned patterns outside of the classroom.

But despite Teresa's good learning results, one might still argue that her interlanguage could not be advanced to include INVERSION because the instruction was inadequate. However, the instruction was adequate for Giovanni. Thus we have to state that the same instruction can influence the natural acquisition process in one learner but fail to do so in another. As both learners were exposed to the same experimental input (same class, same time, same teacher, etc.), the negative result with Teresa cannot be due to learner-*external* factors.

Therefore the consistent conclusion from our findings is that the unequal effect of the instruction on the two learners is due to learner-*internal* factors. The most apparent internal difference between our informants is the acquisitional stage of their L2's. My hypothesis, which will be explained in more detail in the following section, is aimed at exactly this difference: it says that an L2 structure can be learned by instruction only if the learner's interlanguage is close to the point when this structure is acquired in the natural setting.

From this perspective one can easily agree with the view that the same input may have an effect on one learner but not on the other, because one learner may already have acquired the prerequisites for the corresponding learning process while the other has not.

4.   THE TEACHABILITY HYPOTHESIS

The analysis in the preceding section has shown that a given linguistic structure cannot be added through instruction to the learner's interlanguage at any desired point in time in his/her acquisitional career. Rather, the influence of formal instruction is constrained in a specific way: for instance, INVERSION, which is acquired later than PARTICLE, cannot be learned by any means without prior learning/acquisition of the developmentally earlier structure (PARTICLE).

In this section I will outline an explanation of the constrained effect of formal instruction on L2 acquisition. What has to be explained is a learning process. Therefore, the explanation has to be aimed at psychological plausibility.[7] In order to attain this goal I will base my considerations on an explanation of acquisitional processes which is based on a psychologically plausible model of sentence processing.

The approach to explaining L2 acquisition to which I refer has been worked out by the ZISA research group in various publications (see Clahsen, 1978, 1980, 1982, 1984; Clahsen, Meisel, and Pienemann, 1983; Meisel, 1980; Meisel, Clahsen, and Pienemann, 1981). It relies on a model of sentence processing developed by Bever (1970), Fodor, Bever, and Garrett (1974), Bever and Townsend (1979), and Forster (1979). For the purpose of this paper it is necessary to sketch this position briefly.

The model of sentence processing which I mentioned above allows for two different ways of mapping configurations of the underlying structure onto surface forms: (I) through an autonomous linguistic level of processing containing a grammatical processor which is task-specific, and (II) through an additional problem-solving component (GPS) which is not task-specific. This has two important implications:

(a) The strategies which are contained in the GPS "allow *direct* mappings between underlying structure and surface forms thus short-circuiting the grammatical processor" (Clahsen, this volume, my emphasis, MP).

(b) As the GPS is not task-specific, "certain (complex) linguistic structures cannot be processed by the strategies of the GPS" (Clahsen, this volume).

Here we have to consider that it is a general finding of research on sentence comprehension and production that processing capacity – in syntax – "results from reorderings and restructurings of various levels of underlying linguistic units" (Clahsen, ibid.). Therefore, researchers working in this framework conclude that the strategies of the GPS require less processing capacity than grammatical procedures. Against this background the authors cited above assume – in one way or another – a developmental principle which predicts that "rules which require a high degree of processing capacity are acquired late" (Clahsen, ibid.).

Within this framework, Clahsen (1984) has proposed a set of processing strategies which are based on the findings from the above (empirical) research on sentence processing which allow precise predictions about the order of acquisition of L2 structures. The basic idea of this approach is a consistent application of what has been outlined so far: since GPS strategies require less processing capacity than grammatical operations, the learner will first produce structures which conform to these strategies. Among the grammatical processes, those which require the least processing capacity will be acquired first. Clahsen establishes a hierarchy of processing complexity for a number of structures deriving from the number of strategies violated when producing these structures and from the memory load involved in the grammatical operations. His predictions turned out to be correct in longitudinal and cross-sectional studies.

For the purpose of the present study, I quote those of Clahsen's strategies which explain the order of acquisition of the structures which are relevant in our study (i.e., ADVERB, PARTICLE and INVERSION):

(1) *Canonical Order Strategy (COS)*
in underlying sequences
$$[x_1 + x_2 \ldots x_n] \, c_x[\quad]c_{x+1} \cdots [\quad]c_{x+m}$$

in which each subconstituent $x_1, x_2 \ldots x_n$ contributes information to the internal structure of . . . C_x, no subconstituent is moved out of C_x, and no material from the subsequent constituents $C_{x+1}, C_{x+2} \ldots C_{x+m}$ is moved into C_x. (Clahsen, 1984:221)

(2) *Initialization/Finalization Strategy (IFS)*
In underlying sequences $[X \, Y \, Z]_s$ permutations are blocked which move X between Y and Z and/or Z between X and Y. (Clahsen, 1984:222)

Leaving aside the other evidence for these strategies quoted in the literature mentioned above, I briefly want to mention that strategy (2) is supported by investigations of mnemonics, which found that elements in the final and initial position in a sentence can be memorized best (see Neisser, 1967).

If we now compare strategies (1) and (2) with the three acquisitional stages ADVERB, PARTICLE and INVERSION, which are essential in this context (cf. section 2 of this paper), it is apparent that ADVERB requires the lowest degree of processing capacity because it is in line with both strategies as the following drawing indicates:

NP + V + X + $\boxed{\text{PP}}$[8]

The rule PARTICLE can be illustrated as follows:[9]

NP + $\left\{ \begin{array}{c} \text{Aux} \\ \text{Mod} \end{array} \right\}$ V + X

As this illustration shows, this rule violates strategy (1). The same is true for INVERSION:[10]

$$X + NP + [V + NP]_{VP} \; Y$$

The crucial difference between the last two rules is that PARTICLE moves an element into the salient final position, a permutation which is *not blocked* by strategy (2). INVERSION, however, *does* violate strategy (2) and thus requires the highest processing capacity of the three rules.

Thus, what PARTICLE and INVERSION have in common is that they represent grammatical procedures which interrupt basic linguistic units and thus violate strategy (1). They differ in that PARTICLE moves the crucial element into an "easier" position than INVERSION does. As the procedures underlying PARTICLE require the same processing prerequisite as one of the crucial procedures underlying INVERSION (namely the ability to interrupt basic linguistic units), the learner has already acquired one necessary processing prerequisite for INVERSION at the stage PARTICLE, while the order (moving the verb into a less salient position) still has to be acquired.

This explains why it is not possible to reverse the order of acquisition of these two rules or to skip PARTICLE; as one of the processing prerequisites for INVERSION is also the prerequisite for PARTICLE, the learner would automatically be in a position to process PARTICLE as soon as he/she could handle the procedures underlying INVERSION. Thus INVERSION cannot be taught without simultaneously introducing the crucial processing prerequisite for PARTICLE.

Furthermore, the processing prerequisites underlying INVERSION cannot be learned in any desired order, since violating strategy (2) presupposes that (1) can be violated, too, because moving the verb into an internal position (=2) requires (in the case under discussion) that basic units be interrupted (=1). For this reason the interruption of basic units must be learned first.

If we assume that the L2 learner has to abandon the strategies in successive steps, Giovanni was optimally equipped for the learning of INVERSION, since he already had command of the processing prerequisite to be learned first, whereas Teresa would have had to learn both prerequisites during the experiment.

Teresa would have been best equipped for the learning of processes which violate only strategy (1) but not (2) (like PARTICLE or the above-mentioned subject-final strategy) at the actual stage of her interlanguage during the experiment (=ADVERB), because she could only produce structures which conform to both strategies. The instruction did not bring about such learning, however, because it concentrated on INVERSION, thus demanding a procedure which violates both strategies simultaneously.

Such a prediction of the point in the L2 development when PARTICLE can be learned best through instruction is exactly in line with the central hypothesis of this paper. This says that an L2 structure can only be learned through instruction if the learner's language is close to the point when this structure is acquired in the natural setting; and Teresa's interlanguage in fact was at the stage prior to PARTICLE.

In this section we have so far been dealing with the theoretical explanation of one special instance of this general hypothesis concerning the learning of IN-VERSION. The above prediction is another concrete case within our hypothesis concerning the learning of PARTICLE that deserves to be justified theoretically. This is outlined below.

The processing procedures underlying PARTICLE contain a processing prerequisite for the subsequent stage. This also holds for ADVERB and PARTI-CLE: it is characteristic of PARTICLE that it violates the Canonical Order Strategy. Logically, before this strategy can be violated in a systematic way, the learner must have made a hypothesis about the underlying word order of the L2. As Meisel (1980) and Clahsen, Meisel, and Pienemann (1983) show, learners from Romance languages do so by transferring the underlying SVO order of their first language. This process of nonsurface transfer can be witnessed at the two initial acquisitional stages which precede PARTICLE: the learners start out with an exceptionally strict SVO order (see Clahsen, 1982, 1984; Clahsen, Meisel, and Pienemann, 1983; Pienemann, 1981). This initial word order in the acquisition of German as L2, which conforms to both of the above strategies, is characteristic of the two stages preceding PARTICLE.

The processing procedure underlying PARTICLE (moving the uninflected part of a complex verbal group into final position) only functions on the basis of the learner's initial hypothesis about the word order of the L2. If the learner was to start out with an underlying SOV order, he/she would have to produce rather different processing procedures since in this case for the same surface structure (e.g., NP + Aux + NP + V) the inflected part of the verbal group would have to be moved into sentence internal position, a procedure which violates both of the above processing strategies. From this we can conclude that the acquisition of word order rules would be structured quite differently if the learner were to start out with an SOV hypothesis. This is in fact the case in the acquisition of German as L1. Here the learner starts out with an underlying SOV order and thus acquires the separation of discontinuous elements (PARTICLE) and INVERSION at the same stage (see Clahsen, 1982). The reason for this is that on the basis of this underlying word order, both operations require the same degree of processing complexity because, in both cases, the finite verbal element has to be moved into sentence internal position, which violates both of the above strategies.

So far we have been dealing with three acquisitional stages which are represented by three permutation rules of German. I have given empirical and theoretical evidence for these acquisitional stages which makes the teachability hypothesis that is behind this paper explicit. Thus, up to this point in our argumentation, our hypothesis has been operationalized on the basis of some specific acquisitional stages. If we want to generalize this hypothesis and at the same time have it testable in structural domains other than the ones investigated, it is necessary to clarify which device will be used to measure the learner's development in his/her L2.

I shall base the teachability hypothesis on the levels of processing capacity rather than on specific linguistic structures which appear in certain acquisitional sequences. The reason for this is the following: if the hypothesis were related to surface phenomena such as acquisitional sequences, we would not automatically be justified in assuming that, for any acquisitional sequence, the inherent stages are always interrelated in such a way that a given stage contains processing prerequisites for the following stage. Rather, it is necessary to prove that the stages are interrelated in the way outlined above separately for each acquisitional sequence to which the hypothesis is applied. Since such a proof – within the framework we have relied on so far – would have to be based on the processing complexity that the corresponding structures involve, I decided to base my hypothesis directly on this abstract level. As the overall pattern of levels of processing complexity could be shown to underlie quite a number of further acquisitional sequences (see below), this can be regarded as a reliable basis for generalizing the hypothesis.

From the approach outlined above, Clahsen (1984) infers three levels of processing complexity which the learner has to overcome successively when acquiring the word order rules of German main clauses:

I.   the learner conforms to both of the above strategies
II.   the learner violates the COS but not the IFS
III. the learner violates the COS and the IFS.

In this abstract formulation it is apparent that at each stage a necessary prerequisite for the following stage is developed: in order to conform to the COS the learner is forced to establish a fixed word order (=stage I). This is the prerequisite for any type of systematic violation of this order which appears at stage II. The interaction between stages II and III is obvious, since the violation of the COS is the prerequisite for the simultaneous violation of both strategies (for the interrelation between the COS and IFS see above).

So, the fact that at each stage prerequisites for the subsequent stage are developed is not an incidental feature of the structures investigated above, but is brought about by the learner who successively overcomes the processing restrictions represented in the stages I to III. This view is strongly supported by the fact that the above stages of processing complexity are also the underlying pattern in the acquisition of quite a number of other permutation rules. Figure 2 summarizes these rules in their order of acquisition from the top to the bottom. ADVERB, PARTICLE and INVERSION have been mentioned before. SVO refers to the canonical order of the first stage.[11] ADV-VP refers to an optional permutation which moves a PP into a position to the right of the finite verbal element. TOPI stands for another optional permutation which moves an object NP

Stages	V	PP	NP	Neg
I	SVO	ADVERB	—	Neg + V
II	PARTICLE	—	TOPI	Neg-END
III	INVERSION	ADV-VP	—	—

FIGURE 2

into initial position. Neg + V is an "unacceptable" interlanguage structure in German. The other Neg rule moves Neg into final position.[12] (For detailed information, see Clahsen, 1982, 1984; Meisel, 1980; Clahsen, Meisel, and Pienemann, 1983.)

For the acquisition of the rules listed in Figure 2, Clahsen (1984) has shown the following: (a) all rules at stage I conform to both of the above strategies; (b) the rules at stage II violate the COS but not the IFS; (c) all rules at stage II violate both strategies.

Now recall that in the INVERSION case, our argument was that Giovanni was able to learn INVERSION because he already had command of prerequisites for processing this structure which Teresa did not have as a learner from the ADVERB stage. As processing prerequisites for the subsequent stage are developed at each of the stages I to III, our initial line of argumentation can be applied to all structures represented in Table 2. Thus we can predict that a learner at one of the stages I to III can, through instruction, learn only those structures which are in line with the restrictions of the following stage. Therefore Figure 2 represents a broad basis for testing our hypothesis.

Besides the evidence I have presented for the formal learning of INVERSION, there are some further pieces of empirical evidence in our data which favor this hypothesis.

The first type of additional evidence concerns the structure of our informants' interlanguage. If the idea underlying Figure 2 is correct, we should find that Teresa has not acquired any of the structures from stage II or III but only structures from stage I, since we argued that her interlanguage conforms to the restrictions of stage I. This is exactly what we find in the analysis of her interlanguage: as mentioned before, PARTICLE is not applied although she produces contexts for application (cf. Table 2) and INVERSION is not actively applied. Apart from this, the only other rule which appears is Neg + V as the following example sentences illustrate:

(19) *ich nicht spreche* (Teresa)
   "I not speak"
(20) *du nix essen die mann* (Teresa)
   "you not eat the man"
(21) *die kinder nix komm* (Teresa)
   "the children no come"

According to Figure 2, this is precisely the type of negation structures which must be expected at stage I for sentence negation.

Parallel to Teresa, we would predict Giovanni's interlanguage to have the following features before the instructional experiment: PARTICLE, TOPI and Neg-END *but not* INVERSION and ADV-VP. As has been shown in section 3, this prediction is correct for PARTICLE and INVERSION. The following example sentences indicate that this is also correct for TOPI, as in sentence (22), and Neg-END, as in sentences (23) and (24):

(22) *der große bälle er hat gemacht* (Giovanni, interview II)
    "the big balls he has made"
(23) *der schulbus is nich gekommen* (Giovanni, interview II)
    "the school bus has not come"
(24) *der kann nich sprechen* (Giovanni, interview II)
    "he cannot speak"

As ADV-VP is an optional rule, we cannot rely on obligatory contexts to detect whether this rule is definitely acquired or not. But, since there is no instance of a sentence-internal position of a prepositional phrase throughout all the interviews before the crucial instruction, we can safely conclude that this rule is not acquired before this decisive point in time.

This brings us to the other type of evidence for our hypothesis concerning the development of Giovanni's interlanguage: as Giovanni proceeded from stage II to III, the application of ADV-VP should no longer be blocked. In fact, there are some instances which indicate that Giovanni starts to apply ADV-VP from the fifth recording on. Two examples are given below:

(25) *ich kann schon trinken* (Giovanni, interview V)
    "I can already drink"
(26) *der is da oben verstecken* (Giovanni, interview V)
    "it/he is up there hidden"

As the prepositional phrases which appear to the right of the finite verbal element in Giovanni's interlanguage are restricted to short adverbs and as the number of such instances is rather small in a considerable corpus, we may assume that the acquisition of ADV-VP is at its very beginning (see Clahsen, Meisel, and Pienemann, 1983).

So the prediction that ADV-VP can be acquired once a learner has proceeded to stage III can roughly be verified. However, the question of whether the acquisition/learning of these rudiments of ADV-VP is a result of the instruction or of natural acquisition remains unanswered. Probably this cannot definitely be answered on the basis of the available evidence, but I would like to give the following tentative interpretation: The instruction had the effect that the processing restrictions of stage II could be overcome. For the acquisition of ADV-VP, however, the learner needed some evidence that such a structure exists in his target language. Since this evidence was not provided in a systematic way in the instruction, the learner must have drawn it from some natural input to which he was exposed. In order to gain further evidence, the teachability hypothesis will have to be tested with other structures in an experimental setting.

In summary, in this section I have given a theoretical explanation for the observation we made in the preceding section: in the mixed setting of natural and formal L2 acquisition a certain linguistic structure (INVERSION) could be added to the interlanguage by formal instruction only if the learner was close to the point when this structure was acquired in a natural setting. On the basis of studies of sentence processing, I have shown that the learner at the lower stage (ADVERB) has to learn/acquire the processing prerequisites for the stage prior to INVERSION before he/she can process the crucial operation underlying INVERSION.

Since these teachability constraints on INVERSION could be explained on the basis of the processing restrictions being abandoned successively during the acquisition process, our teachability hypothesis was generalized on the basis of the levels of processing complexity underlying a number of acquisitional sequences; thus, it is testable for further structures. This operationalized formulation of our hypothesis was supported by some additional evidence from the data discussed in this paper.

5. DISCUSSION

In this section I will discuss some issues concerning the teachability hypothesis developed above which deserve further clarification. Let us first return to the study's initial question, namely whether or not natural L2 acquisition can be influenced by formal instruction.

In earlier studies this question has been investigated from different theoretical positions which presuppose different ways of interpreting it (cf. section 1). We have to indicate which interpretation we adopt, because in this broad formulation the question cannot be answered unequivocally from our data, which contain both positive and negative results.

As the teachability hypothesis underlying this study is a special instance of the view that all kinds of language development are dependent on a set of shared principles, the study is based on a special interpretation of the above question — namely, whether the process of natural acquisition can be *altered* by instruction. This should not be misinterpreted as a merely technical question since the order of acquisition is the surface manifestation of underlying acquisition principles. Therefore, if it is impossible to alter this order, we may conclude that instruction cannot influence the underlying acquisition process.

Judging from the findings of our experiment, the answer to this specific formulation of the question is definitely negative; although a structure from stage x can successfully be instructed at stage x-2, thus seemingly short-cutting the "natural" order of acquisition, this learning cannot result in actual use of the structure in normal speech (inside or outside the classroom) since processing it is not possible on the basis of the procedures available to the learner at this point in the development. This point is clearly illustrated by Teresa's nonacquisition of INVERSION at the stage ADVERB despite successful instruction.

Thus, the teachability hypothesis negatively constrains the possible influence of instruction on the acquisition process. However, this negative constraint does not imply that formal instruction has no influence on acquisition whatsoever; as was indicated in section 3, instruction can improve acquisition with respect to (a) the speed of acquisition, (b) the frequency of rule application and (c) the different contexts in which the rule has to be applied, *if* the interlanguage development fulfills the requirements for such an influence.

This, of course, only goes part way towards answering the above question because many resulting questions have remained unanswered; above all how the (conscious or unconscious) knowledge given in the instruction is transmitted to the language processing system. This transmission of knowledge is in fact implicitly one of the main issues of theories of language teaching, and there is a long tradition of competition between the different methods of transmission, which we know as foreign language teaching methods.

A crucial assumption underlying all these methods is that language is teachable and that linguistic structures can be taught in many different orders, the most optimal of which has to be selected from a didactic perspective. In the past this assumption has naively been deduced from different learning theories which were not specifically based on the learning/acquisition of language (see Vogel and Vogel, 1975). Our findings as well as other studies (see Felix, 1981; Felix and Simmet, 1982; Hahn, 1983) have provided strong counterevidence against this assumption. Therefore, language teaching methods of every different kind should be closely re-examined for psychological validity.

However, our hypothesis itself does not imply an alternative suggestion for an optimal teaching method, the obvious reason being that it only negatively defines the margin within which instruction in whatever method may have an effect. In order to develop psycholinguistically founded language teaching methods, it will be necessary to more closely investigate the process of transmission of rational knowledge to the unconscious system of language processing.

The second issue concerns the explanation of the teachability constraints described above. The teachability hypothesis is based on the processing prerequisites for the structure which has to be learned. From this perspective we can decide whether the speaker of a certain interlanguage is prepared for the learning of a given structure or not.

Within Krashen's (1981, 1982) theory, there is a hypothesis which implies a similar prediction about what can be taught to learners of a second language. In the following paragraphs I will demonstrate that the two hypotheses are based on different theoretical assumptions which are not compatible.

Krashen's hypothesis is based on the claim that "children progress [in their language development] by *understanding* language that is a little beyond them" (Krashen, 1981:126). This is known as the "$i+1$ hypothesis," "i" representing the actual stage of acquisition and "1" indicating the subsequent step of acquisition. According to Krashen, the child can understand the crucial new items from $i+1$ with the aid of context. From this, Krashen concludes that formal instruction can influence (in the sense of support/promote) L2 acquisition if it contains comprehensible input.

So, like the teachability hypothesis, this approach predicts that at a stage i, elements from $i+1$ can be learned best. The $i+1$ hypothesis, however, is less specific in its scope, since it does not imply that *no elements other than those from $i+1$ can be learned at stage i* and transmitted to the acquired system. Thus it does not address the question whether the process of L2 acquisition can be steered by formal instruction, which is the main concern of the teachability hypothesis.

In Krashen's work, the $i+1$ hypothesis is a central part of the definition of the requirements for formal input to be "optimal": in order to promote language acquisition, formal instruction has to provide input containing $i+1$.

This is not the place to discuss the $i+1$ approach from a teaching point of view (for discussion see Pienemann, forthcoming). Rather, I will concentrate on the crucial psycholinguistic assumption on which it is built. This is the assumption that "children progress by *understanding* language that is a little beyond them" (Krashen, 1981:126), "where 'understand' means that the acquirer is focused on the meaning and not on the form of the message" (Krashen, 1982:21).

Bearing in mind that the $i+1$ hypothesis is at the core of Krashen's theory, from which he derives far-reaching conclusions for formal instruction, it is only very vaguely based on empirical research:

(a) The $i+1$ hypothesis cannot be operationalized or tested, since i, $i+1$, etc., are not defined in Krashen's work at all.

(b) The claim that input containing $i+1$ promotes language acquisition is derived from the assumed learning-aid effect of tuned input to the language learning child. It is, however, questionable whether caretaker talk – not to mention natural L2 input – is in fact tuned to the level of the child's L2 production. Krashen writes that "we see positive, but not strikingly high correlations between linguistic input complexity and linguistic competence in children (Newport, Gleitman, and Gleitman, 1977; Cross, 1977)" (Krashen, 1981:102). However, these positive correlations which are listed in Krashen's book (1981: 126) are selected from a larger number of almost equally distributed *negative and positive* (or zero) correlations in the above author's studies.

(c) There is not much research into the interaction between comprehension and production in L2 acquisition (or in language acquisition in general) which is based on longitudinal comparative studies, but existing findings strongly contradict Krashen's acquisition-by-understanding claim, since comprehension and production were found to develop not as mirror images of each other but as separate abilities (see, e.g., Bever, 1981; Bloom and Lahey, 1978).

Not only may the gap between comprehension and production be more than one acquisitional stage, but there is strong evidence that the interaction between the two sides of language processing does not necessarily have to be such that comprehension precedes production. Rather, it is possible that children *produce* items first and only in a later stage understand them (see Bloom and Lahey, 1978).

Besides this, in Krashen's hypothesis the role of nonlinguistic factors in comprehension is seen as a static one, adding the specific information of $i+1$ to the learner. However, the nonlinguistic factors which contribute to producing and understanding messages play significantly different roles in the two processes and undergo several changes during acquisition (see also Schöler, 1982; Strohner and Nelson, 1974).

As a final issue, I want to touch briefly upon what implications our findings have for the theory of foreign language instruction. I will deal with this matter more explicitly in a forthcoming paper.

The results I presented above very clearly demonstrate what has been claimed by universalist researchers before (see Hahn, 1982; Felix, 1981; Wode, 1981): If formal input is constructed in contradiction to natural sequences, it impedes rather than promotes language acquisition. There are two obvious though opposite conclusions which have been drawn from this finding. One is that the formal instruction of syntax can be abandoned since the child's language acquisition is self-regulating anyway (Dulay and Burt, 1973). The other is that formal input should be presented in the natural order of acquisition (see Krashen, Bailey, and Madden, 1975).

Both proposals are short-sighted. Giving up the instruction of syntax is to allow for the fossilization of interlanguages in a simplified form (see Pienemann, 1978). Such fossilization often appears with natural L2 acquisition in minority groups (see Meisel, Clahsen, and Pienemann, 1981). Of course, it is unclear whether fossilization can be avoided by instruction, but abandoning the instruction of syntax at this point in time is not to care about how this question can be solved.

Teaching syntax along the line of the natural order seems to imply that markedly deviant transitional structures like ADVERB without INVERSION have to be taught, too. At the present time it is simply unknown what effect such a procedure would have on language acquisition. Of course, this problem could be solved without intricate teaching experiments, if it is possible to base the structure of formal input on the natural order in such a way that teaching deviant forms can be avoided. But this, too, is an unsolved problem. Additionally, if it is intended that teaching be based on the process of natural language acquisition, one must take into account the fact that learning problems, which appear at a given acquisitional stage, can be solved in different structural ways ranging between "deviant" and standard oriented – depending on the learner type (see Mciscl, Clahscn, and Pienemann, 1981; Pienemann, 1981). Thus one must decide which of the transitional solutions to learning tasks should be adopted for instruction. This brings us to another problem, namely whether the different types of transitional solutions, which are bound to specific learner types, can be manipulated by instruction aiming at efficiency, nondeviant competence, etc.

These remarks are intended to illustrate that applying L2 research is not just writing acquisitional orders into new curricula. Solving a number of severe and psycholinguistically relevant problems is a necessary part of application.

Besides this, it seems evident to me that a concrete proposal for application has to be embedded in some approach to language teaching. However, I think a "psycholinguistic method" of L2 instruction is far out of reach. After the waves of "direct method," "language lab," etc., the teacher should be spared another "instant application." For the development of instructional methods which go beyond cookbook recipe status, problems remain to be solved whose outlines we may only just have discerned.

NOTES

1. This research was supported from many sides. My thanks go to the Bavarian Department of Education for the permission to conduct the experiment, to the Institute of German as a Second Language at the University of Munich for their invaluable support, and to the University of Passau for the use of facilities in the analysis of data. Invaluable comments on ideas and on an earlier version of this paper came from Harald Clahsen, Rainer Dietrich, Sascha Felix, Kenneth Hyltenstam, Jürgen Meisel and Howard Nicholas. This work could not have been produced without the patient constructive support from my colleague Angela Hahn. My thanks also go to Claudia Wimmer and Jan Wilts who have spent a lot of time on organizing, transcribing and analyzing, not to forget Martin Fee, John Halliday and Michael Knight for lending me their native speaker competence.

2. T. Pica's (1982) recent work, which was not available at the time I wrote this paper, is in fact a comparison of acquisitional sequences in both types of acquisition (M. Long, personal communication). The bibliography includes references to her work which I received after the manuscript was finished.

3. All example sentences are taken from Pienemann (1980, 1981).

4. The reader might at first glance wonder why the experiment was restricted to 10 informants. There are some obvious reasons for this restriction: (I) the number of children who fulfilled the linguistic requirements for the experiment (interlanguage below INVERSION *and* representation of different learner types in the experiment – see below) was relatively small. (II) The somewhat elaborate practical organization of the experiment with its various, temporally coordinated investigational steps did not – with the available financial resources – permit a more broadly-based study. (III) Apart from the 100 interviews for the selection of informants, the data base of a study of this type with 10 informants is equivalent to about 50 hours of recorded speech.

5. The term "pseudoapplication" is used in this context to indicate that, on the one hand, the corresponding structures (e.g. *da* is x "there is x" cf. Table 2) can formally be treated as instances of INVERSION because (I) they meet the structural description for this rule (in the *"da is x"* example especially the preposed adverb is a structural prerequisite for INVERSION) and (II) the verb appears in second position – the standard German position. On the other hand, these structures appear to represent a structural formula *(da is a, da is b, etc.)* at a point in the acquisition of German as L2 when the verb (also "be") remains constantly in its underlying position, as illustrated by example sentence (2) in section 3 (see Pienemann, 1981). Therefore, it has been argued elsewhere (see Clahsen, Meisel, and Pienemann, 1983; Pienemann, 1981) that these structures are not the result of the same interlanguage operations as sentences with INVERSION.

6. As indicated in section 2 the German example sentences are *translated literally* into English in order to demonstrate the word order phenomena of the interlanguage examples. Of course, these "translations" in some cases violate rules of English syntax (as can be seen from the unacceptable word order and missing do-insertion in this example). These translations should be interpreted on the basis of the required word order rules of German explained in section 2.

7. The term "psychological plausibility" is used here in order to indicate that the explanations of learning processes we would like to provide should be based on linguistic operations which do not contradict psycholinguistic findings about the mental processes involved in language process-

ing. This does not imply, however, that the operations discussed below have been proved to be mentally *real* (see Clahsen, Meisel, and Pienemann 1983).

8. All the following descriptions are based on an underlying SVO order for the interlanguages being described. This assumption for the underlying word order is justified in some detail in Clahsen (1983). The main point of this argument is that (a) there is no evidence for SOV order in the data (i.e. all interlanguages conform to an SVO order in the initial stages), (b) that it is plausible to assume some sort of transfer for this initial word order, since the L1's of the corresponding learners are Romance languages which follow an underlying SVO order.

9. This is only part of the structural descriptions of the rule, which can also be applied to separable verbs.

10. This illustration, too, refers to only one of the possible structures to which the rule applies.

11. In Figure 2 ADVERB and SVO appear at the same stage, although these structures are acquired successively by child learners (see Pienemann 1981). The reason for this way of presenting stages of acquisition is that the structuring principle in Figure 2 is not the pure temporal order of acquisition alone but primarily the processing complexity involved in these structures as measured in the way outlined above. Therefore, Figure 2 does not say anything about the temporal relation between the structure at each stage. But, of course, it implies that all structures at stage I are acquired before the structures at stage II which are in turn acquired before the structures at stage III.

12. Note that in sentences in which Neg-END is applied, the negating element does not necessarily have to appear in final position since there are other permutations which may be applied after Neg-END and which also move an element into final position (e.g., PARTICLE, as indicated by example sentence (23)) (see Clahsen, Meisel, and Pienemann, 1983:121ff.).

REFERENCES

Andersen, R. W. (ed.). 1983. *Pidginization and Creolization as Language Acquisition*. Rowley, Mass.: Newbury House.

Berman, R. This volume. cognitive components of language development.

Bever, T. 1970. The cognitive basis for linguistic structures. In J. R. Hayes (ed.), pp. 279-362.

Bever, T. 1981. Normal acquisition processes explain the critical period for language learning. In K. C. Diller (ed.), pp. 176-198.

Bever, T. and D. Townsend. 1979. Perceptual mechanisms and formal properties of main and subordinate clauses. In W. Cooper and E. Walker (eds.), pp. 159-226.

Bloom, L. and M. Lahey, 1978. *Language Development and Language Disorders*. New York: Wiley & Sons.

Burt, M., and H. Dulay (eds.). 1975. *Second Language Learning, Teaching and Bilingual Education*. Washington: TESOL.

Clahsen, H. 1978. Syntax oder Produktionsstrategien? Zum natürlichen Zweitspracherwerb der Gastarbeiter. In R. Kloepfer et al. (eds.), pp. 343-354.

Clahsen, H. 1980. Psycholinguistic aspects of L2 acquisition: word order phenomena in foreign workers' interlanguage. In S. W. Felix (ed.), pp. 57-79.

Clahsen, H. 1982. *Spracherwerb in der Kindheit. Eine Untersuchung zur Entwicklung der Syntax der Kindheit*. Tübingen: Gunter Narr Verlag.

Clahsen, H. 1984. The acquisition of German word order: A test case for cognitive approaches to L2 development. In R. W. Andersen (ed.), *Second Languages: A Cross-Linguistic Perspective*. Rowley, Mass.: Newbury House, pp. 219-242.

Clahsen, H. This volume. Connecting theories of language processing and (second) language acquisition.

Clahsen, H., J. M. Meisel, and M. Pienemann. 1983. *Deutsch als Zweitsprache. Der Spracherwerb ausländischer Arbeiter*. Tübingen: Gunter Narr Verlag.

Cooper. W., and E. Walker (eds.) 1979. *Sentence Processing: Psycholinguistic Studies Presented to Merrill Garrett.* New York.

Cross, T. 1977. Mother's speech adjustments: The contribution of selected child listener variables. In C. Snow and C. Ferguson (eds.), pp. 151-188.

Dietrich, R. T. Kaufmann, and G. Storch. 1979. Beobachtungen zum gesteuerten Fremdsprachenerwerb. *Linguistische Berichte* 64, 56-81.

Diller, K. C. (ed.). 1981. *Individual Differences and Universals in Language Learning Aptitude,* Rowley, Mass.: Newbury House.

Dulay, H., and M. Burt, 1973. Should we teach children syntax? *Language Learning* 23:235-252.

Felix, S. W. 1978. Zur Relation zwischen natürlichem und gesteuertem Zweitsprachenerwerb. In R. Kloepfer et al. (eds.), pp. 355-370.

Felix, S. W. (ed.). 1980. *Second Langauge Development: Trends and Issues.* Tübingen: Gunter Narr Verlag.

Felix, S. W. 1981. The effect of formal instruction on second language acquisition. *Language Learning,* 3.87-112.

Felix, S. W. 1982. *Psycholinguistiche Aspekte des Zweitsprachenerwerbs.* Tübingen: Gunter Narr Verlag.

Felix, S. W., and A. Simmet. 1981. Der Erwerb der Personalpronomina im Fremdsprachenunberricht. *Neusprachliche Mitteilungen.* 3.132-144.

Felix, S. W., and H. Wode (eds.). 1983. *Language Development at the Cross Roads: Papers from the Interdisciplinary Conference on Language Acquisition at Passau.* Tübingen: Gunter Narr Verlag.

Ferguson, C. A., and D. I. Slobin (eds.). 1973. *Studies of Child Language Development.* New York: Holt, Rinehart and Winston.

Fodor, J. A., T. Bever, and M. Garrett. 1974. *The Psychology of Language: An Introduction to Psycholinguistics and Generative Grammar.* New York: McGraw-Hill.

Forster, K. I. 1979. Levels of processing and the structure of the language processor. In Cooper and Walker (eds.). pp. 27-85.

Hahn, A. 1982. Fremdsprachenenunterricht und Spracherwerb. Linguistiche Untersuchungen zum gesteuerten Zweitsprachenerwerb. Ph.D. dissertation, University of Passau.

Hayes, J. R. (ed.). 1970. *Cognition and the Development of Language.* New York: John Wiley and Sons.

Heuer, H. 1976. *Lerntheorie des Englischunterrichts Untersuchunger zur Analyse fremdsprachlicher Lernprozesse.* Heidelberg: Quelle & Meyer.

Hüllen, W., and L. Jung. 1980. *Sprachstruktur und Spracherwerb. Tübingen: A. Francke.*

Jungblut, G. 1974. Terminologie der Lehr-und lernphasen im Fremdsprachenunterricht: *Linuistik und Didaktik.* 17.33-41.

Kloepfer, R. et al. (ed.). 1979. *Bildung und Ausbildung in der Romania.* Vol. II München: Fink.

Krashen, S. 1981. *Second Language Acquisition and Second Language Learning.* Oxford: Pergamon.

Krashen, S. 1982. *Principles and Practice in Second Language Acquisition.* Oxford: Pergamon.

Krashen, S., C. Madden, and Bailey. 1975. Theoretical aspects of grammatical sequencing. In M. Burt and H. Dulay (eds.). pp. 44-54.

Lightbown, P. 1983. Exploring relationships between developmental and instructional sequences in L2 acquisition. In H. Seliger and M. Long (eds.).

Lightbown, P. This volume. Classroom language as input to second language acquisition.

Long, M. 1982. Does second language instruction make a difference: A review of research. Paper presented at the TESOL Research Committee's state-of-the-art session, TESOL Convention, Honolulu, May 1982.

Meisel, J. M. 1983. Strategies of second language acquisition: More than one kind of simplification. In R. W. Andersen (ed.). pp. 120-157.

Meisel, J. M., H. Clahsen, and M. Pienemann. 1981. On determining developmental stages in natural second language acquisition. *Studies in Second Language Acquisition* 3.109-135.

Newport, E., H. Gleitman, and L. Gleitman. 1977. Mother, I'd rather do it myself: Some effects and non-effects of maternal speech style. In C. Snow and C. Ferguson (eds.). pp. 109-149.

Neisser, U. 1967. *Cognitive Psychology.* New York: Appleton.

Pica, T. 1982a. The role of linguistic environment in second language acquisition of the English indefinitive article. MS. University of Pennsylvania.

Pica, T. 1982b. Adult acquisition of English as a second language in different language contexts. MS, University of Pennsylvania.

Pienemann, M. 1979. Erwerbssequenzen und Lernprogression. Überlegungen zur Steurung des Zweitspracherwerbs. In R. Kloepfer et al (eds.). pp. 397-416.

Pienemann, M. 1980. The second language acquisition of immigrant children. In S. W. Felix (ed.). pp. 41-46.

Pienemann. M. 1981. *Der Zweitspracherwerb ausländischer Arbeiterkinder.* Bonn: Bouvier.

Pienemann, M. 1982a. Untersuchungen zur Syncronisierung von natürlichem und gesteuertem Zweitspracherwerb-Projektbeschreibung Deutsch lernen 1.81-87.

Pienemann, M. 1982b. Toward the critical period hypothesis for L2 acquisition. Comparing child and adult acquisition processes. MS University of Passau.

Pienemann, M. Forthcoming. Synchronizing natural and formal L2 acquisition.

Schöler, H. 1982. *Zur Entwicklung des Verstehens inkonsistenter außerungen.* Fechtenheim, Fischer.

Seliger, H. and M. Long (eds.). 1983. *Classroom-oriented Research in Second Langauge Acquisition.* Rowley, Mass.: Newbury House.

Slobin, D. I. 1973. Cognitive prerequisites for the development of grammar. In C. A. Ferguson and D. I. Slobin (eds.). pp. 175-208.

Slobin, D. I. 1975. Language change in childhood and history. *Working Papers of the Language Behavior Research Laboratory,* No. 41 University of California, Berkeley.

Snow, C., and C. Ferguson (eds.). 1977. *Talking to Children: Language Input and Acquisition.* Cambridge: Cambridge University Press.

Strohner, H. and K. Nelson, 1974. The young child's development of sentence comprehension: influence of event probability, non-verbal context, syntactic form and their strategies. *Child Development* 45.567-576.

Swain, M., and S. Lapkin. 1982. *Evaluating Bilingual Education,* Clevedon.

Vogel, K. and S. Vogel, 1975. *Lernpsychologie und Fremdsprachenerwerb.* Tübingen: Gunter Narr Verlag.

Wode, H. 1981. *Learning a Second Language I. An Integrated View of Language Acquisition.* Tübingen: Gunter Narr Verlag.

CHAPTER 8

Classroom Language as Input to Second Language Acquisition[1]

Patsy M. Lightbown
Concordia University, Montreal, Canada

In reports on second language acquisition research it is often specified that the subjects were "natural" or "untutored" learners. When subjects in SLA research have received formal instruction in the second language, they have generally had fairly extensive exposure to the language outside the formal instructional setting as well. Exposure to the target language in communicative settings is deemed necessary to activate language *acquisition* as opposed to language *learning* processes (to use Krashen's terms). There is growing evidence, however, that language acquisition does take place in classrooms – even those which are very formal and in which there is little communicative use of the language (Felix, 1981; Lightbown, 1983a, b).

Second language classrooms, especially those for students receiving little or no informal contact with the language, offer a rare opportunity for studying relationships between input and output in second language development. Whereas the input available in "natural" second language exposure is varied and difficult to describe exhaustively, classroom exposure can be sampled, recorded, described, and analyzed with a reasonable degree of adequacy. This makes it possible, at least hypothetically, to compare input (the teacher's language, the textbook, and the language used by the students in class) with the development of the second language by the students exposed to this input. This comparison has theoretical importance because of its relevance to questions about how learners process the input and how much their developing interlanguage can be explained by characteristics of the input – as suggested, for example, in some foreigner talk studies (see Meisel, 1980, for discussion) and studies of frequency of occurrence of certain structures (e.g., Larsen-Freeman, 1976).

The study of classroom language as input to second language acquisition clearly has practical importance too. Knowing what learners do with the input should be helpful in evaluating certain input characteristics which are considered important in L2 teaching.

The research described in this chapter has been based to a considerable extent on an interest in studying the development of the second language by classroom learners in light of Krashen's (1981) theory of second language development. Krashen has described two ways in which, he hypothesizes, learners internalize the rules of the target language: acquisition and learning. *Acquisition* is described as a nonconscious process comparable with the process by which children acquire their native language (L1), with the focus on meaning while the form is acquired incidentally. Acquired knowledge of particular elements of the L2 is said to develop in essentially the same sequence by all L2 acquirers regardless of age, first language, or kind of instruction. Krashen refers to this as the "natural order" hypothesis. *Learning* is an effortful (conscious) process in which L2 learners focus on the form rather than the meaning of language, attempting to learn the rules of the target language in order to apply them subsequently to construct meaningful utterances. According to Krashen, aspects of language which have been learned – but not acquired – will affect only language used under conditions allowing the L2 learner time and encouraging the learner to focus on the form of the language.

The relative accuracy or order of emergence of grammatical elements in the English of the subjects of this study – L2 learners receiving formal instruction but little informal or "communicative" exposure to the language – has been observed to deviate in some respects from the "natural order," even though procedures for data collection did not encourage learners to focus on form nor did it allow much time for what Krashen has called "monitoring," that is, searching the store of formally *learned* knowledge while carrying out the task. Krashen has suggested that exposure to the target language in communicative settings is necessary for the activation of language acquisition processes. Formal audio-lingual classes like those observed for this study lead learners to focus on form rather than meaning and provide little L2 input outside structured practice of linguistic elements. However, the number and extent of grammatical explanations varies considerably from class to class and within the same class from day to day. In any case, the evidence from this study points to the operation of language acquisition processes in spite of very limited communicative use of the second language. Deviations from a "natural order" of acquisition and other differences between the performance of these learners and those in other studies may be attributable more to differences in and limitations on the input or language model available to the learners than to differences in processing mechanisms. That is, although the subjects' output differs in some respects from the language of "natural" acquirers, such differences cannot be taken as counterevidence for the "natural order" hypothesis or as evidence of the absence of "acquired" linguistic competence. They may instead be due to input factors: what these formally instructed learners are exposed to in the classroom is not the English language but a distorted reflection of it. This appears to be partly due to the fact that some of the teachers are nonnative speakers of English and thus provide learners with certain interlanguage forms as input. Probably more important, however, is the fact that the language is presented in a highly structured linear fashion, requiring practice of one linguistic element at a time, with little regard for communicative use of language.

It should be stated, furthermore, that these findings do not contradict Krashen's current theory of language acquisition. As Krashen has recently said, his is a theory not of *teaching* but of *learning* and *acquisition*. That is, what happens in class is not necessarily what the teacher thinks is happening – or even, for that matter, what the students think is happening. The research reported in this paper seems to reflect, at least in part, the existence of such a mismatch between what teachers intend to teach and what their students do with the input.

In this research report, some characteristics of classroom language are compared with aspects of the second language development of French-speaking pupils (11 to 17 years old) receiving 20 to 60 minutes per day of ESL instruction in Quebec public schools. The input data for analysis include extensive recordings of 11 ESL classes taught by six teachers sampled over a period of several months. (See Appendix A for schedule of classroom recordings.) The language production data include oral and written samples of language from approximately 175 students, 99 of whom were recorded over a period of at least 2 years. The study includes both longitudinal and cross-sectional components which make it possible to examine both short-term and long-term relationships between the learners' development of certain language forms and functions (the output) and such aspects of input as the frequency of use, the intensity of practice, and the presence or absence of "spiraling" of elements in the syllabus.

In several recent papers we have reported on the use of certain grammatical forms and functions by the formally instructed French-speaking adolescents who were the subjects of this research (Lightbown, 1984; Lightbown and Spada, 1978; Lightbown and Malcolm, 1980). The research involved the analysis of speech samples collected from each learner over time in order to trace the development of particular linguistic elements. As noted above, the design involved both cross-sectional and longitudinal components in order to permit us to look at development throughout the period of instruction from grade 6 through grade 11.[2] In addition comparison data were obtained from native speakers of English in the same age groups as the L2 subjects. Table 1 shows the schedule of learner language data collection and indicates the extent of overlap among the groups.

TABLE 1 School Grade and Month of Administration of the Picture Card Game

		School grade	Month
Group I	(N = 36)	6	April/May
		7	December
		7	April/May
Group II	(N = 36)	8	April/May
		9	April/May
		10	October
Group III	(N = 27)	10	April/May
		11	April/May

Comparison data from anglophones were collected one time only from students in grades 6, 8, 9, 10 and 11.

The data-collection procedure involved tape-recorded and transcribed inter-action with each student as he or she was engaged in a game in which the student had to describe each of seven pictures drawn on 3×5 cards and hidden from the interlocutor's view. For each picture described by the student, the interlocutor had four similar pictures (including one identical to the student's) in front of her and had to guess which one the student was describing. Following the picture card game in the second and third administrations, each student was shown a series of five pictures of "a little boy who does the same thing every day" and was asked "What does he do first?" "Then what does he do?" etc. This activity was added because it had become clear in the first administration that obligatory contexts for one of the morphemes under investigation, the third person singular simple present, were rare or nonexistent.

A number of analyses of the learners' speech collected in this manner have been carried out and explanations for the findings have been sought in the target language input available to the students in their ESL classes. The categories of analysis reported below include six grammatical morphemes and a group of lin-guistic forms which learners used to introduce their picture descriptions. There is also a brief discussion of the learners' use of prepositions.

GRAMMATICAL MORPHEMES

One analysis of the transcripts was based on the learners' use of six grammatical morphemes shown in Table 2. We first carried out an analysis in terms of the accuracy of these six morphemes in obligatory contexts. The principal interest here was the possibility of comparing these learners with those who were the subjects of previous morpheme acquisition research (e.g., Dulay and Burt, 1974; Bailey, Madden, and Krashen, 1974; Larsen-Freeman, 1975; Andersen, 1977). Such a comparison appeared useful because these learners differed from the other subjects in terms of three characteristics — first language, age, and type of exposure to the language.

TABLE 2   Grammatical Morphemes Investigated

Copula -s	She's happy.
Progressive auxiliary -s	He's blowing out the candles.
3rd singular -s	He takes a bath.*
Plural -s	The girl wants some cookies.
Possessive -s	The boy's hat has stripes on it.
Progressive -ing	She's wearing a red skirt.

*From the "little boy" sequence.

1. First language: No other study had reported data from a homogene-ous group of French speakers.

2. Age: Previous research dealt with children (5 to 8) and adults. Subjects in this study were 11 to 17 years old.

3. Type of exposure: Subjects of previous research usually had mixed exposure — some "submersion" and some ESL instruction. Subjects in this study were formally instructed learners with little nonclassroom exposure to English.

The results of the morpheme accuracy-acquisition analysis have been reported in two ways: (1) the comparison of these students' accuracy-acquisition sequence with that reported for other subjects and (2) the students' progress over time.

The comparison with subjects of previous research is summarized in Figure 1 where the relative accuracy of our subjects is shown beside an adaptation of Krashen's 1977 summary of morpheme acquisition research up to that time. That figure shows that there are some differences — principally in the place of the auxiliary. The difference may appear to be a small one, but when we look at Figure 2, showing the actual overall accuracy for all the students on these morphemes, the small difference becomes greater. That is, while only the auxiliary is "out of place," it is hard to think of putting the copula (98 percent accuracy) in the same box with plural (61 percent) and -*ing* (50 percent), while placing the auxiliary — with 89 percent accuracy — in a separate, lower (or subsequent) category. However, as we will see, it would be a mistake to conclude that the auxiliary has been mastered by the majority of the subjects.

When one examines their accuracy over time, it seems even less appropriate to group copula, -*ing* and plural for these subjects. (See Figures 3, 4, and 5.)

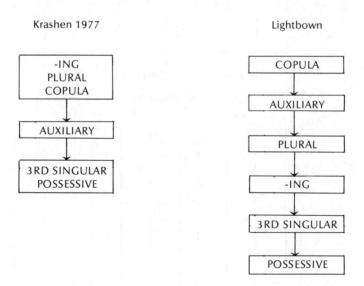

FIGURE 1 Adaptation of Krashen's (1977) "Proposed 'Natural Order' for Second Language Acquisition" compared with accuracy order observed in this study. In Krashen's order, morphemes in the same box are considered to have a fixed order relative to each other.

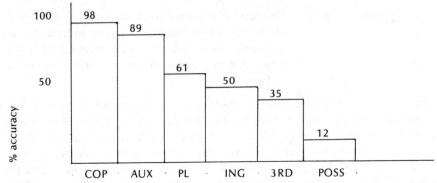

FIGURE 2 Accuracy in obligatory contexts of grammatical morphemes under investigation for all subjects, all administrations, N = 260.

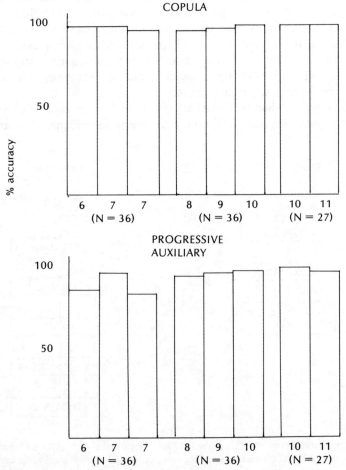

FIGURE 3 Accuracy in obligatory contexts for copula and progressive auxiliary

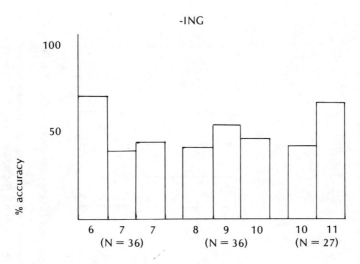

FIGURE 4 Accuracy in obligatory contexts for -*ing*

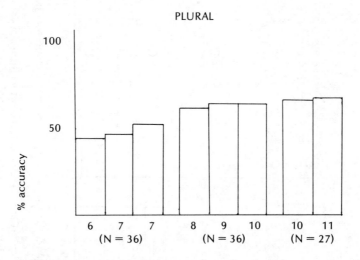

FIGURE 5 Accuracy in obligatory contexts for plural

Accuracy on the copula and auxiliary was high from grade 6 – after 2 years of ESL instruction – and remained high throughout the period of the study. Accuracy on the plural started below 50 percent and rose very slowly, albeit steadily, through the period of the study. Accuracy on -*ing* started at 69 percent but dropped to 39 percent the following year, rising above 60 percent again only in grade 11. Clearly -*ing* and plural were very different from the copula. Furthermore, the proportion of verbs which grade 6 learners marked with -*ing* was dramatically different from the proportion so marked by the other learners or by these same students when they were in grade 7. (See Figure 6.)

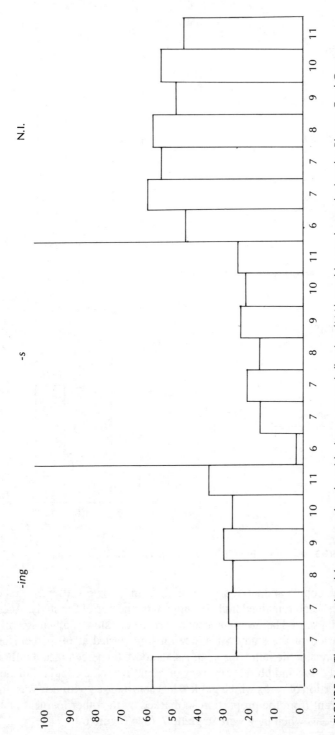

FIGURE 6   The proportional frequency of verbs with -*ing*, -*s*, or no inflection (N.I.) used by students playing the Picture Card Game.

Note: Because of the nature of the Picture Card Game, no inflection other than -*s*, or -*ing* was required on the verb. Verbs without inflection were often correct (for example, with plural subjects). For this figure, all full verbs were counted whether or not the inflection (or the absence of an inflection) was used correctly.

An analysis of the classroom speech for input factors which might explain the difference between these subjects and those observed in other research was not immediately revealing. Table 3 shows the proportional frequency of verbs with -ing, -s, or no inflection in the classroom speech of teachers and students in grades 6, 10 and 11. Except in classes when the progressive -ing was being taught explicitly, it was infrequent in both teachers' and students' speech – although it was somewhat more frequent in students' speech in the grade 6 classes. This might appear to explain the low accuracy on this form, and the preference for uninflected verbs by the secondary students. However, the difference in frequency between grade 6 and secondary teachers' frequency of use of -ing is slight and the students' frequency difference, while larger, does not appear to be great enough to explain the observation that the grade 6 students' accuracy was 69 percent, considerably higher than the other groups' accuracy or than their own later accuracy.

Further investigation and analysis of the grade 6 textbook revealed that in the period prior to our first data collection in the classroom, the grade 6 students had had 11 units – each taking several days of presentation and practice – on the progressive form. They had heard and practiced hundreds of sentences using verbs with -ing. This inordinately high frequency of one grammatical form and the extensive pattern practice apparently did lead the grade 6 students to use the form far more frequently and more accurately than any other group, and this tendency persisted for several months after the form became infrequent in their input. The *function* of the form was far from mastered, however, and the grade 6 students later came to use uninflected verbs far more frequently than any other form. In a natural environment for language acquisition rather than a formal instructional setting, the learners would probably have used a larger proportion of uninflected verbs from the beginning – both because such forms are far more frequent in the language and because inflections other than -ing are hard to hear in the stream of speech. Had students been exposed to a natural language acquisition environment, they, like learners described in other research, would probably have begun using -ing as the first verb inflection, but they would have done so only after an initial period of using uninflected verbs.[3]

With regard to the copula and auxiliary something similar can be observed. The students in grade 6 – in the picture card game interaction – attached 's to 87 percent of the clause initial occurrences of *he, she, it*. With this in mind, high accuracy on the auxiliary may now be seen in a somewhat different light. At the same time, these students were attaching -ing to almost 60 percent of all verbs, creating obligatory contexts for the progressive auxiliary. By attaching 's to 87 percent of their sentence-initial singular pronouns they had a very good possibility of producing a fully correct progressive construction. As -ing was quite infrequent in the speech of the other groups, few obligatory contexts for the auxiliary were created. In the secondary classes, only students whose English was relatively advanced (compared with the others) used the progressive construction. When they did, they tended to use it accurately. Thus accuracy scores on the auxiliary did not fall even though frequency fell considerably.

TABLE 3 Frequency of Verbs With -ing, -s, Other Inflection or No Inflection in Classroom Speech

| | Teacher | | | | | Students | | | | |
	No. of verbs	% -ing	% -s	% O.I.	% N.I.	No. of verbs	% -ing	% -s	% O.I.	% N.I.
Grade 6 (7-1/2 hours of transcript)	2372	14	7	9	69	1062	24	13	2	61
Grade 10 (11 hours of transcrsipt)	4088	8	14	17	61	2887	8	7	15	69
Grade 11 (6 hours of transcript)	3453	10	12	18	59	1682	10	5	31	53

Note: For this table, all full verbs were counted—whether or not the inflection (or the absence of an inflection) was used correctly.

Once again, analysis of classroom input available to the students at the time when 87 percent of their sentence-initial pronouns had *'s* did not immediately provide an explanation for the high frequency of this form. At that time, the grade 6 teacher used *he, she, it* without *'s* far more often (70 percent of all occurrences of *he, she, it*) than she used *he's, she's,* and *it's*. In earlier lessons, however, *he's, she's,* and *it's* were heard and practiced to the point of overlearning (Lightbown, 1984). Thus the proportional frequency of *he's* and *he*, etc., in the students' speech at the time of the picture card game appeared to reflect the influence of extremely high frequency in an earlier period of instruction rather than during the same time period — even when this "same" period is extended to cover several months.

INTRODUCERS

A subsequent analysis of the transcripts was based on the learners' use of certain "introducer" forms in their picture card descriptions (see examples in Table 4). This analysis was prompted by our observation that the French-speaking subjects often used an introducer form which sounded a little strange — but not exactly incorrect — to the research group. The form was what we came to call "*have* as introducer" — for example, *You have a house and two trees*. Because we had had so much contact with French L1–English L2 interlanguage, we did not trust our linguistic intuitions to judge this form as acceptable or unacceptable. We collected data from English L1 speakers in the same age range as our subjects, recording the language they produced in performing the same task — the picture card game. When we compared the introducer forms used by native speakers of English with those used by the ESL learners, we found rather strong evidence to suggest that, at least in this task, native speakers (who are not second language acquisition researchers) have one set of forms which they prefer over all others and, beyond that, a relatively small and narrowly distributed set of alternatives. As Table 5 shows, both elementary (grade 6) and secondary (grades 8 to 11) native speakers use *there's* as the favored form. There was very little difference between the two groups. One thing is quite clear: *have* was not com-

TABLE 4   Introducer Forms Used in Picture Card Game

there's	There's a table and there's a cake.
there are	There are four children.
it's	It's a class.
I see	I see two boys and two girls.
have	You have seven people.
	We have a box green and — uh — decoration red.
other	That's a car and a truck.
	This one is a boy and a girl . . .

TABLE 5   Introducer Forms Used in Picture Card Game
Percent All Introducers Represented by Each Form

	ESL Learners								Native Speakers	
	Group I			Group II			Group III			
GRADE	6	7	7	8	9	10	10	11	6	8–11
	N = 36			N = 36	N = 37	N = 26	N = 27		N = 37	N = 53
	%	%	%	%	%	%	%	%	%	%
There's	35	44	44	18	24	30	26	27	73	73
It's	34	30	22	16	34	32	32	34	13	14
I see	11	0	3	24*	10	8	10	6	7	1.5
Have	2	17	21	35	30	29	25	33	1	1
Other	17	9	9	6	2	1	6	2	6	10
Total no. of occurrences	239	280	322	303	410	292	259	342	457	851
Avg. no. per speaker	7	8	9	8	11	11	10	13	12	16

*Influenced by interviewer's question (What do you see in your picture?) in about half the cases.

monly used in introducer formulas by native speakers. The picture was quite different for the ESL learners: (1) no ESL groups showed a preference for *there's* equal to that of the native speakers; (2) the groups were different from each other; (3) for two of the groups (grade 6-7-7 and grade 8-9-10), there were some changes over time within groups. A first hypothesis was that the members of the research team who administered the task had somehow influenced the forms used by the learners. Analysis of the transcripts did not support this except in the case of one interviewer who asked "What do you see in your picture?" and received "I see . . ." as an answer more frequently than others. Most interviewers used the formula "Tell me about your picture" or simply waited silently for the student to begin his or her description.

Analysis of classroom speech has proved very revealing in explaining the use of *have* as an introducer. First, the absence of the introducer *have* in the grade 6 students' speech is easily explained. They did not know the verb; it had never been formally presented in their textbook (Alexander and Dugas, 1973). Although the teacher used the verb occasionally when she spoke spontaneously, it was very infrequent overall because her "spontaneous speech" was quite limited. She followed the text very closely and her use of English was almost always closely related to the lesson being taught. It is virtually certain that she never formally taught the verb *have* as the text did not require it, and it certainly was not practiced and drilled for weeks and weeks as were certain other structures – including the type "There's a book on the table" "There are some candies in the jar." An interesting footnote to this is that the ESL learners, especially the grade 6 students, were considerably more likely to use *there are* with a plural complement than were native speakers (see Table 6).

The increased frequency of *have* introducers in subsequent speech samples by the same group (in grade 7) and the relatively high frequency of these forms in the speech of the older learners led to some interesting questions and hypotheses about the basis for its use by formally instructed French-speaking learners as opposed to native speakers of English.

We analyzed the presentation of *have* in the textbook series used by the secondary students (Lado, 1970) and found no evidence of *have* as an introducer. We did find a highly structured presentation of the various forms and functions of *have* – with little or no overlap of functions in a given lesson or even in a given book: Table 7 summarizes some of these findings for Books 1, 2, and 3 of the textbook series. In Book 1 – used in grade 7 – *have* was presented only as a main

TABLE 6   Use of *There's/There are* With Plural Complement

	ESL Learners		Native Speakers	
	Grade 6 (N = 36)	Grade 9 & 11 (N = 63)	Grade 6 (N = 37)	Grade 8–11 (N = 53)
There's	72	77	98	91
There are	28	23	2	9

TABLE 7   Occurrences of *Have* in Students' ESL Textbook

	Main verb	Auxiliary	Modal	Total
Book 1	133	—	—	133
Book 2	93	1	85	179
Book 3	205	312	31	548

verb; first appearing on page 116 (Unit 15 of 20); in Book 2, *have* was used as a main verb or in the modal "have to" construction; in Book 3, over half the 548 occurrences of *have* were auxiliaries in the newly introduced perfect tenses. In Book 4, *have* was not a point of focused instruction; thus its use became more natural, integrated into reading material. Clearly there was nothing in the textbook which could have given students evidence for the hypothesis that *have* could be used in English as an introducer.

One plausible explanation for the frequent use of *have* as an introducer was that students, having learned that *have* was equivalent to *avoir* in certain contexts, hypothesized that this might extend to another context where their native language would use *avoir*: the introducer form "il y a."[4] According to this, when students used *have* as introducer, they would reinforce each other's errors in classroom interaction, establishing this as a preferred form. It should be noted, however, that the students' classroom speech was highly constrained, and their opportunities for making errors were surprisingly limited. Indeed, the verb *have* was quite rare in student speech in the classroom corpus, and where it occurred it was almost never as an introducer (see Table 8). Nevertheless, we hypothesized that the "transfer" phenomenon might have been reinforced by another source input: three of the five ESL teachers were themselves native speakers of French.[5]

We first looked at the overall frequency of the verb *have* in the teachers' classroom speech — combining all forms and all functions. The results are presented in Table 9. The table shows (1) total occurrences; (2) the average frequency of *have* in each hour of classroom instruction; (3) the percentage of uses of *have* which were metalinguistic — defined strictly as cases where *have* was being "talked about" (e.g., "What is the past tense of *have*?"). In Table 9, the grade 8, 9, and 11 teachers — the three native speakers of French — stand out from the others as frequent users of *have*.

TABLE 8   Students' Use of *Have* in Classroom Data

Grade	Overall frequency	Percent used as introducer
6	8	0
8	97	11
9	89	6
10	224	3
11	163	0

TABLE 9 All Uses of *Have* by ESL Teachers

	Total occurrences	*Occurrences/ hour*	*Percent Metalinguistic*
Grade 6 (7-1/2 hours of transcript)	163	21.7	5
Grade 8a (10 hours of transcript)	435	43.5	1
Grade 8b (9 hours of transcript)	637	70.7	2
Grade 9 (4 hours of transcript)	268	67	0
Grade 10a (11 hours of transcript)	329	29.9	12
Grade 10b (10 hours of transcript)	284	28.4	2
Grade 11 (6 hours of transcript)	259	43.1	1

We then coded all uses of *have* in terms of a number of form and function categories. In this chapter I discuss only the function categories, which are shown in Table 10.

Table 11 shows the proportional frequency of the various functions of *have* in the speech of these three teachers. What is most immediately obvious is that the grade 8 teacher provided very clear and strong evidence to support a possible

TABLE 10 Functions of *Have* in Classroom Speech

Existential	where *have* was used as an introducer *You have a clock on the wall.*
Main verb	all other main verb uses *She has one dollar.*
Modal	*have to/has to/had to* *I have to study tonight.*
Auxiliary	in the perfect tenses *She has lived here for two years.*
Other	odd and idiomatic usages *Let's have Martine play the storekeeper.*
Have as *be**	where *have* is used in place of *be* *I have hungry. He has 14 years.*
Uncodable	false starts/incomprehensible *I have ... I am ... I don't ...*

*Occurred in teachers' speech only in metalinguistic discussion of this incorrect form.

TABLE 11   Frequency (Percent)* of the Form *Have* in Teachers' Classroom Speech, by Function

	Grade						
	6	8a	8b	9	10a	10b	11
FUNCTION							
Existential	17.0	42.5	42.3	16.4	8.4	11.4	15.9
Main verb	30.0	29.6	23.4	43.3	28.4	51.8	40.9
Modal	19.0	6.3	10.8	6.7	26.2	14.3	10.7
Auxiliary	13.7	4.1	3.3	18.3	28.4	19.5	31.3
Other	15.7	14.8	0.2	15.3	6.3	1.1	1.2
Have as *be*	3.9	2.4	1.1	—	2.2	1.8	—
Total frequency of *have*	153	413	610	268	320	272	252

*Uncodable cases were eliminated before percentages were calculated. The frequency of uncodable cases ranged from 0 (grade 9) to 27 (grade 8b).

interlanguage hypothesis that *you have* or *we have* is an appropriate introducer form in English. Indeed, it is appropriate in some cases. What is striking is that it represents nearly half of all this teacher's uses of *have*. This was very different from the distribution in the speech of all the other teachers – one speaker of English, one Romanian, and the other two French Canadians.

We then analyzed these same transcripts to determine what proportion of all introducers *have* accounted for in the teachers' classroom speech. The results of this analysis are shown in Table 12. Here again, as was the case with *-ing* on verbs and *'s* on pronouns, had we examined the use of *have* as an introducer at the time when its frequency was greatest in the learners' speech, we would have been surprised to find a relatively low frequency of such use in the speech of the grade

TABLE 12   Three Introducer Forms: Frequency Per Hour of Classroom Instruction in Teachers' Speech

Grade	There	It*	Have
6	19.6	3.3	3
8a	2.6	0.2	17
8b	3	0	29
9	12.5	0	11
10a	5.5	0	2
10b	5	0	3
11	7.8	0	7

*Although forms of *it* rarely occurred in the function of introducer, the forms occurred frequently in other functions. Overall frequency for *it* forms in the teachers' speech ranged from 17 occurrences/class hour (Grade 8a) to 29 (Grade 9).

9, 10, and 11 teachers. Grade 8 students, on the other hand, were receiving input which corresponded very well to what the students were doing. It will be recalled that the grade 9 subjects are actually the same students as the grade 8 subjects, recorded a year later. Furthermore, many of the grade 10 and 11 subjects had had the same grade 8 teacher. It seems plausible to suggest that a transfer-based hypothesis that *have* equals *avoir* in introducer constructions and high-frequency confirming information in the input combined to make *have*-as-introducer a very stable interlanguage form for these learners.

PREPOSITIONS

Preliminary results of the analysis of learners' use of prepositions suggest that, while there was very high accuracy in the students' use of prepositions in class, accuracy in the use of the prepositions used in the picture card game showed little improvement over time even though those prepositions which were most frequent in the picture card game also tended to be the most frequently used prepositions in classroom language. Preposition frequency in the classroom language followed patterns already observed for other linguistic elements: a particular form would be intensively practiced for a period of time, and then that particular preposition or group of prepositions would drop back to very low frequency or virtually disappear. High-accuracy "bulges" sometimes appeared in the data following such a period of intensive practice.

The continuing analysis of the data on prepositions is particularly interesting as a contrast to the analysis of grammatical morphemes described above. Prepositions are notoriously difficult to teach as well as for the learner-acquirer to master – both because their use is so highly language-specific that it is usually impossible to transfer L1 knowledge, and because – within a given language – the use of prepositions is so idiomatic that patterns and analogies often cannot be relied on.

CONCLUDING REMARKS

The results of this study suggest that students receiving formal second language instruction in what Krashen calls "acquisition-poor" environments do not simply "learn" linguistic elements as they are taught – adding one after another in neat progression. Rather, the students process the input data in ways which are more "acquisition-like" and often not consistent with what the teacher or textbook intends for students to learn. This is particularly true for students at low levels of target language proficiency whose limited knowledge of the language leads them to make false hypotheses about the elements which are presented to them in isolation from others. Constraining classroom language in such a way that students hear and produce a restricted group of "correct" utterances does not block the process of language acquisition – does not prevent learners-acquirers from generating false hypotheses about the underlying structure of the language. Nor does intensive practice of particular elements prevent these elements from dropping out or becoming confused with others once others are introduced – particularly when those first-learned elements become infrequent in the input. Finally it appears that teachers cannot always control their own language in ways which make available to the students only those elements foreseen by the textbook or syllabus writers.

NOTES

1. This research has been funded by grants from the Social Sciences and Humanities Research Council of Canada and the Secretary of State of Canada. Many people have made valuable contributions to the research since the project began in 1977. Those who have contributed most to the study reported here are Diane Malcolm, Gary Libben, and Jude Rand. We all thank Ann Barkman and Catherine Faure. An earlier version of this paper was presented at TESOL Honolulu, May 1982.

2. Subjects began receiving ESL instruction in grade 4 or 5, having an average of less than 2 hours of instruction per week in grades 4, 5, and 6, and 4½ hours per week in grades 7 to 11.

3. In her M.A. thesis, Spada (1979) showed that students in the grade 6 group who had more contact with English outside school used more uninflected verbs than those whose English exposure was limited to classroom instruction, even in obligatory contexts for the progressive.

4. Another kind of data is needed to give support to this "guess": transcripts of French speakers playing the picture card game – in French.

5. The grade 6 teacher was Romanian and spoke English better than French, and the grade 10 teacher was a native speaker of English. All the teachers spoke English well and fluently.

REFERENCES

Alexander, L. G., and A. Dugas. 1972, 1973. *Look, Listen and Learn*, Books I and II, Centre Educatif et Culturel. Longman Canada Ltd.

Andersen, R. 1977. The impoverished state of cross-sectional morpheme acquisition/accuracy methodology (or: the left-overs are more nourishing than the main course). *Working Papers on Bilingualism*; 47–82.

Bailey, N., C. Madden, and S. Krashen. 1974. Is there a "natural sequence" in adult second language learning? *Language Learning* 24 235–244.

Dulay, H., and M. K. Burt. Natural sequences in child second language acquisition. *Language Learning* 24 37–53.

Felix, S. 1981. The effect of formal instruction on second language acquisition. *Language Learning* 31 87–112.

Krashen, S. 1977. Some issues relating to the monitor model. In H. D. Brown, C. A. Yorio, and R. H. Crymes (eds.), *On TESOL '77* Washington: TESOL.

Krashen, S. 1981. *Second Language Acquisition and Second Language Learning*. Oxford: Pergamon Press.

Lado, R. and R. Tremblay. 1971. *Lado English Series* (Canadian edition). Centre Educatif et Culturel. Longman Canada Ltd.

Larsen-Freeman, D. 1975. The acquisition of grammatical morphemes by adult ESL students. *TESOL Quarterly* 9 409–420.

Larsen-Freeman, D. 1976. ESL teacher speech as input to the ESL learner. *Workpapers in Teaching English as a Second Langauge.* X 45–50.

Lightbown, P. 1983a. Exploring relationships between developmental and instructional sequences in L2 acquisition. In H. Seliger and M. Long (eds.). *Classroom Oriented Research in Second Language Acquisition.* Rowley, Mass.: Newbury House.

Lightbown, P. 1983b. Acquiring English L2 in Quebec classrooms. In S. Felix and H. Wode (eds.), *Language development at the crossroads.* Language and Development Series 5. Benjamins North American.

Lightbown, P., and N. Spada. 1978. Performance on an oral communication task by francophone ESL learners. *SPEAQ Journal,* 2 (4) 35–54.

Lightbown, P., and D. Malcolm. 1980. Evaluating changes in the oral English of French-speaking students. *SPEAQ Journal.* 4 (2) 41–64.

Meisel, J. 1980. Linguistic simplification. In S. Felix (ed.) *Second Language Development: Trends and Issues.* Tübingen: Gunter Narr Verlag.

Spada, N. 1979. Formal and informal learning: some aspects of the ESL development of francophone students who do and do not have out-of-classroom exposure to English. Unpublished M.A. thesis, Concordia University.

APPENDIX A

Schedule of Classroom Recordings

Grade	Total hours Recorded	Date of Recorded Sessions
6	7½	(1977) October 5, 12, 19, 26; November 2, 9, 16, 23, 30; (1978) February 15; March 1, 22; April 5, 11, 25; May 26
8a	10	(1977) October 4, 13, 27; November 7, 21, 30; (1978) February 16; March 7; April 12; June 6
8b	9	(1977) October 21; November 1, 24; (1978) February 22; March 17; April 12, 25; May 31; June 6
9	4	(1978) October 11, 20; November 1; (1979) April 12
10a	11	(1977) October 12, 26; November 4, 18, 29; December 8; (1978) February 23; March 17, 29; April 13; May 31
10b	10	(1977) October 13, 26; November 4, 18, 29; December 8; (1978) February 23; March 30; April 11; May 31
11	6	(1978) September 22; October 17, 26; November 6; December 1; (1979) April 12

Note: Each class session was 60 minutes long except for the grade 6 classes, which met for 30 minutes.

PART THREE

Case Studies of Reference to Past in a Semantic/Functional Framework

CHAPTER 9

A Concept-Oriented Approach to Second Language Studies[1]

Christiane von Stutterheim
Institut für Deutsch als Fremdsprachenphilologie
Heidelberg, Federal Republic of Germany

Wolfgang Klein
Max-Planck Institut für Psycholinguistik
Nijmegen, The Netherlands

1. INTRODUCTION

For some time, second language acquisition research has been primarily concerned with the emergence of specific linguistic forms—lexical items, grammatical morphemes, syntactic constructions—which, like flowers in the spring, were observed to crop up in a certain order, provided that there was enough rain and sun and the soil was sufficiently fertile. Increasing insight, on the one hand, and the unforeseeable meander of linguistic fashion on the other has recently led many SLA researchers to cast off this approach and to replace it by a perspective which is more "functional," more "cognitive," which shifts in emphasis from "product" to "process" and looks into the communicative aspects of the development and usage of learner languages. For further discussion see Pfaff (this volume). We share this view. But clearly it does not say very much to call an approach "functional"—in fact it says no more than that a language cannot be analyzed without also taking its functions into account. The question then is what we should understand by "functions," and apparently authors have quite different ideas about the level on which these functions have to be located. To quote just three examples:

- Littlewood (1979: 125) develops a functional model which should be able to provide for "an account of languages which is sufficiently flexible to allow *human factors* to be discussed." At this level of generality the creation of nonfunctional models seems to require some inventiveness, which doubtless was shown by various authors.
- There is a much narrower usage of the term, for example, in Bates (1981), who talks about the *communicative function* of languages. This usage is

quite common in acquisition studies, both first and second (see, for example, the papers by Clahsen and Kail, this volume).

- There is still a narrower interpretation of "function" and "functional," for example, in Meisel (this volume) where he states that he is "advocating a functional approach," an approach which is characterized as follows: "Instead of searching for possible interpretations of a feature we must define the concepts and the functions which have to be encoded and then analzye the devices used by the different learners." (p. 206)

The examples suffice to show the variety of usages and approaches covered by the label "functional." Note that these definitions are not mutually exclusive; they differ in that they choose quite different levels in locating the functions which make the approach "functional": we might say that it is a function of language to allow people to establish social relations or to store cultural knowledge, but we might also say that it is a function of language to express number agreement or the agentivity of a specific referent. Things do not become clearer if we replace "functional" by another label such as "cognitive," for example. A case in point is a concept of "competing cognitive structures" which is developed in Felix (1981). He starts with a critique of approaches that take meaning and concepts as the major component in the explanation of the acquisition process: "However, language is *more* than *just* meaning and concepts. Any serious theory of language acquisition has to deal with the formal aspects of language." (p. 13). Felix assumes that these formal structures exist and develop independently from meaning or concepts; form and meaning result from *two cognitive* systems that are in principle independent; accordingly he assumes the existence of language-specific cognitive (LSC) and of problem-solving cognitive (PSC) structures. Hence, what Felix, in accordance with many others in the framework of transformational grammar, calls "cognitive" is the opposite of what other authors consider to be a cognitive approach (c.f. Cromer, 1978). Talking about "functional," "cognitive," "communicative" approaches and opposing them to "formal," "structural" approaches does not tell very much, nor is it particularly helpful to look for the common denominator of these approaches. As a consequence, there is little point in evaluating the merits of "functional" versus "formal" approaches on this level of generality. In what follows we present a type of functional approach which we think can answer some questions a strictly form-oriented approach cannot. We call it "concept-oriented." The following examples from learner languages will help clarify how the two approaches differ.

1. One informant in the study discussed below used the German past-tense morphology of regular verbs (the suffix *-te*) quite systematically, for example:

   (1) Beispiel ich krieg*te* Monat 1400, 1500 Mark
       "for example, I (got) 1400, 1500 mark per month"
   (2) Jetzt zahl*te* 400 Mark bloß Miete
       "now (I) (paid) only 400 mark rent"

The context makes clear, however, that what he wants to say is "I *get* 1400 Mark" and "right now I *am paying* . . .". The morpheme-*te* was not used to encode the concept of past time; in about 70 percent of all occurrences, the form *verb* + -*te* referred to the present. A formal morpheme study would have come up with the result that this informant had acquired German past tense. In fact, he marks the fact that something occurred in the past quite differently (past participle forms).

Note that this is a problem not only for morpheme studies in the sense of Dulay and Burt but also for approaches such as that of Felix, i.e., for any approach that looks at the emergence of forms independently of the concepts which they express. A structural analysis will overlook or cannot cope with the majority of those cases where learners have built up a system of their own by using L2 structures with meaning or function other than those of the L2.

All we can say about the example given above is that the speaker adds the suffix -*te* to certain verbs but not that he has acquired the structure of German in this respect.

2. In early learner varieties, the present perfect morphology [in past participles such as *"ge*funden" (found) or *"ge*kriegt" (got)] is used only with verbs whose inherent meaning includes a kind of perfectivity; i.e., the action or event they are talking about is completed, for example, "to find, to get." This differential treatment of verbs in the acquisition of verbal morphology can be accounted for only if concepts such as "perfectivity" are taken into account. A purely structural analysis could never explain why a particular morphological form is acquired and used in such an apparently unsystematic way.

3. There are learners who use the present perfect morphology with the target language function except where backgrounded information is given in relation to some foregrounded event. An example:

(3) 20 *Monate* da *bleiben,* ich *hab* keine Wohnung *gefunden.*
      "20 months here stay, I haven't found a flat"

In this case, the underlying category—backgrounding vs. foregrounding—which is not exclusively temporal—is here responsible for the unequal distribution of morphological forms.

Again, a merely structural analysis of morphological forms and their appearance in learner varieties would miss the crucial point if not related to the underlying conceptual categories.

These examples may suffice to demonstrate the necessity of including conceptual categories if we want to gain a proper understanding of the organization of learner languages and the way in which they develop—that is, into the nature of the acquisition process.

In the following section we briefly explain the idea of the concept-oriented approach, taking temporality, which is clearly one of the crucial concepts expressed in all human languages, as an example. Section 3 illustrates the approach with results from an empirical study.

2. THE CONCEPT OF TEMPORALITY AND TEMPORAL REFERENCE IN LANGUAGE

The basic idea behind what we have in mind is roughly as follows: Every utterance, no matter what communicative purpose it fills, involves the expression of various concepts such as temporality, modality, and locality. It seems clear that in order to produce an appropriate utterance, a speaker must somehow "have" these concepts: he may have acquired them, or they may be innate. In addition he also must have some specific conventionalized means of expressing them; these are provided by individual's language or else by the learner variety. We may assume that a second language learner—in contrast to a child acquiring his first language—does not have to acquire the underlying concepts. What he has to acquire is a specific way and specific means of expressing them. We may then assume that the use he makes of the linguistic means which he has at a given time, as well as the way in which he attempts to enrich his repertoire, depend, in part at least, on the concepts which he already has. Hence, we may gain some insight into the "logic" of the acquisition process as well as into the organization of learner languages by looking at the way in which specific concepts, such as temporality, are expressed at various stages of the acquisition process. Clearly, this picture is somewhat simplified; we will try to make it more concrete and specific by looking at a specific case—that of temporality.

The concept of temporality as used here refers to a fundamental category of human experience resulting from the perception of and reflection on reality, which does not depend on the way in which individual languages encode and thereby categorize time and temporal relations. It is an interesting and clearly disputable question whether there is a basic concept of temporality common to all cultures as some philosophers, such as Kant, have assumed. We are not so ambitious as to give an answer to this question. We merely assume that the people we are dealing with, speakers of Italian, Spanish, Turkish, and German, have a similar concept of temporality, at least on a general level. The concept of temporality when analyzed with respect to its internal, language-independent structure, leads to various categories such as "location on a time axis," "completion of an action," and "temporal relations before/after." For one way of systematizing temporal categories, see Chapter 3 in von Stutterheim, 1984.

Note that the approach is not bound to these particular categories. Other ways of systematizing the basic notions of temporality are possible. The crucial aspect of the approach is that it incorporates a two-tier model. It starts with an analysis of temporality, and then, on the basis of this analysis, any particular language or learner language can be described with respect to the specific means which are used to encode the various categories of temporality in a given context.

In a sense, the whole idea resembles the procedure adopted in some recent studies of linguistic universals, for example, Hopper and Thomson's (1980) study of "transitivity." They describe their procedure as follows:

> The intuitive understanding of transitivity is the one we shall attempt to characterize explicitly and in universal terms. As a first step we propose to isolate the component parts of the transitivity notion, and second, we study how they are typically encoded by languages, and third, we outline an explanation of the grammatical facts within the framework of discourse structure. (p. 252)

The last point is less relevant in the present context. What we are interested in are the effects which (1) the conceptual structure with its various components and (2) the encoding of this structure in the two languages involved may have on the organization and development of learner languages.

The various ways in which the concept of temporality is represented in the different languages involved includes not only the specific forms used for encoding but also the specific weight which is given to the various components of temporality. Some languages play down or even ignore certain components (say "aspect" or "reference to future") which, in other languages, are encoded in a systematic and detailed form. The particular language acts as a filter which foregrounds some features, for example, by expressing them regularly by a grammatical morpheme, whereas other features are treated as less important and marked selectively by lexical means, if the speaker feels the need to do so.

A good example is the feature of "witnessed past," which in Turkish requires obligatory marking by a grammatical morpheme, whereas there is no corresponding marking in German. Note that a speaker of German clearly *can* mark whether an event in the past is witnessed or not. Where this is required, he would choose the appropriate lexical means. He is also free to leave it implicit, however, or to mark it once at the beginning of a longer stretch of discourse with the tacit assumption that the listener would extend this marking to the rest of the discourse. In other words, a speaker is in principle left with three options with respect to the marking of a specific feature:

- Selective vs. obligatory marking within a given utterance; in German, tense marking is obligatory for each utterance, "witnessed" is selective.
- Implicit or explicit marking, where "implicit" means: left to some principle of contextual inference, for example, "maintain the temporal reference which was last marked, until it is marked otherwise."
- The choice of a specific linguistic device, for example, inflectional morpheme, stem change, adverbial.

Obviously these options are interrelated. Thus, selective marking tends to go with adverbials, whereas inflectional morphemes often (though not necessarily) are obligatory; i.e., the speaker must decide in each utterance how to specify the feature and does not have the option of simply ignoring it.

Both source and target language constrain these options in a specific way. Learner varieties, on the other hand, at the early stages at least, do not provide options with respect to different linguistic devices. There is often no obligatory marking at all; the balance between what is made explicit and what is left to a "clever" use of parallel contextual information *may shift,* and there are no strong syntactic restrictions on the use of forms which constitute the learner's repertoire at a given point in time. It seems reasonable, then, to assume that the way in which the learner organizes his utterances is heavily influenced by the conceptual structure present and by the way in which this conceptual structure is encoded in the source language. In many cases, this provides a guideline for answering questions on *why* a learner builds up his utterance in a specific way, on *why* he acquires a specific form of marking something before another one, on *why* he ignores certain features that might be important in the target languages, and consequently, on *why* the acquisition process proceeds in the way that it does. This is admittedly all very global. In the next section we try to show how this general idea may be put to use in a concrete investigation of learner varieties.[2]

3.   SOME ILLUSTRATIONS OF THE CONCEPT-ORIENTED APPROACH

The following examples are taken from an extensive study of the expression of temporal reference in learner languages (c.f. von Stutterheim, 1984).[3] The analysis was carried out within the framework sketched above. The questions addressed in that study correspond to what we have formulated as the explanatory goals of the concept-oriented approach at the end of Section 2:

Why does a learner acquire specific forms and items in a specific order?
How does the learner build up his utterances?
How does he communicate complex temporal structures in discourse?

We first make a few observations with respect to the initial question and then focus on strategies for conveying temporal concepts in discourse.

3.1.   THE INFLUENCE OF CONCEPTUAL CATEGORIES ON THE ACQUISITION OF LINGUISTIC DEVICES

The explicit linguistic devices for temporal reference used in the different learner systems were compared on the basis of a set of language-independent temporal categories (c.f. p. 194). The picture which arose showed a high degree of consistency with respect to the referential functions covered by the linguistic devices at different stages of the acquisitional process. Differences appear in the selection of a *particular* lexical item or grammatical form.[4]

Conceptual categories seem to play a role in a number of different ways in the learner's choice of a specific L2 form at a particular stage of the acquisition process. We will mention three ways in which conceptual categories influence these choices.

- One criterion for the selection of a specific L2 form as a productive part of the learner's system is given by the degree to which a particular temporal category can be conveyed implicitly. Establishing a temporal reference point, for instance, must in most cases be explicit. (An exception would be a question-answer sequence where a temporal reference point is introduced by the question.) A distinction which requires explicit representation is the one between background and foreground in discourse.[5] To some extent this distinction can be inferred from the inherent temporal properties of the verb (durative vs. punctual). In those cases, however, e.g., where a punctual verb appears in the background, the distinction has to be marked explicitly. That is why we find an aspectual distinction in early learner languages long before a tense system emerges (cf. Kumpf, 1982; von Stutterheim, 1984).

- The first language certainly plays a role and forms a further *constraint* governing the learner's choice of devices. Dominant conceptual categories—the grammatically marked ones, for instance, as well as specific structural patterns in the first language—form the "equipment" of the learner at the beginning of the acquisitional process and lead to a certain form of selectivity in dealing with the L2 input. Two examples taken from a comparative study of Italian, Spanish, and Turkish learners of German serve to illustrate the L1 influence.

The Turkish verbal system makes a twofold distinction between "near past" and "remote past." (The "remote past" is not relational like the German past perfect.) Some Turkish learners appear to acquire a twofold adverbial system *vorher* "before" and *ganz vorher* "very before" which corresponds to the Turkish categories, which they apply systematically. No trace of this was found in the data of the Italian and Spanish learners.

The second example shows L1 interference on a more structural level. Whereas the Spanish and Italian speakers use the temporal conjunction *wenn/wann* or *quand* (c.f. Trévise) even in very restricted varieties, the Turkish informants do not acquire any conjunctions until a high level of language proficiency is reached. They rely instead on specific forms of discourse organization (see below) or, as in the case of the more advanced speakers, on a nontargetlike use of tense marking: unmarked verbs in subordinate clauses and marked verbs in the main clause, e.g.:

(4)   20 Monate da *bleiben,* ich *hab* keine Wohnung *gefunden.*
      "20 months here stay, I haven't found a flat."

A plausible explanation of these observations lies in the structural differences between German and Turkish in this respect, differences which do not exist in the other pairs of languages mentioned.[6]

- The learner's choice of linguistic forms is also influenced by the need to express *complex* temporal structures in discourse. The adult learner who, as pointed out in sections 1 and 2, has the conceptual categories at his disposal is faced with the problem of establishing some kind of temporal coherence between utterances whenever he wants to go beyond a question-answer discourse type. This is the reason why we find means for expressing one type of temporally structured discourse among the first devices acquired for temporal reference. The basic type seems to be a temporal sequence which requires specification in three respects: the initial reference point, the relation "following-in-time," and the end point. The specific forms which serve these functions are very restricted:[7] *erstemal/erste* "first, at first" as a discourse marker for the beginning of a sequence; calendaric and a few deictic expressions (*jetzt* "now," *früher* "before," etc.) for establishing a temporal reference point; *und dann* "and then" for expressing the temporal relation (this could also be done implicitly, see below); *ende, fertig* "end, finish" as a discourse marker for the end of a temporal sequence.

3.2. TEMPORAL REFERENCE IN DISCOURSE

We now turn to the third question raised at the beginning of this section: "How do learners communicate complex temporal structures in discourse?" Basically there are two ways of encoding temporal reference, the explicit representation by means of lexical or grammatical devices and different kinds of pragmatic devices where the temporal component is not represented overtly. In the following discussion the focus lies on the pragmatic devices, *discourse organization principles* and *implicit reference,* both of which convey temporal meaning in L2 discourse.

Discourse organization principles (DOP)   By DOP we understand all those strategies which make use of a particular *order of elements* in discourse. The most important is the "principle of chronological order." It is well known that the order of reported events has a function for encoding meaning in natural language (cf. Klein, 1981), but its weight among the different means for expressing temporality is different in learner languages. For the beginner or early fossilized L2 speaker, this principle forms the basic means whereby temporal relations are established between utterances.

(5) Schule fertig, Deutschland komm.
     "school finish, Germany come."
(6) Deutschland komm, Schule fertig.
     "Germany come, school finish."

In sentence (5) we get the interpretation "after school I came to Germany"; in sentence (6) the different order of elements changes the sequential relation of the events: "after I came to Germany I finished school." That this principle should not be violated is shown by the fact that the speaker has to repair those cases where the principle was not obeyed.

(7) diese Kinder 3 Jahre komm immer deutsche Schule gehen türkische Schule gehen
     inglische nicht verstehen
     "these children 3 year come always German school go Turkish school go English not
     understand"

repair/new start

7 Jahre Türkei Schule gehen und dann Berlin komm 3 Jahre Schule gehen aber nicht
verstehen inglische
"7 years Turkey school go and then Berlin come 3 years school go but not understand
English"

In the acquisition process the communicative role of the "chronological order
principle" changes. The low-level speaker is *tied* to it, whereas with the
advanced L2 speaker it is but one of several possible pragmatic devices. The
reason for this change lies in the acquisition of more differentiated forms. A fully
developed language frees the speaker from this tie. He can, for example, say
"after I finished school I came to Germany" or "I finished school after I had
come to Germany."

The second principle discussed here is the "bracketing principle," which is
used for temporal embeddings on both discourse and utterance level. In the
former case, an utterance is repeated in identical or similar form after some
intervening utterance; we may represent this as   *a b c . . . a*. In the latter case
an utterance *a* is broken down into two parts *a*^I and *a*^{II} with some intervening

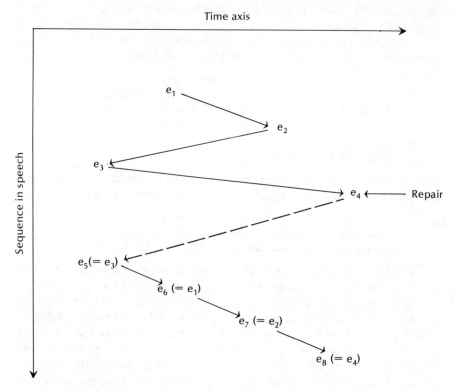

FIGURE 1 The schematic diagram of the temporal relation between the events shows
that the speaker reorganizes the sequence e_1 to e_4 such that it forms a chain—e_5 to e_8—
along the time axis, because the switch of the referential domain back into past carried out
between e_2 and e_3 could otherwise not have been followed by the interlocutor.

part *b*. Obviously these structures violate the chronological order principle. The repetition or continuation of an element forces the listener to exclude sequential order in forming a temporal interpretation.

The following two examples show how this strategy is used for expressing temporal embedding (8) and temporal subordination (9).

(8) a ich wie Meister
        "I (am) like boss"
    b jetzt ist Maschine kaputt
        "now is machine broken"
    c ich alleine gemach
        "I alone made (repaired)"
    a ich wie Meister
        "I (am) like boss"
(9) dann nachher — daß Kinder groß — Kinder arbeiten.
          a^I b   a^{II}
    "then afterward — that children big — children work"
    Meaning: Then later on, *when* the children are grown up they will have to work.

Implicit reference   In early learner languages the listener's inferencing capacities are heavily taxed. Inference in language understanding has to have a counterpart in language production, and this is referred to here as implicit reference. Any kind of implicit reference works on the basis of shared world knowledge, which can be drawn from different sources.[8]

world knowledge

(10) Atatürk, ja Atatürk gut, Türkei viel Fabrik, Türkei alles Kapitalist.
     "Atatürk, yes, Atatürk good, Turkey much factory, Turkey all capitalist."

situational knowledge

(11) Türkei Rente, meine Wohnung schön.
     "Turkey pension, my house nice."

Here the speaker relies on mutual knowledge about the fact that he is working at the moment and "pension" therefore implies reference to future.

contextual knowledge

(12) Arbeitsamt, Türkei Arbeitsamt, alles Vertrag, Siemens arbeit.
     "labor exchange, Turkey labor exchange, all contract, Siemens work."

For the interpretation of the last two utterance units the speaker expects the listener to maintain the reference Turkey, implying past time reference.

It is not satisfactory to say only that the interpretation is based on mutual knowledge. What must be analyzed are the different ways in which the listener is guided in deciding what kind of knowledge should be drawn upon to assist understanding. There must be some clues in the learner language which tell the listener what kind of information to add at what place. Guiding the listener in this way is certainly less precise than an explicit formulation, but it has to be more specific than just a simple "call" for world knowledge.

There are two kinds of implicit reference in the expression of temporal reference which we will call *inherent temporal reference* and *associative temporal reference.* By inherent temporal reference we mean those cases where the temporal properties can be inferred from the specific semantics of a verb or noun group, without being explicitly established. In establishing the temporal connection between events on the discourse level, the inherent temporal properties of the reported events play a crucial role. This is also true of fully developed languages, and quite a number of studies have dealt with the interrelation of the inherent temporal properties ("Aktionsarten") primarily of verb and grammatical devices for temporal reference (cf. Kamp and Rohrer, 1983; Kamp, 1981; Hopper, 1979). Again the relative weight of these devices with respect to the linguistic "Gesamtsystem" is different in learner language and standard language. In learner languages the inherent temporal properties of the reported events provide crucial information about temporal relations, whereas in standard language inherent meaning can be overruled by explicit marking. The following example may help to illustrate the point. Compare the two sentences:

(13) Türkei Urlaub zurückkomm, meine Mann krank.
"Turkey vacation come back, my husband ill."
(14) Türkei Urlaub, meine Mann krank.
"Turkey vacation, my husband ill."

There is no overt marking of the temporal relation between the two events, but the relations are clearly interpreted differently. The second case will be interpreted as "when he was on vacation in Turkey my husband was ill." That is, the information contained in the second half of the utterance has to be embedded temporally into that contained in the first half, whereas the first sentence (13) will be understood as reporting a temporal sequence of events, "after he came back from holidays. . .".

The reason for the varying interpretation lies in the different temporal properties of the first parts of the utterances. *Türkei Urlaub* describes a *state*, which will function as a background or frame for an embedded event because there is no internal temporal boundary which establishes a reference point for the following part of the sentence. In contrast to sentence (13), the first part of sentence (14) establishes such a temporal reference point by its inherent temporal properties. "Come back" implies a temporal boundary. This is the reason why sentence (14) will be interpreted as a temporal chain of events.

Observations of this kind seem to prove that in contrast to what Meisel says in his paper (this volume), *aspectual* categories as semantic concepts are highly relevant for learner language. This does not mean that one has to look for explicit grammatical aspect markers but that the aspectual properties of the lexical items provide a guideline for understanding temporal relations in restricted L2 speech. The different ways of structuring discourse by means of the temporal organization of the utterance units—chaining, framing, contrasting—operate to a large extent on the basis of the inherent aspectual characteristics of lexical items denoting events, states, and processes.[9] Analyzing second language data according to these criteria will give insight into how temporal coherence is made transparent for the listener without the essential linguistic devices.

The second form of implicit reference, which we call *associative temporal reference*, is found in examples like:

(15) Türkei große Haus, Deutschland Wohnung ganz kleine.
"Turkey big house, Germany flat very small."

What this sentence means in the given context is "in Turkey I *had* a big house, in Germany I *have* a small flat." The semantics of the words do not convey anything about the possible temporal location. Only if the listener can associate the local expression "Turkey, Germany" with specific reference times (Turkey "meaning" past, Germany present) is he able to make sense of the given utterance.

The information has to be added from the outside, and this is what puts so much burden on the factor "shared knowledge" in this type of conversation.

Both forms of implicit reference can be found in the speech of all the informants studied, but the role changes with increasing fluency. Whereas for the low-level speaker they are an indispensable means for reporting a series of events, the advanced speaker has sufficient expressive devices to override them. Hence the application has become almost a question of style.

To conclude, let us see how these principles are used in combination, that is, how they interact with explicit linguistic devices in the construction of complex temporal structures on the discourse level. This will be illustrated by a short narrative.[10]

I: du hast gekündigt?

1. das ist Firma kündigen—das Krankenhaus
2. aber ich liebe Arbeit
3. Schwester gesag, das ist bei mir helfen arbeiten
4. *dann* Leute gesag, das ist Türkin, Ausländer, komm warum Schwester helfen arbeiten, muss deutsche Frau oder Fraulein arbeiten helfen
5. *dann* alles Ärger Ärger
6. *und dann* gehen, das ist Chef sagen, warum Türkin Schwester helfen
7. *und dann* was ist/was gesag
8. *und dann* weiss nicht
9. schlechte gesag, gute gesag
10. *und dann* gleich meine Kündigung komm
11. und Schwester ganz weinen
12. warum gehen, warum kündigen?
13. weiss nich, keine Ahnung
14. *dann nachher* ich gehen andere Firma
15. *nachher* bei mir Brief komm
16. und bitte bitte komm nochmal Arbeit

I: Did you hand in your notice?

1. it was the firm that dismissed me—the hospital
2. but I like the work
3. nurse said, she help me work
4. then people said, that is Turk, foreigner, come, why nurse help, German woman or girl should help to work
5. then everything trouble, trouble
6. and then go, to tell boss, why Turkish woman help nurse
7. and then, what said
8. and then (I) don't know
9. bad said, good said
10. and then immediately my dismissal come
11. and nurse all cry
12. why go, why hand in the notice?
13. I don't know, no idea
14. then afterward I go to another firm
15. afterward I get a letter
16. and please, please come back to work

The temporal structure of the narrative is relatively simple, if we ignore direct speech for a moment. There are two types of temporal relations: events can be either sequential or (partially) parallel in time (cf. Figure 2). The informant strictly adheres to the principle of real time order by using an additional lexical device *(und) dann* almost systematically for marking temporal shift from a given reference point to the next one.

The relation between the utterances which do not refer to a temporal sequence must be inferred from the specific content. In (2) we get a comment without a specific temporal value. It is introduced by *aber*. This is quite typical: the adversative conjunction is used by learners to "mark" a cut in the temporal flow of the narrative (cf. von Stutterheim, 1984). The other cases [internal structure of (4) and (6), (8–9), (11–13), (15–16)] of nonsequential relations follow a consistent pattern, i.e., a form of implicit reference. In these cases the speaker introduces a frame for quoted speech, quoted thought, and even quoted writing (15–16) by lexical means. Taken in terms of the overall temporal organization, the quoted parts must be interpreted as a form of embedding. They do not shift the temporal reference point. The *und dann* which follows a quotation links the utterance to the sentence which introduced the quote. This strategy of quotation is frequently used in learner languages to build up a temporal "relief."

After the illustration of what has been called the "concept-oriented approach" we would like to add just one final remark. We are not claiming that a

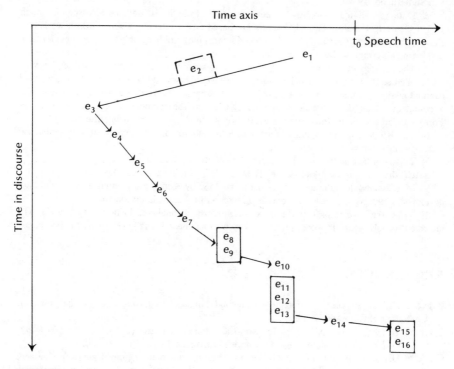

FIGURE 2

concept-oriented analysis can come up with an all-round explanation for second language learning and usage. But we think that this field has been widely neglected for a long time and that first studies carried out within that framework have proved that it is worth pursuing.

ACKNOWLEDGMENTS

Thanks are due to Mary Carroll, Clive Purdue, and Colette Noyau for their help.

NOTES

1. This chapter is a slightly revised version of the talk given by the first author at the Göhrde conference, 1982.

2. Taking the conceptual structure as a starting point obviously raises a number of methodological problems. How can we be sure what the speaker's conceptual structure really looks like? How can we know what he really intended to express in a given situation? There is no easy solution for all these problems. However, there are a number of methods, none of them always applicable, none of them reliable in every case. They include "rich interpretation," as often applied in first language acquisition studies, self-confrontation, bilingual interviews, selected experimental controls by spontaneous translations, and other (cf. Tarone, 1981; Heidelberger Forschungsprojekt, 1979; von Stutterheim, 1984).

3. Data on Italian and Spanish workers were taken from the Heidelberger Forschungsprojekt Pidgin Deutsch. Data on Turkish workers are based on 20 interviews with Turkish workers in Berlin. The workers (7 female/13 male, 25 to 45 years old) had lived at least 5 years in Germany and learned German without formal instruction.

4. The findings fit very nicely with other data presented in this volume; cf. Meisel, Trévise.

5. We use these terms in a strictly temporal sense: backgrounded utterances are those which cannot function as a temporal reference point R_t but rather function either as a temporal frame or as a comment which does not constitute an element of the temporal discourse organization. Foregrounded events, on the other hand, function as an R_t for the following utterance.

6. Turkish does not have temporal conjunctions; subordination is expressed by norminalized, tenseless verb forms.

7. This is in fact a stage at which learners may already fossilize.

8. Cf. the term "mutual knowledge" (Clark, 1977; Clark and Marshall, 1981).

9. Mention should be made here of the work done by Kamp and Rohrer (1982), who have developed a suitable model for systematizing temporal relations in discourse.

10. The narrative is part of the data von Stutterheim analyzed in her study (1984). The informant is a 42-year-old woman from Turkey who has been living in Germany for 10 years.

REFERENCES

Bates, E. 1981. Processing strategies in second language acquisition. Unpublished paper. University of Colorado, Boulder.

Clark, H. H. 1977. Bridging. In P. N. Johnson-Laird and P. C. Wason (eds.), *Thinking: Readings in Cognitive Science*. Cambridge: Cambridge University Press, pp. 411–420.

Clark, H. H., and C. R. Marshall. 1981. Definite reference and mutual knowledge. In A. K. Joshi, B. Webber, and I. Sag (eds.), *Elements of Discourse Understanding*. Cambridge: Cambridge University Press, pp. 10–63.

Cromer, R. F. 1979. The strengths of the weak form of the cognition hypothesis for language acquisition. In V. Lee (ed.), *Language Development*. London: Croom Helm.

Dittmar, N., W. Klein, and C. von Stutterheim. 1982. The expression of temporality in learner varieties. Unpublished paper. Max-Planck Institute for Psycholinguistics, Nijmegen.

Felix, S. W. 1981. Competing cognitive structures in second language acquisition. Paper presented at the European-North American Workshop on Cross-linguistic Second Language Acquisition Research, Los Angeles.

Givón, T. 1982. Tense-aspect modality: The creole prototype and beyond. In P. J. Hopper (ed.), *Tense and Aspect Between Semantics and Pragmatics*. Amsterdam: John Benjamins, pp. 115-163.

Heidelberger Forschungsprojekt. "Pidgin Deutsch." 1978. Zur Erlernung des Deutschen durch ausländische Arbeiter. Arbeitsbericht Nr. IV. Universität Heidelberg, German Department.

Heidelberger Forschungsprojekt. "Pidgin Deutsch." 1979. Studien zum Spracherwerb ausländischer Arbeiter. Arbeitsbericht. Nr. V. Universität Heidelberg, German Department.

Hopper, P. J. 1979. Aspect and foregrounding in discourse. In T. Givón (ed.), *Syntax and Semantics 12*. New York: Academic Press, pp. 213–241.

Hopper, P. J., and S. A. Thompson. 1980. Transitivity in grammar and discourse. *Language*. 56. 251–299.

Kamp, H. 1979. Events, instants and temporal reference. In R. Bäuerle, U. Egli, and A. von Stechow (eds.), *Semantics from a Different Point of View*. Berlin: Springer, pp. 376–417.

Kamp, H. 1981. Discourse representation and temporal reference. Unpublished paper.

Kamp, H., and C. Rohrer. 1983. Tense in texts. In R. Bäuerle, C. Schwarze, and A. von Stechow (eds.), *Meaning, Use and Interpretation*. Berlin: De Gruyter, pp. 250–269.

Klein, W. 1981. Knowing a language and knowing how to communicate. In A. Vermeer (ed.), *Language Problems of Minority Groups*. Tilburg: Tilburg University Press, pp. 75–95.

Kumpf, L. 1982. Tense, aspect and modality in interlanguage: A discourse-functional approach. Unpublished paper, UCLA.

Littlewood, W. T. 1979. Communicative performance in language-developmental contexts. *IRAL* 17. 123–138.

Tarone, E. 1981. Some thoughts on the notion of communicative strategy. *TESOL Quarterly*. 15. 285–295.

von Stutterheim, C. 1984a. Temporality in learner varieties. *Linguistische Berichte* 82. 31–45.

von Stutterheim, C. 1984b. Der Ausdruck der Temporalität in der Zweitsprache. Unpublished dissertation, Freie Universität Berlin.

CHAPTER 10

Reference to Past Events and Actions in the Development of Natural Second Language Acquisition[1]

Jürgen M. Meisel

University of Hamburg, Federal Republic of Germany

1. SOME THEORETICAL CONSIDERATIONS

Research on second language acquisition has been able to contribute to a general theory of language acquisition over the last years. Results show that it can help us to gain a better understanding of the human capacity to acquire and use language. It is more likely that underlying mechanisms may be discovered by contrasting second language (L2) acquisition to other types of language development, e.g., first language acquisition, language loss, pidginization, and creolization than by restricting one's attention to one type, such as first language acquisition. The importance of L2 data for the study of principles and strategies of language acquisition can, in fact, be seen in the specific choice of options the L2 acquirer has available during the whole process of acquisition. Since the development of the concepts which are to be conveyed through communication represents less of a problem for the L2 learner (especially the adult) than for the child acquiring the first language, L2 researchers' attention is appropriately focused on the changing ways in which they are expressed. Longitudinal studies of L2 development should therefore be able to reveal cognitive and communicative constraints on the use of morphological and syntactic devices to code the intended message.

To achieve this goal, however, it is necessary to go beyond the mere description of surface phenomena. Viewing L2 acquisition as a psychological *process*, instead of limiting one's analysis to a description of the *product* of L2 speech, is a step in the right direction but is not sufficient. What needs to be done is that the usual perspective has to be reversed; instead of searching for possible "interpretations" of a feature, we must define the concepts and functions which have to be encoded, and then analyze the devices used by different learners or types of learners to express these concepts and functions at different points on the developmental continuum.

In other words, I am advocating a functional approach to L2 acquisition. Although such an approach has been used quite successfully in L1 research, a similar change of perspective is not yet established in L2 studies. Even some of the more sophisticated works stick very closely to the usual criterion of appearance or nonappearance of grammatical devices. Quite frequently this criterion is defined in terms of surface features of the target language: correct functor supplied, wrong functor supplied, no functor supplied. This has been criticized repeatedly (see Wode et al., 1978), but it is nevertheless an approach which is almost always followed in L2 research.

To clarify this point, I will use our own work as an example and will try to show very briefly how it might be affected by the suggested change in perspective.[2] We have argued in several publications (see Meisel, Clahsen, and Pienemann, 1981), that a number of developmental phases can be defined in terms of word order rules which are acquired in the following sequence by learners of different L1 backgrounds: (1) ADV-FRONTING, which moves adverbials from the previously preferred sentence-final (equivalent to canonical SVX order) into sentence-initial position; (2) PARTICLE, which moves particles, infinitives, and participles to the end of the clause, as in sentences (1) to (3):

(1) ich *sehe* das Buch *an*
     "I am *looking at* the book"
(2) du *willst* das Buch *ansehen*
     "you *want to look at* the book"
(3) er *hat* das Buch *angesehen*
     "he *has looked at* the book"

(3) INVERSION of subject and verb, obligatory in German after preposed elements, e.g., interrogatives, fronted adverbials, topicalized clauses, or simple noun phrases; (4) ADV-VP, which moves adverbials into the verb phrase, as in (4):

(4) er kauft *morgen* das Buch
     "he buys *tomorrow* the book"[3]

(5) V-END, which moves the tensed verb to final position in certain embedded clauses.

We suggested to explain this sequence in terms of increasing complexity of the operations involved in the production of each of the constructions (see Clahsen, 1980; Meisel, 1983). Although we did not limit our attention to surface phenomena and still maintain that this explanation is basically correct, it may misrepresent the process of L2 acquisition in at least one respect. It implies that the same kind of operation is used by the learner in each case. We will need to modify our hypotheses if suggestions like the following by MacWhinney are correct. MacWhinney (in press) suggests that *initialization* of linguistic material is a pragmatic device which, along with morphological and syntactic devices, is used to set the stage for the interpretation of the following main predication. Such "stage setting" is also important for L2 learners. For L2 acquisition this implies that a learner who has only a limited number of syntactic devices and practically no morphological ones at his disposal may tend to rely heavily on the one option of initialization. The question to ask, then, is "how does a learner set the stage?" rather than asking for the number of past tense morphemes which are supplied or for the number of time adverbials which are used in various positions in the sentence.

If this is true, it follows that certain syntactic operations, like ADV-FRONTING and TOPICALIZATION OF NP, which can be described as initialization, do not have to be acquired in the same way as, for example, PARTICLE; they could be regarded as the pragmatically most plausible solutions to a communicative problem of the learner. Thus, it may be misleading to postulate a developmental sequence (such as the one mentioned above) which does not distinguish among such solutions. Note, however, that our original claim, namely, that ADV-FRONTING is performatively less complex than the other operations, can nevertheless be maintained. This is why it *can* be employed in an early phase, even by learners who use a rather restricted variety of L2 interlanguage. On the other hand, an approach which is limited to pragmatic aspects without considering performative complexity of syntactic construction cannot explain such phenomena. In fact, it can be shown (see Clahsen, 1984) that learners initialize adverbials far more frequently than object NPs. This is predicted by the claim that verb-object constructions form a psychological unit, the interruption of which increases the performative complexity significantly (see Slobin, 1973). In other words, for an operation to be carried out during early phases of L2 development, it is a necessary but not sufficient condition that it be performatively simple.

L2 acquirers apparently have more options and can choose among a range of devices to express a function; in L1 child language, variation of this kind also exists. A very interesting point is made by Givón (in press), who distinguishes between structure ("code") and function ("message") and, furthermore, between two communicative modes, the pragmatic and the syntactic. The latter is said to follow the former "ontogenetically, diachronically and probably also phylogenetically" (p. 14). This is explained as a consequence of the following facts:

> the pragmatic mode is a slow means of processing. . . . It is a more *transparent* communicative system, with a simpler 1:1 correlation between code and message. The syntactic mode . . . is a *faster, semiautomated* mode of processing, but it has lost a certain amount of *fidelity* and tends to exhibit either a lower correlation between code and message or a more complex correlation.

It may, indeed, be reasonable to assume that children first acquire the pragmatic mode and then gradually syntacticize it, since this permits them to be initially "clear" and "processible," and then, during later phases, "quick and easy" and "expressive" (see Slobin, 1977). Such a development seems to reflect the needs of the child learner. In the case of natural L2 acquisition, these needs may vary considerably as compared with L1 acquisition, and this variation may partially determine different learner types (see Meisel, Clahsen, and Pienemann, 1981). As pointed out by Felix (1978), L2 acquirers also differ from L1 learners in that they are able to use their implicit knowledge of syntactic organization of language from the beginning of the acquisitional process, and it is to be expected that at least some learners will focus on the syntactic mode even during the early phases and will give it more importance during the entire process of L2 acquisition than others do.

These remarks should suffice to set the stage for discussion of how adult learners of German, acquiring the language in a natural setting, make use of various devices to express reference to events or actions which are situated in the "not-here," "not-now," prior to the time of utterance.

2. THE DATA

The following observations are based on data collected in two research projects studying the acquisition of German by adult immigrant workers from Italy, Portugal, and Spain. After a number of preliminary studies and a pilot study (1974–1976), we carried out a cross-sectional study with 45 learners from age 15 to 65. Most of them had had little formal education, and their social and cultural background was fairly homogeneous. They had emigrated from their countries of origin because of economic necessity. The study was based on tape-recorded interviews which consisted mainly of informal free conversation. Occasionally, additional formal elicitation techniques and oral language proficiency tests were used. The recordings were subsequently transcribed and analyzed.

In a subsequent longitudinal study, twelve immigrants to Germany from Italy, Portugal, and Spain were interviewed for at least 57 weeks, some for well over 80 weeks, usually starting within a few weeks after immigration. At the time of the first interview, they were between 14 and 37 years of age; the social and educational background was similar to the population of the cross-sectional study, with the exception of two women who had more than average formal instruction. The main purpose of the longitudinal study was to test the hypotheses developed during the preceding studies, especially the claims concerning developmental sequences. Basically, the same techniques and methods were used; in addition, tests to assess language proficiency, linguistic awareness, ability to detect errors in their own speech in earlier recordings, etc., were administered.

The linguistic analysis attempts to describe the development of German as a second language, focusing on syntactic and morphological aspects. We also tried to distinguish between developmental patterns which can be predicted to be followed by all learners, and others which are claimed to be specific to certain types of learners only. In an effort to explain learner-type-specific linguistic variation by means of external and internal factors, our studies included an analysis of social-psychological factors. Computer-aided statistical methods were applied in the cross-sectional study. In the longitudinal study, individual factors were examined with special care. Case studies containing demographic information and reports about the individual's contact at work, activities after working hours, etc., were prepared for each of the twelve learners. In addition, we carried out IQ and personality tests and administered an assertion analysis to determine motivations and attitudes. Detailed information about these studies is given in Clahsen, Meisel, and Pienemann (1983) and in Clahsen et al. (forthcoming).

We believe that these analyses enable us to determine the learning orientation of each individual, resulting from the network of social-psychological factors, and we also think that we can show how learning orientations influence the choice among the different strategies of L2 acquisition and processing. With respect to the topic of the present paper, explanations of this kind still require broader empirical verification and a more thorough analysis. For the time being, the focus will be on a description of what we expect will turn out to be a developmental sequence. Analyses of learner-type-specific variation and explanations in terms of underlying mechanisms determining both general development and variation should follow after the establishment of developmental patterns. Explanations will have to be based on comparisons with other types of language acquisition, particularly L1 acquisition.

In what follows, examples will be given from one learner studied longitudinally, José SL.[4] The results obtained by a detailed examination of his linguistic development over a period of 80 weeks have been compared with careful analyses of six other learners in the longitudinal study. In addition, they have been compared with data from the cross-sectional study. In quoting from José's speech, roman numerals refer to the number of the interview; arabic numerals refer to the length of residence, e.g., II (1;7) stands for the second recording, taken after 1 year and 7 weeks of residence.

3. REFERENCE TO PAST EVENTS AND ACTIONS IN THE TARGET LANGUAGE

Standard German, "Hochdeutsch," offers a choice among a number of devices to refer to past events, but there is considerable disagreement as to what exactly the functions of the so-called tense forms are, whether they also carry aspectual value, etc. To simplify matters, I will only mention some basic facts.

1. A number of tense markings can be used to refer to past events:
   a. PRETERITE is claimed to be the "basic form" which refers to the past, and grammar books state that it expresses an event accomplished in the past without relation to present state of affairs. The "regular preterite" is constructed by means of the suffix -te, e.g., er

sagte "he said"; the so-called "strong forms" make use of the "ablaut," e.g., *du gehst—du gingst* "you go—you went."

b. PRESENT PERFECT is constructed by means of an auxiliary (most frequently *haben*, sometimes *sein*) and the past participle, frequently in the following form: *ge + verb stem + t* or *ge + verb stem + en; er hat gesagt* "he has said," *du bist gegangen* "you have gone." Grammar books usually state that this tense refers to past events which are somehow related to the present state of affairs; e.g., you step out of the door and realize the street is wet and say *es hat geregnet* "it has rained" but never *es regnete* "it rained."

c. PAST PERFECT refers to past events which occurred prior to other events in the past; formally it resembles the present perfect except that the preterite forms of the auxiliary (*hatte, war,* etc.) are used.

Other tense forms may also be used to refer to past events if special conditions are set, e.g., "historical present tense" *44 v. Chr. wird Caesar ermordet* "Caesar was assassinated in 44 BC" or present tense referring to immediate past, e.g., *letzthin komme ich ins Büro, als . . .* "the other day, I enter the office when suddenly . . .".

2. Adverbials (i.e., adverbs and adverbial prepositional phrases) also establish reference to events which occurred prior to the time of utterance. This is obvious in the case of time adverbials, but locatives may serve a similar function if the speaker can assume that the listener knows that the people or objects involved in the action (event) used to be in the place mentioned at some point prior to the time of discourse.

3. Principles of discourse organization. Included here are some devices which are usually not mentioned in traditional grammar books and which would need more careful analysis: knowledge shared by the interlocutors, discourse structure, etc. One such device which is of prime importance for L2 studies is "order of mention"; i.e., events are sequenced such that the order of mention corresponds to order of occurrence.

This picture of "Hochdeutsch," however, may be misleading since the different forms listed under 1—although far from being described in a comprehensive manner—are not used in colloquial German in this way, especially not in dialectal varieties which provide the input for the learners studied. In spoken German, the preterite has virtually disappeared except with the copula, auxiliaries, and some modals. It is more likely to be used (with main verbs) in northern than in southern dialects, but it is safe to assume that such forms are extremely rare in the input of the learners. On the other hand, in the spoken colloquial German of some regions there is a form which looks like past perfect but which is used in contexts where Hochdeutsch would require present perfect, e.g., *gestern war ich im Kino gewesen* "yesterday I have (had) been to the movies."

Summarizing, we may expect the learners to acquire preterite forms with modals and auxiliaries, present perfect forms with all verbal elements, past perfect forms (including those with present perfect meaning) with all verbal elements, and we can expect to find that adverbials will be used as well as special principles of discourse organization. The use of present tense forms to refer to past events is less likely to be found, since it is restricted to specific discourse types, e.g., dramatic narratives, etc.

4.   REFERENCE TO THE PAST IN L2 DEVELOPMENT

In what follows, I will try to show which of these devices are actually used, and I will address the question of the developmental sequence in which such devices for reference to past events and actions appear.

As a first general remark, I want to point to the fact that during early phases of L2 acquisition, adult learners do not make systematic use of the inflectional system of the target language. In fact, many of those who acquire the language under the unfavorable conditions characteristic for many immigrant workers never use anything which comes close to the German system of verb inflection. José is one of the most successful learners of those studied by our research team; many others never get beyond the first of the phases discussed below. As long as inflectional forms have not been acquired, the verbal element (main verbs, modals, auxiliaries, and the copula) is used in an *invariant form*. There is, however, a huge amount of individual variation as to which one is used: infinitives, third person singular of the present tense, etc. Often it is hard to decide which form the learner is aiming at, especially since phonetic problems also intervene. Furthermore, the infinitive is identical to 1 pl. and 3 pl. present, e.g., *schlafen* "(to) sleep"; so, in cases where the subject pronoun is omitted, the intended meaning cannot be identified. In dialects which delete the final *n* in unstressed syllables, these forms merge with 1 sg. pres. *ich schlafe* "I sleep."

Quite frequently, even an invariant form is lacking as a result of learners' employment of simplification strategies which permit omission of verbal elements entirely (see Meisel, Clahsen, and Pienemann, 1981; Meisel, 1983). The use of these strategies depends on learner types. Although we found in the longitudinal study that all learners delete during the early phases, only some do so after they make progress toward the target variety. In general, nouns are deleted more frequently than verbal elements. Some learners, e.g., Zita PL, however, delete verbal elements categorically during early recording sessions. José, on the other hand, starts out with a lower probability of deletion of verbal elements of .75 during the first interview but subsequently never goes beyond .5. As of XII (1;44), he stays below .2. He uses main verbs and copulas from the beginning, while auxiliaries appear subsequently and modals even later.

How, then, does an L2 acquirer establish reference to the "not-here," "not-now" if during early phases verbal elements are either omitted or not systematically marked? One way to do this is by means of what has been called *scaffolded discourse* (see Slobin, 1981); there is considerable interaction between the learner and the interlocutor, the latter asking questions and frequently also providing possible answers. Occasionally, this looks like a multiple-choice procedure, and the learner merely has to pick the right point of reference among the several suggested by the native interlocutor. There are good reasons to suspect that there is, quite generally, a significant amount of cooperation with the interlocutor without the parties involved necessarily being aware of this. More detailed analyses are needed to answer questions such as what are the conditions for successful cooperation and what are the linguistic devices used?

The second principle for establishing reference to nonactual events and actions might be called *implicit reference*. In this case, the L2 speaker mentions an event assuming that the interlocutor will be able to infer that it has to be situated at a specific point in the past or in the future, for example, as in (5):

(5) meine schwester klein meine mutter ni arbeit
    "my sister small my mother not work."

The hearer interprets this as *"as long as"/"when"* my sister was young, my mother did not go to work. This presupposes shared knowledge or simply relies on the situational context, as in (6) taken from the first interview, I (1;2):

(6) hier wohne ich/ fünf kilometer Portugal
    "here I live/ five kilometers Portugal"

When uttering this, José and his interlocutors were looking at a map of Spain; so it is obvious that he was referring to the time before emigration.

A third possibility is to *contrast two or more events*. This is related to the second principle, since it can be used successfully only if the speaker can presuppose that the interlocutor will be able to establish that they have to be related temporally. This may be achieved by referring to the same kind of event, e.g., mentioning places where the speaker is or was employed, adding that one pays/paid better than the other. If the listener knows that the speaker was or was not employed at two places simultaneously, he will have to sequence the events or actions chronologically. If this appeal to the listener's knowledge does not yield the correct intepretation, and the speaker realizes this, he will have to use explicit temporal markings. I will return to this later.

A fourth principle of L2 discourse organization: *order of mention follows the natural order*, i.e., the order of actual occurrence is familiar from conversational analysis and studies of L1 acquisition. This strategy is not limited to cases where relating the different events to each other is unavoidable. Rather, the learner may replace one past event by a sequence of events ordered as they actually occurred, thus situating in time the point of reference in question, as in (7) from V (1;17): in this example the interlocutor asks how José found his job; J. does not understand; I. gives a possible answer.

(7) I: der don M. hat dir gesagt: kommt José ich habe 'ne arbeit
        "don M. told you: come on J., I have a job for you"
    J: nein nein
        "no no"

I: wie dann?
     "then how?"
J: de don M. ist der geschäftsführer von se (de) Lazo ne?
     "this don M. is the manager of the "Lazo" right?"
     und der andere geschäftsführer von de Chaparral hat mir gesagt komm du für mir/und
     de andere jetzt aufmachen hier eine in Oberkassel bei de Belsenplatz eine Steakhouse
     "and the other manager of the Ch. has said to me: you come for(= to) me. and the other
     now open(ing) one here in Oberkassel near the Belsen square a steakhouse"

Instead of just answering how he found his job, José mentions three restaurants, Lazo, Chaparral, and the new steakhouse where he used to work, is currently working, and will be working, respectively. He locates the events in time by mentioning names and locations of the restaurants, finally succeeding in explaining how he found the new job. He also uses adverbials, *hier,* and one instance of verbal marking, a correct present perfect, *hat mir gesagt.* In this interview, the first instances of verbal inflection appear in José's speech. The different events are related by means of a conjunction, *und.* Finally, reference to the immediate future is expressed by the adverbial *jetzt.* This is a very complex example; although cases like this one are not very frequent, it is by no means the only instance. It shows cooperation between learner and native interlocutor, the latter offering a possible answer to his previous question; the learner then replacing one event, how he found his new job, by a sequence of events given in their natural order. Implicit reference is also used but plays a minimal role here. A number of formal linguistic devices are also employed to refer to the past: verbal marking, adverbials, and conjunctions.

This leads us to the next point, the kinds of explicit linguistic devices available to the learner, i.e., free and bound morphemes. We have already seen that different discourse principles and different linguistic devices can be combined. In early phases, it appears to be quite usual that no such linguistic device is used; i.e., there is no explicit linguistic reference to the time of the event under discussion. All the principles mentioned allow this avoidance of marking. Thus, initially, learners tend to let the native speaker supply the necessary markings, and they appeal to his ability to make inferences based on previous knowledge about an event. Only if the native interlocutor fails to set the scene in an appropriate way will the learner provide the necessary information. It is not certain, however, that this kind of behavior will be found in all learners; rather, I suspect that this feature of early second language acquisition is specific to particular learner types. This remark also applies to the following observation: in initial stages, temporal markings seem to be limited to one instance per conversational unit, defined as a sequence of utterances dealing with the same topic and not changing the temporal reference. In other words, redundant marking of temporal reference appears to be drastically reduced by eliminating verbal inflections which are obligatory in the target language, and by giving other kinds of information only if there is the risk of misunderstanding.

During early phases of L2 acquisition, reference to the past, when expressed explicitly by the learner, is established by means of one linguistic device exclusively, namely, adverbial expressions. Learners differ with respect to the internal structure of the adverbials. Whereas, for example, José prefers adverbial proforms, others predominantly use prepositional phrases. (Lina IL); Ana SL uses both, and Zita PL uses adverbs more categorically than José SL. Quite frequently, the preposition is deleted from prepositional phrases. The inventory of prepositions itself is strikingly limited for a fairly long period: *in* is by far the most common, followed by *von* "from." We will not go into this since the phenomena do not seem to be restricted to temporal expressions. Similarly, we will not discuss the placement of adverbials in much detail. Roughly speaking, German, as well as the three Romance languages, which are the native languages of the learners studied, offers three possibilities: sentence-final, sentence-initial, and internal (i.e., within the verb phrase, immediately following the verb). As mentioned above, adverbials first appear in final position, but very early many learners begin to place them in initial position. If MacWhinney is right, this means that adverbials and topicalized noun phrases "set the stage" for the following proposition. This seems to be a very plausible explanation and might partly account for the frequent initialization of adverbials, given that temporality and modality are not yet expressed by means of verb inflection. Findings in other areas of morphological development indicate that there is, in fact, a relation of this kind between bound and free morphemes. To mention one example, Zita PL, a Portuguese learner, usually supplies verb inflection for the 2nd sg. only in sentences where she omitted the subject pronoun; the converse apparently also holds true; i.e., omission of subject pronouns usually entails verbal marking. We might expect to find a similar relationship between adverbials and verb inflection.

In our cross-sectional study we found that some learners tend to place adverbials immediately after the subject, preceding the verb (see Clahsen, Meisel, and Pienemann, 1983: 180–184). This results in constructions which are ungrammatical in German. Note, however, that no other ungrammatical placements of adverbials were observed in our studies and, furthermore, that it was temporal and modal adverbials almost exclusively which occurred in this position. One might hypothesize that they are attracted by the verb to replace the missing information conveyed by the target language suffix. This would support our suggested explanation concerning the relationship between word order and the use of bound morphemes. What might appear to be strange, then, is that the internal position of the adverbial next to the verb is acquired late and used very infrequently. This position could have been expected to be attractive for the learner who uses adverbials instead of verb inflection. But here again, one has to take into account the fact that the internal position is performatively more complex (see Clahsen, 1984; Meisel, 1983). This complexity outweighs the gain in expressiveness. These remarks must suffice as far as the position of adverbials is concerned; we have not found specific placement restrictions for adverbials establishing reference to past events.

I would like to add a few observations about the kind of adverbials used in these cases. During the first 12 weeks of recording, the adverbials found in

José's speech are almost exclusively locative. He uses them to refer to events or actions occurring before or after the time of conversation, e.g., *in Spanien, in Deutschland, in Orense.* Although their preponderance may be due to the specific situation and type of conversation—an immigrant talking about what happened before and after emigration from his country of origin—it is striking that locatives are also used to refer to more immediate past or future events. Comparing José with other learners, we found, however, that this, again, is a feature characteristically used by certain acquirers. Zita PL and Bongiovanni IL behave similarly to José SL in using locatives to set time, while Ana SL and Lina IL also use temporal adverbials right from the beginning. It remains to be seen whether this is systematic for some learner types or whether this is only a chance distribution due to individual acquisitional strategies.

Occasionally, calendric expressions like *in August* and relational temporal expressions like *sechs Monate* appear as in example (8)III(1;11): talking about J's girlfriend

(8) I: und mit der triffst du dich so/ seit wann denn/
           "and you meet her occasionally? since when?"
     J: das is en . . . de de von Asturias
           "this is en . . . the the from Asturias"
     I: ne nich wo/ wann/
           "no, not where, when!"
     J: *cuando, cuando la conoci*/eh . . .sech monat oder so
           "when, when I first met her? eh . . . six months or so."

Here, José mentions only the time span, deleting the preposition *vor* "ago," which is left to the listener's interpretation. This kind of expression appears repeatedly. I would like to hypothesize that during early phases, learners who otherwise prefer locative expressions use more elaborate devices such as calendric expressions, relational temporal expressions, and perhaps all temporal adverbials predominantly when their reliance on the interlocutor's intuition has led to misunderstanding or lack of comprehension. This hypothesis requires further testing.

Note that the use of adverbials is frequently combined with the above-mentioned principle of contrast, as in example (9), I (1;2): asked whether he plays soccer,

(9) J: hier in Deutschland nis/ in Spain ja aber hier nis/
           "here in Germany not/ in Spain yes but here not/"

Another class of linguistic devices used to refer to past events which appears as early as adverbials is connectives. The most frequent ones are *und, dann, aber* "and, then, but," sometimes combined as in *und dann.* They play an important role in connection with the principles of sequencing events in their natural order and of contrasting two or more events, as in examples (7) and (9) above.

This very limited set of linguistic devices, together with the principles mentioned, seems to suffice to express, in a very rudimentary but often sufficient manner, the functions discussed so far. Several principles and several devices may be combined, but sometimes reference is only implicit and none of these linguistic expressions is used. The inadequacy of these means becomes apparent as soon as more than reference to just one event in the past is necessary, i.e., when different events, all occurring in the past, have to be related, or when, in a narrative, a change of perspective is appropriate or necessary. This can be illustrated by example (10), V(1;17): talking about J's girlfriend whom he does not see any more, supposedly because they only had time to meet once a week. I asks whether the real reason was not another girl.

> (10) J: nächste montag isch andere frau auch. deutsche—italianisch-deutsche/sprechen/
> italianisch eh sprechen kein italianisch, nur sprechen deutsch/
> "next Monday I also other woman, German—Italo-German. Speak . . Italian eh
> speak(s) no Italian, only speak(s) German."

What J. meant became apparent as the conversation went on: the Monday after he had last seen his former girlfriend, he met another girl, an Italian born in Germany who spoke only German. The interlocutor did not understand this, asking (very surprised) "you are going to break up with her next Monday, this coming Monday, you know already?" Thus, he failed to interpret *nächste Montag* "next Monday" as referring to a point of time in the past.

To express this function, i.e., relating events in the past, it seems to be necessary to have a more complex system of linguistic devices available, namely, the ones mentioned plus verbal inflection. Except for one occurrence in III(1;11)—apparently an imitation of the native interlocutor's immediately preceding utterance—the first instances of verbal markings establishing temporal reference appear in José's speech in V(1;17). In fact, in earlier recordings, no main verb appears in more than one form, usually the infinitive. The only two inflected verbs can be interpreted as routine formulaic utterances acquired at work (as a waiter): *weiß ich nicht* "I don't know" and *trinkst du?* "do you (want to) drink (something)?" Some other verbs do carry inflectional marking, but these are invariant forms, irrespective of tense and person.

As soon as verb inflection appears, it results in great confusion. In fact, almost all inflected verbs now violate the target norm, even those which were invariantly used before, and therefore sometimes looked like standard usage, e.g., *versteh' ich nich* "I don't understand" which now becomes, in V(1;17), *verstehst ich nicht*, marked as 2nd pers. sg. *-st.* This confusion is occasionally also extended to auxiliaries. Up to this point, the auxiliary/copula *ist* "is" is always used correctly; similarly, J. uses *(ich) habe(n)* "I have" for a certain period of time. This continues to be used but, in addition, forms like the correct *(du) hast* "you have," *(er) hat* "he has" and the nonstandard forms *ich hats, ich hat, ich hatte,* are all used as 1st sg. present tense. Thus, as a consequence of the beginning acquisition of verb inflection, there is considerable variation instead of previous invariance, but also great uncertainty. Nevertheless, this should be interpreted as an indication of development in the L2 grammar.

As might be expected (compare section 3), the first form used with main verbs to refer to past events in learners' speech is the present perfect. The verb is always used in the past participle form, and the auxiliary may be omitted by some learners, for example, by José. But even when the auxiliary is missing, the main verb is moved to the end of the clause, as required in German. There is a strong tendency to overgeneralize the use of the auxiliary *haben* "have" in cases where *sein* "be" would be appropriate. Similarly, the *ge + verb stem + t* past participle form tends to be overgeneralized at the expense of the *ge + verb stem + en* forms. Some learners, however, like Ana SL, choose the other alternative, preferring *ist* "is" as the auxiliary and *ge + verb stem + en* as past participle. It remains to be seen whether this is an idiosyncrasy or whether other learners do, in fact, behave like Ana. In José's speech, the first instance of a standard perfect form appears in V(1;17), see example (7) above. In subsequent interviews, he uses constructions of this kind more and more consistently, often in accordance with the German target norm, deviating, however, where *sein* would be required or where *-en* participles would be appropriate, e.g., *ich habe bekommt* "I have received," in XXII (2;30).

Before the next step in José's L2 development of the expression of reference to past events, a rather long time elapsed. One should bear in mind that J. is one of the most successful learners in our study; many never get as far as using present perfect constructions as he does. The next step is the use of past tense constructions with *sein* "to be"; see example (11), XII (1;44): talking about J's last holidays in Spain:

(11) I: was hast du denn gemacht da?
          "so, what did you do there?"
     J: alles
          "all (kinds of things)"
     I: alles, nur nicht gearbeitet?
          "everything but work?"
     J: auch ein bisken, aber nich so viel/ war zwei tage in de ganze urlaub/
          "also a little, but not so much. was two days during the holidays"

He is saying that he only worked two days, using the past tense of *sein* correctly except for failure to mark the plural, which would have been *waren*.

During the first recording, José never used a modal verb. When they begin to appear in his speech, they expressed obligation, possible events in the future, etc., but they were never used to refer to past events. This began only much later and was rather rare; see example (12) XXII(2;30):

(12) I: hast du nicht krach gehabt mit Toni oder wie war das?
          "didn't you get into an argument with Toni, or how was that?"
     J: ja, der Toni wollte nix. dass ich gehe. ne †was soll der machen †
          "yes, the Toni [possible in German] didn't want me to leave, uh? what should he do?"

Another development related to the acquisition of verb morphology but not to the expression of reference to prior events concerns plural markings. By the time modals are used in the past tense form, *haben* "have" and *sein* "be" are occasionally marked for plural, e.g., *haben wir, (sie) sind* "have we, they are."

A consequence of the acquisition of a more elaborate system of linguistic devices is that the importance of principles of discourse organization mentioned above declines; learners are able to give reports without the support of the native speaker; reference to points in time is frequently made explicit, and the order of mention may reverse the natural order of occurrence period. This also means that reference not only can be made to specific points in the past, but different events in the past can be related to each other; the speaker may change perspective within the narrative; all this implies that one event can be introduced as background for another occurring later but still taking place in the past. Thus, it is possible for the L2 acquirer to express a range of functions all concerning reference to past events and actions; some of these could not be expressed as long as the whole set of devices was not available. Consider example (10) above, where J. did not succeed in relating two past events in a way comprehensible to the native interlocutor. Now, compare this with example (13), XII(1;44): Explaining how useful the knowledge of German might be for him as a waiter, even if he goes back to Spain, J. recounts an event which happened during his holidays in his native village, Verin:

(13)   und jetzt. ich habe in Verin net mit drei. mit drei deutsche hier von Düsseldorf/hat(te) ein. eine in ein café net/ich habe 'raus zwei motorrad geguckt net/ . . ./Deutschland Düsseldorf/ ich komm da reint. und der muss äh, die tss frühstück net/ un' kann ich mit de kellner sprechen net/ (kann ich sagen) was möchten sie haben?/ *was* hat der gesagt. uuuh sprecht auch deutsch/
"and now, I have (talked?) [verb missing] in V. huht with three, with three Germans here from D. Had (there was) one, one in a café, uh? I have out(side) two motorbikes seen, uh? Germany Düsseldorf. I come [present] in there, and this guy has to [pres.] eh, the tss breakfast, right? And I can [pres.] talk to the waiter, right? (I can say) What would you like to have? *what* has he said [correct use of perfect in German], (you) also speak German?"

Although the sequence of events recounted in this example does correspond to the chronological order, J. is able to switch tenses. He first uses the perfect to set the stage (backgrounding), beginning with *und jetzt* to indicate that this happened fairly recently; then he switches to the present tense, *ich komme, der muss, ich kann;* and then back to perfect, *er hat gesagt.* The following example shows that J. no longer has to follow the natural order of events, XXII(2;30):

(14) I: hast du ne telefonnummer von mir oder von H.?
          "do you have my phone number or H's?"
     J: nee. hab ich kein/ von H. hab ich verlort/hab ich gehabt
          "no, I have none. H's I have lost. I (used to) have had it"

The order of mention reverses the natural order: I have none of these numbers, I lost the one I had, I used to have H's.

A remark should be devoted to the hypothesized use of aspectual marking in learners' interlanguages. When referring to past events and actions, the learner might use aspectual markings to indicate that an event has been accomplished rather than using temporal markings expressing reference to points prior to the time of utterance. The study of creole languages, which have similar systems, supports predictions of this kind. In creoles the temporal systems of the substrate languages tend to be replaced by aspectual systems proposed by

Meisel (1977) and others. The hypothesis is that, like creoles, an early phase of L2 acquisition might be characterized by a distinction between perfectivity and nonperfectivity in the actions expressed by the verb. The perfective could be coded by means of adverbials or morphological markings, the latter using the inflectional system of the target language which there expresses temporality. A first look at some data appeared to support this hypothesis. One learner studied in our cross-sectional study, Franco I, seemed to use an opposition between past participles of verb (usually omitting the auxiliary) and "other verbal forms," which varied depending on the verb, infinitives, and 3rd sg. present forms predominating. A few other learners seemed to use adverbials or other expressions like *fertig* "finished," *ende*, "end" to express perfectivity, as in (15):

(15)   Giovanni IL: meine vater *fertig* arbeiten deutsch zurück in Italien
        "my father finish work Germany back in Italy" (When my father stops working in
        Germany, he will go back to I.)

A more careful analysis, however, revealed that learners do not systematically use an aspectual system. It may well be that this is a very marginal phenomenon, occurring only occasionally, which has received too much attention by researchers who based their expectations on findings in L1 studies or on creole studies.

It might also be the case that it is a learner-specific characteristic. My guess is that aspectual notions play a marginal role in the development of L2 interlanguages. They may be used occasionally, just as standard languages with temporal systems do, in some instances, make use of aspectual notions. Anyone who wants to claim that an aspectual system is characteristic of certain phases of L2 acquisition or of specific types of learners will have to give solid empirical evidence. Citing isolated examples will not suffice; quantification is indispensable in this case.

5.   CONCLUSIONS AND PROBLEMS FOR FUTURE RESEARCH

The picture which emerges from this description is not yet entirely clear, and certainly not definitive. The results are summarized in Figure 1, which shows that some functions can be expressed only during the later phases of L2 development—after a sufficiently elaborate set of linguistic devices has been acquired. As for the principles of discourse organization which help to express references to past events and actions, they are quite obviously not given up altogether, since they also belong to those conversational principles used by native speakers, but they play a less important role after the acquisition of the linguistic devices listed at the top of the diagram. These are ordered, from bottom to top, as they appear chronologically in the speech of L2 learners. Note that this refers to the beginning of systematic usage; it does not make any claims about how successfully they are used (80 or 90 percent) of all possible occurrences, or some similiar criterion).

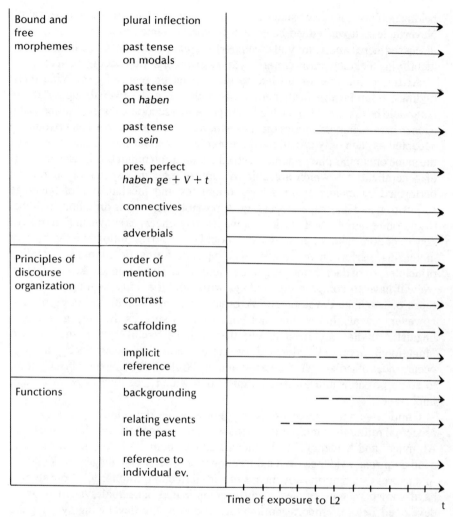

Bound and free morphemes	plural inflection	
	past tense on modals	
	past tense on *haben*	
	past tense on *sein*	
	pres. perfect *haben ge + V + t*	
	connectives	
	adverbials	
Principles of discourse organization	order of mention	
	contrast	
	scaffolding	
	implicit reference	
Functions	backgrounding	
	relating events in the past	
	reference to individual ev.	

Time of exposure to L2   t

FIGURE 1 Preliminary developmental chronology: Reference to past events and actions

The arrows indicating the periods during which functions are expressed and morphemes or discourse principles are used are sometimes drawn as broken lines (see Figure 1). This represents the fact that the empirical evidence available is not sufficient to decide exactly when a certain function is first expressed and, with respect to the principles of discourse organization, shows that these are never really abandoned, but rather that their relative importance decreases.

At any rate, I do not attempt to pinpoint the exact onset of usage. It would be premature to make strong claims regarding this question. What I hope will turn out to be correct is the developmental sequence established, ranging from adverbials to past tense of modals. Plural inflection, strictly speaking, does not belong to this category, since it is not a means of expressing temporality. Nevertheless, it was added because it is closely related in form to the devices discussed here, and it may also support the expression of these functions by identifying the noun phrase referring to the event or action occurring in the past.

At this point, one would like to turn to the problem of explaining these findings, assuming that further empirical evidence can be given to support them. As should be apparent from what has been said in section 1 above, the approach chosen in this chapter implies that an *explanation* of the observed facts would be accepted as such only if it allowed for predictions about further occurrences of the same or similar phenomena. Such an explanation might be phrased in terms of generalizations, which are able to capture relevant aspects of operations performed by means of underlying principles and mechanisms of language acquisition and language processing. A possible step in this direction could be, to give one example, that the developmental sequences (as shown in Figure 1) of new functions and of new devices could be said to follow hierarchies of increasing performative complexity (e.g., in terms of Slobin's operating principles) or of decreasing pragmatic usefulness. To be able to take such a step, we will have to compare our findings with similar studies dealing with other types of language development. A brief glance at available research results, however, reveals that we may not hope for easy success. Rather, more cross-linguistic studies are needed; but they will be useful only if they take a "functional approach," instead of merely counting occurrences or non-occurrences of isolated surface phenomena. To close this chapter, I briefly point to some possible future research questions which I believe to be of crucial importance.

Child language researchers more or less agree that children first express aspectual rather than temporal notions when acquiring their first languages (see Antinucci and Miller, 1976; Bronckart and Sinclair, 1973). Further, there is good empirical evidence from a fair number of different languages that children first express such notions by means of verb inflection. Similarly, creole studies have shown that in creoles a fairly complicated aspectual system may be developed before temporal notions are coded in the developing system; the expressive devices are usually verbal elements, never adverbials. Pidgins, on the other hand, use adverbials, frequently clause-external, and these are not integrated into a later developing creole system; instead, the first-generation creole speaker may use verbal elements to construct an aspectual system (see Bickerton, 1981). Summarizing, we may expect to find that children—in L1 acquisition as in creoles—differ markedly from our adult L2 acquirers with respect to the functions expressed as well as to the formal devices used. Thus, if we want to explain our findings in terms of performative complexity or pragmatic usefulness, we have to account for the fact that children appear to have different notions of complexity or usefulness.

The questions to be asked, then, are: "what exactly are the differences among these types of language development?" and "what causes these differences to appear?" As for the former question, we need to know whether children really first refer to aspectual distinctions. If this were the case, could we say that verbal elements are more adequate means to express aspect, while adverbials more easily render temporal notions? An answer of this kind must appear to be somewhat unsatisfactory as long as one cannot say *why* this should be the case. But it would enable us to give at least a partial answer to the above question; the difference would then be one of semantic notions expressed, rather than one stemming from specific coding problems. This leads to the second question: the causes for the observed similarities and differences. Do adults differ from children in their speech behavior because of differing conversational strategies, varying communicative needs, etc.? Or do children make use of some kind of innate knowledge, preprogrammed notions, etc., which make aspectual distinctions more easily accessible to them than a temporal organization of the world?

A number of these questions could be answered, I believe, if we had comparable results from naturalistic L2 acquisition by children. We would need longitudinal data from children who already use and comprehend temporal (as opposed to aspectual) reference in their first language. In fact, I would tend to interpret such findings as evidence in favor of theories which claim that there is a language-specific innate program which is accessible only until a certain age. This discussion will have to wait until we possess at least some of the evidence asked for above. At any rate, this kind of research not only would tell us more about second language acquisition but should also be able to contribute significantly to our understanding of language development in general.

NOTES

1. This paper is based on research conducted during the workshop; on Principles and Strategies of Language Acquisition, Max Planck-Institut für Psycholinguistik, August 15–September 13, 1981. The workshop was directed by Dan I. Slobin, Eve Clark, and Brian MacWhinney. Some of the findings presented here have been discussed in working groups chaired by Eve Clark and Dan Slobin. I want to thank all participants for their help. Thanks are also due to Klaus-Michael Köpcke, who is responsible for the detailed analysis of the longitudinal study informants discussed here. A first version of this chapter was presented at the Second European–North American Workshop on Cross-Linguistic Second Language Acquisition Research, Göhrde (Hamburg), August 1982.

2. "Our own work" refers to publications by the present author and by other members of the research group ZISA (Zweitspracherwerb spanischer, italienischer und portugiesischer Arbeiter). The research was supported by two research grants to J. M. Meisel. In 1977/78, a cross-sectional study was funded by the Minister für Wissenschaft und Forschung des Landes Nordrhein-Westfalen; part of the work on the cross-sectional study as well as a longitudinal study were supported by a grant from the Stiftung Volkswagenwerk, 1978–1982. During the period when the research on this chapter was carried out, ZISA consisted of four researchers, Harald Clahsen, Klaus-Michael Köpcke, Howard Nicholas, Maryse Vincent, and myself. I want to thank all four for the very interesting discussions and the pleasant time we spent together.

3. The English versions of the German sentences are not always exact translations; they are not even always grammatically correct in English. They have been constructed in a way which should help in understanding the German grammatical phenomena being discussed.

4. The abbreviation after a person's first name refers to the nationality: S = Spanish, P = Portuguese, I = Italian. The second letter, L, indicates that this person was interviewed longitudinally.

REFERENCES

Antinucci, F., and R. Miller. 1976. How children talk about what happened. *Journal of Child Language* 3. 167–189.

Bickerton, D. 1981. *Roots of Language.* Ann Arbor: Karoma.

Bronckart, J.-P., and H. Sinclair. 1973. Time, tense and aspect. *Cognition* 2. 107–130.

Clahsen, H. 1980. Psycholinguistic aspects of L2 acquisition: Word order phenomena in foreign workers' interlanguage. In S. W. Felix (ed.), *Second Language Development—Trends and Issues,* Tübingen: Gunter Narr Verlag, pp. 57–79.

Clahsen, H. 1984. The acquisition of German word order: A test case for cognitive approaches to L2 development. In R. W. Andersen (ed.), *Second Languages.* Rowley, Mass.: Newbury House, pp. 219–242.

Clahsen, H., J. M. Meisel, and M. Pienemann. 1983. *Deutsch als Zweitsprache. Der Spracherwerb ausländischer Arbeiter.* Tübingen: Gunter Narr Verlag.

Clahsen, H., K.-M. Köpcke, J. M. Meisel, H. Nicholas, and M. Vincent. Forthcoming. *Sprachentwicklung in der zweiten Sprache,* Tübingen: Gunter Narr Verlag.

Felix, S. W. 1978. *Linguistische Untersuchungen zum natürlichen Zweitsprachenerwerb,* Munich: Fink.

Givón, T. In press. Function, structure and language acquisition. In Dan I. Slobin (ed.), *Cross-Linguistic Study of Language Acquisition.* Hillsdale., N.J.: Lawrence Erlbaum.

MacWhinney, B. In press. Point-sharing. In R. Schiefelbusch and J. Pickar (eds.), *Communicative Competence: Acquisition and Intervention.* Baltimore, Md.: University Park Press.

Meisel, J. M. 1977. Linguistic simplification: A study of immigrant workers' speech and foreigner talk. In S. P. Corder and E. Roulet (eds.), *The Notions of Simplification, Interlanguages and Pidgins, and Their Relation to Second Language Pedagogy.* Geneve: Droz, pp. 88–113.

Meisel, J. M. 1983. Strategies of second language acquisition. More than one kind of simplification. In R. W. Andersen (ed.), *Pidginization and Creolization as Language Acquisition.* Rowley, Mass.: Newbury House, pp. 120–157.

Meisel, J. M., H. Clahsen, and M. Pienemann. 1981. On determining developmental stages in natural second language acquisition. *Studies in Second Language Acquisition* 3(2). 109–135.

Slobin, D. I. 1973. Cognitive prerequisites for the development of grammar. In C. A. Ferguson and D. I. Slobin (eds.), *Studies of Language Development.* New York: Holt, Rinehart and Winston, pp. 175–208.

Slobin, D. I. 1977. Language change in childhood and in history. In J. Macnamara (ed.), *Language Learning and Thought.* New York: Academic Press, pp. 185–214.

Slobin, D. I. 1981. Reference to the not-here and not-now. Pre-Workshop Paper, Nijmegen: Max Planck-Institut.

Wode, H., J. Bahns, H. Bedey, and W. Frank. 1978. Developmental sequence: An alternative approach to morpheme order. *Language Learning* 28. 175–185.

CHAPTER 11

Toward an Analysis of the (Inter)language Activity of Referring to Time in Narratives

Anne Trévise

University of Paris, France

The study of temporality implies the analysis of the links between temporal linguistic markers and the notional value of time. When studying temporality, linguists first analyze grammatical tenses and their links to time (past, present, and future being ambiguous terms which refer both to grammatical forms and to notional time values) and also temporal and spatial adverbials (i.e., adverbs, conjunctions, prepositional phrases, and subordinate clauses). Tenses alone rarely play an unambiguous part in determining these links, since a present tense may well refer to past time as in the so-called "historical present" or to future time, or it can be atemporal. Thus tenses must be studied within the utterance situation and/or the preceding or following context (adverbials, complements, negation, nature of the subject and of the determiners, etc.) and also in relation to verb categories ("aktionsart") and aspects. All these extralinguistic and linguistic elements enable the speaker and the hearer to build up the temporal meaning of the text and to assign a semantic representation to it. It is always difficult to establish an exact correspondence between notional time and grammatical tense. Temporal reference is achieved through a double function: first, situations and events have to be chronologically ordered (anteriority, simultaneity, posteriority) and second, this order has to be linked to the moment of utterance, or the absence of a link has to be explicitly marked as in historical or scientific texts (see Benveniste, 1966). Apart from these cases where no form of deixis is used (first and second persons, deictic adverbs), the moment of utterance serves to differentiate among present, past, and future time.

Moreover speech is developed along a time axis, with a preceding and a following context. The construction of meaning is not punctual, is not even due to a group of words, but it can make use of anaphoric and cataphoric markers and of the preceding and following pieces of information. This construction of meaning by the speaker (and reconstruction by the hearer, which may or may not be a symmetrical process) works backward and forward along the speech flow. If a temporal adverbial occurs at the end of a text, the hearer has to reconstruct, i.e., to close some of the doors he left open, in order to eliminate ambiguities present in tense and determiners until the final determining forms occur. If some of the doors were wrongly closed, that is, if further determination was not expected and no space was left for any ambiguity, the hearer has to readjust the relations he built between the preceding forms and the values he wrongly assigned to them, and also to readjust the relations among these values. This is constantly done in language activity. A text is not simply the linear addition of one mark after the other, but its meaning is built (and rebuilt) by the subjects by means of the network of all the determinations brought about by the markers. A specific temporal marker, such as a tense or an adverbial, serves to determine the other markers of the context and to restrict the ambiguities due to the fact that a form corresponds to several values.

The semantic value and determinative capacity of a marker cannot be described a priori. It depends on the concrete occurrence of the marker in each context and/or utterance situation. Although the speech stream is linear, the activities of production and comprehension are not linear. Methodologically speaking, one cannot assign one function and one value to a form: these functions and values are only the result of the relation of this form to other forms.

Interlanguages (ILs) are interesting to study because they may help to analyze the intricate maze of forms and values and the relations among the different values. Adults acquiring a second language are cognitively developed; i.e., they have, for instance, a full grasp of notional time: what they are acquiring is a "new" network of markers, which have to be related to notional time. This leads to more ambiguity and, in extreme cases, to communication breakdowns. What factors are responsible for this additional ambiguity?—"missing" markers[1] or "lack" of redundancy resulting in a system in which the markers which do occur have a greater determinative value and different scope than in the target language. When listening to an IL narrative, one does not have the same backward-forward activity along the speech line. Additional readjustments are necessary when, for instance, no verbal morphology is used.

ILs certainly allow for a more analytical study of the construction of temporal determination because they reveal exactly where problems do occur and whether they are due to a particular "missing" morphological or lexical element (determiner, adverbial, temporal, or aspectual marking) or to the "wrong" use of such an element. ILs show, for instance, that when verb forms have no morphological markers, temporal reference is nonetheless achieved through other elements and other relations between these elements (including the "aktionsart" of the verb itself). ILs can thus help to understand how temporal reference is constructed and reconstructed in language activity, for they allow us to isolate factors which are all at work together in adult native speech and to appraise the degree of their relevance or usefulness in the construction of temporal reference.

When analyzing temporal reference in texts, for instance, narratives, whether native speech or foreigners' IL, whether cross-sectional or longitudinal studies of first language acquisition or ILs, one needs an analytical frame, or grid, which necessarily takes the form of a list of headings. The fact that it is presented as a list should not be misleading; it is an analytical tool which by its nature does not explain the functioning of the system when it is actively used by a speaker, or the network of relations he establishes between the items. Such a list can obviously be used to analyze temporality in native speaker speech as well as in ILs. It must simply be noticed that more caution is needed in the case of ILs because the links between forms and values are not necessarily the same as in the target language (TL), and they are not the same as in the source language (SL) either, except in the cases where transfer may have occurred. Therefore, the list is mostly based on notional items, the aim being, given an oral or written text, to be able to analyze the means used by the speaker to refer to the notions. We are not saying that such notions are cognitively or culturally invariant, but at least in many languages (including Spanish and French, the two languages referred to in this chapter), these notions are relevant in the analysis of temporal reference.

The frame of analysis presented here was established after many detailed analyses of different narratives, both of native speaker (NL) speech and of IL speech, and it may help to disentangle the maze of relations between forms and values as regards temporal reference. The framework can be applied cross-linguistically to any NL or IL narrative.

ANALYTICAL FRAME

1. *Reference point operations by means of:*
   1.1.   *Utterance situation, i.e., deixis*
      1.1.1. Tenses and aspects
      1.1.2. Adverbials (temporal and spatial)
      1.1.3. Persons
[Very broadly speaking, the utterance situation includes the extra linguistic knowledge (or "world knowledge") that both speech partners, in the canonical exchange, bring to this exchange; the amount of this knowledge which is shared can of course be crucial; cf. 1.2.]
   1.2.   *Self-reference operations*
      1.2.1. Proper nouns
      1.2.2. Full dates
      1.2.3. Names of places
   (For such operations to be fully self-sufficient, shared knowledge is a prerequisite)
   1.3.   *Textual relations* (anaphora and cataphora)
      1.3.1. Tenses and aspects
      1.3.2. Adverbials (temporal and spatial)
      1.3.3. Person (third person)
      + ruptures/ time of utterance
      + mixed cases

1.4.   *No deictic or textual reference point operations*
    1.4.1.   Generic use of NPs (determiners, person and number)
    1.4.2.   Atemporal use of tenses + aktionsart of verbs
    1.4.3.   Adverbials
1.5.   *Ambiguous forms* (like *the, this, now, today, here,* etc.)
1.6.   *Direct and indirect speech, verba dicendi* shifts (in the Jakobsonian sense of "shifter")
    1.6.1.   Persons
    1.6.2.   Tenses
    1.6.3.   Adverbials
2. *Structure of the narrative* (type of narrative: proximal vs. remote, experiential vs. historical)
2.1.   *Introduction and conclusion* (orientation)
2.2.   *Body of the narrative: discourse organization principles*
    2.2.1.   The story line
    Order of mention / sequence of events vs. chronology
    Degree of redundancy (repetitions, number, and discourse scope of temporal adverbials)
    Aktionsart and aspectual values of verbs
    Implicit reference and, generally, supposed shared knowledge (choice of lexicon)
    2.2.2.   Comments, explanations, and descriptions
    Generic comments (cf.1.4)
    Narratives inside the main narrative
    2.2.3.   Use of direct and indirect speech (cf.1.6)
(Concerning 2.2.1, 2.2.2, and 2.2.3, how is the transition from one to the other made clear? How are the three modes distributed inside the narrative?)
    2.2.4.   Turn taking in the canonical encounter

PROBLEMS OF INTERPRETATION OF IL NARRATIVES

This grid requires some addenda and comments. First of all one should note the occurrences of metalinguistic comments, questions, rises in intonation, self-repairs, etc. On the distinction between deictic and textual reference point operations (cf.1.1, 1.2, and 1.3): adverbs, tenses, or personal pronouns are empty, or underspecified, until they are "filled" semantically by deictic or textual (anaphoric or cataphoric) determination. Deictic forms take a referential value only when they occur in a specific utterance situation (e.g., *this morning, I, you, I'm eating now*). Anaphoric forms are also notionally empty until the context (preceding or following) assigns a value to them (example: *the previous day, two days before*). Both the speaker and the hearer (and also the linguist a posteriori) make use of these external characteristics when constructing the meaning of the text: world knowledge, utterance situation, and/or context. In the case of adverbs, the distinction between anaphoric and deictic is quite clear. Adverbs are deictic when it is the time of utterance which allows the hearer to assign a referential value to them. But there are cases of ambiguity: when the speaker uses the term *Sunday,* the hearer needs another clue in the context ("normally" a tense) to know whether the speaker meant *last Sunday* or *next Sunday.* Some expressions are not completely deictic: *the next 14th of July* needs a partly "objective" reference point operation (i.e., it is partly a self-sufficient date) and it also needs a "subjective" operation in the sense that at least the year of the time of utterance must be known to assign the full referential value to the expression.

In some cases, the reference is circular in the sense that it needs the moment of the event/state to be determined: *then, the other day, one day.* These adverbs are neither deictic nor anaphoric; they refer to the moment of the event/state itself, which in its turn refers to the adverb.

Complete dates (*10th of May 1981*) are neither deictic nor anaphoric (cf.1.2). They are self-determined within a shared culture. They do not require the time of utterance or the context to be assigned a referential value. Proper nouns of persons or places belong to the same category of self-determination.

In narratives some contextual determinations are not real anaphora: this is the case when a process (event or state) takes its reference point from another process, for instance, when a process is marked as anterior or posterior to another process of the context (e.g., *having drunk coffee, he left*).

There are other cases of ambiguity which are due to the fact that, in language, a form can be assigned different values (and often, a given value is represented by different forms). An adverb like *now* or determiners like *this* or *the* can be either deictic or anaphoric, and it is important to analyze the other contextual cues which determine which of the two values is to be selected. In the speech of native speakers tense generally helps the hearer to assign to *now* a present or a past value (e.g., *he was now reading the paper*). Besides, an adverb like *today* (1.5) can be assigned a narrow (i.e., the day of the time of utterance) or a broad value (*nowadays*), and then determiners (nongeneric vs. generic) and number are some of the cues which help to determine the value to be assigned to that adverb. The speaker can also use contrastive expressions such as *in these days* vs. *today.* A spatial adverb like *here,* for instance, can be "purely" deictic; i.e., it can refer to the exact place of utterance, or it can have a broader meaning (i.e., *in France*), or else it can be contextually determined and refer to the place of the event/state mentioned.

In narratives one often finds general comments which do not make use of deictic or contextual reference point operations (cf.1.4): the markers are present forms referring to atemporal present time (the present of general "truths"), singular or plural generic determiners, a switch to third person singular or plural. These markers are cues which point to a rupture or parenthetical break in the story line with a concomitant break in the determinative value of the preceding temporal (or spatial) markers. On resumption of the story line, either the parenthesis is ended and the previous temporal markers (adverbials, possibly tenses, nongeneric determiners, switch to other persons) are still valid, or else they are reintroduced. The intonation pattern generally plays a part in this determination and may add to the redundancy of markers.

In direct speech, the deictic elements (cf.1.6) shift according to the speakers in the situational or textual dialogue; this shift requires of course less of a (cognitive?) effort of calculation than that necessitated by indirect speech, with its supplementary relays (sequence of tenses, shifters, etc.). Thus introductory verbs in French (and other languages) L1 oral narratives are often in the present, possibly because of some kind of attraction when the speaker wants to make the dialogue more vivid (or to give himself less work!). These present forms can be cases of historical present, very frequently found in newspapers, résumés of novels, film scenarios, scenic indications, etc. (cf. Weinrich, 1973). The historical present requires the presence of other temporal clues to be assigned a past time value, and it has a different aspectual value from the "normal" present, either "real" or atemporal.

Narratives seem to obey general structural laws. They often have an introduction (setting the stage, orientation) and a conclusion (cf.2.1), which have a qualitatively different function from the main story line. As regards the distinction between the story line itself (cf. 2.2.1) and comments, explanations, and descriptions (cf.2.2.2), some scholars like Weinrich (1973), Givón (1982) or Kumpf (1982) have made use of the opposition "foreground"/"background." Events in the foreground push the line of the story chronologically, whereas backgrounded elements are often general comments, explanations, descriptions, i.e., further information designed to help one to follow the story line. Kumpf claims that narrative "is the best source for revealing the tense and aspect relations of a language. Narrative is by definition a story line" (p. 2). The line of event clauses, which she calls "foreground," "can be contrasted with clauses which elaborate on the event line" (p. 2), which she calls background." "The background consists of clauses which set the scene, make digressions, change the normal sequence of events and give evaluative remarks" (p. 2). In her case, study of a Japanese acquiring English, she discovered that "completed action in the foreground is expressed with the base-form. There is no tensing of these verbs. In the background are many marked forms, and most verbs are marked for tense. Virtually all statives are tensed. Active verbs in the background are marked for habitual and continuous aspect, and irregularly for tense" (p. 16). The results were totally different in the case of a Russian acquirer of English, where marked forms appeared in the foreground, whereas background forms were unmarked (1982b). These results could be accounted for, according to her, by the nature of the Russian aspectual system and its transfer as a semantic category.

Whatever the results and their possible explanation, it seems that this distinction between the main story line and "the rest" must certainly be taken into account, because it might entail different use of tenses, aspectual marking, temporal (and spatial) adverbials, and persons. The terms "foreground" and "background" should be handled carefully, however, since they do not represent linguistic concepts and their definition easily runs the risk of being tautological or purely psychological. Considering linguistic markers only, one can define different types of texts or modes of discourse: narratives in which a story is told and general comments are those which can be distinguished most easily, because, at the level of markers, they reveal differences in the use of pronouns, determiners, tenses, etc. (cf. 1.1, 1.3, and 1.4). But why should comments be labeled "background" information? Speakers may make a general comment, which is what is important to them, and then tell a story as an anecdote. Methodologically speaking, at least, the linguist should start from the forms and their links to the values (presence or absence of deictic forms, for instance; cf. Simonin, 1977), and more generally from the relation between utterances and the utterance situations, and not from the speaker's supposed attitude. Narratives inside narratives (sometimes referring to anterior time), descriptions, and general comments all reveal complex and different aspectual values and aktionsart of the verbs. Thus "background" may cover heterogeneous elements in this regard.

Concerning ILs more specifically, it might be useful to repeat that the links between a form and a value are not necessarily the same for an IL speaker as for a native. The IL speaker may transfer, simplify, even code-switch. The redundancy and variety that morphological marking allows in native speaker speech will be expressed (qualitatively and quantitatively) differently. Furthermore, it must be noticed again here that the task of the hearer and that of the linguist are different—a temporal value that seemed "obvious" at the time of the interview may turn out to be false (i.e., the hearer misunderstood at the time) in the light of the analysis of the learner's system or microsystems of oppositions and (variable) rules. As an example of this last case, consider the pronunciation of Spanish learners of French. It is often the case that it is impossible to interpret the value of the verbal ending /e/ in terms of the TL system. It can be either an infinitive (like *chanter*, "to sing," a past participle (*chanté*), an imparfait (*chantais, chantait, chantaient*), or the first person singular of the passé simple (*chantai*). The passé simple hardly ever occurs in the oral input but, as the preterit is often used in Spanish, the acquirers might well use it in French IL.

Things are made even more complex because of the French silent /ə/, which Spanish does not possess; so that *je* "I" is often pronounced /ʒe/, which can be interpreted as *je* or *j'ai* "I have," i.e., the auxiliary used to construct some of the passé composé forms. Moreover, a subject may also pronounce as /e/ the final silent e of certain verbs like *chanter*, for instance (first group), as in *je chante, tu chantes, il chante, ils chantent*, which are then all pronounced as /ʃ āte/. So that /ʒeʃ āte/ can be either a present tense (*je chante*), a passé composé (*j'ai chanté*), a passé simple (*je chantai*), or else the pronoun followed by a past participle or an infinitive (*je chanté, je chanter*, which are not standard French (SF) forms).

The same phonetic ambiguities are found when non-SF preverbal negation is used as in /ʒenekõtinue/. The same applies when the clitic pronouns *me* or *te* are used as in the example /ʒeteʃāte/ *une chanson* "sang you a song," constructed by the author. In terms of SF or non-SF, it could be either a passé composé, a passé simple, a present, an imparfait (all SF forms), or the pronouns followed by a past participle or the infinitive (non-SF forms) ("I have sung you a song," "I sang you a song," "I sing you a song," "I was singing you a song"). Such ambiguities can sometimes be removed when the acquirer's whole pattern of morphological marking is considered. This may reveal, if not an invariant system, what at least may be consistently contrasted forms and oppositions of meanings. For instance, if it is the case that the subject uses the two forms /ʒeʃāt/ and /ʒeʃāte/ somewhat systematically, then it is sometimes possible to assign a past value to /ʃāte/ as opposed to /ʃāt/. But it is impossible to know, in terms of TL morphology, whether it is an imparfait, a passé simple, an infinitive, a passé composé, or a past participle. Even if the subject produces forms like /tvaʃāte/ (*tu as chanté*, SF) or /ilaʃāte/ (*il a chanté*, SF), i.e., standard passé composé forms, one cannot take it for granted that /ʒeʃāte/ is a standard passé composé.

This example underlines the methodological importance of assigning values to IL verbal forms in context, rather than attempting to establish a relationship between an IL form and a TL form, assigning a TL value to its associated IL form. The latter approach can lead (and has led) to false conclusions concerning the IL system of a learner. As Perdue (1980) pointed out, a "correct" form used "appropriately" can be both correct and appropriate for the wrong reasons.

Methodologically speaking, then, the two notions of hearer and linguist should be clearly differentiated; the linguist's comprehension a posteriori is different from the *hic et nunc* comprehension by the hearer. The linguist has to reconstruct all the deictic values which have obviously changed since the *hic et nunc* of the interview. These two types of "comprehension" should not be mixed.

This is all the more important since more or less successful comprehension is the only criterion we have to assign certain values to certain forms (apart from elicitation tasks which change the nature of the language activity), and it is subject to a great deal of variation according to individuals, shared knowledge, foreign accent, motivation to understand, etc. It is by no means an objective measure of the speaker's achievement, since it is also a measure of the hearer's activity of reconstruction.

DATA ANALYSIS

In this chapter I merely try to apply the analytical frame to short narratives to see how temporal reference is actively constructed and reconstructed by the speech partners and also by the linguist. For analysis, I have chosen three short narratives (L1: Spanish; L2: French). The first two are taken from the data of the cross-sectional pilot study conducted by the GRAL, University of Paris VIII (see Dubois et al., 1981; Noyau, 1982; Trévise, in press). The third one is taken from the data collected for the European Science Foundation project by the French team (see Perdue, 1982). It is drawn from the first interview of a longitudinal study. Thus, the present analysis will not yield any conclusion on the acquisition process. The E.S.F. longitudinal study will hopefully answer some of the questions concerning developmental stages in temporal reference (cf. also Meisel, 1982; von Stutterheim, 1982; Noyau, 1982).

THE FIRST INFORMANT

M1 is an Argentinian political refugee. At the time of the interview, he was 49 and had spent 3½ years in France. He came to France with his wife (referred to as F2 here and in the articles mentioned above), aged 30. They do not know how long they are going to stay in France.

M1 went to primary school in Argentina, but he is primarily self-taught. He used to be a trade-unionist in his country. He is interested in politics and sociology. He has few contacts with French natives but reads *Le Monde* every day. He often resorts to the help of his wife when speaking "French," because he knows her French is much better than his. In France, he has been employed as a janitor and as a printer. He reads a lot in Spanish and writes political and economic articles in Spanish. He is a militant in Amnesty International and also works for the Latin-American refugees in France.

He took the 3-month course in French for refugees at the Alliance Française which he found too childish; he did not get on well with the teachers or the teaching and gave up before the end of the course.

The extracts analyzed here are taken from a standard linguistic interview of M1 and his wife by C. Noyau and C. Perdue. Although M1 is aware of the fact that his French is not "good," he enjoys speaking a lot. As a former trade-unionist and a person deeply interested in politics and sociology, he always intermingles autobiographic narratives with general comments about Argentina, France, the French, England, exile, and even linguistic problems. This yields very interesting shifts from atemporal comments to story line. Given the importance that these comments obviously have for him, one hesitates to call them "backgrounded" information (cf. p. 230). I nevertheless use the term sometimes for lack of a better one[2] in describing the links between aspectual characteristics (including aktionsart), pronouns, number, and determiners in the two different modes of discourse.

M1's inflectional oppositions (as revealed by the whole interview[3]): After more than 3 years in France, M1 knows quite a lot of vocabulary; he uses a certain number of "frequent" verbs which are in the main inflected, for instance, *être* "be," which he uses most often as the copula, *avoir* "have," which he uses to express age as in *X a 30 ans*—"X is 30," and sometimes as an auxiliary in the construction of what may be called a passé composé (cr. pp. 231-232) as in *elle a donné* – "she has given."

In all M1's productions, the verb *être* occurs only three times in the past form, /ɛtɛ/, which looks like an imparfait, and three times in the third person singular: twice as *c'était* (*c'est* also appearing in past contexts) and once in an interesting self-appraisal of the inadequacy of the form he used followed by a metalinguistic question to his wife. When talking about a French lady who has become one of their friends, M1 asks for his wife's help:

(1) M1:   *elle est ... elle era ... /lera/?*
          "she is ... she *era*"
    F2:   *elle était*
          "she was"
    M1:   *elle était journaliste dans l'Humanité*
          "she was a journalist"
          (i.e., she worked for the communist newspaper *l'Humanité*).

Here he was obviously aware that a past tense was needed to underline the important fact that the woman no longer worked for the newspaper at the time of the utterance. He was thus also aware that he was wrongly using a present.

However, a past form of the verb *être* never occurs in the first person; either singular (*j'étais, j'ai été, je fus*), or plural (*nous étions, vous avons été, nous fûmes*); the third person singular never occurs in a SF passé composé form either (*il/elle a été*).

Among the "frequent" verbs M1 uses are the modal verbs *pouvoir* "can," *vouloir* "want," *aller* "go," which is most often used as an auxiliary for the periphrastic future,[4] and the verbs *faire* "do/make," *travailler* "work," *dire* "say," *venir* "come," also used to express immediate past as in *je viens de me souvenir* "I have just remembered," SF: *Je viens de me souvenir—connaître* "know," *parler* "talk/speak," to give the most frequent verbs he uses.

For a certain number of verbs, the first and third person singular and the third person plural take the same form /travaj/ as in SF *je travaille, il travaille, ils travaillent*. But M1 also uses the same form for verbs of other groups like *dire* where for the three persons mentioned above he uses the form /di/ in cases where the context makes it clear that /ildi/ is indeed a plural (SF: *ils disent*; *il* "he" and *ils* "they" are pronounced in the same way in SF when the following verb starts with a consonant). Other occurrences of the same type are /ʒevjen, il vjen/ where in the latter case /il/ is a plural anaphoric pronoun (SF: *ils viennent*), /ʒekone, ɛelkone, vukone/ (SF: *je connais, elle connaît, vous connaissez*), or /ʒefe, ilfe/ where again it is sometimes the case that /il/ is a plural anaphoric (SF: *je fais, il fait, ils font*). These forms may come from an overgeneralization of the first and/or third person singular, or they may reveal the use of a "base form." On the contrary, the first person plural is inflected "correctly," i.e., *-ons*. It might be because *-ons* is more salient as an ending than a silent *e*. Besides, M1 uses the first person plural extensively, with the pronoun *nous* "we" referring to either himself and his wife in narratives or to political refugees or the Argentinians in comments, where it obviously has a kind of political meaning for him. The same form *-ons* is also used in past contexts. Thus first person pronouns, which have a "privileged" deictic status, are often treated differently by speakers.

In present contexts, the first and third person singular forms M1 uses do not "violate" the target norm, as regards verbal morphology, at least phonetically. In past contexts, the "past" form /e/ M1 uses for certain verbs sounds like an imparfait for the first, second, and third person singular and also for the third person plural (*-ais, -ait, -aient*). In an utterance like (2):

(2) *les professeurs me /sorte/*
"the teachers threw me out"

the verb form sounds like an imparfait for a French native, especially since the distinction /e-ɛ/ is not always made in French. In SF, the context would have required a passé composé here.

It seems that M1 uses a single past tense form, /e/, which is not an imparfait or a passé simple or a passé composé, so that one cannot tell whether, when he uses what sounds like an SF imparfait in the right context, he really chooses to make the aspectual distinction. His "real" uses of the passé composé as in *le groupe a venu* "the group has come" never occur in contexts where they are opposed to the "past" form /e/. For instance, the forms /a done/ "has given?" and /done/ "gave?" or /a peje/ and /peje/ "has paid/paid?" occur in exactly the same contexts, where SF would have used the passé composé. This fluctuation might be the sign of the emergence of a distinction between different aspects and tenses. *Donner* and *payer* are the only (active) verbs which are used in the two forms. The other verbs used in a passé composé form (*a venu* "has come," *a demandé* "has asked," *a disparu* "has disappeared," *a dit* "has said") never occur in the past form in /e/. I have no explanation for this phenomenon. Rote learning? Unanalyzed chunks? Some of these verbs, however, occur in the present form as well.

As regards the first person singular, at least with verbs constructed with *avoir* in SF, and belonging to the first group (like *chanter*), the verb forms used by M1 "sound" correct for the hearer in a past context, e.g., /ʒedemãde/, *j'ai demandé* "I have asked" or /ʒetravaje/, *j'ai travaillé* "I have worked." As M1 uses a lot of first person singular forms, it is hard to describe his verbal inflectional oppositions, since the two forms could be either a passé composé, a present with no silent *e*, or one of his "past" forms. It could also be an imparfait or a passé simple, a past participle, or even an infinitive (cf. pp. 231-232), although he never seems to use infinitives as invariant forms.

It is thus difficult to say whether M1 had acquired past tenses at the time of the interview. One could say that they are partly acquired, depending on the verb (first group vs. others) or on frequency, depending also on whether they are used in the first person singular or plural, etc. The presence of (clear?) cases of passé composé forms, primarily in active verbs such as *donner*, might mean that at least some of the occurrences of /ʒe/ + /-e/ verb ending are real passés composés (i.e., *j'ai* + past participle), which would speak in favor of the existence of a few microsystems of aspect and tense inflections for certain verbs.

With respect to choice of the auxiliary, the passé composé is constructed only once with the SF auxiliary *être* in *nous sommes arrivés* "we have arrived" (cf. p.

238). It is true that in Spanish the present perfect is always constructed with the auxiliary *haber* which takes the form *ha* in the third person singular and might then account for the overuse of *avoir* as an auxiliary.

There are also a few occurrences of what sounds like plus-que-parfait forms as in /nuavefe/ (SF: *nous avions fait*), /ilvefe/ (SF: *il avait fait*), /ilavevy/ (SF: *il avait vu*), in contexts which clearly require the expression of anteriority (cf. p. 243). This form mainly appeared with the verb *faire* as in (3) to (6):

(3) *-nous* /avefe/ *amis à Londres*   "we had made friends in London"
   (SF: *avions fait*)

(4) *-nous* /avefe/ *avec son mari . . . toute la*   "we had done with her husband" . . .
   famille /avefe/   "all the family had done"
   (SF: *avions fait; avait fait*)

(5) *-nous* /avefe/ *un voyage*   "we had made a journey"
   (SF: *avions fait*)

(6) *-nous* /avevjy/ *Yves Montand*   "we had seen Yves Montand"
   (SF: *avions vu*)

M1's construction of this form always makes use of /ave/. M1 uses the whole inflectional system of the verb *avoir* in the present but not in the past (i.e., imparfait in the plus-que-parfait form). This /ave/ + PP form might be partly the result of rote learning. M1 has perhaps not analyzed the construction of the French plus-que-parfait yet, and he may be using an invariable auxiliary because he does not know the past forms of the auxiliary; (/ave/ also appears as a SF present form in *vous avez* "you have"). There are not enough occurrences of passé composé forms other than /a/ + what sounds like a past participle to prove that M1 knows that he is using the auxiliary *avoir* when he constructs the passé composé or the plus-que-parfait. [There is only one occurrence of /õvenu/ (SF: *sont venus*) apart from the problematic /ʒe/ forms.]

One of the devices M1 uses to "avoid" using past tenses is the expression *venir de* which is not used as a spatial movement verb but refers to M1 and F2's personal life history, as in (7) to (10):

(7) *nous venons de la mort*   "we come from death"
(8) *nous venons d'une expérience très*   "we come from a very deep experience"
   profonde
(9) *nous venons de beaucoup d'espoir*   "we come from a great hope"
(10) *il vient de la prison*   "he comes from prison"

(The expression *venir de* was also used once as an auxiliary of the periphrastic immediate past.) Here the expression is followed by a noun phrase; the tense used is the present but the semantic information is past, or rather its aspectual value expresses a link between the past and the present through this verb of movement. In SF, one would have "normally" used the passé composé (*nous avons échappé à la mort*—we have escaped death, *nous avons eu une expérience très profonde, nous avons connu beaucoup d'espoir, il a été en prison*). Thus M1 expresses the aspectual value, not through the choice of a passé composé, but rather by choosing a verb of movement expressing the same resultative value, which does not hamper comprehension at all.

Narrative 1: analysis   The text of M1's narrative is given in (11). I did not use the phonetic transcription systematically here for all ambiguous forms, except /done/ for simple reasons of legibility. The English translation will be given word for word:

(11) M1:   *nous sommes arrivés... non parqué il y a une grande différence dé âge ... (F2) a trente ans ... et l'autra chosa très important c'est qué quand nous arrivons ici comme nous sommes refugiés ... la ... la chose toutes réfugiés comme R. et sa femme... va à la autorité française donne un foyer... mais nous ... nos salvamos?*

"we have arrived... no because there is a great difference of age ... (F2) has thirty years... and the other thing very important it is that when we arrive here as we are refugees...the the thing all the refugees like R. and his wife... go to the French authority gives a hostel... but we ... nos salvamos?"

F2:   *nous nous sommes sauvés parce –*

"we have escaped bec –"

M1:   *parcé qué nous trouvons un Brasilien ... ici... qué il est aussi refugié et qué il sorte de Brasil et il va à Buenos Aires ... et dans cette époque il est ... ensemble ... il est ami il dit dé un Français séparé avec des des petites... il dit bon cette dame francesa euh ... cherche quelqu'un pour qu'il garde lé petit enfant... et nous fait un combination... il nous donne nous /done/ un chambre mais c'est une chose intéressante ... cette dame qué c'est une dame qué aujourd'hui très très amie de nous...*

"because we find a Brazilian...here ...who/that he is also refugee and who/that he goes out of Brazil and he goes to Buenos Aires... we know from Buenos Aires... and in this period he is ... together... he is friend he says of a French separated with small (kids) ... he says well this French lady euh ... looks for someone for ... for that he looks after the small child ... and makes us a combination... he gives us gave us a a room but it is an interesting thing...this lady who/that it is a lady who/that today very very friend of us..."

This short piece of narrative will be analyzed starting from the beginning in order to show how the story line intermingles with the comments and the narrative inside the narrative and how temporal relations are established.

As was mentioned earlier, M1 often makes comments on autobiographical events, thus giving them a more political and social value, or explaining part of what "shared knowledge" should include. In this narrative the comments and the narrative inside the narrative make use of anaphora: they take up one or several elements explicitly or implicitly present in the upstream context which has already established some determination. Thus, comments are "rooted" or so to speak "have their landmarks" in the determined elements of the upstream context. Often in the interview, these comments are either subordinate clauses introduced by *parce que* "because" or by a relative pronoun, or else independent clauses (cf. *nous connaissons de Buenos Aires*), sometimes introduced by *bon* "well" and a change in intonation.

How can the hearer understand that M1 is making a comment and not going on with the story line? The landmarks are, apart from intonation and rhythm changes, *non*, which signals a rupture (*non parqué*) or the determiner *toutes* in *toutes les réfugiés* (generic). The determiner *la* in the expression *la chose* is cataphorically determined by the following subordinate clause, and the expression is used as a topicalization device (see Trévise, in press).[5]

The third comment is different in nature since it begins with an explanation (*qué il est aussi refugié*) and goes on with a narrative inside the main narrative, with an anteriority value (*qué il sorte de Brasil et il va à Buenos Aires*). The *aussi* is implicitly anaphoric and also signals a change in the mode of discourse. We come back to this later. This narrative inside the main narrative is followed by yet another kind of comment or explanation: *nous connaissons de Buenos Aires*, where *Buenos Aires*, a self-determined spatial proper noun, is repeated. Such a repetition is probably used because M1 is not yet able to use the anaphoric *là-bas* "there." He never uses it to speak about Argentina. The mention of Buenos Aires gives an anteriority value to the clause, since being in Argentina obviously belongs to a period anterior to the moment of utterance, and he refers to the place of utterance contrastively by using the deictic adverb *ici* "here," i.e., in Paris or, more broadly, in France. Although SF would allow a present in *nous le connaissons de Buenos Aires* (i.e., *nous l'avons connu là-bas et nous le connaissons toujours* "we met him there and we still know him," it is not certain that the value M1 assigns to this stative verb form is present time (even inclusive present) in his system (or several microsystems) of oppositions, as the verb *connaître* never occurs in a past form, whatever the person, singular or plural. But, whatever the value assigned by the speaker to the verb tense he uses, the meaning is clear and the mention of Buenos Aires implies a left boundary mark to the state expressed by the verb.

What is striking at the beginning of the narrative is the occurrence of *nous sommes arrivés* (i.e., SF passé composé constructed with the correct SF auxiliary, which occurs only once in the corpus), followed by *quand nous arrivons ici* (i.e., present form), which refers to the same event but perhaps from a different aspectual point of view. When using the only temporal conjunction he ever uses (in its different meanings), and after having set up the past situational frame, M1 does not use a redundant morphological marker. The contrastive deictic spatial adverb *ici* "here" enhances the temporal relation to the moment of utterance.[6] The following verb is also stative and used in a present form (*sommes*-copula) and might refer to a present state since they still are refugees (inclusive present). In argumentation of this kind, however, with the conjunction *comme* (as), a native speaker would probably have used the imparfait (*étions*— a form M1 never uses), since the speaker considers the past state in relation to the temporality of the subordinate clause.

The following atemporal comment breaks up the formal construction of the argumentation, if not its purpose. It also interrupts the chronology of the narrative, as well as its relation to the speaker of the utterance; the first person pronoun *nous* is no longer used and is replaced by the third person pronoun *toutes les refugiés, la autorité française* (self-determined reference point), until the *nous* is used again after a contrastive connective (*mais*). This conjunction takes up the narrative thread, and the story reenters the determinative values of the upstream temporal markers.

Thus the shift from the main story line, using the present tense with a past value (historical present?), to an atemporal stative comment in the present with a general meaning is achieved by means of determination devices (generic values) and a shift from the first person plural (i.e., identity with the speaker of the utterance) to third person. The interlocutor understands that the story line goes on after the parentheses when he hears the conjunction *mais* and the first person *nous* again.

Thus, in one "sentence" (pragmatic unit?), M1 intermingles the two different modes of discourse: past story line and "the rest," i.e., comments, explanations with present time values (atemporal present or inclusive present) and a narrative inside the main narrative with an anterior value. This complex construction is achieved without the help of any strictly "temporal" markers, neither temporal adverbials nor changes in tense morphology. The only "truly" temporal markers used are the conjunction *quand* and the passé composé in *nous sommes arrivés*. The present tenses are overused (from a TL standpoint); they no longer have a temporal determinative value attached to them. Contrastive references to places (self-determined as *Buenos Aires*, or deictic as *ici*), determiners, persons, and aktionsart of verbs play an important part in determining the relation to the moment of utterance (or the absence of relation). Even the temporal conjunction *quand* is ambiguous: it can mean "whenever," "after," or "at the time when," and here it is the aspectual information (aktionsart) contained in the verb *arriver* which enables the hearer to assign the value *after* to *quand*. Thus M1 does use some redundancy here, apart from the repetitions of *ici* or *Buenos Aires*, although the redundancy is far less important than in native speaker speech.

The change over to Spanish (*nos salvamos* "we escaped") is confusing here, at least for the linguist, because it could be either a present or a preterit in Spanish. It must be noticed, though, that F2, when translating, uses a French passé composé. M1, however, goes on explaining how they were able to "escape," and the active verb he uses (*trouvons*) is a present form. He does not make use of the input provided by F2 directly. This is a case of scaffolding. He does not repeat the new lexicon or the verbal marking. His linguistic consciousness urged him to ask for the help of his wife, but he is less interested in the metalinguistic task of repetition than in the communicative activity, i.e., pushing the story line ahead. The fact that he repeats the deictic *ici* might be a sign that he is aware that the tense he is using, and the mention of the man's nationality (*Brasilien*), may lead to some ambiguity. He probably felt that the determinative capacity of the first occurrence of *ici* was ended. *Nous trouvons un Brasilien* refers to a recent past, but the fact of his being a Brazilian was obviously valid at the period preceding exile so that the hearer implicitly knows that the man must have been in Brazil once. The present form of *trouvons* cannot be referred to the time of utterance; it has the aspectual value of perfectivity because of the aktionsart of the verb *trouver*. It can thus be understood only as a present form with a past value (in SF it would be called a historical present).

The relative clauses about the Brazilian build up a narrative inside the narrative. The anteriority value is mainly brought about by the shared knowledge of the world. The implicit reference is built up by means of the upstream context, i.e., the contrastive opposition between *Brasilien* and *ici*, which helps the hearer to reconstruct the meaning. The first relative clause contains a present state (*qué il est aussi refugié*) which refers to both the past and the time of utterance; it was valid at the time of the event (*trouvons*) and it is still valid at the time of utterance. The two following verbs, on the contrary, are active verbs (*sorte* and *va*) which have a present form but a past value. Their aktionsart certainly helps the hearer to assign a past value to them. The two events of *sortir* and *aller* are mentioned one after the other, which corresponds to the extralinguistic chronological order. But it is not only this "unmarked" order of the two clauses which enables the hearer to understand the chronology; it is also the shared geographical knowledge of the world. Given the lack of morphological redundance to express anteriority (in SF, one would have said: *nous avons trouvé un Brésilien qui était aussi réfugié et qui était sorti du Brésil et était allé à Buenos Aires. C'est là-bas que nous l'avons connu*), the hearer has to be more "active" in his reconstruction of meaning. He has to make a fuller use of the determinative elements which do occur.

It must be noticed that the connective *et*, which M1 uses frequently (he does not use *et puis* in the way a lot of children do), might also be ambiguous. It does not necessarily mean "and then" (cf. narrative 2, pp 242-243).

The two different modes of discourse (story line vs. "the rest") are not only intermingled. They interfere one with the other as regards anaphoric values, implicit reference, and shared knowledge of the world. The mention of the words *la autorité française*, for instance, clarifies the temporal meaning of *nos salvamos* which is part of the main story line. Without this information, the action of "escaping" could have been misunderstood and might have been related to Argentina.

In the phrase *et dans cette époque*, the anaphoric *cette* is ambiguous at first for the hearer, who is led to think that it refers to the time when they were in Buenos Aires, even if the intonation break implies that the narrative inside the narrative is finished. This phrase cannot be understood immediately with the value that M1 assigns to it. In fact, a posteriori, the hearer understands that *époque* refers to the more recent past, whereas in SF *à cette époque* always establishes a rupture from the moment of utterance, and a certain temporal distance. The hearer thus has to reconstruct and readjust the meaning of *époque* and thus the meaning of the anaphora by means of the downstream context. More precisely, he can do so when the element *un Français* occurs. By using this phrase, M1 introduces a break, but it is not a temporal break, it is a landmark he uses to signal that he is reentering the main story line after the "parenthesis." The occurrence of *un Français* allows the hearer to place the sentence in the chronological order. It belongs to the same period as *trouvons*, that is to say, to a more recent past, in Paris. This is a case of delayed comprehension which requires an active backward reconstruction. It would not have occurred in a native conversation, and it shows that temporal adverbials (especially anaphoric adverbials), when used with a different form: value relation, are not the best help in establishing temporal reference.

The end of the narrative contains sentences which could be either direct or indirect speech. There is no way to tell because M1 might well not have used *que* and still report speech. It is true that elsewhere in the data, direct speech seems to be a very common device he, like many IL and native speakers, uses to "avoid" reference to the past through syntactic shifts. The use of verbs dicendi in the present *(il dit)* is quite common in SF to refer to a past dialogue (cf. p. 230). The hearer knows when the direct or indirect speech comes to an end *(pour qu'il garde le petit enfant)* because of the occurrence of the first person plural *nous (et nous fait une combination, nous donne)*. Here the temporal frame is established, so that what follows the mention of the French lady is easily understood, although, as M1 uses *il* instead of *elle*, it is not very clear who gave the room. Some ambiguity remains here. A readjustment was already needed with the change from *un Français* (masculine) to the anaphoric *cette dame francesa*. In this case, the repetition of the nationality gives the necessary clue for the semantic readjustment.

The self-correction *nous donne... nous* /done/ is interesting. It would not have been possible with the verb *trouvons*, since M1 never uses a "past" form with a first person plural (except for the occurrence of *nous sommes arrivés*). *Donner* is one of the few verbs for which M1 makes a distinction between present and "past" forms. Here again his metalinguistic self-repair shows that he is aware of the necessity of morphological oppositions (cf. p. 234).

In the conclusion of the narrative, M1 uses the contrastive deictic temporal adverbial *aujourd'hui* (vs. *cette époque*), which is thus understood to mean "at present" and not to refer to the exact day of utterance (cf. p. 237).

When looking at the narrative "skeleton" in Figure 1, one cannot help wondering about the terminology "background", "foreground," simply first of all because the "background" column is fuller than the so-called "foreground" one. On the other hand, if the story line column is rather homogeneous [active verbs, although with aspectual differences (punctual vs. perfective, for instance)], the right column is far from being homogeneous (cf. p. 242). The first two verbs (*a*) refer directly to the moment of utterance; the explanation introduced by *comme* refers both to the past and to the present. This is followed by an atemporal comment with active verbs, and then by a narrative inside the narrative, with active verbs, to which the geographical knowledge of the world assigns an anteriority value. Among the "stative" verbs, some imply a left boundary mark like *il est aussi réfugié* and *nous connaissons de Buenos Aires*, and some a right boundary mark (example: *dans cette époque*, which suggests that the following statement is no longer true). (I have put the indirect/direct speech string in the right column, but maybe it should be in the left one.)

The whole narrative reveals a very intricate chronological structure, even though M1's morphology is so reduced. The aspectual values are complex and should not be reduced to the simplistic active/stative distinction.

Story line	Comments, explanations, narratives inside the main narrative
nous *sommes arrivés* (active) 3 (perfective)	il y a une grande différence d'âge (stative)
	F2 *a* 30 ans
quand nous *arrivons* ici (active) (punctual) 3	comme nous *sommes* réfugiés (stative)
	la chose toutes les réfugiés *va* à la autorité, *donne* un foyer (active, atemporal, generic)
mais nous nos *salvamos* (active) (punctual or perfective) 4	parce que nous *trouvons* (active) (perfective) un Brasilien ici
	qué il *est* aussi réfugié (stative)
	qué il *sorte* de Brasil et *va* (active, narrative inside the narrative + anteriority value)
	nous *connaissons* de Buenos Aires (stative with left boundary marker)
	il *est* ensemble dans cette époque il *est* ami (stative)
il *dit* (active) 4	il *cherche* pour qu'il *garde* (Direct or indirect speech; stative)
nous *fait* un combination (active) 5	
nous *donne* . . . nous/*done*/(active) 6	Conclusion: mais c'est une chose intéressante c'est une dame qué aujourd'hui très amie de nous

(NB: the numbers stand for chronological order)

FIGURE 1   "Structural skeleton" of M1's narrative 1

Narrative 2: analysis

Interviewer: *vous avez été dans le sud de la France vous avez dit?*

you have been in the South of France you have said?

M1:   *hm . . . porqué il y a une dame française que . . . il /ave/ vu . . . un . . . un grand intimité dé Argentin et el fait un voyage à Buenos Aires . . . bon y et aussi il fait dé . . . un peu de solidarité argentine avec notre exil . . . avec le comité de solidarité argentine latino-américan . . . il fait un invitation à*

hm . . . because there is a French lady who . . . he had seen . . . a . . . a . . . great great intimacy of Argentinian and he makes a journey to Buenos Aires . . . I know her from solidarity with our exile . . . with the committee of solidarity argentina Latin-American . . . he makes an invitation to us to

nous pour faire un voyage à . . . Bar-	make a journey to . . . Barcelona and
celona et quand nous retournons de	when we come back from Barcelona
Barcelona il il dit non nous pouvons	he he says well we can make a ride for
faire un promenade pour lé. Sur dé la	the South of France . . . and we stay
France . . . et nous restons quatre non	four no one week for the region of
un semane pour la région de la Lozère	Lozère . . . and we stay in a small how
. . . et nous restons dans un pétite	one says *granca*? farm?
comm'on dit granca? fermé?	

F2:   *ferme*   farm

M1:   *fermé et bon de paysan . . . et dans ce*   farm and well of farmer. . .and in this
      petit peuple toutes les Français et bon/   small people all the French and well/

F2:   *village*   village

M1:   *nous sommes toutes les les les après-*   we are all the afternoons in the bar and
      midi dans lé bar et y vient les Français he/they comes the French *y* they
      y /parle/ avec nous et très bien . . .   spoke with us and very good

M1 frequently begins statements with *il y a* (58 occurrences in the first hour of recording). This is a very common way of introducing a new situational frame in SF. (M1 never uses it in the past but here the present form does not violate the target norm.) Here he uses it as an introduction to his narrative. The mention of *une dame* makes it possible for the hearer to readily interpret the following occurrences of *il* as *elle*.

The following verb *(/ave/vu-avait vu)* takes the form of a plus-que-parfait (cf. p. 236), and it is part of the narrative inside the narrative. In spite of the "error" in the choice of the verb (*voir* instead of *avoir*—but the proximity of the word *intimité* and the gender/sex of *Argentin* enable the hearer to reconstruct the meaning here), M1 wants to express anteriority explicitly. In this short narrative inside the narrative, the order of the statements does not really follow the extralinguistic sequence of events, since the "period of intimacy" lasted during the trip to Buenos Aires. The temporal and aspectual values are complex here (an active event took place during the time expressed by the stative verb). By means of the use of the plus-que-parfait, M1 seems to express the fact that the "state of intimacy" was valid before he himself met the woman. Then the connective *et* is followed by a present tense form, *fait* (active verb), which has a past value. The hearer can assign the past value to this present form because of the mention of Buenos Aires, to which presuppositions indirectly assign a past value (i.e., M1 and F2 are no longer in Buenos Aires). The reference to the past becomes even clearer when the mention of Buenos Aires is related to the pronoun *je*. As in the preceding narrative, the stative verb *connaître* receives a left boundary mark by means of the mention of Buenos Aires (cf. p. 238). the same analysis applies here as in the case of *nous connaissons de Buenos Aires* in narrative 1).

Apart from the very short narrative inside the narrative, which expresses anteriority, and from the comments referring to the time of utterance, the order of sentences follows the chronological order, with a sequence of simultaneous processes (stative and iterative), all introduced by the connective *et* at the end of the narrative.

M1's comments often begin with *bon* "well" and a rupture in the intonation pattern of the story line. The second occurrence of *il fait* (in *il fait... un peu de solidarité*) reveals a different aspectual value, iterative and even more "stative" in fact. It is understood as a present form referring to a present value because of this aspectual value due to the verb complement and also because of the mention of the word *exile* in the downstream context, which obviously cannot refer to the period when M1 was in Buenos Aires. In this narrative the verb *faire* occurs four times: *faire un voyage, faire une invitation, faire une promenade*, and *faire un peu de solidarité*. In all four cases, the form is *fait*, but the temporal and aspectual values change and only the "more stative" verb is a present form referring to a present time. It is clear here that the aktionsart does not depend on the verb alone but also on the links between the verb and its complement (and the determiners of this complement: countable/uncountable in this case).

In the same passage, M1 expresses a future in the past by means of *pour faire* together with the mention of the self-determined spatial adverbial *à Barcelona*—for which the presupposition is that it is different from the place of utterance, Paris. The name of the city is repeated twice, perhaps because M1 does not control the anaphoric forms *là-bas* or *en* (SF: *quand nous sommes revenus de là-bas* or *quand nous sommes revenus*).[7]

The temporal conjunction *quand* is used here to express the quasi-simultaneity of the two events *retournons* and *dit*. As was mentioned above, M1 does not always assign the same value to the only temporal conjunction he uses (cf. p. 239). Merely counting up the occurrences of a given form does not explain the values assigned to it in discourse by the activity of the speaker.

Il dit could be SF as regards the tense form chosen (cf. p. 241). The following modal *(nous pouvons faire)* could be either direct or indirect speech, since the pronoun is in the first person plural and does not require a shift. M1 often "deletes" the conjunction *que* (cf. p. 241). M1 does not think it is necessary to say explicitly that they actually did go to the south of France.

The following repetition of *nous restons* would not be considered SF. This device allows M1 to determine the place of the process progressively without using a complex noun phrase "south of France," *Lozère*, "farm," "small people"—which means "small village," as F2's interpretation shows—and finally *bar*). M1 uses the anaphoric *ce* here.

The end of the narrative is temporally complex: the stative verb *restons* is repeated twice and followed by iterative verbs. The aspectual meaning of these verbs is given by the determiner *toutes (toutes les Français, toutes les après-midi)*. All these processes belong to the same period of time (i.e., *un semane* "one week"). M1 then uses a "past" form for the last verb:/parle/. Nowhere in the data do any of the other verbs used in this narrative occur in the "past" form, at least in the persons used here (*restons, sommes, vient*—although *ont venu* and *a venu* occur once but to refer to a punctual event). This could suggest that as soon as M1 masters a "past" form, he uses it rather systematically, even if all the other verbs in the passage have the present form.

The last *et,* in the conclusion, is assigned a specific value: neither "and then" nor simultaneity. It introduces a concluding synthetic comment on M1's experience in the south of France. Here he does not use *c'est,* as he often does (123 occurrences in a present context, but only 2 in a past context during the first hour of recording). He does not use *c'était* either, which would be SF. (He uses this form only twice in the data and perhaps has not automatized it yet.) It might be the case that M1 wants to avoid a present form here again (as he does on several occasions; cf. pp.234 and 241) and chooses to delete the verb and the subject (avoidance strategy?). This would then be due to his linguistic consciousness. One might add that comprehension does not suffer from this deletion of the copula and of the anaphoric *c'.* The "structural skeleton" for this narrative is given in Figure 2 (p. 246). The processes expressed in 6 revealed that the story line is not pushed ahead chronologically and that durative and iterative processes become the "foregrounded" elements of a more stative description.

In this narrative there is no atemporal comment (apart from the metalinguistic one). The distinction foreground/background seems difficult to make here from the point of view of the linguistic markers. The last "foregrounded" description reveals some of the markers usually present in the so-called "background," i.e., stative and iterative verbs (nonactualization). It is always difficult to use a concept which is not based on linguistic elements present in the text itself. This is not the case when one makes the distinction between atemporal comments with no deictic forms and utterances which make use of the utterance situation as a reference point. Aspectual distinctions, notably not based on supposed psychological distinctions, however, certainly play an important part in the structural construction of narratives.

The Second Informant

The last narrative, from the second informant, Emilio, reveals a less developed stage of IL.

Emilio is Chilean, and he is interesting to compare with M1, because he has about the same "profile." At the time of the interview, he was 46 and had been in France for 6 months. He has no schooling. On his arrival in France, he had attended the 3-month French course. In Chile, he was a mason, then a fisherman, then an adviser for Indian communities, and a very active trade-unionist. He is a self-taught man who reads *Le Monde* and books on recent history. When we interviewed him, he was still living in one of the Paris homes for political refugees.

The interview was conducted as part of the E.S.F. Project (see Perdue, 1982) by C. Noyau, who spoke only Spanish with Emilio, and myself, who spoke only French to him and was not supposed to understand any Spanish, which perhaps accounts for his frequent use of foreigner-talk expressions. His IL was difficult to understand, but, like M1, he was eager to talk. As a former trade-unionist, he is used to talking, and "building up" stories. Here is one of his narrative pieces:[8]

Introduction: il y a une dame française (stative)

Story line	Comments, explanations, narrative inside the narrative
	1 il/ave/vu un grand intimité (stative)
	1 et il *fait* un voyage à Buenos Aires (active) = narrative inside narrative (anteriorité)
	je la *connais* de Buenos Aires (stative with left boundary mark)
	il *fait* un peu de solidarité avec notre exil
	(iterative/more like a state) (process = time of utterance)

il *fait* un invitation (active)   2

(pour *faire* un voyage à Barcelona)   3
   (future in the past-active)

quand nous *retournons* de Barcelona
   (active)   4

il *dit* (active)   5

> nous *pouvons* faire un promenade
>   pour le Sud
>
> (direct or indirect speech + modal)

6
> nous *restons* une semaine
> nous *restons* dans une ferme   (stative)
> toutes les Français
> nous *sommes* toutes les après-midi   (stative) +
> y *vient* les Français   (iterative) +
> y /*parle*/ avec nous   (active)

Conclusion: et très bien (stative)

NB: metalinguistic activity: comm'on dit granca? (implies a change of interlocutor, i.e., F2 and not the interviewer)

FIGURE 2   "Structural Skeleton" of M1's narrative 2

Narrative 3

E: *...une expérience moi* vivir *à* quince   ... an experience me *vivir* at *quince* days
     jours/a Rive/ *à la France eh...un ami*   arrive/d/al at the France eh ... a friend
     invita *à Besançon et* el/*done/passage le*   *invita* at Besançon and *el* gave passage the
     train et moi no/konƐse/pas eh...gare de   train and me no knew not ch ... Gare de
     Lyon eh...*c'est* desconocido eh como   Lyon eh ... it's *desconocido eh como*
     haber una jungla *(XXX)* no se   *haber una jungla* (XXX) *no se*

Int:	*une jungle*	a jungle
E:	...*et/ ʒe/moi/a*Rive/*à la station à la gare gare de Lyon et avant train/e/*termino *à la sortie/de/train/de/train/*ʒeℝ ə *garde*... *d ə màde/ (XXX) eh* el *numero/de/train et/cet/*problema *pour demade à una/ d ʒena/à* otro/ dʒena/...*n'a pas* informar *(XXX) et/kop ende/*yo...*il informa* yo *n'a pas/kõprende/et* por *deduction*...	and I me arrive/d/al at the station at the Gare de Lyon and before train is (?) *termino* at the way out of train of train I looked ... asked (XXX) ah *el numero* of train and it's *problema* for ask to *una* people to *otro* people did not *informar* (XXX) and understand *yo* ... he *informa yo* did not understand and *por* deduction
Int:	*par déduction d'est ca*	yes by deduction
E:	*oui et/ʒe a*Rive/*à train correct*	yes and I arrived to/at train correct
Int:	*et c'était le bon train?*	and it was the right train?
E:	*bon train et sans* problema...	right train and without *problema*

The episode could be summed up by the "structural skeleton" in Figure 3, where chronology is again indicated by numbers.

Here it is even more obvious that the hearer and the linguist have different status. When listening to Emilio's narrative I had certainly understood that it was a narrative, but I had not understood much of what he was saying.

What is striking in this narrative, apart from the comments in Spanish, is the rupture in the otherwise chronological order at event 8. This rupture is made possible, at this very early stage, by the knowledge Emilio has of the temporal conjunction *avant* (which M1 never used).

Two passages can be classified as metalinguistic verbalization: *no se* "I don't know" and the repetition/self-repair—with the introduction of the negation: *il informa yo n'a pas*/kõpℝende/. The anaphoric pronoun *il/ils* is probably anaphoric and plural and refers to *una/d ʒena/* and *otro/d ʒena/* "one people" and "other people." (In SF, *gens* cannot be used in the singular.)

It must be noticed here that the self-determined reference point is also implicitly deictic: *invita à Besançon* is understood as "to go to Besançon" because the place of utterance is not Besançon but Paris, and because I knew that he had never lived in Besançon (shared knowledge of the speaker's life story). The *hic* of the utterance situation plays a part here as regards reference point operations.

Concerning temporal reference point adverbials, *à quinze jours/*a ive/*à la France* is also interesting since in SF, *à quinze jours dè faire quelque chose* means "fifteen days before doing something" and here the knowledge that the experience he is telling happened in France selects the value *après* "after" instead of *avant* "before." The use of the preposition might be due to transfer here (cf. *a los quince dias*). Not much can be said about verbal morphology in the narrative, especially since Emilio uses only one form for the verb (or noun *arriver/arrivée* ?) /aℝ ive/, which could be an infinitive (cf. his Spanish use of *vivir* and *informar*) or a past participle. All the verbs he uses and either in /a/ or in /e/, or else they are (foreigner talk?) Spanish infinitives. In the data there was no meaningful opposition at this stage.

Thus, with two prepositions (*à* and *de*), three verbal endings, the connective *et* used between the "units," one conjunction (*avant*), Emilio is able to build up a

Introduction: une expérience moi *vivir* à quince jours /aRive/ à la France (cataphoric)

Story line	Comments, explanations
un ami *invita* à Besançon (active) 1	
et el /done/ passage le train (active) 2	
	et moi ne /konɛse/ pas Gare de Lyon (stative)
	c'est desconocido como *haber* una jungla (stative + Spanish)
	no se (metalinguistic?) (stative)
et /ʒe/ moi /aRive/ à la station (active) 3	
et *avant* train /e/ termino (active?) 8	
à la sortie de train	
/ʒe RegaRde/ (active) 4	
/ʒe demãde/ el numero (active) 5	
	c'est problema pour *demander* (iterative) (stative)
n'a pas informar (active) 6 /kõpRende/ yo (active)	
	repetition-self repair (negation) il *informa* (active) yo n'a pas /kõpRende/
	et por deduction (comment on strategy)
et /ʒe aRive/ à train correct (active) 7 et /aRive/ à Besançon (active) 9	
Conclusion: et sans problema (no verb)	

FIGURE 3   "Structural Skeleton" of E's narrative

rather complex narrative with a chronological rupture, comments, a real introduction, and a conclusion.

CONCLUDING REMARKS

The analytical tool developed here for narratives (with the three necessary headings: analysis of SL, TL, and IL systems, of reference point operations and of the structure of narratives) can be used cross-linguistically to discover how acquirers (and, more generally, speakers) spontaneously refer to time (in both cross-sectional and longitudinal studies).

This is precisely what we are doing now in the E.S.F. Project. In France, we are also studying the acquisition of French by Arabic speakers (in Aix-en-Provence). We will therefore be able to do paired comparisons with data collected in Sweden (SL: Spanish, TL: Swedish) and in Holland (SL: Arabic, TL: Dutch), and then to the other L1s and L2s involved in the project (see Perdue, 1982). As the analytical tool is based on (possibly invariant) semantic—and not simply syntactic—criteria, it can be adapted to many languages and will hopefully yield a clearer view of the impact which a particular SL has on the second language acquisition of an adult learner. **It may allow scholars, when they are applying the analysis to more typologically different languages, to identify potentially generalizable phenomena in the acquisition of temporal reference, even if all languages do not have the same underlying conception of time. It seems that before analyzing data, one must have, if not a theory, at least a few theoretical criteria which give a coherent and analytical frame.**

In the case of temporality, any study must account for the complex way in which temporal reference is actively constructed and reconstructed by means of all the network of relations the subjects establish between forms and values, and among the values themselves.

At each stage of the acquisition process, as in final stages, statistics and neat tables do not tell us all of what we want to know.

NOTES

I have greatly benefited from the lively discussions on temporality that took place in the workshop at Göhrde (August 1982), and which regularly take place within the French team working on the E.S.F. Project. I am also grateful to Clive Perdue for long talks.

1. "Missing" is used here with regard to the target language. We are aware of the fact that ILs should be studied in themselves and not compared with TLs, but a native *hearer* will not notice "missing" elements which interfere with her reconstruction of meaning. Here again, the linguist and the hearer do not have the same type of "comprehension."

2. I return to the inadequacy of this term in p. 241 below.

3. See Borillo (1982), Nef (1980), Simonin (in press), Simonin (1977), Vet (1980), Guillemin-Flescher (1981), Fuchs and Leonard 1980), and Weinrich (1973) for an analysis of the French tense-aspect system.

4. There were very few references to the future in M1's productions. The future tense morphology appeared once in a self-repair: *nous restons . . . nous resterons* "we stay . . . we will stay." Otherwise, in the very few future contexts, the modal auxiliary *aller* (periphrastic future, cf. going to) was used under two of its forms only: *vais* (first person singular, example: *je vais dire* "I'm going to say") and *va* (SF: first person singular (*je va donner* "I'm going to give") and for other persons as well: *tu va(s) voir, il jamais va lire, il(s) va travailler.* This use of the modal periphrase may be a strategy to avoid the future inflectional system (cf. *venir de* to express reference to the past, p. 236). Adverbials were used to assign some determination to the utterances, as in *je vais faire le prochain mois* "I'm going to do next month."

Consider this other example:

l'autre problèma, c'est l'âge ... je suis un homme qué lé mois qué vient/ʒ e/ (je/j'ai) ... vous savez l'âge qué/ʒ e/(j'ai) ... quaranteneuf ans.	"the other problem, it's age...I am a man who the month which comes I/I am ... you know the age which I have ... 49 years."

Obviously, M1 does not know how to say *je vais avoir*. He never uses the verb *avoir* in the infinitive. He does not use the future tense *j'aurai*. The semantic content of the upstream context *(age, next month)* succeeds in making the statement meaningful.

5. For lack of space, I will only briefly mention the landmarks which signal the transition to atemporal comments in the whole interview:

Deactualized present tense (no reference to the *nunc* of the utterance situation ("general truth" present).

Adverbs like *en général* "in general" (vs. *par exemple* "for instance" which often leads to a narrative/anecdote).

Use of generic determiners: *le, la, les, toutes,* etc.

NB: in French, a sentence like *le lion mange de la viande* is ambiguous. It can mean either "lions eat meat" or "the lion is eating meat," and here it is obvious that the generic or definite value of the determiner is not independently selected from the atemporal or on the contrary actualized value of the present tense. Either the speaker/hearer chooses the two values which imply no relation to the moment of utterance, or he or she chooses the two values which imply such a relation. Any linguistic theory necessarily needs this concept of relation between utterances and utterance situations.

6. Consider also the following example:

-*Quand je suis jeune je suis ouvrier* "when I am young I am worker" taken from another of M1's narratives. Semantic information comes not only from the conjunction but also obviously from the relation between the first person pronoun *je* and the semantic information carried by the adjective. Without the conjunction, the utterance would still have been clear, because of the shared knowledge of M1's age: he is 49. This lexical item and this knowledge play a role in the successful construction of temporal reference here (SF: *Quand j'étais jeune, j'étais ouvrier*).

7. In a longitudinal study, one of the questions the linguist might ask would be: are self-determined and anaphoric references to time and space different developmental stages? i.e., does the repetition of proper nouns and dates tend to disappear when the corresponding anaphoric markers are mastered? A parallel question would be: what happens as regards self-determined expressions(especially dates) vs. the corresponding deictic marker? One possible hypothesis would be that there might be an order of acquisition from deictic and self-determined toward anaphoric expressions (18 Janvier 1982 being "easier" to say than *le 18 Janvier de l'année dernière* or *il y a un an—one year ago*).

8. I did not use the phonetic transcription systematically here for reasons of legibility. The transcriptions we use for the analyses try to take all ambiguous forms into account (cf. p. 247 for the ambiguity of the preposition à (French)/a (Spanish).

REFERENCES

Benveniste, É. 1966.*Problèmes de Linguistique Générale.* Paris: Gallimard.

Borillo, A. 1982. Temps notionnel, temps grammatical: quelques faits linguistiques concernant la durée. In*Approches formelles de la sémantique naturelle,* CNRS, UPS, UTM ADI, Toulouse.

de Lemos, C., and J. Bybee. 1981. The development of backgrounding devices coded on the verb. Workshop Paper, Nijmegen.

Dubois, C., C. Noyau, C. Perdue, and R. Porquier. 1981. A propos d'une pré-enquête sur l'utilisation du français en milieu naturel par des adultes hispanophones. *GRECO 13,* numéro spécial, 57–78.

Fillmore, C. J. 1982. Towards a descriptive framework for spatial deixis. In R. J. Jarvella and W. Klein (eds.). *Speech, Place, and Action.* Chichester: Wiley, 31–59.

Fuchs, C., and A. M. Léonard. 1979. *Vers une théorie des aspects. Les systèmes du français et de l'anglais,* Mouton, La Haye.

Givón, T. 1973. The time axis phenomenon. *Language* 50: 890–925.

Givón, T. 1982. Tense-aspect modality: the creole proto-type and beyond. In P. J. Hopper (ed.) *Tense-Aspect: Between Semantics and Pragmatics.* Amsterdam: John Benjamins. pp. 115–163.

Guillemin-Flescher, J. 1981. Syntaxe comparée du français et de l'anglais. Problèmes de traduction, Paris: Ophrys.

Kumpf, L. 1982a. Temporal systems and universality in interlanguage: a case study. Paper presented at the 11th Annual University of Wisconsin, Milwaukee Linguistics Symposium.

Kumpf, L. 1982b. Tense, aspect and modality in interlanguage. Discourse-functional approach, ms.

Meisel, J. M. 1982. Reference to past events and actions in the development of natural second language acquisition. This volume.

Nef, F. 1980. Les verbes aspectuels du français: remarques sémantiques et esquisse du traitement formel. *Semantikos,* Paris, vol. 4.

Noyau, C. 1981. The acquisition of French by adult Spanish-speaking immigrants: transfer of LI structures and individual systems. Paper presented at the 1st EuNam Workshop on Cross linguistic SLA Research, Lake Arrowhead.

Noyau, C. 1982. The expression of temporality in French L2: stability/evolution of an L2 system long after the initial acquisition phase. Paper presented at the 2nd EuNam Workshop on Cross-Linguistic SLA Research, Göhrde.

Perdue, C. 1980. L'analyse des erreurs: un bilan pratique, *Langages* 57, Larousse, Paris, 87–94.

Perdue, C. (ed.). 1982. *Second Language Acquisition by Adult Immigrants: A Field Manual.* E.S.F. Strasbourg.

Reichenbach, H. 1947. *Elements of Symbolic Logic.* New York: Macmillan.

Simonin, J. 1977. Linguistique textuelle et étude des textes littéraires. A propos de *Le Temps* de H. Weinrich, Pratiques 13, Paris.

Simonin, J. In press. Les repérages énonciatifs dans les textes de presse, In *Interlocution et référence,* Presses Universitaires de Lille.

Traugott, E. Closs. 1978. On the expression of spatio-temporal relations in language, In J. H. Greenberg (ed.), *Universals of Human Language,* vol. 3: *Word Structure,* Stanford University Press, 369–400.

Trévise, A. 1984. Adult Spanish-speakers and the acquisition of French negation forms; individual variation and linguistic awareness. In R. Andersen (ed.) *Second Languages* Rowley, MA: Newbury House, pp. 165-190.

Trévise, A. (ed.). 1982. *Acquisition d'une langue étrangère, II. Encrages,* Université de Paris VIII.

Trévise, A. (In press.) Topicalization, is it transferable? In E. Kellerman and M. Sharwood-Smith (eds.). This volume.

Vet, C. 1980. *Temps, aspects et adverbes de temps en français.* Genève: Droz.

von Stutterheim, C. 1982. Temporality in learner varieties. Paper prepared for the 2nd EuNam Workshop on Cross-linguistic SLA Research, Göhrde.

von Stutterheim, C., and W. Klein. A concept-oriented approach to second language studies. This volume.

Weinrich, H. 1973. *Le Temps.* Paris: Le Seuil.

Wunderlich, D. 1982. Langage et espace, *DRLAV* 27, Centre de Recherche de l'Université de Paris VIII, 63–82.

CHAPTER 12

Reference to Past Events and Actions in Narratives in L2: Insights From North African Workers' French

Daniel Véronique

University of Provence, France

This chapter is mainly based on narrative excerpts from seven 45-minute conversations in French between a target language (TL) speaker and Arabic and Berber speaking workers living in southern France (Marseilles). This cross-sectional study addresses the following research questions:

- How do L2 users with a varying command of the TL morphosyntax achieve the communicative task of recounting past events to TL speakers?
- What are the devices used to establish temporal reference, and in what way does spatial reference interact with them in narratives about past events and actions?
- To what extent do speakers whose degree of proficiency in L2 differs vary in their narration of past events and actions?

It seems fairly obvious that the native speaker's contribution to the conversation should also be assessed, especially his degree of cooperation in accomplishing the communicative act of past reference. However, it is our contention that the TL speaker's behavior in the type of setting we used for data collection is strictly determined by the nonnative language user's communicative competence in L2. Hence we concentrate mainly on the nonnative speech.

In the first sections of this chapter, we present our informants and give an outline of the morphosyntactic means available to them as a group in TL. A description of the methodology used to process the data available is also given. In the following sections, the findings for each informant are reported. These are discussed in the final section, where an attempt is made to survey some of the issues involved in a functional approach to the study of temporality in interlanguage.

TABLE 1 Informants

Subjects	L1	Arabic spoken	Schooling	Literacy Arabic	Literacy French	Place of learning of French	Duration of stay in France	Places of stay in France	Occupation
T(unisian) 1	Arabic	+	−	−	−	France	7	Marseilles Center of France	mason
T2	Arabic	+	−	−	−	France	6	Coralen Marseilles	unskilled worker
A(lgerian) 3	Berber	+	−	−	±	Algeria	11	Paris Marseilles	unskilled worker
A4	Berber	+	−	−	−	France	11	Marseilles	unskilled worker
A5	Arabic	+	−	−	±	serving in the army	11	Marseilles	unskilled worker
A7	Arabic	+	−	−	−	France	19	Marseilles	unskilled worker
A8	Arabic	+	−	−	−	France	25	Lille Marseilles	unskilled worker

SUBJECTS

The informants for this study were chosen among the eleven subjects studied in Véronique (1984). All of them are practically illiterate (in L1 and L2) unskilled workers. They were long-term residents in France (length of stay varying between 5 and 25 years) at the time data were collected. All lived in Marseilles and had been exposed, except for A8, mainly to the southern variety of French as spoken in Marseilles and its surroundings.

The subjects' communicative and linguistic proficiency in French was assessed by the investigator (who also held the interview sessions) to be as follows:

- Low level: T1, A7
- Intermediate level: T2, A5, A8
- Advanced level: A3, A4

It is to be noted that this subjective assessment[1] is partially at variance with the quantitative indices available for the same subjects (see below).

OUTLINE OF THE USE OF MORPHOSYNTACTIC FEATURES OF TL

Only features relevant to this study are outlined in this subsection (for further details, see Véronique, 1984):

- Errors on the verb phrase are few in number. Only approximately 7 percent of the tokens of VP contain one or more errors. Thus the morphology of VP, if we omit covert errors and avoidance strategy, seems to be mastered. Note that the percentage of errors on VP does not follow our assessment of the subject's proficiency and that some of the intermediate-level informants have a better mastery of aspects of the TL verb morphology than more advanced users (see, for example, the use of *être + Verb of movement,* in Véronique, 1984).

TABLE 2   Errors on the Verb Phrase

Informant	Proficiency level	Tokens	Total no. of errors	Percent
A7	Low	141	15	13
T1	Low	562	50	8.9
T2	Intermediate	999	38	3.8
A8	Intermediate	1112	54	4.8
A3	Advanced	1657	69	4.1
A4	Advanced	998	108	10.8

- Most of the errors on VP concern tense marking. In all the transcripts, there is an overwhelming use of a form which corresponds to the unmarked present tense in TL. This leads to errors in some contexts. For morphophonemic and other reasons, there is a prevailing confusion between the forms of the TL progressive past *(imparfait),* usually represented by an -e form, and of the compound past *(passé composé),* an auxiliary + past participle (also usually ending in -e). There is thus available to our informants for reference to past events and actions a verbal form which is in most cases V stem + e. It should be remembered that in TL, the difference between *imparfait* and *passé composé* is temporal and aspectual; the former is [- perfective] and [+ progressive] and the latter is [± perfective] and [- progressive].[2]

- If overt errors according to TL norms on VP are few in number, the overuse of two verb forms, V stem (comparable with TL present) and (aux) + V stem + e (henceforth, V + e) (comparable with TL compound past), and the reduction of the TL morphological verbal stem alternation indicate the existence of a simplification strategy on the part of the subjects. In A3's transcript, for instance, out of 214 different verbs, 135 belong to the category of nonalternating verbs[3] and account for 38 percent of the occurrences of verb form.

- It should be added that in the interlanguage (IL) of North African workers, auxiliary *avoir* tends to supersede *être* in those few instances where the latter is required according to TL norm.

As will be shown through the analysis of the subjects' narratives, mastery of TL morphology does not preclude the possibility of specific nonnative uses of these forms to achieve a given function.

PROCEDURES FOR DATA ANALYSIS

Data were analyzed according to the following procedures (see Andersen, 1982):

- The transcript is reviewed for passages containing reference to past events; this identification is based primarily on the contents of the subject's answers and secondarily on the clues provided by the interviewer's questions.

- Among the suitable passages, preference is given in the final selection to narratives over dialogues, whenever possible. As a rule, three passages are retained per informant. According to Kumpf (1982), specific differences are manifested by these two discourse types: conversation reveals irrealis/modality forms whereas narratives are more structured when it comes to time and aspect. We primarily examine narratives, but where the relevant data are not available, we also take conversation into account.

In analyzing these passages, we make use of the background-foreground dichotomy as defined in Hopper (1979) and we apply the methodology for the study of temporality in IL outlined by Klein, Dittmar, and von Stutterheim. We thus have the opportunity to test the validity of these tools for a functional approach to temporal reference.

FINDINGS

We devote more space to the analysis of narratives by the informants of lesser proficiency, since the devices employed by these subjects are also found in narratives by more advanced informants. In the analysis of narratives by the latter, we stress only those formal means which are specific to that type of subject. A subset of the narratives is included in the appendix.

LOW-LEVEL INFORMANTS

A7 Except for one short narrative, this informant talks about past events only in response to queries from the investigator. Thus, the communicative task of setting the frame for reference to past events and states rests partly on the latter, who does whatever "scaffolding" is required for the conversation to be smooth and intelligible.

Conversation In answering queries by the TL speaker, A7 marks past reference by three main devices, anaphoric adverbials and calendric expressions (which are partially or totally self-sufficient in terms of temporal reference; see Kerbrat-Orrecchioni, 1980) on the one hand and verb morphology on the other. Examples from the transcript are given in (1) and (2):

(1) Q. *Ça fait longtemps que tu habites Mar-*   "You've been living in Marseilles for long?
     seille? depuis dix ans peut-être?   for ten years perhaps?"
   A. *Peut-être.* [3 ekite] *Marseille trois ans là*   "Perhaps. I left Marseilles three year
     après [3 eturne] *et puis* [3 erεst] *ici.*   (ago?) then I come/came back and then I
       stay here."

(2) Q. *T'es allé à l'école coranique là-bas?*   "You've been to Koranic school there?"
   A. *Jamais.*   "Never (been)"
   Q. *Jamais?*   "Never (been)?"
   A. *Jamais* [3 ete] *à l'école* [3 ete] *à l'école*   "Never been to school I've been to school
     jamais.   never"

In (1), the use of adverbials *trois ans là, après, puis,* and the formal difference between V + e forms, [3 ekite], [3 eturne], conveying perfective meaning and V stem forms, [3er ε st], with imperfective meaning, should be noted. The deletion of an obligatory preposition between [3ekite] Marseilles and *trois ans,* which could be either *pendant* "during," *il y a* "ago" or *depuis* "since" in the TL should also be mentioned. It is unclear whether A7 means "three years from the here and now"—time of utterance being the reference point—in which the whole clause would be [+ durative], or whether "three years" is the sum total of the time spent away from Marseilles. This could then be regarded as a case of unspecified temporal reference in the sense that the time elapsed is quantified but not referred to from a specific vantage point. The latter interpretation may be preferable, as tokens of *depuis* "since" + N (temporal) expressing duration implicitly are found elsewhere in the transcript.

In (2), note the use of adverbial *jamais* to give perfective meaning to the otherwise ambiguous [ʒete] (*j'étais* imparfait or *j'ai été* compound past). In addition, the nature of turntaking between the investigator and the informant is of interest. Interaction between the two partners is quick, the informant being reluctant to hold the floor. In 20 minutes of conversation, 475 turns were counted. The subject's attitude leads the investigator into taking a leading role in the conversation, introducing new topics and supporting whatever is introduced as theme by the subject.

Narrative   In his one narrative (see Appendix), A7 answers the investigator who had set the scene by hinting that being unemployed, he could take it easy for one year (*pendant un an tu es tranquille*), by using anaphoric adverbial *après un an* (after one year) which shows *en passant* that he understands durative prepositions. Then he goes on with an indexical adverbial *maintenant* "now." The rest of the narrative is organized in a chronological order, according to the discourse principle "first happened, first mentioned." Background is marked especially through the use of adverbials, whereas the foreground is made up of V stem verb forms. In this passage, eleven out of the sixteen tokens of VP are of the form V stem.

Each of the six temporal units in both the background and the foreground is constructed in the following frame:

$$\left\{ \begin{pmatrix} \text{Adverb} \\ \text{Quand} \\ (\text{Si}) \end{pmatrix} + \text{VP} \right\} + \text{Main clause}$$

Seen from a semantic point of view, the subordinate temporal clause sets the frame of action or describes the process, whereas the main clause is resultative in meaning. This binary construction, which is used by all the subjects and probably, with some differences in verb morphology, by native speakers too is a discursive device furthering temporal reference.

T1   Conversation between T1 and the same investigator is different. During an interaction of approximately 45 minutes 403 turns were counted and T1 produces at least six narratives.

Conversation   Outside narratives, T1 answers the investigator's questions by using calendrical expressions, for example, in (3):

(3) Q: *Ça fait longtemps?*
     "Been (here) for long?"
  A. *24 juillet 70.*
     "24 July 70."

Calendrical expressions appear both to the left and to the right of the VP. There are nine tokens of the syntactic frame calendrical expressions + VP such as (4):

(4)   *76* [ʒ eãntre] *chomage*
      "76 I enrolled (because of) unemployment"

as well as five tokens of VP + calendrical expressions.[4] In those 14 sentences, VP is marked for compound past (i.e., auxiliary *avoir* + V past participle) in 12 cases; in the remaining cases V stem is used. Verb morphology is probably used here to distinguish between duration in the past (V stem) and punctual reference to a past event (V + e) (see below).

Besides calendrical expressions, adverbials are also used; *avant* "before" occurs by itself or introduces a calendrical expression seven times. In each of these cases, the adverbial is to the left of VP. In contrast to sentences where reference to past events and actions is expressed partly through calendrical expressions, utterances containing *avant* "before" are always unmarked as for verb morphology. This could be interpreted in one of two ways: the first possibility is that syntactic frames with calendrical expressions are perceived as needing an explicit grammatical marker, hence [-e], whereas *avant* is analyzed as a grammatical form bearing past temporal meaning so that an additional marker seems unnecessary; the second possibility is that syntactic frames with calendrical expressions are distinctly [+ perfective] whereas, in *avant* + VP, the focus of temporal reference changes from the aspectual feature of perfectivity to the temporal feature of actualness in a past framework; i.e., the temporal space between the time of occurrence of the event denoted and the time of utterance is deleted. Examples are given in (5) to (7):

(5) *avant j'écris la date*   "before I write the date"
(6) *avant 59, je compte tout seul*   "before 59, I count by myself"
(7) *avant d'entrer la France, je calcule* "before entering France, I knew how to count."

A further explanation following Hopper (1979: 215) that foreground has punctual verbs could also be considered. However, in this particular case, that discourse constraint does not explain the facts, since *avant* +V form occurs in both background and foreground units.

Duration or repetition of past events is expressed by lexical means, as in (8):

(8) *Ça fait 6 ans je travaille*
    "It's been 6 years I work"

or through the functor *jusqu'à* "up to." Note that in a way similar to A7, T1 juxtaposes VP + calendrical expression (without using one of the appropriate TL link words *depuis, il y a,* or *pendant*) to express duration in the past. In that context, V is unmarked (V stem).

Narratives   In narrative 1, all sentences setting the background are in the TL compound past tense form, auxiliary + V past participle (mostly V + e) while the foreground verbs are unmarked (V stem form). T1 uses indexical (for instance, *cette là . . .nuit* "that night") as well as anaphoric adverbials (*le premier jour même,* "the very first day"). The informant does not, however, properly master the morphological changes associated in TL with adverbials in either role. For instance, he uses indexical *demain matin* instead of anaphoric *le lendemain matin* in (9):

(9) *je reste quatre heures l'après-midi jusqu'à demain matin*
    "I stay (from) four in the afternoon till tomorrow morning."

Reference to "two days after" or "two days before" in (10) from narrative 3 is also unclear to a TL hearer.

(10) *je travaille là-bas trois ans jusque le dernier jour*
    "I work there (for) three years until the last day"
    [ʒe antre] *la France/Je prends le trente* [ž urdwi]
    "I entered France/I start on the 30th today"
    demain après-demain je prends le bateau je m'en vais
    "tomorrow after tomorrow I get on board I leave"
    [ãntre] *ici la France*
    "got here (in) France"

TL anaphoric forms for "the day before" would be *la veille,* for "the day after" *le lendemain,* for "two days before" *l'avant-veille,* and "two days after" *le surlendemain.*

In narrative 1, the story follows chronology and is anchored by a parallel set of temporal and spatial referents.

TABLE 3   Sequencing in Narrative 1

Temporal reference	Event/Action	Spatial reference
• *le premier jour même* the very first day	1. Arrival	• *La France* • *La Vieux Port* Marseille
• *quatre heures et demie* (at) four and a half		
• *cette nuit-là* that night	2. Departure for Toulouse; stop over	• *Toulouse*
• *quatre heures du matin* four in the morning	3. Leaves for Guéret in the early morning	• *Guéret*
• *du matin huit heures* eight in the morning	4. Starts work there	• *avec l'entreprise* with the firm

Narrative 2 is performed by T1 as a result of a question posed some turns before by the investigator, *Comment avez-vous fait pour apprendre le français?* "How did you manage to learn French?" All the verbs, except for one alternation (*le demande cendrier/j'ai demandé paquet de cigarettes* "I ask for ash-tray/I asked for cigarettes") are unmarked (V + ∅). There are two occurrences of adverbial *avant,* but as mentioned before, it does not require past marking. The whole passage with its many action verbs (*je parle, je (di)scute* "I talk with"/"I speak to"; *j'écoute* "I listen"; *je demande* "I ask" is [+ punctual]. Note that although the events recounted have passed, verb morphology seems to be that of TL present tense.

In narrative 3 (see Appendix), 13 out of the 15 verbs are in the unmarked V stem form. The perfectivity of the events and actions being described has been established two turns before by a question from the investigator: *Tu travaillais en Tunisie? Dans quelle entreprise? Toujours maçon?* "Did you work in

Tunisia?" "In what firm?" "Always (as) a mason?" Shared knowledge of the world—the interview is taking place in France—also helps to set the narrative in the past; thus the naming of places and towns in Tunisia can only be associated with past (or future, but this reading cannot apply here) events.

As mentioned before in the analysis of conversation, T1 never uses a preposition having possible durative meaning such as *pendant* "while" with adverbials. This holds true for narratives also. *Jusqu'à* "until" is used in adverbial clauses, but it indicates the limits of a given process or state; it is [+ progressive] [+ bounded]. *Ça fait* "it's been" or *y a* "there's" which are also used can be analyzed as [+ perfective] [+ bounded]. Time NPs such as *trois ans* "three years" and calendrical NPs are placed in the immediate vicinity (left or right) of the VP by which they are governed.

INTERMEDIATE-LEVEL INFORMANTS

A8 The first narrative selected is a very short one dealing with the settlement of A8 and his family in France. It is a factual account, and backgrounding takes up a large part of the passage. This is achieved through the simultaneous use of four devices:

- An anaphoric adverbial clause, *la première fois* "the first time"
- A calendrical expression, *en cinquante-deux* "in fifty-two"
- Verb morphology, [ʒ erãtre] "I came in"; in TL it should be *je suis rentré*, [ʒ ite] "I was"
- Reference to shared knowledge, *dans le nord de la France* "in the north of France"—recording is taking place in the south of France, years later.

The foreground is introduced by *et pi* " and then," but verb morphology remains unchanged, V + e as in parts of the background.

One striking feature is the way in which once it is established that the narrative is about past events, A8 goes on talking about these using V stem forms. This he does through the use of anaphoric *à ce moment là* " at that time." Through this device, which is also frequently used by TL speakers (who would, however, in that case use the *imparfait*), A8 is able to switch his temporal "origo" from the here and now of the time of utterance to some point in the past and to talk anew from there employing V stem forms.

Narrative 2 is also characterized by digressions, which seem typical of more advanced L2 users. The scene is set by indexical *avant* "before" + V + e verb morphology. The foreground is introduced and developed by means of *après* " afterward" + V stem morphology. Comments are marked either through verb form contrast, e.g., in (11):

(11) *avant* [sete] *wagons des petits wagons*
    "before there were wagons small wagons"
    [se] *interdit pour le personnel*
    "it is prohibited for the personnel"

by means of an anaphoric linkword, e.g., *aussi* in (12):

(12) *après on part pour travailler et* [ʒ rev ə nɛ] *par le wagon aussi*
"then we leave for the work site and we came back with the wagon so"
y en quelqu'un en retard et i vient à pied
"there's somebody late and he comes by foot"

or through asyndeton, e.g., in (13):

(13) *après ça commence moderne i fait des wagons*
"then it starts (becoming) modern they start (running) wagons"

Narrative 3 (see Appendix) is the most intricate of these narratives. The background is established by two parallel statements in (14):

(14) *en 54* [ʒete ãbo ʃ e] *comme mineur de fond*
"In 54 I was employed as miner"
en 56, ça commence la guerre en Algérie
"In 56 the war starts in Algeria"

Then there occurs a pattern of regular switching between background and foreground which is typical of A8 and of more advanced learners in general, which can be thus summarized:

Background	Foreground
1a Sets the scene: 54, A8 starts working in the mines 56, war breaks out in Algeria	
1b Comments on bombing in Algeria *(ça commence + V + e form)*	
	2a French and Algerians in the military service leave for Algeria *(à ce moment-là + aux + V + e form)*
2b Comments on working conditions in France during the Algerian War *(à ce moment là + V stem form)*	
	3a Changing working conditions in France as a result of war ($\left\{ \begin{array}{l} alors\ 55 \\ à\ 57 \end{array} \right\}$ + V stem form)
3b Explains why economic situation has improved in France as a result of war *(uses parce que (because) + aux + V + e morphology)*	
	4a End of Algerian war *(aprés 62 + aux + V + e morphology)*
4b Comments on the change in the attitudes of Frenchmen towards North African immigrant workers *(après + V stem morphology occassional aux + V + e morphology)*	

In A8's narratives, background and foreground are differentiated by means of a binary verb morphology distinction V + e vs. V stem as is the case in narratives by less proficient speakers. Note however, that the 5 V + e verbs (out of a total of 45) are all foreground verbs. As a matter of fact, A8 relies more heavily on discursive means such as asyndeton than on explicit marking to contrast background and foreground. *A ce moment là* "then" is used as a means both to switch time "origo" and to further the story line. *Ça commence* is employed in an idiosyncratic way to introduce comments and to keep the story going. It could be interpreted as [+ inchoative] in meaning.

T2   The theme of narrative 1 (see Appendix) is: arrival of the informant in France and his whereabouts. Though less intricate than narratives by A8, a pattern of regular switching between background and foreground can be observed. Comments are introduced either by *parce que* "because" or by asyndeton. As with A8, differentiation between the story line and the comments is not strictly based on verb morphology. However, all (aux) + V + e forms do occur in the foreground, except for three which occur at the opening of the narrative. In the foreground, a contrast between V stem forms and V + e forms should be noted. The latter forms occur after *alors* "then," *alors après* "thereafter," or *ensuite, alors* "then," whereas *après* "after" is followed by V stem with a resultative meaning. As is the case with less advanced informants, progress in the story line is enhanced by spatial deixis through reference to the various places where the informant has stayed and worked.

In narrative 2, T2's use of verb morphology is akin to that of informants of lower TL proficiency. He uses unmarked V stem forms in the foreground while both V stem forms and V + e forms are used in the background. One tentative rule which provides some explanation for the use of both types of forms in background units could be the following: once expressed through a V + e form, the perfective meaning need not be marked in the clause or clauses immediately following. However, in this narrative, V stem forms in background units are also used to convey imperfective meaning, either referring to timeless truth as in *dans l'été i fait quatre ou cinq ouvriers après il a/ après Octobre ils ont fermé* "during the summer he has (V stem form) four or five employees then he/ after October they have closed (V + e form)" or to an action originating in the past and extending to a near past—in this context, the *imparfait* (imperfect) form is used in standard French and it is often the case, though not always, in the informant's IL.

Of note in T2's narrative is the coupling of anaphoric adverbials *après* "afterward" and *alors* "then," e.g., in (15):

(15) *après je viens ici alors je trouve pas le travail*
   "Afterward I come here then I find no work"

This seems to be a variation on the binary construction signaled in the data from A7 (see above). Sequences with *après* and *alors* are used independently of the organization of information in terms of background and foreground. They may occur in either type of narrative unit or cut across these. In this narrative, a certain amount of variation should be noticed in the use of verb morphology +

adverbials, V stem forms occur at least three times after *après*, and V + e form at least once in the same context.

In narrative 3, all foreground sequences contain V + e forms. In the background, V stem and V + e forms occur according to the type of temporal contrast which the informant wants to achieve with the foreground. V stem forms convey an atemporal meaning while V + e forms are used when the temporal frame of the preceding foreground unit is shared by the following background unit. Besides verb morphology, comments are marked by T2 as with A8 through the use of link words (*mais* "but," *parce que* "because") and asyndeton. Quotations of the discussion that went on between the characters involved in the narrative are found in the background. Those are introduced by *il dit* "he said"; then the quotation with V stem forms follows. Unlike the less proficient informant T2, A8 (although the latter does use *en* + calendrical expressions) seems to distinguish between 73 [ʒe travaje] "73 I worked" or [ʒ ale] *vivre là-bas peut-être 3 ans* "I went/I was going to live there maybe three years" and *en 73 que [ʒete] là-bas* "in 73 when I was there." *En* + calendrical expression is [+ punctual], whereas mention of the date or the number of years alone would be respectively [+ durative] or atemporal, a sum total. Note that this distinction is not strictly determined by backgrounding or foregrounding.

A5   A5's transcript, as is the case with advanced informants, contains many narratives about past events and actions. The first narrative selected shows that A5 uses the same array of devices as the other informants for reference to past events and actions. As for verb morphology, most of the background clauses are V stem forms whereas 8 out of the 12 V + e forms are found in the foreground. Adverbials *après* "afterward" and *alors* "then" are used to introduce foreground clauses. In narrative 1, which is about the life of the informant's relatives during the Algerian war, temporal reference is reinforced by shared knowledge of the world and spatial deixis. Thus the story opens with *la guerre d'Indochine* "Indochinese war 1950s" and *Guerre des Allemands* "Second World War," then continues with the Algerian war (1957–1962). Reference is also made to Algeria and Egypt where one of the characters fled during the Algerian war, and these places are contrasted through the respective use of *ici* "here," though the recording is taking place in Marseilles) and *là-bas* "there." Note that duration is expressed in verb morphology through *va* + V infinitive where TL would require V stem. This could be a case of transfer from L1[5] and could be compared with idiosyncratic inchoative *"ça commence"* of A8.

In narratives 2 and 3, various features already observed in data from other informants are employed. As in the previous narrative, V + e forms tend to occur mainly in the foreground while verb morphology in the background is more varied. It contains both V stem and V + e forms. Clauses introduced by *un jour* "one day" and *après* "afterwards" are contrasted. In this type of binary construction, the *après* clause is always second and has a resultative meaning (see above). Here again, this coupling of clauses cuts across the background/ foreground distinction. Note that A5, like A7, T1, and A8, omits *pendant* "during" before calendrical expressions where TL would require it. Lastly, adverbials are as a rule followed by V stem forms.

ADVANCED-LEVEL INFORMANTS

The most striking feature of the narratives by these informants is their degree of intricacy. Greater mastery of TL seems to give greater freedom to those informants *vis à vis* the discursive principle "first happened, first mentioned." It should also be mentioned that all the devices indentified up to now for the expression of reference to past events are used by the advanced-level informants. Their use of TL verb morphology is more targetlike in that they seem to differentiate between *imparfait* (imperfect) and compound past. They also use various prepositions such as *pendant, depuis,* and *jusqu'à* + calendrical expressions to signify duration.

A4   In two out of the three selected narratives, foreground clauses have V + e forms, whereas comments and direct quotations from past conversations have a V stem form. The constraint that adverbial *après* should be followed by V stem whether it occurs in the foreground or in the background, observed in narratives by other informants, applies here too. Note that the final clause (coda) of the narrative has a V + e verb. Inside foreground units, binary constructions contrasting *alors* "then" and *après* "afterward," etc., are used to distinguish between a distant past and a more recent past.

Narrative 2 (see Appendix) is noteworthy because it contains two subnarratives very distinctly marked in terms of verb morphology. Subnarrative 1—how he did not attend school—has V + e verb forms, whereas subnarrative 2—working with his father in the fields—uses V + Ø forms. The final clause has a V + e form.

A3   Narratives by A3 also display all the temporal devices and constraints identified so far and the same degree of intricacy in structure. Narrative 1 (see Appendix) opens with a short story which sets the scene; then a second narrative is inserted. The two episodes are contrasted through verb morphology. The distribution of verb forms seems to obey the following TL rule: if compound past is used in the foreground, then *imparfait* (imperfect) should be in the background.

In narrative 2, the foreground is made up of *imparfait* verb forms which convey an imperfective meaning—it is all about getting ready to leave the work site. This episode ends with a V + e perfective form—in the street, a tile fell from a roof, missing the informant by chance. Then a subnarrative is started with mainly V stem forms giving a detailed account of what happened when the tile crashed in front of the informant. This second episode ends by remembering with V + e form that the tile really broke into pieces when it crashed down. Narrative 3 does not reveal any new peculiarity in the reference to past events and actions.

Summary of Findings

The following list of devices for expressing past reference is common to all informants:

- Lexical means, reliance on calendrical expressions and adverbials
- Verb morphology, V stem forms, and (aux.) + V + e forms regularly contrasted
- Discursive means, binary constructions used to contrast background information and processes; chronology relied upon as well as asyndeton
- Spatial deixis and shared knowledge of the world enhance reference to past actions and events

The informants differ on the following points:

- The way V stem forms and V + e forms are distributed between background and foreground
- The expression of duration in the past
- The modification of the temporal reference "origo"
- The intricacy of narratives or the degree to which the chronological sequence is violated

DISCUSSION

In this section, we would like to raise some theoretical and methodological questions first and then discuss our findings. Although looking at the use of L2 from a functional angle is a good departure from the morpheme-bound approach, this change of perspective entails some new questions. Thus, in the functional approach to temporality adopted in this paper, the very notion of reference to past events and actions seems somehow fuzzy. It has been understood to mean the designation of events, states, and actions set in the past: denotation provides the clue for interpretation.[6] Everybody will agree that this type of external facility is not always available when it comes to temporal or other reference for that matter. For instance, it is not quite clear to us whether the substitution of the notion "prior to" for that of past reference would yield a different analysis. In effect, universes of discourse can be so construed that events of the real world are or should be organized in a different sequence linguistically. Our contention is that for the conceptual approach (see von Stutterheim and Klein, this volume) to L2 use to be viable, the semantic and pragmatic notions which structure linguistic organization need to be closely scrutinized and defined at least from the speaker's and the hearer's perspectives as those may not always coincide.

Further, classification of the various formal, semantic, and discursive devices which help to build a given reference without explaining the type of cognitive space achieved lends support to the criticisms of those who consider the functional approach to be taxonomy of another kind. Yet the question of how the array of devices listed is structured is not an easy one. At least two levels are important here:

- The level of information organization which affects large units of discourse such as the paragraph and which can be analyzed through the background-foreground dichotomy
- The level of local constraints, sentence or clause bound such as V stem after adverbials

Analysis of the data has shown that difference in the expression of reference to past events in narratives between the informants is dependent on the way they contrast background and foreground as well as on the type of local constraints they bring to bear on given clauses following the rules of their interim grammar. While low-level informants are quite systematic in their use of verb morphology, V stem forms occurring in foreground units and V + e forms in the background, this is not the case with intermediate-level informants. A8 and A5 tend to use V + e forms in the foreground, whereas T2 makes use of either V stem or V + e but never both at the same time. In background units, both verb forms occur. The latter has to do with the fact that narratives tend to be more intricate as proficiency increases in TL and as temporal contrasts in the background become more elaborate.

Viewing temporal reference in narratives from another angle, it is striking to note that such an apparently simple notion as past reference is achieved by a variety of means belonging to different linguistic realms and working contradistinctly. For example, it was observed that contrast of verb morphology or use of binary constructions cuts across the sequencing of information in terms of background and foreground. To use Halliday's (1970) triple distinction among textual, interpersonal, and informational functions, one can consider that although these grammatical and semantic means work toward the same goal, let us say, reference to past events, each set of devices in so doing abides by its own rules of function.

In addition to those general points, this cross-sectional study provides some insights into the way TL forms and rules are used by L2 speakers to achieve a given communicative purpose. Two features must be commented upon. One is the development of specific local constraints such as: calendrical NPs co-occur with V + e forms whereas given adverbials *(après, avant)* are found with V stem forms, and variation in the use of TL constraints such as imperfective *(imparfait)* or perfective *(passè simple/passè composè)* marking on the main verb is obligatory according to whether a calendrical expression is to the left or to the right of V. Those constraints which are common to all the narratives examined[7] partly explain certain specific uses of verb morphology, such as apparently random marking of past reference on the verb. The second noteworthy feature is the difference between the low-level proficiency informants A7 and T1 and all the others in the distribution of V stem and V + e between background and foreground. This difference could be explained by the fact that these two less proficient speakers are more dependent on a limited set of devices, to which one of them resorts systematically.

Viewed from another perspective, those remarks may seem to be critical of Hopper's notions of aspect, of the foreground-background distinction, and of its application in IL study by Kumpf(1982). In effect, we have shown that the use of IL verbal morphology is not determined by backgrounding or foregrounding as is the case in TL (see Benveniste, 1966; Hopper, 1979). It seems to us that the expression of temporality is not exclusively contrived by the need to bring certain events into the foreground and to shunt others to the background. Local clause level constraints must also be taken into account. Rather than an all-encompassing principle, we would rather consider foreground-background as one level, maybe the most important one, of the organization of narratives.

It would appear that beyond a set of quasi-universal devices such as reliance on chronology, shared knowledge of the world and spatial deixis, the amount of information about past events conveyed (as measured by the intricacy of the narratives and the switches of temporal "origo") is directly related to the mastery of temporal marking on the verb, especially the expression of duration in the past. This means that notwithstanding differences in performance strategies, there exists in the subfield of reference to past events a continuum of development whereby the L2 speaker acquires greater freedom in the use of the interplay between the information organization level and that of local constraints and is therefore able to progress beyond the simple perfective-imperfective dichotomy.

CONCLUSION

This study has shown that L2 speakers of varying proficiency in L2 placed in a similar situation, that of recounting past events to a TL speaker, used partially similar devices. These are:

- Reliance on the discursive principle: first happened, first mentioned
- Reliance on shared knowledge of the world and asyndetic relations between clauses
- Use of calendrical expressions and spatial reference
- Use of indexical and anaphoric adverbials
- Use of an elementary V stem $\sim$ (aux.) V + e verb morphology contrast

The more advanced L2 speakers built more intricate narratives because they were also able to switch reference points in their expression of temporality. They could also express duration in the past either by some idiosyncratic means or by the use of TL morphology.

This study has also pointed to some of the questions raised by a functional approach to the expression of temporality:

- Manner of definition of the notion under survey
- Principles that organize the array of devices used to convey a given notion
- The divergence between L2 speakers of different TL proficiency in the use of all the means — textural, informational, and interpersonal — available to achieve a given reference.

ACKNOWLEDGMENT

I would like to thank Philippe Soghomonian for his help with the data and Tansy Thompson for improving my IL. All errors are obviously mine.

NOTES

1. This assessment is based on such cues as nature of turn taking in the interaction, propensity of the informant to take the lead in the conversation and to hold the floor, and average length of the utterances of the informants in response to queries from the investigator. For all intents and purposes, a low-level informant is defined as a person who never takes the initiative in the interaction, who does not hold the floor, and whose replies to the investigator are short and possibly erroneous by TL standards. An advanced-level informant has a near-native command of conversational interaction and is able to produce long stretches of speech in L2. An intermediate-level subject shares the communicative skills of the advanced-level informant, but his linguistic competence is not targetlike. Admittedly this characterization mixes linguistic criteria (degree of approximation to TL norm) and a broad evaluation of the learner type (eagerness to communicate vs. careful style), but it proved to work in this particular study.

2. The difference between *imparfait* and *passé composé* in TL has been variously analyzed. Benveniste (1966: 237 ff.) considers that in standard French *imparfait* and *passé composé* differ in that the former belongs to both of two different tense systems: historical enunciation *(énonciation historique)* and discourse enunciation *(énonciation de discours)*, whereas the latter occurs in discourse only. Historical enunciation is used by Benveniste to refer to the system which allows impersonal historical narratives, whereas discourse enunciation refers to the here-and-now speech acts. Contrasting *imparfait* and *passé simple/passé composé,* Kamp and Rohrer (1982) insist on the fact that for *imparfait* to introduce an event occurring at a time other than the reference time, a temporal adverbial is usually needed, whereas that is not the case with *passé simple* and *passé composé.*

3. Alternating verbs are those verbs of TL whose stem varies according to tense and person. This is the case with *aller,* for instance, which is *je vais* "I go," *tu vas* "you go," *nous allons* "we go" in the present tense, indicative mood but *j'allais* "I was going" in *imparfait* and *j'irai* "I shall go" in the future tense, indicative mood. Nonalternating verbs are those whose stem is not subject to such variation. Take, for instance, *manger* "to eat," which is *je mange* "I eat" in the present tense, *je mangeais* "I was eating" in the *imparfait,* and *je mangerai* "I shall eat" in the future.

4. Following Maingueneau (1976: 107) in TL the following order of constituents is compulsory with *imparfait:* date + verb + subject in narratives of past events, e.g., *le 2 avril 1974 mourait G. Pompidou* "on the 2nd of April 1974 died G. Pompidou," whereas *passé simple/passé composé* would require obligatory order: subject + verb + date, e.g., *G. Pompidou mourut (est mort) le 2 avril 1974"* G. Pompidou died (was dead) on the 2nd of April 1974." According to Maingueneau, the difference of placement and the choice of tense are linked: left dislocation of the date NP + *imparfait* tense emphasizes the relationship between the time of utterance, the reference point, and the chronology of the event described, whereas right disclocation reinforces the perfectivity of the event. One may wonder whether this type of constraint is also at work in IL.

5. Note that *aller* "to go" + V infinitive is used in TL to express futurity. In L1, participial verb forms such as *meši, zāj* "going/ gone" + V imperfective or full verb forms such as *bda* + perfective "to begin" + V imperfective are [+ inchoative] (see Marçais, 1977: 75–78).

6. Definitions of what past reference implies vary. Benveniste (1966: 239) defines narratives of past events—his *énonciation historique* which is exclusively used in the written medium—as accounts of events having taken place at a given moment without any intrusion on the part of the speaker in the narrative. Von Stutterheim and Klein (this volume) on the other hand advocate an analytical-synthetical approach to temporality rather than an a priori definition. They suggest that one should start from the meaning of utterances but, also following Hopper, try to make the intuitive representation of the notion in question explicit. For reference to past events, this would mean both scrutiny of given utterances and analysis of past reference as a notion. This could easily be circular.

7. Quantification would be needed here.

APPENDIX

Narratives

A7

Q. *C'est bon ça pendant un an tu es tranquille*
That's fine   you can take it easy for one year

A. *eh oui   mais après un an xxx et maintenant i*
yes   but after one year   and now they
te disent pas   i te convoquent il dit voilà [ʃɛr ʃ e
don't tell you they call you he says look for a
travaje] et quand tu arrives là-bas i dit vous
job   and when you get   there he says you
vous [ʃɛr ʃ e travaje] i demande un salaire (?) c'est normal si tu
you are looking for a job he asks for wages (?)   that's normal if you
vas là-bas tu vois je sais pas moi xxx Paris ou Lyon ou
go there you see I don't know   Paris or Lyon or
St Etienne tout ça tu demandes un frais de déplacement
St Etienne   you ask for   transport allowance
tu sais   i dit   non tu dis non et quand tu
you know   he says no you say no and when you
tout seul   tu trouves la lettre à la fin tu [ladi] (?)
are by yourself you   get   a   letter finally you say it (?)
tu   [e] pas droit au chômage   et alors
you   can't get unemployment(pay) and then

T1 (Narrative 3)

Q. *Tu travaillais en Tunisie? Dans quelle entreprise? Toujours maçon?*
Did you work in Tunisia? In   what   firm?   Always as a mason?
C'est tunisienne oui mais lui habite loin   Sfax je
It is Tunisian   yes but   he lives far away Sfax I
travaille à côté chez moi Le Kef et à l'essai   Le Kef je
work near my place   Le Kef and on probation Le Kef I
travaille trois ans avec lui pour l'essai   l'essai pour [pase]
work   three years with him for probation probation to become
professionnel tout l'examen   tout   là-bas tu vois professionnel
skilled worker everything exams   everything there you see skilled
[pase]   stage là-bas Tunis Le Kef je travaille là-bas trois ans
followed course there Tunis Le Kef I worked   there three years
jusque le dernier jour [ʒeãtre] la France je prends le 30
until the last day   I came to France   I start on the 30th
demain   après demain   j'ai je prends le bateau je m'en vais
tomorrow after tomorrow   I   I take the boat   I   leave
[ãtre] ici la France.
came here France.

A8 (Narrative 3)

Ouais en 54 [ʒete ãbc ʃ e] comme   mineur   de fond pas
Yes   in 54 I got a job   as   miner   not
beaucoup de travail à   56   ça commence   la   guerre en Algérie
much   work   in 56 it starts   the   war   in Algeria

ouais   ça commence bien bombarder   là-bas   eh ben   à ce
yes   it starts   bombing quite a lot there   so   at that

moment-là   les français   sont partis   à la guerre d'Algérie
time   the Frenchmen left   for the Algerian War

la plupart   des Algériens ici en France   que au moment
most of   the Algerians here in France who (had to be)

de service militaire sont partis   à la guerre   en Algérie
in service   left   for the war   in Algeria

et pis à ce moment-là   ça commence le travail
and then at this time   it starts   the work

beaucoup   tu   dis même au chef merde i   te dit   merci
a lot   you   say shit to the foreman he   says   thank you

parce qu'il manque d'ouvriers   alors 55   ça commence   i travaille
because there is not enough workers so 55   it starts   it works (i.e., there are jobs)

rien que dans les usines à 57   commence   sur
only in the factories   in 57   begins   in

toute la France   c'est vrai c'est pas vrai 57 ça   commence   56 ou
the whole of France it's true or not   57 it   starts   56 or

57 ça commence   en toute la   France   parce que   l'argent de
57 it   starts   in the whole of France because   the money

l'Algérie   les pieds noirs   [sɔpɔrte]   ici ça   commence
from Algeria the "pieds noirs" have taken [it] here it starts

aussi entre   la France parce que   je   connais hein   [sepa]
also coming to France because   I   know anyway even

que la police [ãtã]   mais [ʒ l ə kone]   bien
if the police   listens but I know that   well

ça   commence   l'argent de l'Algérie   [saputrãvenir]   ici
it   starts   the money from Algeria it is coming   here

ça   commence   en France ça   monte   et à l'Algérie   ça   descend
it   starts   in France   it is growing up and in Algeria it is going down

après 50/62 la guerre   en Algérie elle   est finie   après   faut
after 50/62 the war   in Algeria it   is   over   afterward   must

parler avec un   européen qui dit   que si t'es pas content t'as qu'à
talk   with a   European   who says that if you are not happy go

aller chez toi totalement   l'argent de l'Algérie   qui monte en
back home   all   the money from Algeria that comes in

France c'est   les gens   de l'Algérie   sont venus   ici [s ʒ m ʒ t] la France.
France it's   people   from Algeria came   here have built   France.

T2 (Narrative 1)

Voilà   c'est ça   [ʒ earive] à la France   en 69/1900 alors   [ʒete]
So   that's it   I came   to France   in 69/1900 then   I was

en Corse [ʒ ale]   vivre là-bas peut-être 3 ans   je vais travailler
in Corsica I was going to live there maybe   3 years I am going to work

et tout parce que je suis un immigré   c'est   pas riche [ʒ ə travaje]
and all because   I am   an immigrant it's   not rich   I have worked

là pour gagner mon morceau de pain je cherche pas des histoires ni
there to earn   my piece   of bread I am not looking for trouble nor

rien   alors après j'ai/ là-bas c'est   trop méchant tu vois les
anything else and then I/ there   it's   too tough   you see the

patrons [siltravaj] là-bas [ldeklar] pas   i [dɔn] pas un
bosses if he works there   he does not declare he does not give

congé c'est vrai je t'ai vu   beaucoup   le patron là
leave it's   true I have seen many   bosses there
peut-être [i travaj]   pour 4 ou 5 là-bas mais tous   il est
maybe   he works   for   4 or 5 there   but they/he are/ is all
même chose il est pareil ensuite alors [ʒerãtre] ici au continent
the same   then   I came   here on the main land
[ʒ eparti]   à Paris   non mais première fois [ʒ ete] à Toulon [ʒ ereste]
I left   for Paris no but (the) first time I was   in Toulon I stayed
là-bas peut-être un an et demi   après je retourne à la Marseille
there   maybe   one and a half year then I come back to the Marseilles
j'y vais à l'embauche de là où on travaille plus   [kiljaye la kjave]
I go to look for a job   there where people work more where there was
le Métro   je travaille je l'ai embauché le 13,   le 13 janvier
the underground I work   I start work   on the 13, the 13 January
74, le 13 premier 74 jusqu'au 15 mars en 76.
74 the 13 first   74 until the 15 March in 76.

A4 (Narrative 2)

Quand je suis jeune je suis petit à l'âge c'est-à-dire que je
When   I   am   young I   am small at age   that is   I
crois 7 ans quand j'ai 7 ans alors [sak ɔ mãse] à faire l'école
think 7   when I was 7   then it starts running   a school
où est-ce que j'habite moi ouais ils [ak ɔ mãse] faire à
where I live   yes   they start   to run
l'école   alors quand ils ont fait l'école alors moi je me suis
(a) school then   when they run a school   then   I was too
déjà c'est-à-dire l'âge alors mon père   il a essayé c'est-à-dire
old that is age   then my father   he tried   that is
de me l'apprendre parce qu'il prend pas   c'est-à-dire de 6 ans
to teach it to me   because he does not enroll that is after 6
alors y   a mon frère [kilerãtre] à l'école et moi j'ai pas
then   there is my brother who went to school and I   I did
rentré alors moi qu'est-ce que je fais y a mon père   qu'il a
not go then   I what do   I do   there's my father that he has
la terre alors   il achète il a deux boeufs et me fait une petite pioche
soil   then   he buys   he owns two oxen and makes a small hoe for me
je viens derrière à les boeufs et on met des blés des blés tout ce
I walk behind   the oxen   and we put wheat wheat   all that
qu'il faut quoi alors je travaille on plante les fèves on plante c'est-à-
is needed   then   I work   we plant beans   we plant   that is
dire les olives on plante c'est-à-dire des jardins alors je travaille
olive plants we plant   that is   gardens   then   I work
comme ça je travaille c'est-à-dire à la maison jusqu'à l'âge c'est-à-dire
like that   I work   that is   at home   until I am   that is
què j'ai au moins 17 ans et y a mon père   il était là c'est
I am at least 17 years old and there's my father he was here that's
ce qu'il faut   c'est-à-dire de la guerre après mon père il est
what's necessary that is   war   then my father   he
venu ici c'est moi qu'il est resté c'est-à-dire responsable de la maison.
came here it's I   who   became   that is   responsible for the household.

A3 (Narrative 1)
  Q. Tu   es allé   à l'école   en Algérie?
  You   went   to school in Algeria?

  A. Oui   [ʒ ete] un peu   mais   j'ai pas été   tellement même
  Yes   I have been   but   I was not   so much (there) not even
  pas un an voyez   7 ou 8 mois comme ça   après   j'ai abandonné
  one year you see 7 or 8 months approximately then   I left
  j'avais tellement la tête   dure le matin   je fais semblant d'aller
  I was so dumb   (in) the morning I pretend to leave for
  à l'école   je prends mes cahiers   je pars à l'école   mais
  school   I take my exercise books I leave for school but
  on était   4 ou 5 comme des sauvages on allait à la plage   le midi
  we were 4 or 5 like savages   we went to the beach at noon
  on rentre à   la maison on va manger   à 1h30 on ressort de la maison
  we go back home   we go to eat   at 1:30 we leave home
  on fait semblant d'aller à l'école   on allait encore à la
  we make believe we are going to school we went again to
  plage et à la pêche.
  the beach fishing.

REFERENCES

Andersen, Roger W. 1982. The expression of temporality in interlanguage. ms.

Benveniste, Emile. 1966. *Problèmes de Linguistique Générale.* Paris: Editions Gallimard.

Dittmar, Norbert, Wolfgang Klein and Christiane von Stutterheim. 1982. The expression of temporality in learner varieties. Unpublished paper. Nijmegen: Max-Planck Institut für Psycholinguistik.

Halliday, Michael. 1970. Language structure and language function. In John Lyons (ed.), *New Horizons in Linguistics,* Harmondsworth: Penguin Books, pp. 140–165.

Hopper, Paul J. 1979. Aspect and foregrounding in discourse. In Talmy Givón (ed.), *Discourse and Syntax. Syntax and Semantics.* Vol. 12. New York: Academic Press.

Kamp, Hans, and Christian Rohrer. 1982. Tense in texts. ms.

Kerbrat-Orrecchioni, Catherine. 1980. *L'Énonciation de la Subjectivité dans la Langue.* Paris: Armand Colin.

Kumpf, Lorraine. 1982. Tense, aspect and modality in interlanguage. A discourse-functional approach. ms.

Maingueneau, Dominique. 1976. *Initiation aux méthodes de l'analyse du discours.* Paris: Hachette Université.

Marçais, Philippe. 1979. *Esquisse grammaticale de l'arabe maghrébin.* Paris: Adrien Maisonneuve.

Meisel, Jürgen. Reference to past events and actions in the development of natural second language acquisition. This volume.

Noyau, Colette. 1982. The expression of temporality in French L2: stability/evolution of an L2 system long after the initial acquisition phase. Paper presented at the 2nd EuNam Workshop on Cross-Linguistic SLA Research, Göhrde.

Trévise, Anne. 1982. Toward an analysis of the (inter)language activity of referring to time narratives. This volume.

Véronique, Daniel. 1984. The acquisition and use of French morphosyntax by native speakers of Arabic dialects (North Africa). In Roger W. Andersen (ed.). *Second Languages.* Rowley, Mass.: Newbury House.

Von Stutterheim, Christiane. 1982a. Temporality in learner varieties: A first report. Paper prepared for the 2nd EuNam Workshop on Cross-Linguistic SLA Research, Göhrde.

Von Stutterheim, Christiane and Wolfgang Klein. A concept-oriented approach to second language studies. This volume.

AUTHOR INDEX

LANGUAGE INDEX

NL = Native Language, Native Language Acquisition
L1 = First Language of second language learner
L2 = Second Language

SUBJECT INDEX